DB2® Universal Database™ v8 Handbook for Windows®, UNIX®, and Linux®

IBM Press Series—Information Management

DB2 Universal Database v8 for Linux, UNIX, and Windows Database Administration Certification Guide, Fifth Edition
Baklarz and Wong

Advanced DBA Certification Guide and Reference for DB2 Universal Database v8 for Linux, UNIX, and Windows
Snow and Phan

DB2 Universal Database v8 Application Development Certification Guide, Second Edition
Martineau, Sanyal, Gashyna, and Kyprianou

DB2 Version 8: The Official Guide
Zikopoulos, Baklarz, deRoos, and Melnyk

DB2 Universal Database v8 Certification Test 700 Study Guide
Sanders

Teach Yourself DB2 Universal Database in 21 Days
Visser and Wong

DB2 UDB for OS/390 v7.1 Application Certification Guide
Lawson

DB2 SQL Procedural Language for Linux, UNIX, and Windows
Yip, Bradstock, Curtis, Gao, Janmohamed, Liu, and McArthur

Business Intelligence for the Enterprise
Biere

DB2 Universal Database v8 Handbook for Windows, UNIX, and Linux
Gunning

Other Complementary DB2 Titles

DB2 Universal Database for OS/390 Version 7.1 Certification Guide
Lawson and Yevich

DB2 Universal Database v7.1 for UNIX, Linux, Windows and OS/2—Database Administration Certification Guide, Fourth Edition
Baklarz and Wong

DB2 Universal Database v7.1 Application Development Certification Guide
Sanyal, Martineau, Gashyna, and Kyprianou

DB2 UDB for OS/390: An Introduction to DB2 OS/390
Sloan and Hernandez

DB2 Universal Database v8 Handbook for Windows, UNIX, and Linux

IBM Press™

DB2® Information Management Software

Philip K. Gunning

PRENTICE HALL
Professional Technical Reference
Upper Saddle River, New Jersey 07458
www.phptr.com

Editorial/production supervision: *MetroVoice Publishing Services*
Cover design director: *Jerry Votta*
Cover design: *IBM Corporation*
Manufacturing manager: *Alexis Heydt-Long*
Publisher: *Jeffrey Pepper*
Editorial assistant: *Linda Ramagnano*
Marketing manager: *Debby vanDijk*
IBM Consulting Editor: *Susan Visser*

Published by Pearson Education, Inc.
Publishing as Prentice Hall Professional Technical Reference
Upper Saddle River, NJ 07458

Printed in the United States of America

Second Printing

ISBN 0-13-066111-2

Pearson Education LTD.
Pearson Education Australia PTY, Limited
Pearson Education Singapore, Pte. Ltd.
Pearson Education North Asia Ltd.
Pearson Education Canada, Ltd.
Pearson Educación de Mexico, S.A. de C.V.
Pearson Education — Japan
Pearson Education Malaysia, Pte. Ltd.

Contents

CHAPTER 8 Tuning Bufferpools 175

CHAPTER 9 Tuning Configuration Parameters 191

APPENDIX A DB2 Catalog Views 323

Foreword

In 2003 DB2 celebrated its 20th anniversary, which is significant in this day and age of disposable, ever-changing software. But what exactly does this mean? The term "DB2" has meant a lot of things over the course of its 20-year history. Way back in the dark ages of DB2 version 1, back in 1983, DB2 very clearly meant "IBM's mainframe database management system."

But times change, and so has DB2. There are five platform (or operating system) choices for DB2: mainframe, Linux/UNIX/Windows, AS/400 (iSeries), VSE/VM, and PDA (Palm/PocketPC). My background is primarily from working on the mainframe edition of DB2, but I have had the opportunity to use DB2 UDB on Linux, UNIX, and Windows, too. And there is a lot to learn—even for veterans of DB2 on other platforms.

Whether you are a DBA or an application programmer using DB2 UDB for Linux, UNIX, and Windows, this book will provide you with much valuable information. It offers a treasure trove of information. From logical and physical database design to high performance I/O strategies to database system tuning to running DB2 utilities, Phil offers practical and useful advice to simplify your DB2 UDB experience.

I think my favorite chapter is Chapter 11 where Phil takes you on a guided tour through the minefields of identifying and correcting DB2 problems. The diagnostic tools and tips he covers in this chapter are essential knowledge for anyone who uses DB2 regularly. I mean, how many of you can relate to getting that strange problem that just won't go away—and the manuals aren't any help? Well, now you'll have a place to turn.

But really, this whole book is valuable. Phil Gunning has written this comprehensive new book to offer you the benefit of his hard-won "in the trenches" knowledge of DB2 UDB. You really need to own this book so you can take advantage of learning from the battles Phil has fought over the years because few can approach Phil's years of hands-on experience. Between these pages you will find exhaustive coverage of just about everything you'll need to know as you design, build, and manage your DB2 UDB applications on Linux, UNIX, and Windows platforms.

Importantly, this is not a book for pure novices. Phil assumes that you've had some exposure to relational databases, so he doesn't waste any time teaching the syntax basics that most people already know. And I also have to note that you will enjoy Phil's writing style. Sometimes when I read software books and manuals I get lost in the arcane and convoluted writing style frequently employed by technicians. You know what I'm talking about—when you're sure the information is there but it just doesn't seem like English anymore. Well, you won't have that problem here. This book is well written and in a style that is easy to read and understand.

I am pleased that Phil asked me to write the foreword for this great new book. I enjoyed reading it, and I am sure you will enjoy reading it too.

—Craig S. Mullins
Director, Technology Planning
BMC Software
June 2003

Preface

I wrote this book to provide you with the necessary knowledge with which to accomplish business objectives with DB2 UDB v8.1 for Windows, UNIX, and Linux. After all, as a developer or DBA, your primary mission is to accomplish business objectives by providing a database environment that provides the requisite performance, availability, and scalability required in today's demanding 24 × 7 highly competitive business environment.

To that end, I have focused this book on key areas of DB2 UDB v8.1 that will enable you to meet those objectives. Some of the features covered are: the new Development Center, multidimensional clustering, online reorganization and online load, Type-2 indexes, tablespace enhancements, block-based bufferpools, tuning bufferpools, new commands and utility options, dynamic configuration parameters, autonomic computing features, write-to-table event monitors, SQL snapshot functions, `QUIESCE` command, and the database partitioning feature with new partitioning terminology updates. And, almost all new DB2 UDB v8.1 features and enhancements are covered in this book. Also, I have included a chapter on logical and physical design to help you in designing top performing databases.

In the following chapters, I will show you how to design, maintain, monitor, and tune high performing DB2 UDB v8.1 databases.

If, after you read this book, I have helped you do that, then I have accomplished my mission.

ACKNOWLEDGMENTS

I have had a lot of help in writing this book. I would like to thank the following people from Prentice Hall: Mike Meehan, for helping me get started on this book; Jeff Pepper, for continued support and patience; Scott Suckling, for producing the final manuscript; and all the people behind the scenes in the marketing and publication of this book.

Without the support of IBM it would have been difficult to write this book. Special thanks to Susan Visser for her patience and positive attitude and for providing access to DB2 Developers and technical writers. I also want to thank Brad Cassells for providing technical assistance and clarification when needed. I also want to thank my reviewers: Bob Harbus, who did a yeoman's job reviewing the book while on the road; Sam Lightstone; and Dwaine Snow, who rearranged his schedule to review Chapter 13.

I also want to thank Scott Hayes for providing some of the material for Chapter 8, and to Martin Hubel, who dropped what he was doing to review Chapter 10, 11, and 12.

Thanks to my mentor, Doug French, who took me under his wing many years ago; and to Polly Mathys, Professor of Information Systems at Alvernia College, for her outstanding teaching ability, and for setting the example for all to emulate.

Of course, although I have tried to be as accurate and complete as possible, any errors are strictly my own.

I also want to thank my fellow IDUG North America Conference Planning Committee members who put up with me over the last year and a half!

To my wife, who's constant support and encouragement were instrumental to the completion of the book. And finally, to my daughters Paula and Katie, who helped a lot with keyboarding and completing my drawings, tables, and examples. They finally have their Dad back!

—Philip K. Gunning
Sinking Spring, Pennsylvania
June 2003
pgunning@gunningts.com
www.gunningts.com

C H A P T E R 1

What's New

DB2 Universal Database (UDB) version 8 for Linux, UNIX, and Windows is packed with new features that provide for unprecedented performance, manageability, and availability. The new version incorporates a host of features requested by DB2 customers, from the ability to start DB2 in single-user mode to the new infinite logging capability.

As a participant of the closed BETA program and the open BETA test program, I was able to test and evaluate many of the new features in DB2 v8 that I am writing about. I hope that you find the multitude of features and enhancements as exciting as I do!

DB2 v8 is the culmination of several years of research by IBM Labs. DB2 v8 incorporates technology developed as part of the LEO (Learning Optimizer) project, SMART (Self Management and Resource Tuning) project, and the eLiza project, which is increasing the reliability and availability of IBM servers.

Current and future business practices demand that data be available 24 hours a day, 365 days a year. DB2 v8, through its many enhancements in the areas of maintainability and availability, meets or exceeds these demanding requirements through its new online reorganization capability, infinite logging capability, online index reorganization capability, and online load capability, to name a few.

Self-management enhancements are evident throughout the product. Autonomic computing enhancements have been made in the area of new and improved Wizards, Advisors, and a complete suite of database management tools. These enhancements are in response to the ever-increasing business requirement to do more with less in an environment where highly skilled DBAs are hard to come by. Self-management will help companies meet the ever-demanding day-to-day business challenges, now and for the forseeable future.

DB2 v8 takes the already existing XML support to new levels. The XML Extender has been enhanced to support Web services with the Web services Object Runtime Framework (WORF), which is a set of tools for implementing Web services with DB2. Web services are XML-based functions that can be started from the Internet and enable DB2 to be the platform of choice for companies conducting B2B Web transactions. The v8 XML Extender also lets users send or retrieve XML documents from MQSeries™ message queues. These enhancements make it easy for developers to work with XML documents.

DB2 v8, through the new Development Center, offers tight integration with Microsoft C++, Visual Basic, and Visual InterDev, making it easy for developers to develop and incorporate stored procedures and user-defined functions into the development environment.

The DB2 v8 Universal Developer's Edition incorporates WebSphere Studio and WebSphere Application Server. WebSphere Studio makes it easy for developers to create, publish, and maintain dynamic Web applications. And with WebSphere Application Server, developers can create enterprise Java applications that access DB2 databases.

There are many performance improvements in DB2 v8. Multidimensional clustering (MDC) enables indexes to be automatically created on multiple dimensions. This is especially useful for data warehousing and business intelligence environments where data is frequently analyzed over multiple dimensions. The optimizer can use these new dimension indexes for fast data access. Because MDC indexes guarantee 100% clustering, they never have to be reorganized. New block-based bufferpools improve prefetch performance as blocks of noncontiguous pages can now be fetched into blocks of contiguous memory.

The new compression of nulls and defaults enhancement will benefit companies with data warehouses and large databases. This new feature can be enabled with the `VALUE COMPRESSION` and `COMPRESS SYSTEM DEFAULT` clause of the Create Table statement. This enhancement can reduce disk storage requirements and can increase the performance of large table scans. Once enabled, a new data row format will be used, which provides efficient storage of null and 0 length values. By enabling this new feature, significant disk space can be saved. Note that only system default values are compressed, not user defined.

PRODUCT CHANGES

Along with feature changes, v8 introduces several changes in product names and characteristics. IBM combined the former Enterprise Edition and Enterprise-Extended Edition into DB2 UDB Enterprise Server Edition (ESE). The base ESE product lets you create multiple database partitions on a single SMP server. If you want to create multiple database partitions in a clustered environment, then you need to order the Database Partitioning Licensing Feature (DPF). Product changes are covered in more detail in Chapter 2.

MANAGEABILITY ENHANCEMENTS

SMART technology appears in v8 in the form of new wizards and tools that greatly simplify DB2 maintainability and operability. Examples include the following:

Load Enhancements

Online Load enables load operations to take place at the table level, allowing concurrent access to other tables in a multiple-table table space. This change particularly benefits ERP and CRM applications, which often have many tables per table space. If you specify the `COPY NO` option for a recoverable database, the table space will be placed in a backup pending table space state when the load operation begins. With the `READ ACCESS` option of the load command, preexisting data can be queried while new data is being loaded. A new option, `LOCK WITH FORCE`, lets you force applications to release locks on a table so that a load operation can proceed.

Autoloader functions have been incorporated into the load utility, and the autoloader control file is no longer needed.

The v8 load utility now generates column values for generated columns and no longer requires the `SET INTEGRITY` statement on a table that only has generated columns and no other constraints. The `LOAD QUERY` command now returns the status of the target table, in addition to the status information previously included. `LOAD QUERY` can also query table states whether or not a load operation is in progress.

Wizards

In addition to the Load Wizard, IBM added eight wizards to DB2 v8. They are:

- Memory Visualizer
- Redistribute Data Wizard
- Backup and Restore Wizard
- Configure Database Logging Wizard
- Add Partition Wizard
- Alter Database Partition Group
- Storage Management View
- Design Advisor (an enhanced form of the previous Index Advisor).

Flush Package Cache

A new `FLUSH PACKAGE CACHE` SQL statement lets you remove cached dynamic SQL statements by invalidating them. Queries currently using dynamic SQL statements will continue to use the previously cached statement; however, any new request for the same statement will be prepared and a new statement entry cached.

Logging Enhancements

DB2 v8 supports dual logging on all 8.1 platforms, which means you can now specify the log-path through the MIRRORLOGPATH DB CFG parameter. This new parameter replaces the previous registry variable DB2NEWLOGPATH2.

The maximum amount of log space increases to 256 GB from 32 GB. Infinite logging allows a current unit of work to span across active and archive logs. Previously, log records for a unit of work had to fit into the primary and secondary log space. This change will accommodate large units of work that require more log space than that allocated for the primary and secondary logs. The BLK_ON_LOG_DISK_FUL registry variable has been replaced with the new database configuration parameter BLK_LOG_DSK_FUL, which tells DB2 not to fail on a log full condition. Instead, DB2 will retry the write to the log every 5 minutes, giving you time to resolve the disk full condition.

Backup and Recovery Enhancements

A new tablespace history file identifies log files needed for a particular table space recovery. Log files that aren't needed are skipped, resulting in faster tablespace recovery.

You no longer have to specify Coordinated Universal Time (CUT) for rolling forward to a point-in-time. Instead, you can now specify local time. This improvement eliminates the confusion that can result when converting local time to CUT time.

The *DB2DIAG.LOG* has been split into two files. The Administration Notification Log will contain messages for use by DBAs and systems administrators. Additional information will supplement SQLCODE error information. The level of information is controlled by the new NOTIFYLEVEL database configuration parameter. Detailed diagnostic information will still be written to the *DB2DIAG.LOG* file. The DIAGLEVEL configuration parameter will still control the level of information (primarily for DB2 Support) written to that file.

New Database Maintenance Mode

This new feature is akin to the ACCESS(MAINT) command available for some time on DB2 for z/OS and OS/390. You can use the DB2 v8 QUIESCE command to force all users off an instance or database and place them in quiesced mode so maintenance can be performed. This feature solves the problem of application servers or transaction monitors immediately reconnecting to the database after a FORCE APPLICATIONS ALL command has been issued. The UNQUIESCE command takes the database or instance out of maintenance mode so users can connect to the database without requiring a shutdown and restart.

REORGCHK Enhancements

REORGCHK now includes an ON SCHEMA option to specify a particular schema.

`RUNSTATS` Enhancements

`RUNSTATS` can now collect statistics on column combinations, on prefetching on a table, and on index and index-to-table relationships. `RUNSTATS` can now also accept lists of indexes and columns on which statistics are to be collected. Refer to Chapter 11, "Problem Determination," and Chapter 7, "Commands and Utilities," for detailed information.

Management by Exception Monitoring

The new Health Monitor is a server-side tool that can raise alerts when predefined thresholds are exceeded or when it detects that an instance is down. Based on the alert generated, the Health Monitor can send an email or issue a page to a predefined email or pager address, trigger a script, or run a task through the new Task Center.

Health indicators are used by the Health Monitor to evaluate specific aspects of database manager or database performance. Refer to the *System Monitor Guide and Reference* for additional details on Health indicators. The Health Monitor checks the state of the system against these health indicators when determining when to issue an alert. Health Beacons are located on all Control Center windows. You simply click on a Beacon to access the Health Center, a GUI for configuring and interfacing with the Health Monitor.

Event Monitor and Snapshot Enhancements

Event monitors can be created that write to tables instead of files or pipes. This enhancement will make it easier for DBAs to correlate event monitor data. You can write customized queries to query tables containing event monitor data and produce reports for your items of interest. In conjunction with this, snapshots can now be taken via SQL table functions, the output of which can be joined to other tables or written to a file, whereas previously they could only be embedded in programs that used the Administrative API. This will make it easier for you to take and correlate snapshot data. Monitoring is covered in detail in Chapter 10.

PERFORMANCE ENHANCEMENTS

Many performance enhancements have been incorporated into v8 that will enable companies to meet the ever-increasing business requirements demanded of companies in a 24 × 7 × 365 environment. DBAs and developers alike will be able to take advantage of these performance enhancements by incorporating these enhancements into new and existing applications and databases.

Performance enhancements are highlighted and covered in detail throughout the book. Some of the most important performance enhancements are:

Multidimensional Clustering (MDC)

MDC is new clustering technology that provides a method for automatic, continuous clustering of data along multiple dimensions. And MDC tables don't require database maintenance operations such as reorganization. MDC primarily benefits data warehousing type queries and large database environments; however, it can also be useful for transaction processing. MDC is covered in detail in Chapter 5.

Prefetching Enhancements

You can now use block-based bufferpools to improve prefetch performance. The `BLOCKSIZE` parameter of the `CREATE` or `ALTER BUFFERPOOL` statement is used to define the size of the blocks and number of pages to be read from disk in a single I/O. When a block-based bufferpool is defined, DB2 will recognize this and may use block I/Os to read multiple pages into the bufferpool in a single I/O. This enhancement will benefit data warehouse and large database environments where significant prefetching is used.

Catalog and Authorization Caching

For databases with multiple partitions, an extension of catalog cache will be provided at each partition. Cached information will include `SYSTABLE` and authorization information. For applications with multiple coordinator partitions, this feature will improve performance significantly, as the local cache will service trips to the catalog partition.

Asynchronous I/O Enhancements

Version 8 exploits AIX asynchronous page cleaning performance. Because asynchronous I/O isn't always enabled on AIX, it must be enabled before v8 installation. Two AIX asynchronous I/O parameters that you can tune are minservers and maxservers. Configure these parameters using SMIT. Refer to the *AIX Performance Guide* for additional information.

Java SP and UDF Performance Enhancements

Java routines are now implemented using a thread-based model, which results in significant performance improvement for multiple routines executing simultaneously. Thread-based models, or lightweight threads, share process memory and control blocks and can block without causing a context switch. Additionally, routines share the Java Virtual Machine (JVM); previously, a JVM was created for each executing routine.

Connection Concentrator

Connection concentration enables many transient connections, such as Internet connections, to share the same logical coordinating agent. This results in DB2 being able to accommodate many concurrent users because of the reduced memory requirements. Previously, DB2 would create a coordinating agent for each connection. With connection concentration, new connections coming in can use the same logical coordinating agent, which results in less memory being used as the coordinator agent does not have to be created. This greatly reduces memory requirements for each connection and improves performance by reducing the number of context switches (context switches require that the previous execution state and memory structures be saved and restored later, which is a lot of overhead). You can enable this new feature by setting `max_connections` greater than the value of `max_coordagents`.

Common Client Enhancement

The new DB2 client uses DRDA and replaces the previous private protocol, known as DB2RA. This common client can connect to all other DB2 databases using the same protocol, eliminating costly data conversion, which had to be performed in previous releases. The protocol stack has been significantly optimized and offers significant performance improvements for client applications. Version 8 clients will be able to connect to all other members of the DB2 family without additional code.

Full 64-bit Support

Version 8 is 64-bit capable. This will allow DB2 to provide the super-scalability needed by demanding business requirements today, and into the foreseeable future. Full 64-bit capability enables DB2 to make full use of large real memories, which can be exploited for larger bufferpools, sort memory, and other DB2 memory areas. This capability is urgently needed by some of the larger DB2 installations and will provide immediate relief to memory-constrained systems in use today. The common client plays a key role in this regard, as it provides 64-bit capability for client applications as well as connectivity to 32-bit versions of DB2.

Declared Global Temporary Table (DGTT) Enhancements

Version 8 adds rollback support of data changes to DGTTs. The `NOT LOGGED` clause, which was mandatory in v7, is now optional. You can now create an index on a temporary table and `RUNSTATS` can be run.

Materialized Query Table (MQT)

New in v8, MQTs are tables whose definitions are based on the result of a query that uses precomputed results derived from tables on which the MQT definition is based. Summary tables, previously known as ASTs, are now a subset of MQTs in which the AST has a fullselect that contains a `GROUP BY` clause summarizing data from the tables referenced in the fullselect.

Queries can now be routed to MQTs whose definitions contain a join that is not aggregated. The optimizer will recognize that the MQT contains the requested information and will use the MQT instead of the base tables. MQTs can now be incrementally maintained, resulting in improved performance.

User-Maintained MQTs

IBM recognized the need to provide a mechanism for users to maintain and load tables that contain precomputed data. The user-maintained MQT is the solution. These MQTs are managed by the user (not the system) and are distinguished by the `MAINTAINED BY USER` option of the `CREATE SUMMARY TABLE` statement. This enhancement makes it easier for existing Oracle users to migrate to DB2.

Nickname Support

MQTs can now be defined on nicknames, resulting in the remote data being cached on the local DB2 instance. This can result in huge performance gains for federated queries as the remote data is accessed locally. And, if the remote table is not available for some reason, DB2 can use the MQT defined on it if it meets all routing criteria, resulting in improved availability and performance.

Type-2 Indexes

Type-2 indexes improve performance by eliminating most next-key-share locks, as entries are marked "deleted" instead of physically deleted from the page. Type-2 indexes are required for online load, online reorganization, and MDC. A table cannot have a mix of type-1 and type-2 indexes. Tables can be migrated to type-2 indexes via index reorganization. Type-2 indexes let you create an index on a column that is longer than 255 bytes. Type-2 indexes are covered in more detail in Chapter 5.

AVAILABILITY ENHANCEMENTS

Customers demand access to their accounts anytime, anywhere, from anyplace. Businesses must provide this pervasive capability or risk losing customers. The availability of DB2 is significantly enhanced in v8 and those demands can be met. Online table reorganization, as well as online index reorganization, will greatly reduce scheduled and unscheduled outages. IBM has taken this a step further by providing new capabilities for DB2 to adjust to changing business needs. DB2 can automatically set and adjust several configuration parameters online, and over 50 configuration parameters can now be changed online by DBAs. Previously, these changes required an outage and a restart of DB2.

Online Table Reorganization

Online table reorganization offers a significant opportunity for DBAs to improve the availability and performance of supported databases. No longer will reorganizations have to be scheduled for off-hours or during maintenance windows. Online reorganization works by reorganizing a table in place for regular tables. There is no requirement for temporary space. New commands give you the capability to monitor the status of the reorganization.

Online table reorganization allows applications to access the table during the reorganization. Reorganization can also be paused and resumed later, if needed.

> **NOTE**
> Online table reorganization is only allowed on tables with type-2 indexes.

Online Index Reorganization

Online index reorganization allows a table to be read or updated during an index reorganization. During the reorganization all indexes on the table are rebuilt using a "shadow copy." During the time that the shadow copy is being made available, no access is allowed to the table. A new `REORG INDEXES` command has been provided with which to run online index reorganization. Unlike online table reorganization, online index reorganization is not done in-place and requires temporary space. The Reorganization Utility is covered in more detail in Chapter 7.

Dynamic Online Configuration Parameters

You can set 50 configuration parameters online without having to stop and restart the instance or database. Parameters that control key memory areas can be changed dynamically, and the results of these changes monitored using the Memory Visualizer. Changes can be deferred so that they take effect at the next instance or database start. The `GET DB CFG` and `GET DBM CFG` commands now feature a `SHOW DETAILS` option that shows the current and deferred parameter values. A few of these parameters can be set to automatic, and DB2 will adjust the value automatically as the workload changes. Configuration parameters are covered in detail in Chapter 9.

Online Bufferpool Enhancements

You can now create, drop, or alter bufferpools online as well as defer changes. And if a bufferpool is dropped, DB2 will immediately make the memory available to the database shared memory so that it can be reused for other memory allocations.

With these new capabilities, a DBA could create a script that would run after the business day and alter parameters for nightly batch work or DB2 loads, and then run another script after nightly processing has completed to alter the parameters back to the day settings. This scenario should sound familiar to experienced DB2 for OS/390 DBAs as it is quite common on that platform. Detailed information on bufferpools is covered in Chapter 8.

DMS Container Enhancements

You can now drop an existing container, reduce the size, and add new containers to avoid a rebalance. To add containers to a DMS tablespace to avoid rebalance, use the new `BEGIN STRIPE SET` option of the `ALTER TABLESPACE` command. This forces new containers to be added above the high-water mark. These operations can be performed online and the new container is immediately available for use.

SERVICEABILITY ENHANCEMENTS

A new `INSPECT` command lets you check the architectural integrity of tablespaces and tables online. `INSPECT` can also be used to identify the types of indexes on a table. Additionally, the DB2 trace facility has been rearchitected to significantly reduce overhead so that it can be used to capture important diagnostic information for DB2 Support. A new command in v8, `db2support`, can be used by a DBA to provide DB2 Support with a "support bundle" of diagnostic and problem determination information. This new command makes it a lot easier for DBAs to collect and provide diagnostic information to DB2 Support.

The Database Analysis and Reporting Tool (DB2DART) is now fully supported in v8. db2dart can be used to diagnose and repair structural problems with underlying database objects.

Data Warehouse Enhancements

The DB2 Warehouse Manager, once limited to Windows platforms, now supports AIX and Linux. The warehouse server, logger, initialization, external trigger, and mail notification programs are all available on AIX, and Warehouse Manager capabilities have been extended to Linux (32-bit Intel) with Linux Kernel level 2.4.7 and glibc 2.2.4.

APPLICATION DEVELOPMENT ENHANCEMENTS

Version 8 tightly integrates application development tools and add-ins into the new Development Center. This results in improved productivity for application developers and enables Rapid Application Development (RAD). The Development Center offers a central point from which all application development can be completed. Developers can easily create applications that use DB2 stored procedures and UDFs. The Development Center fully integrates DB2 Websphere application development. SQL Assist has been enhanced to include an easy to use interface, assistance with writing table joins, SQL syntax checking, and the ability to copy and paste SQL statements.

SQL in External UDFs and Methods

External UDFs can now contain read-only SQL statements. Both static and dynamic SQL are supported. The limit of 90 parameters has been removed from `PROGRAM TYPE MAIN` stored procedures.

`CALL` Statement

The `CALL` statement is now fully compiled, which means that it can now be dynamically prepared in command line interface, open database connectivity, embedded SQL, Java database connectivity, and SQLJ. You should not use host variables for procedure names when invoking a stored procedure with the `CALL` statement if you want to use package cache efficiently and preclude additional compilation and reads to the catalog.

Development Center

The Development Center replaces the Stored Procedure Builder and includes more features and functions. With the Development Center you can:

- Create, build, and deploy Java and SQL stored procedures
- Create, build, and deploy SQL table and Scalar UDFs and UDFs that read MQ Series messages, access OLE DB data sources, or extract data from XML documents
- Deploy Stored Procedures using the integrated debugger
- Export and import routines and project information

The Development Center also provides an add-in for each of these development environments:

- Microsoft Visual C++
- Microsoft Visual Basic
- Microsoft Visual InterDev

With these add-ins a developer can pick and choose from a wide variety of development options and easily incorporate stored procedures and UDFs into a development effort.

You can launch the Development Center as a stand-alone application or from the Control Center, Command Center, or Task Center.

SQL Enhancements

The new `INSTEAD OF` trigger provides an extension to the ability to update views. Using an `INSTEAD OF` trigger, the update operation against the view gets replaced by the trigger logic, which performs the operation on behalf of the view.

New Informational Constraints are rules that can be used in query rewrite but are not enforced by the database manager. You can use Informational Constraints where applications have verified the data and you want to let DB2 use the constraint for query optimization. New options on the Alter Table statement, `ENABLE QUERY OPTIMIZATION` or `DISABLE QUERY OPTIMIZATION`, instruct DB2 whether or not to use this new capability. Application Development and SQL enhancements are covered in detail in Chapter 4.

SUMMARY

DB2 v8 is one of the most complete DB2 releases to date. In fact, it has so many new features and enhancements that this chapter is just an introduction to some of them. Through Autonomic Computing and the SMART initiative, IBM has made DB2 v8 very easy to operate and manage.

Some configuration parameters can now be automatically configured by DB2. These changes, along with the new wizards and tools, will help make DBAs more productive. With the new Development Center, application development has been tightly integrated into DB2 with support for a myriad of development tools. The availability enhancements—which include infinite logging, online index and table reorganization, online configuration parameters, and online table load—precisely positions DB2 to be able to handle the tough demands of today's businesses, and to grow with them into the future. And lastly, v8's full 64-bit capability will enable DB2 to not only handle today's demands, but handle them well into the future. You'll find lots of information on enhancements and new features in v8 throughout the book.

CHAPTER 2

DB2 v8 Product Overview and Architecture

With the release of v8, IBM continues to refine and improve the DB2 Architecture. IBM continues to integrate new patented technology, such as Multidimensional Clustering (MDC), and XML and Web Services into the DB2 engine. (MDC is covered in detail in Chapter 5.) The DB2 v8 architecture is fully capable of providing complete availability through the introduction of MDC, online reorganization, infinite logging, dynamic configuration parameters, and online index reorganization.

DB2 can now be found in small businesses with just a few employees and in Fortune 500 companies running mission-critical applications. As is typical with any software product, IBM has changed the name of various DB2 product offerings to be more in keeping with the way they are used and with the value provided to the enterprise. DB2's penetration of the small business area is a direct result of its low cost of ownership and superior performance. The integration of Self Management and Resource Tuning (SMART) and autonomic computing will only enhance DB2's ease of use and growth in both small and large companies alike. The former EE has been merged with EEE and has been renamed Enterprise Server Edition (ESE). DB2 Satellite Edition has been merged with DB2 Personal Edition. See Figure 2.1 for an overview of ESE capabilities.

ENTERPRISE SERVER EDITION

ESE meets the needs of midsize to large businesses. ESE is the product of choice for data warehousing, e-commerce, online transaction processing (OLTP), supply chain management (SCM), enterprise resource planning (ERP), and customer relationship management (CRM) applications. ESE includes the DRDA application server and requestor functions, which enable connectivity to other products in the DB2 family. With ESE, the capability to create partitioned databases on SMP servers is included.

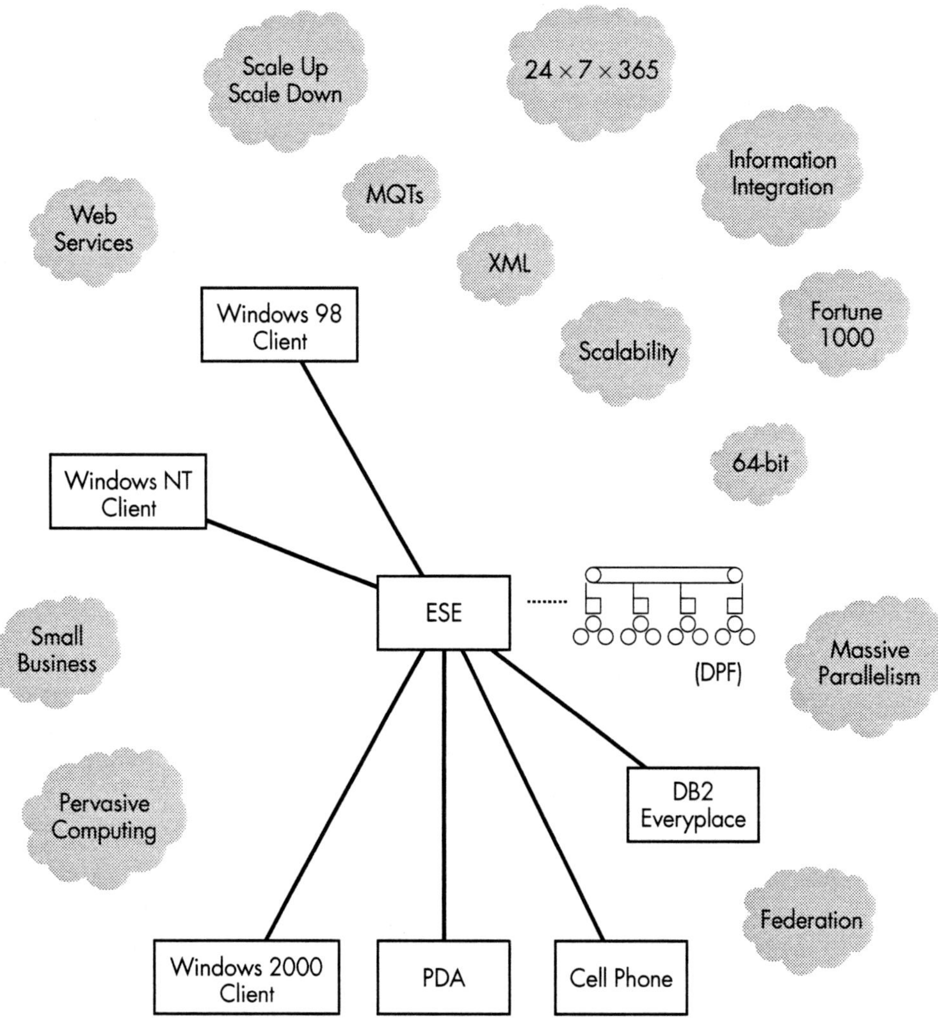

Figure 2.1
Enterprise Server Edition.

Database Partitioning Feature (DPF)

Through the use of DPF you can create multiple partitioned databases over multiple physical machines in a single system or cluster. This enables companies to scale DB2 as data requirements increase. This is built into ESE and an uninstall of the code is not required to enable partitioning over multiple physical machines. Simply enable the licensing feature by purchasing the appropriate entitlement.

> **NOTE**
> The former EEE has been merged with EE, which provides partitioned database functionality in the base ESE products.

DB2 Workgroup Server Edition (WSE)

WSE was formally known as Workgroup Edition. WSE is for small businesses or departmental requirements. WSE provides full DB2 functionality at a reduced cost. It can be used on servers with up to four CPUs. See Figure 2.2 for an overview of WSE.

Workgroup Server Unlimited Edition (WSUE)

This version of WSE offers a simplified per-processor licensing model. This version offers more attractive licensing costs for small companies with Internet users or a large number of users.

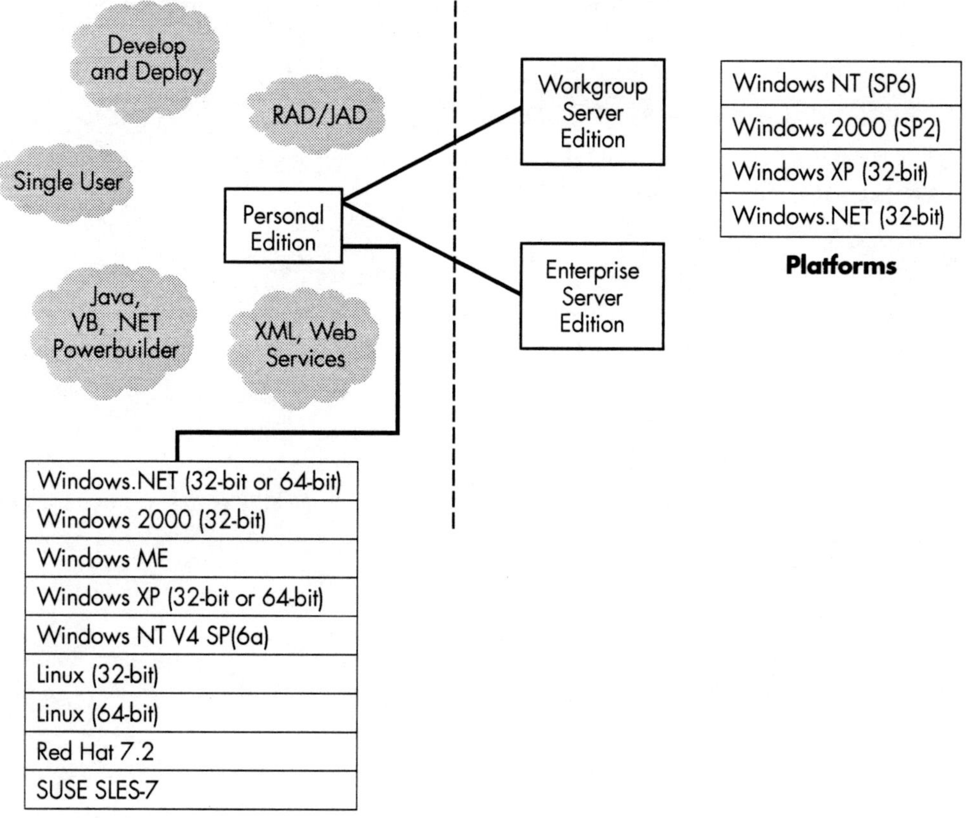

Figure 2.2
Workgroup Server Edition, Personal Edition (PE), and Enterprise Server Edition.

NOTE
DB2 Satellite Edition has merged with DB2 Personal Edition.

DB2 Personal Edition (PE)

PE is for single users developing on PCs. Satellite Edition has been merged with PE and PE can serve as a satellite. PE provides connectivity to ESE and WSE and can be remotely administered. PE can be used for occasionally connected or remote office implementations that don't require multi-user capability. See Figure 2.2 for an overview of PE.

DB2 Universal Developers Edition (UDE)

UDE is designed for use by application developers who design, build, and deploy DB2 applications. It includes all DB2 client and server editions as well as DB2 connect, DB2 Extenders, Warehouse Manager, and Intelligent Miner. UDE is available at low cost to enable application developers to easily develop many types of DB2 applications. It cannot be used for production systems.

DB2 Personal Developers Edition (PDE)

PDE enables a developer to design and build single-user desktop applications. PDE is available for Windows and Linux and includes the DB2 Extenders.

DB2 Warehouse Manager

Warehouse Manager extends the scalability, manageability, and accessibility of DB2 data warehouses and data marts built using the Data Warehouse Center. It provides tools for complete management of data warehouses.

DB2 Intelligent Miner Products

Intelligent Miner products provide a complete set of analysis capabilities that help you make informed business decisions.

DB2 Spatial Extender

DB2 Spatial Extender allows you to analyze spatial data. You can store location-based data in DB2 tables and use the power of SQL for spatial data analysis.

DB2 Net Search Extender

DB2 Net Search Extender enables an application to include powerful in-memory search capabilities for text-based data. The integration of these advanced searching capabilities into the database provides the speed and flexibility in text searching demanded by e-commerce applications.

DB2 v8 is fully 64-bit capable; 64-bit addressing enables the use of large bufferpools, sort heaps, and exploitation of large main memories. DB2 v8 is capable of scaling with the business demands of today and well into the future. See Table 2.1 for a list of DB2 64-bit clients, platforms, and products.

Table 2.1 DB2 64-Bit Product Platforms

64-bit Support	AIX PPC	Sun	HP	Linux IA64	Windows IA64
Personal Edition	N/A	N/A	N/A	Yes	Yes
EE/ESE	Yes	Yes	Yes	Yes	Yes
Connect Enterprise	Yes	Yes	Yes	Yes	Yes
App. Dev. Client	Yes	Yes	Yes	Yes	Yes
Administration Client	Yes	Yes	Yes	Yes	Yes
Run-time Client	Yes	Yes	Yes	Yes	Yes
Relational Connect	Yes	Yes	Yes	Yes	Yes
Datalinks Manager	No	No	No	No	No
Spatial Extender	Yes	Yes	Yes	Yes*	Yes*
XML Extender	Yes	Yes	Yes	Yes	Yes
Warehouse Manager	Yes	Yes	Yes	Yes	Yes

* Support to be provided in a planned fix pack.

New Client

The DB2RA protocol stack has been replaced with a leaner and faster Distributed Relational Database Architecture (DRDA) protocol stack. DB2 client applications will see significant performance improvements using the new protocol. The older protocol and drivers had been modified significantly over time as new APIs emerged. Hence, it had become slow and unwieldy.

> **NOTE**
> DRDA is a protocol that has been used for some time to enable clients and servers to communicate with DB2 on Z/OS either directly or indirectly through a DB2 connect gateway.

The new client will provide for future driver enhancements without major modifications. As such, there are some restrictions on client communications. This will be covered in more detail in Chapter 4. See Table 2.2 for a list of restrictions.

Table 2.2 Client Compatibility Matrix

Client	UNIX 32-bit	UNIX 64-bit	Windows 32-bit	Windows 64-bit
v7 32-bit Client (Windows)	Yes	No	Yes	Yes
v7 32-bit Client (UNIX)	Yes	No	Yes	No
v8 New Client	Yes	Yes	Yes	Yes

The new v8 client can connect to all versions of new servers. It can also connect to all other members of the DB2 family without the need for additional code. However, there are restrictions on down-level feature support to v7 databases.

DB2 Architecture

DB2 uses semaphores and shared memory for interprocess communication. This has enabled DB2 to be the first Relational Database Management System (RDBMS) to support the new InfiniBand storage architecture.

The DB2 Process Model (Figure 2.3) consists of clients or applications connecting to DB2 databases where a coordinating agent is assigned to process all requests for a particular application. Subagents can be assigned if using the ESE Database Partitioning Feature (DPF) or intrapartition parallelism. Bufferpools are used to store frequently accessed data and I/O servers process prefetch requests. I/O cleaners flush dirty pages from the bufferpools to disk. The logger process records changed information and at the appropriate time writes committed changes to disk in coordination with the bufferpool manager.

Communication protocols supported are TCP/IP (the most common), NETBIOS, Named Pipes, and APPC. Work in DB2 is accomplished by Engine Dispatchable Units (EDUs). In UNIX, EDUs are implemented as processes and in Windows, EDUs are implemented as threads. The *ps* (process status) command can be used on UNIX to display DB2 processes. Use the db2_local_ps command to return a list of all DB2 processes to standard output. Operating system processes will not be shown; only DB2 processes will be shown, which makes it easier to quickly see what DB2 processes are running. On Windows, DB2 threads can be monitored using the TASK MANAGER. See Table 2.3 for a partial list of DB2 processes on UNIX platforms. (For a detailed list, refer to the "Everything You Wanted to Know About DB2 VDB Processes," *DB2 Developer Domain* tech article by Snow and R. Chung).

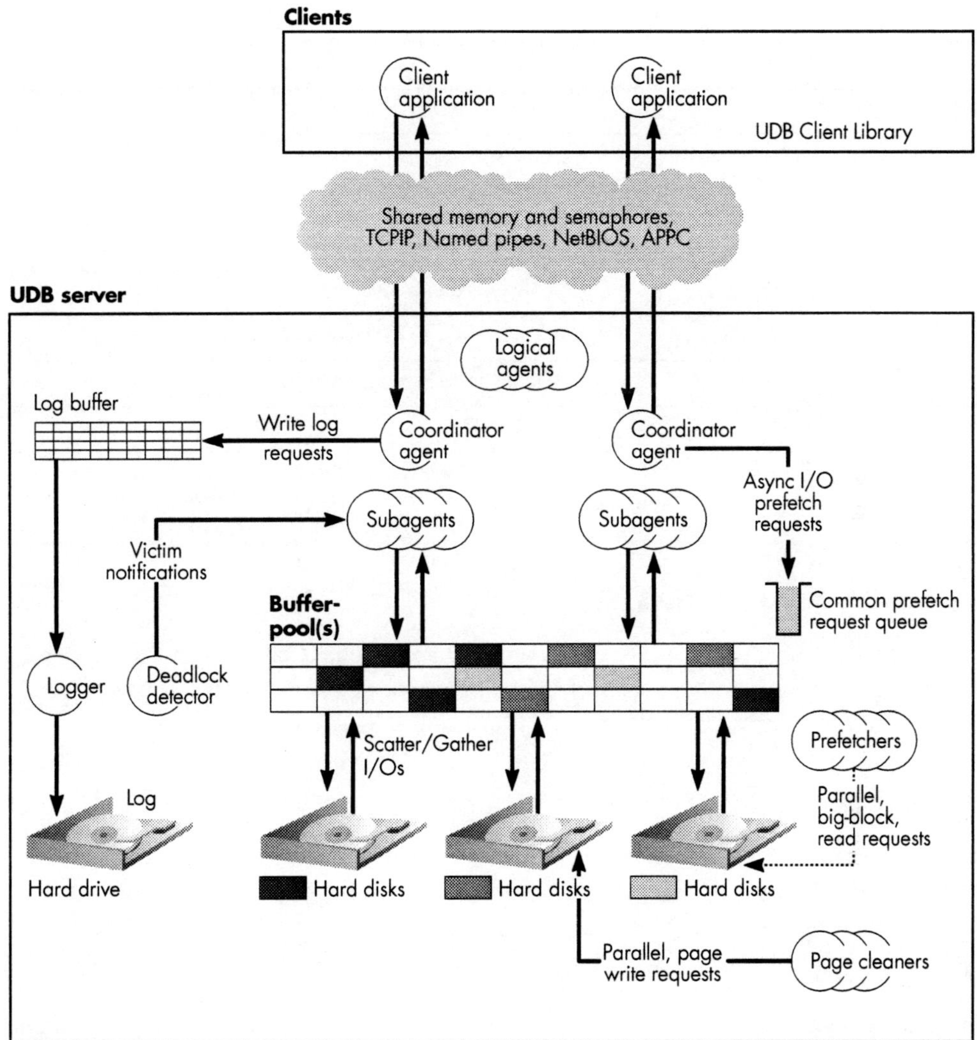

Figure 2.3
Overview of DB2 architecture.

Table 2.3 DB2 AIX Processes

Process Name	Function
`db2agent`	Coordinator agent
`db2agentp`	Subagent processes
`db2pfchr`	Prefetching

Table 2.3 DB2 AIX Processes (Continued)

Process Name	Function
db2pclnr	Page cleaning
db2loggr	Log reader
db2loggw	Log writer
db2logts	Tablespace logger
db2glock and db2dlock	Global and local deadlock detector, one per partition
db2fmp	Fenced process for UDFs and SPs
db2reorg	Online inplace reorg process
db2sysc	DB2 engine
db2tcpcm	TCP communication manager
db2ipccm	IPC communication manager

Coordinating Agent (db2agent)

DB2 assigns a coordinating agent for each connected application. Coordinating agents coordinate the work associated with an application. Coordinating agents create subagents in a partitioned database environment or if intraparallel is enabled, as well as the work of subagents.

Subagents (db2agntp)

Subagents are created by coordinating agents to do work in parallel. Subagents are used in partitioned database environments or if the `intra_parallel` DBM CFG parameter is enabled.

BUFFERPOOLS

Bufferpools are one of the most important tuning areas in DB2 and are the single most important resource in DB2. Bufferpools are used to cache frequently accessed indexes and data in memory. Agents read and modify data pages in the bufferpools. If needed data is not found in the bufferpool, it must be retrieved from disk. Bufferpools are covered in more detail in Chapter 8.

PREFETCHERS (db2pfchr)

Prefetchers are used to fetch data from disk into the bufferpool in anticipation of the application needing it. Agents send asynchronous prefetch requests to a common prefetch queue. Prefetchers process these requests from the prefetch queue using big-block (extent) reads or scatter I/O to bring the required pages into the bufferpool from disk. Prefetching performance is covered in more detail in Chapter 6.

PAGE CLEANERS (db2pclnr)

Page cleaners are used to write updated (dirty) pages to disk so that free space is available for new pages to be brought into the bufferpool. If there are not enough page cleaners configured, agents must write the dirty pages to disk. This will impact performance because the write operation is synchronous. It is important to configure enough page cleaners to perform asynchronous writes. See Chapter 8 for additional information on configuring page cleaners.

> **NOTE**
> When a page cleaner flushes a dirty page to disk, the dirty flag is removed but the page remains in the bufferpool. This page will remain in the bufferpool until a prefetcher or agent overwrites it.

LOGS (db2loggr)

All changes to data pages in the bufferpool are logged. As data is updated, agent processes write a log record to the log buffer. The log records in the log buffer are flushed to the log files asynchronously by the logger. Neither updated data pages in the bufferpool nor the log records in the log buffer are written to disk immediately to optimize performance. They are written to the disk by page cleaners and the logger, respectively.

The logger and the bufferpool manager coordinate and make sure that the updated data page is not written to disk before its associated log record is written to the log. This is known as "write-ahead logging." Refer to Chapter 10 for more information on logging.

DEADLOCK DETECTOR

Deadlock detection is one of the most important functions in DB2. A deadlock occurs when two applications are holding locks on data that each application needs. Both are waiting for each other to release the lock. This is also known as a "deadly embrace." If a deadlock situation is not resolved, the applications involved could wait forever. Plus, they could and usually do cause many other applications to wait on this same data. This results in a clogged system that could stall or hang. Fortunately, DB2 has a deadlock detection mechanism that runs in the background and checks for deadlocks. When DB2 finds a deadlock, it chooses one of the applications to receive a terminal SQL error code and then conducts a rollback for the application. Once the rollback is complete, the locks previously held are released and the deadlock is resolved.

The *dlchktime* DB CFG parameter controls the interval for deadlock checking. The default is 10 seconds. This should be adequate in most situations. If a deadlock is encountered, the higher this setting is the longer deadlocked resources are locked. This decreases database concurrency. Usually, this is a sign of an application sequencing problem. Fix application design problems before changing *dlchktime* to accommodate a poorly written application. If running ERP, CRM, or SCM packaged applications, check the vendor documentation for recommendations. Many of these vendors test their applications in conjunction with IBM and arrive at recommended settings for this parameter.

> **NOTE**
> Lock snapshot information has been significantly improved in v8. Snapshot on locks now provides details on the SQL involved, lists only the connections involved, and provides more granularity on locks involved.

Information on resolving locking problems is covered in more detail in Chapter 11.

CONNECTION CONCENTRATOR

Connection concentrator allows many applications to connect to DB2 while minimizing the amount of memory and processes needed to process and maintain large numbers of connections. This is especially beneficial for Internet applications with many transient connections or similar applications. The new connection concentrator architecture reduces the amount of memory used for each connection and decreases the number of context switches by using an *n:m* architecture. This offers significant performance improvements.

> **NOTE**
> Enable Connection Concentrator by setting the value of `max_connections` greater than the value of `max_coordagents`.

As depicted in Figure 2.4, Connection Concentrator works like this:

After the first connection, the connection concentrator reduces the connect time to the host. When a disconnect is processed, the inbound connection is dropped, but the outbound connection to the host is kept in a pool, where it becomes a logical subagent that is controlled by a logical coordinator agent with an active connection to the remote host. When a new request is made to connect to the host, DB2 tries to reuse an existing outbound connection from the pool.

SUMMARY

DB2 comes in several editions to enable businesses to select the right edition for their needs. The former EE and EEE have been merged to form Enterprise Server Edition. ESE includes the capability to partition databases on SMP machines. With the ESE Database Partitioning feature, you can create partitioned databases across multiple physical machines. This enables DB2 to scale as your business requirements increase. The DB2 process model provides for a client/server architecture. DB2 processes such as prefetchers and page cleaners process work in the background so agents and applications do not wait for data. Connection concentrator paves the way for DB2 to be able to efficiently process thousands of connections.

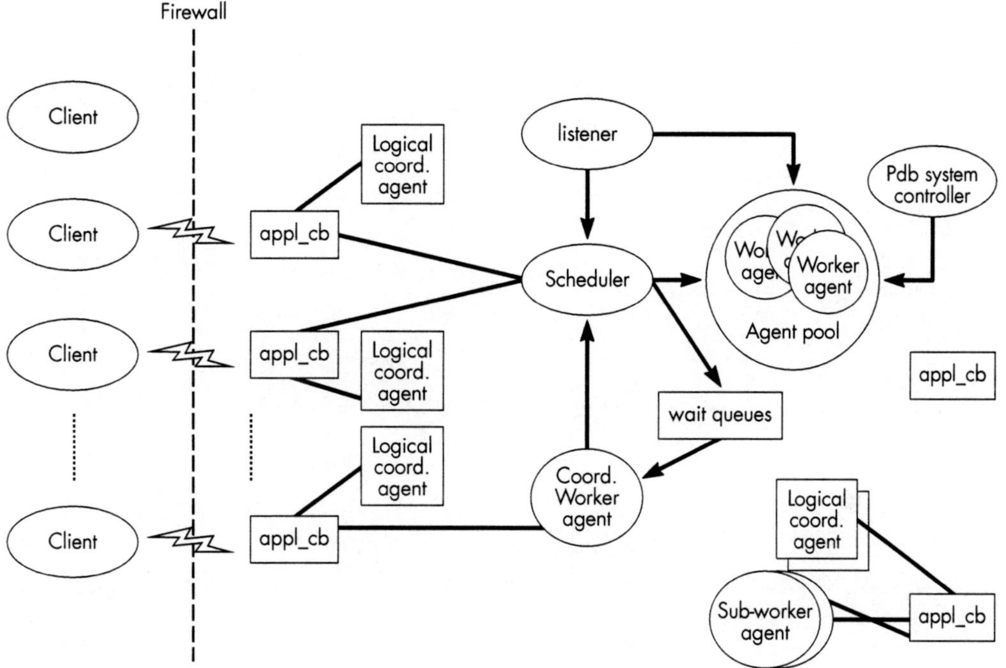

Figure 2.4
Connection Concentrator.

CHAPTER 3

Logical and Physical Design

Logical design is the process of identifying entities and the relationships between those entities. It begins with the business model that is transitioned to a logical model as part of the logical design process. All new database projects and modifications or improvements to existing applications require a logical design. A logical model is used to document the logical design. There are several data modeling tools on the market (e.g., Erwin from CA, ERstudio from Embarcadoro, PowerDesigner from Sybase, and Rational Rose from Rationale Software). The logical design process and availability and upkeep of the logical model are key ingredients to a successful project and database implementation. Without them a project is doomed to failure. The process can be customized or tailored for enhancements or maintenance projects but it cannot be skipped.

Logical design is the most important step in designing a database. If you don't do it in the beginning and if it is not done right, then typically an implementation will fail and require serious modification to the application and database structure in production, usually at the expense of loss of business due to the new system not working at all, or providing only limited function.

I have never worked on a project that skipped logical design and was successful and I doubt you have or ever will either. So let's get on with the details.

BUSINESS MODEL

A business model is a description of business entities, functions, relationships, and the business rules associated with them. The business model is essential to logical design and is the primary input to the logical design process. Business architects and analysts are responsible for developing and maintaining the business model. See Figure 3.1 for an example of a business model.

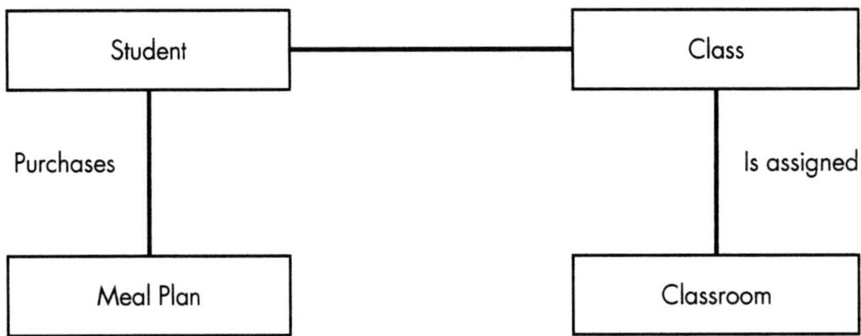

Figure 3.1
A business model.

The business model in Figure 3.1 identifies business entities and the basic relationships between them. In addition to a diagram, the business model consists of data flow diagrams, state diagrams, business rule documentation, and other documents that help to further define the functions of the business. The business model reflects the business practices of an organization independently of any requirements for the underlying structure of a RDBMS. The business model is further refined into a conceptual model. The following rules should be used in developing and defining business models:

- Each entity should have a self-describing name that is acceptable throughout the organization
- A complete definition for the entity that defines what is included and excluded
- An identifier for a business entity to discern it from other entities or multiple occurrences of the entity type

Business Entities

Business architects are responsible for identifying and documenting business entities, relationships, and business rules. This is often documented in a tabular form. See Table 3.1 for an example of business entities.

Table 3.1 Business Entities

Entity Name	Abbreviation	Identifier	Description
STUDENT	STUDENT	Unique Student ID	A registered student
CLASS	CLASS	Unique Class Number	Class offered
INSTRUCTOR	INST	Unique Instructor ID	Instructor ID

A series of models are used to document and depict business rules, entities, relationships, constraints, and physical database implementation. There are three types of data models: conceptual, logical, and physical.

In the following sections we will discuss the details of each model. Once we have identified and documented business entities, we can convert the business model to an entity–relationship diagram (conceptual model), as shown in Figure 3.2.

Once we have an entity–relationship diagram, we can convert it to a logical model by using the following steps:

1. Convert business entities to data entities
2. Represent the degree of the relationships between entities
3. Identify conditional relationships
4. Convert many-to-many relationships
5. Convert repeating groups to characteristic entities

In Figure 3.3, we converted the conceptual model in Figure 3.2 to a logical model using the steps provided.

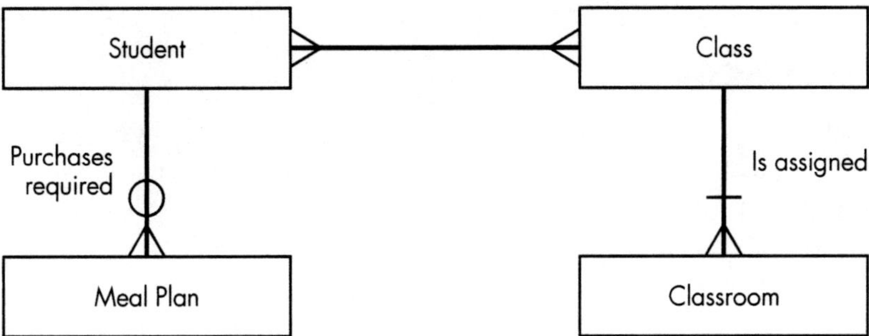

Figure 3.2
An entity–relationship diagram.

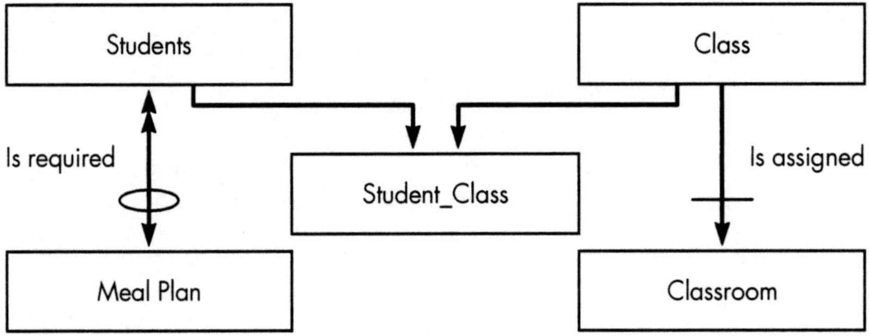

Figure 3.3
Entity–relationship diagram converted to logical model.

In Figure 3.3 we have defined the cardinality of the relationships between entities and have created the `Student_Class` *associative entity* to eliminate the many-to-many relationship between Student and Class. We will understand the reason for this later in this chapter. In Figure 3.3, notice the circle close to the Meal Plan entity. This denotes an *optional relationship* between Student and Meal Plan. A student can exist without having a meal plan, as is the case at times with students that commute. The solid line across the connecting line between Class and Classroom identifies a *mandatory relationship.* A Class cannot exist unless it is assigned to a Classroom. Optional and mandatory relationships are useful for documenting and enforcing business rules.

BUSINESS RULES

Business rules define how a business operates. An example is that a customer can only have one charge account, an invoice cannot be paid unless associated with a valid purchase order, and each customer charge account must be associated with a valid social security number. These types of business rules are known as *constraints.* Business rules also define the degree or cardinality of the relationship between business entities. Business rules are unique to each business and can vary widely from business to business.

ENTITIES AND RELATIONSHIPS

Once we have identified business entities, relationships, and rules, we can document them as part of the logical design process using entity–relationship (ER) diagrams. The conceptual model, as previously illustrated in Figure 3.2, is represented using ER diagrams. It is as close to a real-world view of an organization's data as possible. Entity-relationship diagramming was invented by P. P. Chen in 1976.

However, before you can develop ER diagrams and conduct the normalization process, it's helpful for you to understand some key terms.

Entity

An *entity* is a person, place, thing, concept, or event. You can think of it as a noun.

Relationship

A *relationship* is used to describe the relationship between entities. Relationships are defined in terms of action words. You can think of it as a verb. A relationship can be *optional* or *mandatory,* as previously described.

Candidate Key

A *candidate key* is an attribute or combination of attributes that uniquely identifies an instance of a relation.

Primary Key

A *primary key* is a candidate key that is selected as the unique identifier of a row.

Relation

A *relation* is a two-dimensional table consisting of attributes (columns) and tuples (rows).

Foreign Key

A *foreign key* is used to record the relationships between entities. The primary key of the entity on the one side of a one-to-one or one-to-many relationship is placed in the entity on the one or many side. Foreign keys are used to implement referential integrity and can have additional rules associated with them. For example, if the parent entry in a parent–child relationship is deleted, the associated entries in the child entity will be deleted. This is known as "cascade delete."

Cardinality

Cardinality is the degree of the relationship between entities. We can also identify certain relationships or attributes using functional dependencies by observing two attributes, for example, A and B, which can be related in three ways indicated by fd notation in the headings (A => B and B => A, etc.). The cardinalities that will be sufficient for our purposes are: one-to-one, one-to-many, and many-to-many.

One-to-One Relationship (A => B and B => A)

A single instance of one type is related to a single entity of the other type, In Figure 3.4, the `EMPLOYEE–CUBICLE` relationship associates a single employee with a single cubicle. According to the relationship, no employee has more than one cubicle and one cubicle cannot be assigned to more than one employee.

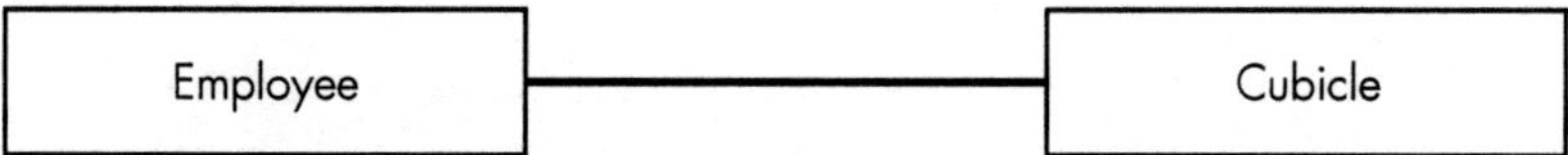

Figure 3.4
A one-to-one relationship.

One-to-Many Relationship (A => B but B not => A)

A single instance of one type is related to many instances of the other type. In Figure 3.5, the `DEPARTMENT–EMPLOYEE` relationship shows that an employee is assigned to one department and that a department has many employees.

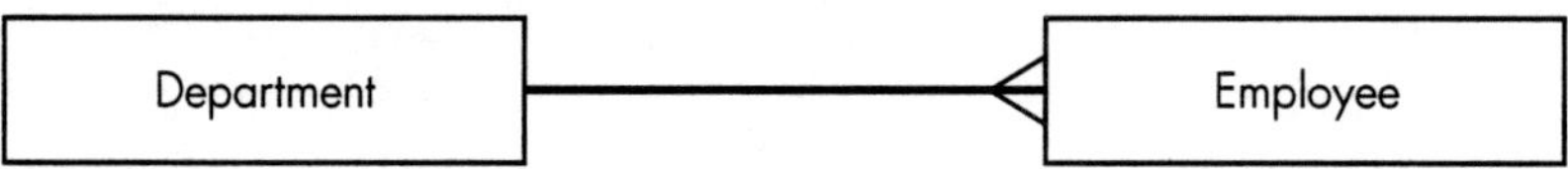

Figure 3.5
A one-to-many relationship.

Many-to-Many Relationship (A not => B and B not => A)

Many instances of one type are related to many instances of the other type. In Figure 3.6, the STUDENT–ORGANIZATION relationship associates many instances of Student to many instances of Organization. A student can join more than one organization and an organization can have many students as members.

Figure 3.6
A many-to-many relationship.

SPECIAL ENTITY RELATIONSHIPS

Characteristic Entity

Repeating groups present a problem to relational databases. This is caused by the storing of redundant data and the loss of flexibility if additional elements have to be added.

Therefore, you will need to create a characteristic entity, which will essentially involve creating another entity using the primary key from the original entity and adding columns to the primary key to ensure uniqueness.

In the following relation, a manager can receive more than one bonus, thus we have a repeating group, the attribute MGR_BONUS:

```
MANAGER (MGR_ID, MGR_NAME, MGR_BRANCH, MGR_HIRE_DATE, MGR_BONUS1,
MGR_BONUS2,...MGR_BONUS5)
```

As shown in the MANAGER relation, a Finance Company manager can get up to five bonuses in a year. The MANAGER relation has five columns defined to store this BONUS information. However, if the company decides to give a manager a sixth bonus, BONUS6, it will not be able to. In the following relation, we created a new characteristic entity as follows:

BONUS (**MGR_ID**, **BON_DATE**, BON_AMOUNT)

With MGR_ID and BON_DATE as the primary key, this will resolve the repeating group problem and is much more flexible, allowing a manager to receive any number of bonuses without the underlying table requiring any changes. However, the business rule in this case only allows one bonus to be issued per day. That certainly is a reasonable business rule!

Associative Entity

An associative entity is used to resolve many-to-many relationships. Many-to-many relationships are difficult to support in a RDBMS and are subject to modification anomalies. In the following example, we have a many-to-many between STUDENT and CLASS:

```
STUDENT (ID, NAME, ADDRESS, PHONE_NMR, EMERG_CONTACT)
CLASS (CLASS_NAME, NBR_CREDITS, PREREQUISITES, CLASS_NBR)
```

We resolve the many-to-many relationship by creating an association entity (STU_CLASS) that serves as a "go-between" for the two related identities.

```
STU_CLASS (ID, CLASS_NBR, NAME)
```

This is done by creating a new entity, STU_CLASS, which contains the primary key from STUDENT and CLASS (ID and CLASS_NBR) as the new primary key. These columns are also foreign keys, which point to the parent table.

The new relationship contains two one-to-many relationships, which are much easier to understand and more accurately reflects how the data is used.

NORMALIZATION

Once you have identified business entities and converted them to a logical model, the logical model needs to be normalized. *Normalization* is the process of identifying and eliminating redundant data elements in the logical design to avoid update and delete anomalies. The normalization process uses a series of forms (CODD,1970) that have defined rules, and these rules are applied to each entity in an iterative approach.

For our purposes, we will discuss five types of normal forms. They are First Normal Form (1NF), Second Normal Form (2NF), Third Normal Form (3NF), Boyce-Codd Normal Form (BCNF), and Domain/Key Normal Form (DK/NF). DBAs should also become familiar with Elementary Key Normal Form (EKNF) and Project-Join Normal Form (PJNF), but they are beyond the scope of this chapter.

Functional Dependencies

A *functional dependency* is a relationship between or among attributes. An example would be that if we are given the value of one attribute, we can obtain the value of another attribute. For example, if we know the value of STUDENT_ID we can find the value of GRADE_LEVEL. We can restate this using the following notation:

```
STUDENT_ID => GRADE_LEVEL
```

which can be read as the attribute STUDENT_ID determines the attribute GRADE_LEVEL or GRADE_LEVEL is determined by STUDENT_ID. The attributes on the left side of the arrow are called *determinants*.

We will see later in this section how functional dependencies can be used to normalize relations.

Key

A *key* is a group of one or more attributes that uniquely identifies a row. Every relation must contain a primary key. It should be noted that keys and functional dependencies are not determined by some arbitrary set of rules but are determined by the *business rules* of the organization.

First Normal Form

A relation is in first normal form (1NF) if it contains no repeating groups. That is, each attribute (or column) must have only one value. Neither arrays nor repeating groups are allowed. Let's take a look at the CUSTOMER_ACCOUNT relation:

CUSTOMER_ACCOUNT (**CUST_ID**, **ACCT_NBR**, CUST_NM, ADDRESS, TYPE, DESCRIPTION, BRANCH_NBR, BRANCH_ADDR)

where:

CUST_ID = customer identifier
ACCT_NBR = account number
CUST_NM = customer name
ADDRESS = customer address
TYPE = account type
DESCRIPTION = account description
BRANCH_NBR = branch number
BRANCH_ADDR = branch address

This relation is in 1NF since it has no repeating groups, but has some inherent modification anomalies. What happens if a customer closes their account? All data regarding a customer such as customer identification, account number, and customer address will be lost. Also, inserting new data is a problem. The type of account, description, and branch address cannot be inserted until a customer opens an account.

The problem with the CUSTOMER_ACCOUNT relation is that nonkey attributes are dependent on parts of the primary key, but not the entire key. We can see this by identifying the functional dependencies involved:

```
CUST_ID => CUST_NM but ACCT_NBR => CUST_NM
CUST_ID => ADDRESS but ACCT_NBR => ADDRESS
CUST_ID => TYPE but ACCT_NBR => TYPE
ACCT_NBR => DESCRIPTION but CUST_ID => DESCRPTION
ACCT_NBR => BRANCH_NBR but CUST_ID => BRANCH_NBR
ACCT_NBR => BRANCH_ADDR but CUST_ID => BRANCH_ADDR
```

In order to eliminate modification anomalies, relations in 1NF must be normalized to 2NF and 3NF. This will result in more entities being created throughout the normalization process.

SECOND NORMAL FORM

A relation is in second normal form (2NF) if it is in 1NF and all of its nonkey attributes are dependent on all of the keys. Therefore, if the key has only one attribute, the relation must be in 2NF.

The CUSTOMER_ACCOUNT relation from our previous example can be decomposed into four new relations as follows:

```
CUST_MSTR (CUST_ID, CUST_NM, ADDRESS)
BRANCH_LOC (BRANCH_NBR, BRANCH_ADDR)
ACCT_TYPE (TYPE, DESCRIPTION)
CUST_ACCT (CUST_ID, ACCT_NBR)
```

These new relations are in 2NF. The CUST_MSTR, BRANCH_LOC, and ACCT_TYPE relations have primary keys with just one attribute. And the CUST_ACCT relation contains no nonkey attributes. Customer information can be inserted into the CUST_MSTR relation before an account is opened. Deletion of all customers assigned to a certain branch will not result in branch information being deleted. Deletion of all accounts for a customer will not result in loss of customer data.

Relations that are in 2NF can still have modification anomalies. For example, the relation

```
BANK_FEES (ACT_NBR, TRAN_TYPE, FEE)
```

is in 2NF, since the primary key ACT_NBR only has one attribute, but there is a dependency involving a nonkey attribute (TRAN_TYPE) on another nonkey attribute (FEE). By identifying functional dependencies, you can identify the anomalies as follows:

```
ACCT_NBR => TRAN_TYPE
ACCT_NBR => TRAN_TYPE => FEE
```

We have dependencies between nonkey attributes; the TRAN_TYPE and FEE.

```
TRANTYPE => FEE
```

The fee charged is determined by the transaction type. What happens if we delete an account number from the BANK_FEE relation? We lose the fact that a certain transaction type is associated with a specific fee.

Another method that can be used to normalize relations is the concept of themes. Generally, if there are multiple themes in a relation, the relation can be decomposed further into relations with single themes to eliminate modification anomalies. Using the following relation, we can see that this relation has two themes, one containing student activity information and one containing activity cost information.

```
STUD_ACTIVITY (STU_ID, ACTIVITY, FEE)
```

We can decompose these relations into additional single-theme relations:

```
STU_ACT (STU_ID, ACTIVITY)
ACTIVITY_COST (ACTIVITY, FEE)
```

So you can use whichever technique you are more comfortable with.

Third Normal Form (3NF)

A relation is in 3NF if it is in 2NF and has no *transitive dependencies*. Another well known definition for 3NF is a situation in which an attribute is "a function of the key, the whole key, and nothing but the key."

In the BANK_FEES relation, the transitive dependency between TRAN_TYPE and FEE was illustrated. To resolve the transitive dependency, the relation can be decomposed into two new relations as follows:

```
BANK_FEE (TRAN_TYPE, FEE)
ACTIVITY (ACCT_NBR, TRAN_TYPE)
```

Boyce-Codd Normal Form (BCNF)

Another level of normalization is BCNF. Relations in 3NF can still have modification anomalies. Hence, we can continue to normalize relations in our search to eliminate modification anomalies.

A relation is in BCNF if every determinant is a candidate key. In the following relation

```
ADVISER (SID, MAJOR, FAC_NAM)
```

a student can have more than one major (MAJOR). A major can have several faculty members (FAC_NAM) as advisers, and a faculty member (FAC_NAM) advises in only one major area. The combination (SID, MAJOR) determines FAC_NAM, and the combination (SID, FAC_NAM) determines the major. Hence, both of these combinations are candidate keys. Additionally, FAC_NAM determines MAJOR (any faculty member advises in only one major; therefore, given the FAC_NAM, we can determine MAJOR). So, FAC_NAME is a determinant. But ADVISER is in 3NF because it is in 2NF and there are no transitive dependencies.

However, ADVISER still has modification anomalies. Suppose a student drops out of school. If we delete the row with the SID of 500, we lose the fact that the assigned adviser advises in psychology. This is a deletion anomaly. Similarly, we cannot store the fact that an adviser advises in history until a student majors in history. This is an insertion anomaly. As with previous examples we can decompose ADVISER into two relations to resolve the anomalies. The two new relations are:

```
STUDENT_ADVISER (STU_ID, FAC_NAM)
ADV_SUBJ (FAC_NAM, SUBJECT)
```

These two new relations are now in BCNF normal form and have no anomalies in regard to functional dependencies.

DOMAIN KEY/NORMAL FORM (DK/NF)

This normal form was defined in 1981 by R. Fagin. A relation is in DK/NF if every constraint on the relation is a logical consequence of the definition of keys and domains. In order to understand DK/NF form it is important that you understand the following definitions.

Constraint

A *constraint* is any rule governing static values of attributes that is precise enough to enable us to determine whether or not it is true. Note that time-dependent constraints are excluded from this definition. Valid constraints are edit rules, functional, multi-value dependencies, and inter- and intra-relational constraints.

Key

A *key* is a unique identifier of a row (tuple).

Domain

A *domain* is a description of the allowed values of an attribute. Check constraints are an example of this in DB2. A domain has two parts: a physical description that defines the set of values the attribute can have, and a logical description that defines the meaning of the attribute.

A relation is in DK/NF if enforcing key and domain restrictions causes all of the constraints to be met. This is especially important to an RDBMS, since they can prohibit modification anomalies by enforcing key and domain restrictions.

A straightforward approach for converting relations to DK/NF has not been defined. However, in a RDBMS the facilities for doing it are usually provided as part of the RDBMS. If the constraints cannot be implemented by the database, then they can be coded into the application logic.

In the following relation

```
CUSTOMER (CUST_ID, ACCT_LEVEL, ACCT_TYPE, FEE)
  CUST_ID = Customer identifier
  ACCT_TYPE = Account type
  FEE = FEE charged based on type of account
```

`CUST_ID` functionally determines `ACCT_LEVEL`, `ACCT_TYPE`, and `FEE` so `CUST_ID` is the key. Our business rules in this relation place domain constraints on each of the attributes and we know that `ACCT_TYPE` => `FEE`. In accordance with the rules for DK/NF, we need to make the functional dependency `ACCT_TYPE` => `FEE` a logical consequence of keys. If `ACCT_TYPE` were a key attribute, `ACCT_TYPE` => `FEE` would be a logical consequence of the key.

`ACCT_TYPE` cannot be a key in Customer because more than one customer can have the same account type. But it can be a key of its own relation. So, we define the following domain definition, relations, and attributes:

```
DOMAIN DEFINITIONS
  CUST_ID in DDDDDD, where D is a decimal digit >0<999999
  ACCT_LEVEL in  ("PERS", "CML", "INTB")
  ACCT_TYPE in CHAR (3)
  FEE in DEC (4)
RELATION AND KEY DEFINITIONS
  CUSTOMER (CUST_ID, ACCT_LEVEL, ACCT_TYPE)
  KEY:  CUST_ID
  ACCT_FEE (ACCT_TYPE, FEE)
KEY:  ACCT_TYPE
```

We know that by converting the relation to DK/NF, the relations have no modification anomalies whatsoever. We could have arrived at this result by converting from 2NF to 3NF to remove transitive dependencies. However, using DK/NF we just need to make all the constraints logical consequences of domain and key definitions.

Unified Modeling Language (UML)

The Unified Modeling Language (UML) was adopted by the Object Management Group (OMG) in November 1997 as a language for object-oriented analysis and design. The OMG received input regarding the UML specification from industry leaders such as Microsoft, IBM, and Oracle.

In addition to being used for designing object-oriented programs, it has made in-roads into logical database design. This is a natural evolution as UML-capable tools are widely used to model, construct, and deploy enterprise applications.

UML class diagrams are similar to entities in ER diagrams and can be used for conceptual and logical design. Many UML-capable tools can input and convert ER diagrams to object class diagrams. Since it is so full-featured, UML is well positioned to become the enterprise application development and data modeling tool of choice. This will be appealing to IT organizations because the entire enterprise from business architects to database administrators will all be able to work from the same model and tool set. As a DBA or data modeler, you should become familiar with the use of UML and associated outputs. I anticipate that it will eventually see widespread use in logical design.

Logical Design Outputs

A logical model identifying the entities, relationships, and attributes for the data being modeled is the primary output of the logical design process. The logical design is complete with primary and foreign keys and constraints defined on the data, and should contain data at least normalized to 3NF, or DK/NF if possible. The logical model is the primary input to physical design.

Physical Design

Once the logical design has been completed, physical design can begin. Physical design consists of the following five steps:

1. Denormalization
2. Creation of indexes
3. Creation of tablespaces and tables
   - Container layout
   - Disk strategy
4. Tablespace breakout strategy
5. Bufferpool strategy

Denormalization

Normalized relations eliminate or reduce modification anomalies. However, the process also results in many more relations, which will be subsequently converted (in most cases) to DB2 tables. Sometimes the costs (query runtime and complexity) outweigh the benefits of normalization.

With continued enhancements to the DB2 optimizer, cost is not as much a factor as it used to be (in terms of processing many table joins, etc.), but it still can be a factor to consider when trying to optimize the physical design. Denormalization is the process of combining relations or attributes from relations to reduce the number of relations to be processed and to reduce the complexity of queries. Denormalization is sometimes referred to as "controlled redundancy." Denormalization is primarily done for performance gains, to provide read-only tables for decision reports, or for ad hoc reporting, but like "caveat emptor" the DA or DBA must be aware of the redundancy subsequent modification anomalies that can be produced. Denormalization can be done just using the logical model but it is done much better if the DBA has the SQL so that they are aware of the relationships and joins involved. A DBA must have the SQL queries associated with the logical model in order to develop a proper physical design.

> **HINT**
> Many logical modeling tools can generate Data Definition Language (DDL) to create the physical objects. Use this generated SQL (you can modify it, if necessary) to save time and increase productivity.

Creation of Indexes

Unique (primary key) indexes and indexes on foreign keys should be created based on the logical model. Secondary indexes, to support SQL queries, join operations, and business reports, should be created as part of physical design. In order for this to occur the SQL needs to be provided to the DBA staff at this time, although too often this is not the case and the SQL is not available. Therefore, it is very difficult to identify all the secondary indexes required. What usually happens in this case is that the application does not meet performance expectations in production, and significant modification is required to programs and indexes.

If the SQL is available at the initial physical design, then the DBA can create indexes to meet the needs of the business.

Follow these guidelines when creating secondary indexes:

- Create indexes to eliminate `SORTS` required by `ORDER BY`, `GROUP BY`, and `DISTINCT` SQL statements.
- Create indexes on joined columns.
  - Failure to do so could result in a cartesian product, which is not always desirable.
- Create indexes on local predicates to get index-only access.
- Consider using `INCLUDE` columns to obtain index-only access.
- Create indexes including the `ALLOW REVERSE SCANS` clause to eliminate sorts.
- Create indexes on foreign keys.
- Create a clustering index on every table.
- Consider use of `APPEND ON` for highly inserted tables.
- Use Multidimensional Clustering (MDC) indexes for data warehousing environments and consider MDC for online transaction processing (OLTP) environments.

For more information on indexes, refer to Chapter 7.

Creation of Tablespaces and Tables

A tablespace and table strategy needs to be developed: the type of space that will be used, SMS or DMS, as well as the size and number of tables per tablespace, along with the number of containers to be used.

> **HINT**
> Prior to creation of tablespaces, remember to enable the `DB2_PARALLEL_IO` environmental variable so that it is applied to any tablespaces you create.

File systems must be built or drive assignment verified and raw logical volumes requested if DMS device containers are being used. This requires coordination with system, storage, and possibly network or InfiniBand administrators if storage area networks (SANs) or InfiniBand networks are being used or planned.

Tablespace Breakout Strategy

A tablespace breakout strategy consists of the following:

- Assigning high priority tables to a single tablespace.

- Placing high priority tablespaces in dedicated bufferpools and/or on separate physical disks or disk arrays.
- Creating separate tablespaces for indexes and/or assigning indexes to separate bufferpools.

Bufferpool Strategy

Objects should be assigned to bufferpools based on business priorities and access type. Business priorities are contained in or derived from business needs. Access type pertains to whether or not access is sequential or random. Place objects with different access types into different bufferpools. That way, an object with lots of sequential prefetch against it will not compete for bufferpool space with randomly accessed objects. Refer to Chapter 8 for more information on bufferpools.

Summary

Logical design is the single most important step in database design. It cannot be skipped. It can be customized to support specific development efforts.

Business architects identify business entities and business rules and develop the conceptual model. Data administrators or DBAs develop the logical design and normalize it to meet business objectives. This is typically to 3NF or DK/NF. The importance of identifying and eliminating modification anomalies has been discussed. UML was introduced and identified as a future modeling language. The importance of having well-defined and documented business rules was presented.

The logical model is important to the physical design process. Most modeling tools can generate DDL for use in building the physical design. Tablespace design, as well as container strategy and disk layout, need to be planned and coordinated with UNIX, SAN, and network administrators. Finally, business priorities need to be used in developing a tablespace breakout and bufferpool strategy.

CHAPTER 4

Application Development

DB2 v8 is rich in application development features. The new Development Center makes it easy for developers to use their development tool of choice. Important changes to various drivers has resulted in improved performance for client applications. XML enhancements enable DB2 to act as both a provider and a consumer of Web services. SQL enhancements such as `INSERT` through `UNION ALL VIEWS`, `INSTEAD OF TRIGGERS`, `ORDER BY`, and `FETCH FIRST` in subqueries will enable substantial productivity improvements for application developers. New plug-ins for the Websphere Studio integrated development environment are available for integration with the new Development Center along with new add-ins for Microsoft Visual Studio development products (Visual Basic, Visual C++, and InterDEV). This chapter covers the new DB2 v8 enhancements and also addresses the establishment of the DB2 development environment and how the DB2 provided tools can be used to develop your applications of choice.

GETTING STARTED

Getting started with developing DB2 applications is very easy. The primary enabler to getting started is the Run-Time Client. The Run-Time Client provides the driver required for the following APIs:

- ODBC
- DB2 CLI
- OLE DB
- JDBC
- SQL J

The Run-Time Client is included with the base DB2 ESE product. It is also provided with the following components:

- DB2 Administration Client
- DB2 Application Development Client
- DB2 Universal Developers' Edition (UDE)

The Run-Time Client enables DB2 clients to communicate with DB2 UDB servers.

> **NOTE**
> For v8 clients to work with DB2 UDB v7 servers, you need to enable the use of the DRDA Application Server capability on the DB2 UDB v7 server and the DB2 UDB v7 server needs to be at Fixpack 8 or above.

Although access from v8 clients to v7 DB2 UDB databases is supported, it is not recommended. This is due to the number of restrictions involved.

DB2 Administration Client

The DB2 Administration Client provides all the features of the DB2 Run-Time Client and includes all the DB2 Administration GUI tools, documentation, and support for Thin Clients. Developers can use the Control Center component to browse DB2 schemas and objects, which can aid them in developing applications.

> **NOTE**
> In Windows, the installer needs to make sure the user account used to install the Administration Client is defined on the local machine, belongs to the Local Administrator's group, and has the *Act as part of the operating system* advanced user right.

DB2 Application Development Client

The DB2 Application Development Client provides all the features of the DB2 Administration Client and also includes libraries, header files, documented APIs, and sample programs to build all kinds of applications.

DB2 Personal Developers' Edition (PDE)

PDE enables a developer to design and build single-user desktop applications. PDE is available for the Windows and Linux platforms and includes the DB2 Extenders.

DB2 Universal Developers' Edition

UDE offers a low-cost package for a single application developer to design and build applications for deployment to any of the DB2 UDB platforms. It is for development use only and cannot be used in a production environment. UDE includes all client and server editions, DB2 Extenders, Warehouse Manager, and Intelligent Miner.

DB2 Development Center

The DB2 Development Center is a new integrated development environment in DB2 v8. The Stored Procedure Builder has been replaced and its functions incorporated into the Development Center. Application developers can use the Development Center to build, debug, teat, and deploy JAVA and SQL stored procedures, SQL functions, and table functions that can read MQSeries messages, access OLE DB data sources, and extract data from XML documents. We will look at the Development Center in more detail later in this chapter.

DB2 Visual Explain

DB2 Visual Explain is an excellent tool for developers to aid them in developing efficient SQL. Visual Explain is integrated with the DB2 Control Center, Command Center, and Development Center. Visual Explain is used to explain and analyze SQL statements and display the access plan in a graphical format. It should be used by developers and DBAs to review SQL from unit test, acceptance test, and system test through post-implementation.

DB2 Visual Explain should be available to all developers to use in developing SQL. Although there are other forms of DB2 Visual Explain available, my experience is that using Visual Explain in conjunction with Design Advisor is a very powerful combination that is hard to beat. Visual Explain is definitely a tool that improves the productivity of developers and DBAs alike and should be used throughout the system development life cycle.

For a complete list of DB2 Developer Tools and components, refer to the DB2 *Application Development Guide: Programming Client Applications.*

As noted earlier, Visual Explain can be launched from the Control Center and Command Center. See Figure 4.1 for an example of how to launch Visual Explain from the Control Center.

Figure 4.1 shows how to launch visual explain by right-clicking on the database of interest and selecting *Explain SQL*. After making the selection, the input window appears as shown in Figure 4.2.

The SQL statement in the window was retrieved from a local file. Note that you can change the optimization class to see how various optimization levels affect the performance of the SQL. After making any changes, select the OK button, which causes an explain to be run and the access plan returned in the next window, as shown in Figure 4.3.

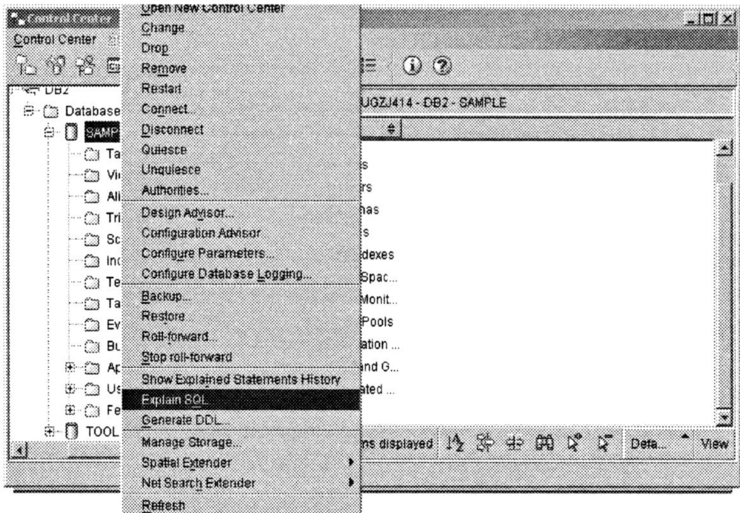

Figure 4.1
Launching Visual Explain from the Control Center.

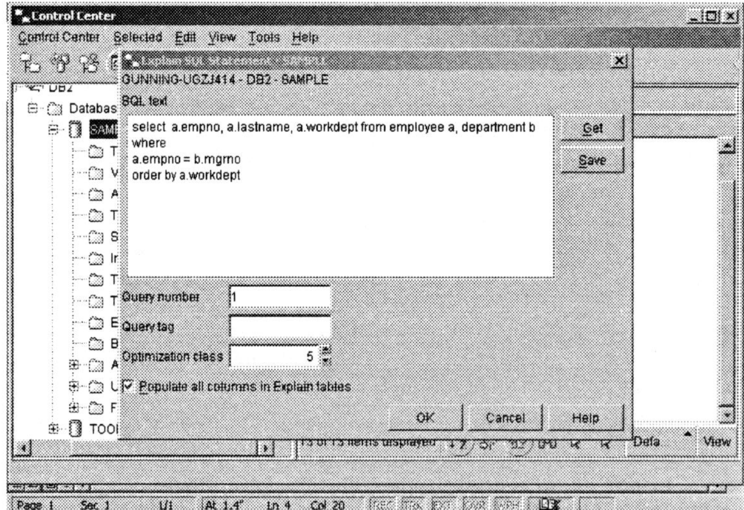

Figure 4.2
Visual Explain Input window.

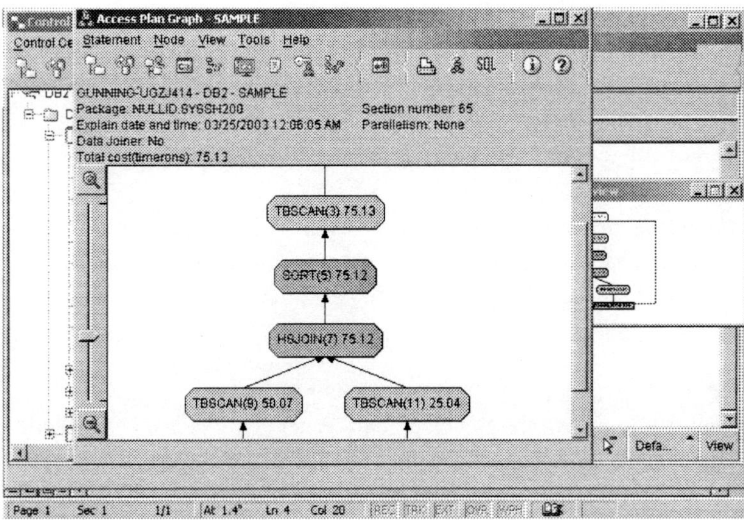

Figure 4.3
Access plan graph.

In Figure 4.3, we can observe from the access plan graph that was returned that a hash join is being used and that a sort is involved. By selecting the sort object, we can get additional details on the sort operation being performed. See Figure 4.4 for details on the sort operation.

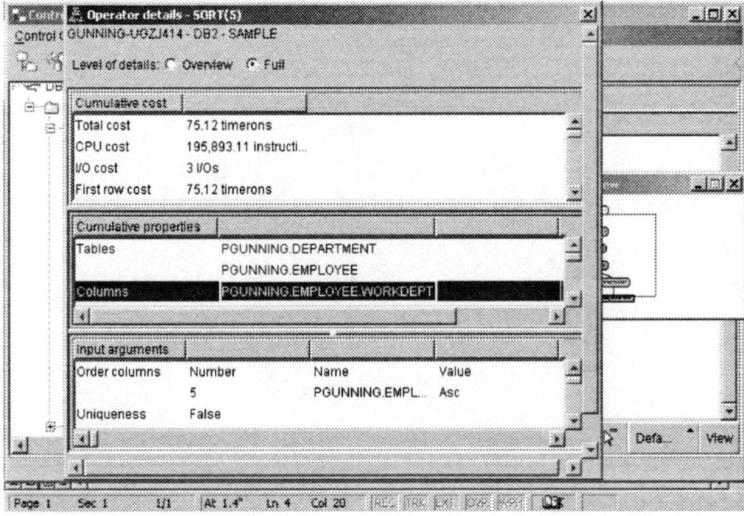

Figure 4.4
Sort details.

The sort details pane provides you with detailed information regarding the sort. You can analyze these details, such as columns involved and statistics, and use this information to eliminate the sort. You can take the statement and run it through Design Advisor to arrive at an optimal solution.

DEVELOPMENT CENTER

The Development Center (DC) is launched from the Control Center. The DC can be used to easily develop SQL or Java stored procedures and user-defined functions and structured data types. While it supports developing and debugging server-side logic in Java and Procedural SQL, stored procedures written in any language can be tested within the Development Center.

The Development Center allows developers to browse the contents of remote databases, as well as containing project management features. The Development Center also provides a DB2 add-in for Visual C++, Visual Basic, and Visual InterDev. With these add-ins, you can easily develop DB2 server-side logic without leaving your Microsoft development environment. A central theme to the Development Center is the concept of a project. The first action that you need to take when launching the Development Center for the first time is to create a project. In the next several examples, I take you through the steps necessary to create a project and build an environment where you can create or import SQL and Java procedures on UDFs. See Figure 4.5 for the initial Development Center panel.

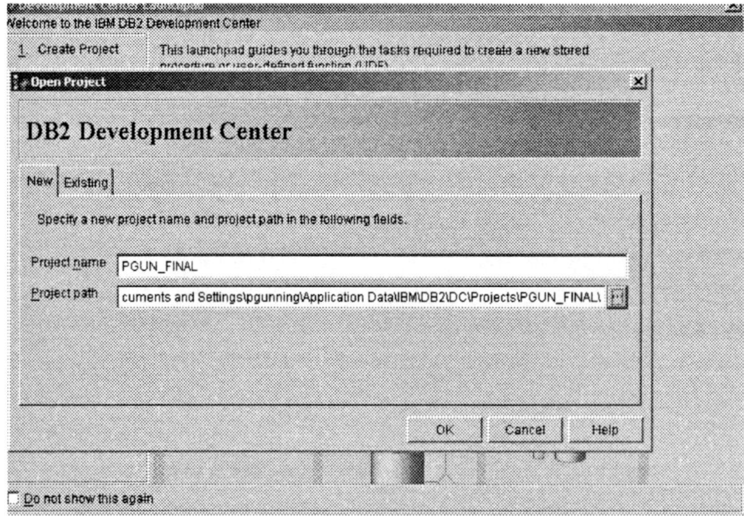

Figure 4.5
DB2 Development Center.

After providing a project name and path, you can click on the Select button and the Connection panel is displayed, as shown in Figure 4.6.

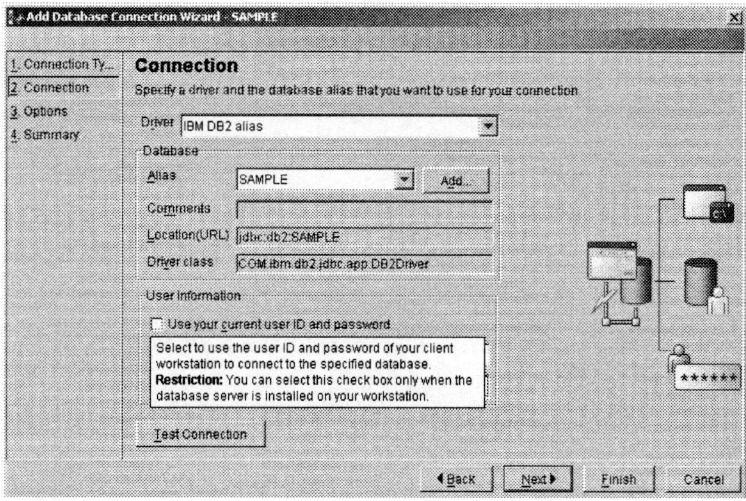

Figure 4.6
Connection Panel.

The Connection Panel is used to specify the type of driver you want to use and the database that you want to work with. After verifying or changing this information, select the Next button to proceed to the Options Panel, as shown in Figure 4.7.

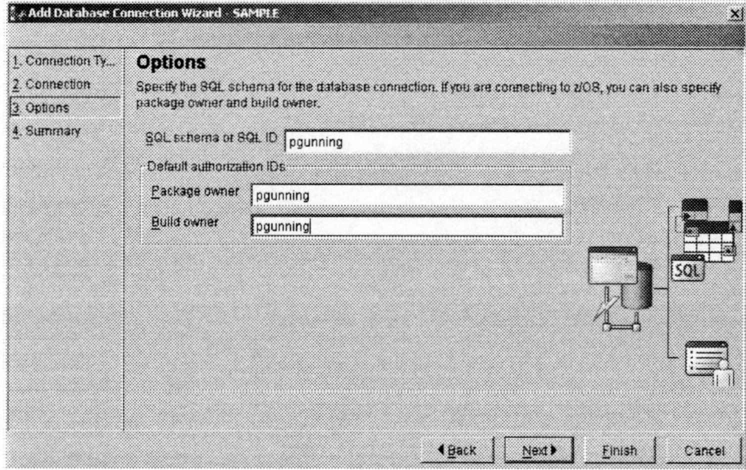

Figure 4.7
Options Panel.

The Option Panel is where you specify the schema for the database connection as well as default authorization IDs. Once you have done this, select Next to proceed to the summary panel, as shown in Figure 4.8.

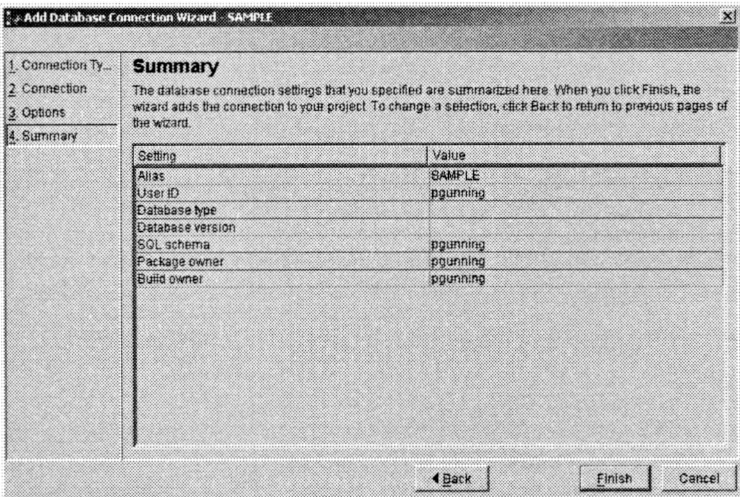

Figure 4.8
Summary Panel.

The Summary Panel displays a list of all your selections. Select the Back button to go back and change settings or select Finish if no changes are required. After selecting Finish, the Development Center Launchpad is launched, as shown in Figure 4.9.

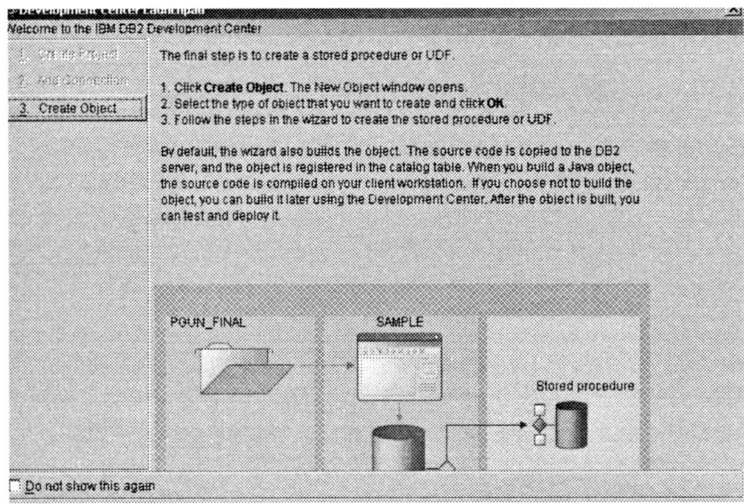

Figure 4.9
Development Center Launchpad.

The final step is to create a Stored Procedure or UDF. You then select Create Object and the New Object selection panel is launched, as shown in Figure 4.10.

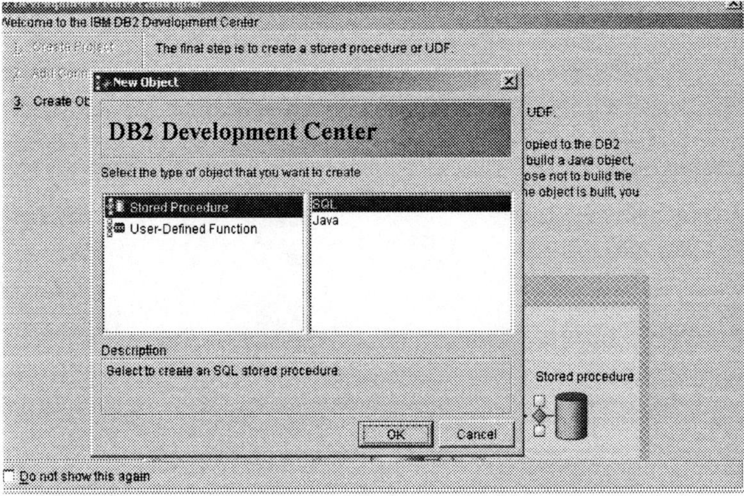

Figure 4.10
Development Center New Object panel.

After we make our object selection by selecting the OK button, the name panel is launched, as shown in Figure 4.11.

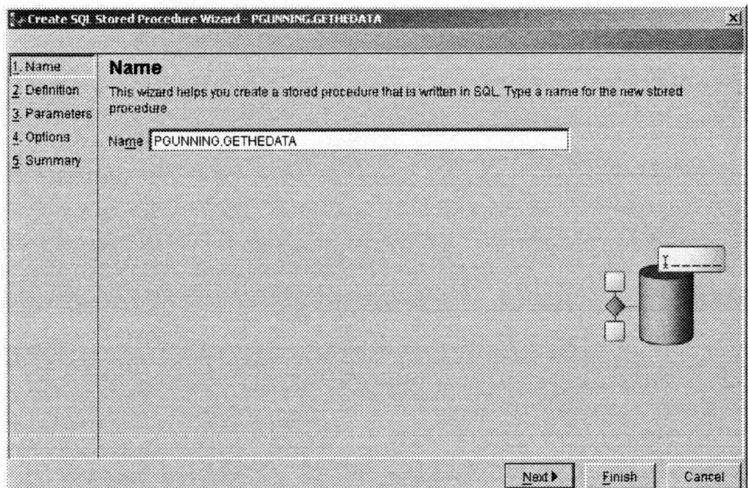

Figure 4.11
Name panel.

The Name panel requires that we give our stored procedure a name. Use a name that follows your company naming standards. Select the Next button and the Definition panel is launched, as shown in Figure 4.12.

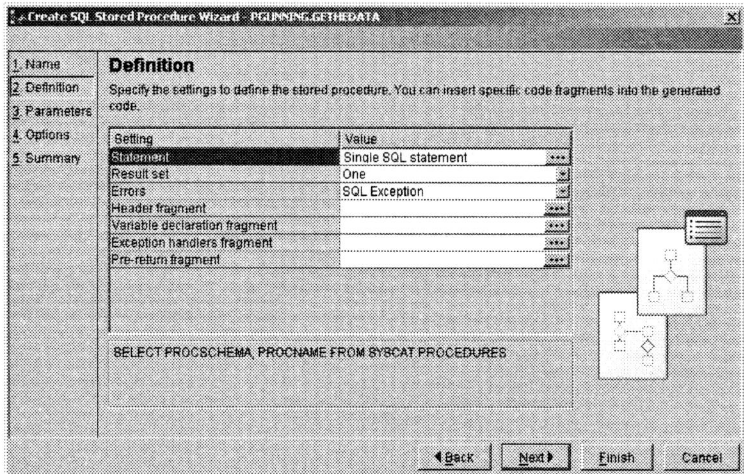

Figure 4.12
Definition panel.

The Definition panel is used to define the stored procedure. The number of statements, result sets, and error handling can be specified. After defining the stored procedure or UDF, select the Next button to display the Parameters panel, as shown in Figure 4.13.

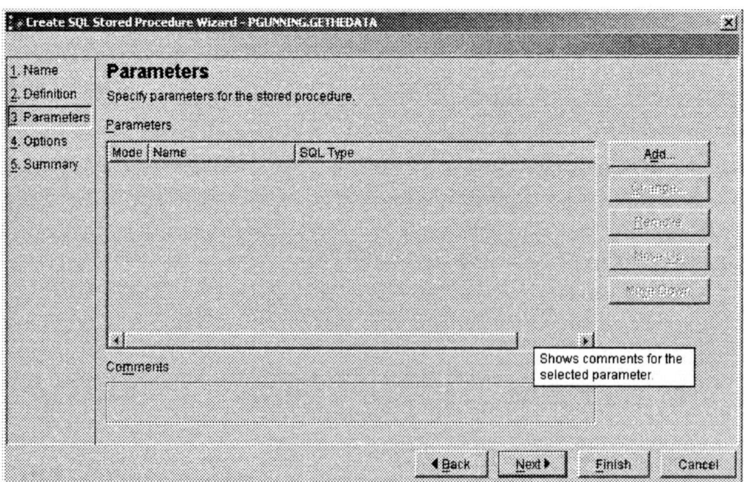

Figure 4.13
Parameters panel.

The Parameter panel of the Create SQL Stored Procedure Wizard helps you to define input and output parameters for your SQL stored procedures. After adding the necessary parameters, select the Next button and the Options panel is displayed, as shown in Figure 4.14.

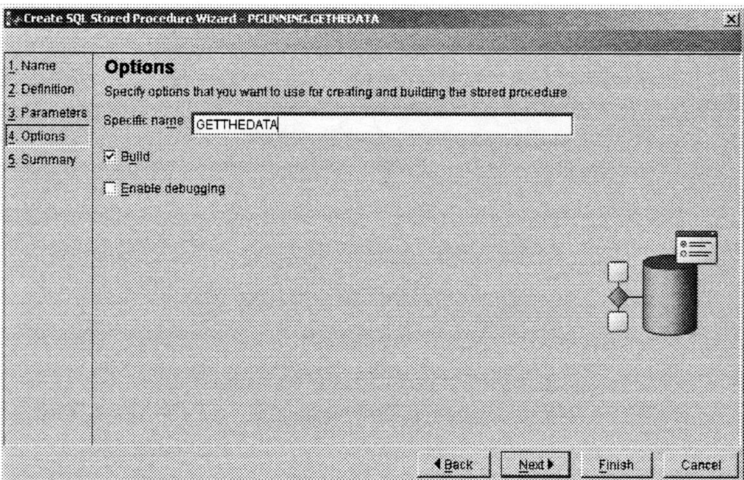

Figure 4.14
Options panel.

The Options panel enables you to provide a specific name for the SP and to determine whether or not debugging is enabled. Once we complete the entries on this panel, select the Next button and the Summary panel is displayed, as shown in Figure 4.15.

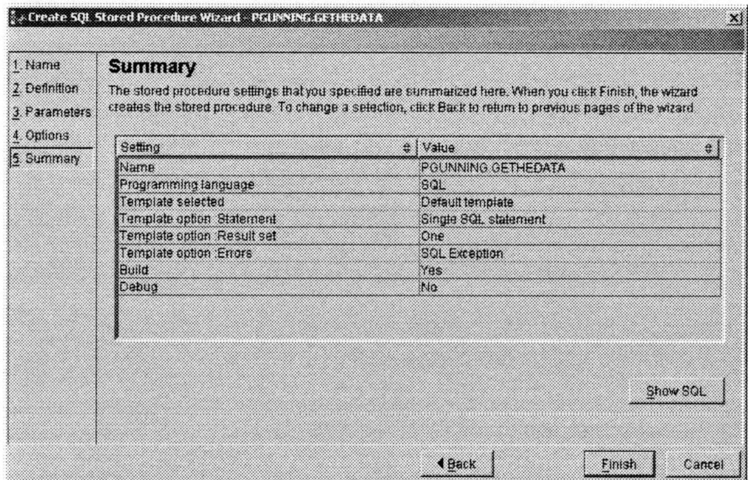

Figure 4.15
Summary panel.

The Summary panel enables us to review the settings that have been specified and to go back and make changes if necessary. By selecting the Finish button, the SP is built and the project view of the DB2 Development Center is displayed, as shown in Figure 4.16.

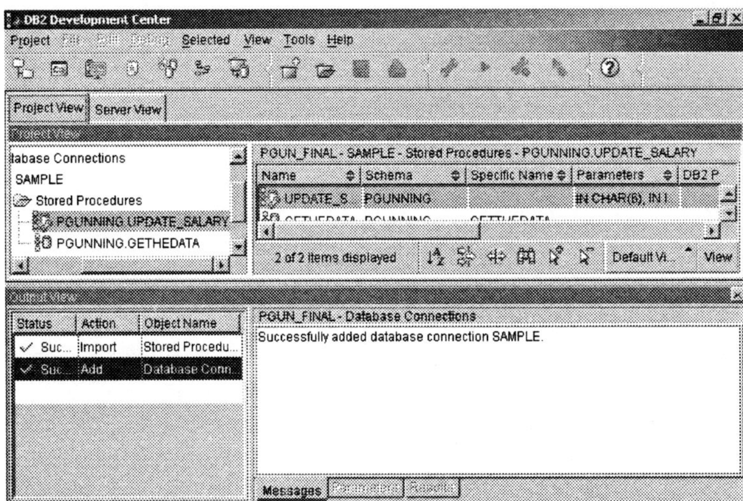

Figure 4.16
Development Center Project View.

As is shown in Figure 4.16, the Project View displays a list of SPs under the SP folder. You can choose which one to work with and you can import procedures from a text file. In Figure 4.15, two SPs are defined. We created the GETHEDATA SP and imported the DB2-provided sample SQL procedure, UPDATE_SALARY, from the DB2 SAMPLES directory. The import process is started by right-clicking on the SP folder, as shown in Figure 4.17, and selecting Import, which launches the Import Wizard, as shown in Figure 4.18.

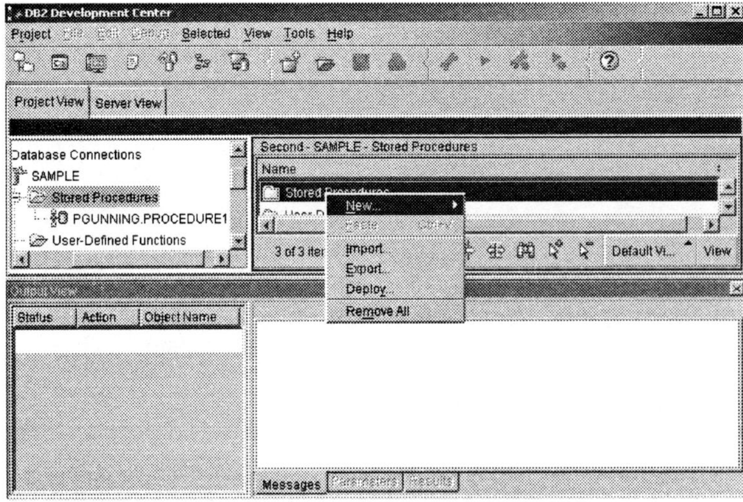

Figure 4.17
Importing a procedure.

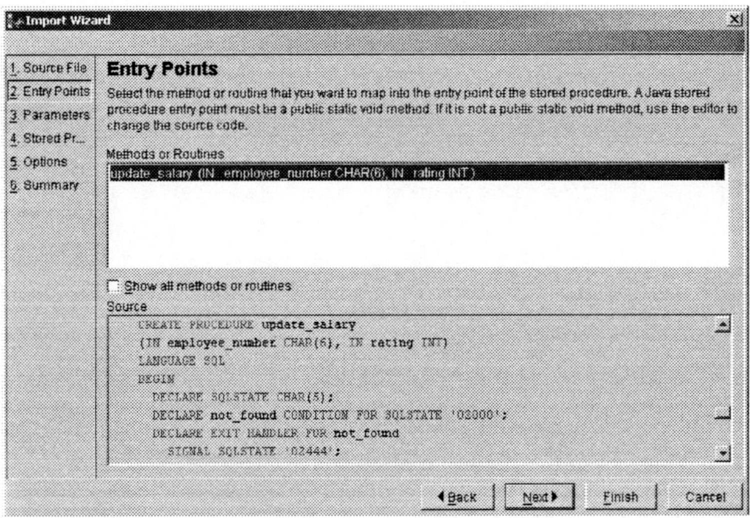

Figure 4.18
Import Wizard.

After successfully importing the UPDATE_SALARY sample SQL procedure, we are returned to the Development Center, as shown in Figure 4.19.

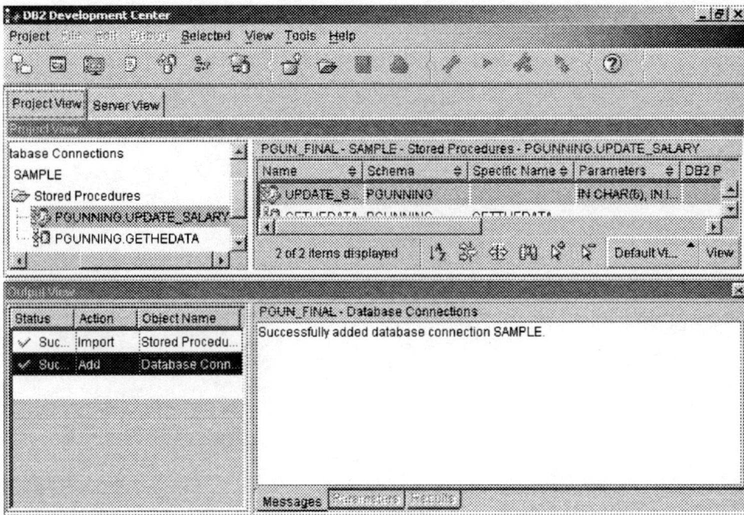

Figure 4.19
Development Center.

Help is available throughout the Development Center. By selecting Help from the toolbar, you are taken into the appropriate help page in the DB2 Information Center, as shown in Figure 4.20.

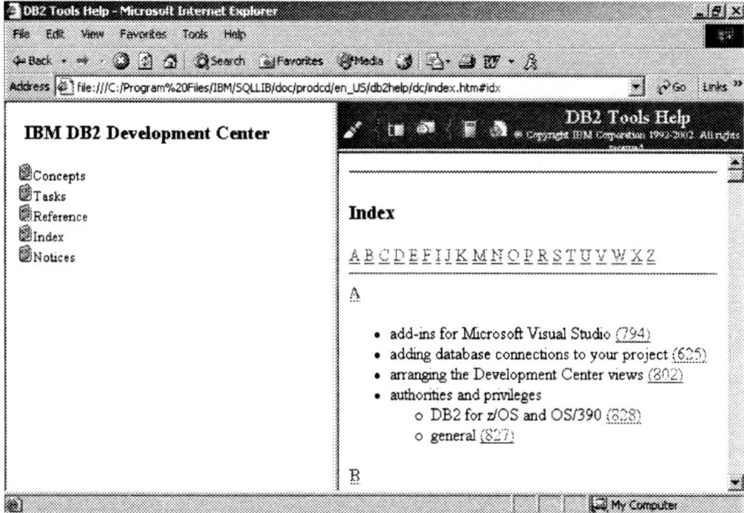

Figure 4.20
DB2 Development Center Help.

By selecting your area of interest in the DB2 Information Center, you can drill down to specific help details for your item of interest.

In addition to integrated help, you can set breakpoints in your stored procedure to aid in your development and debugging efforts, which is shown in Figure 4.21.

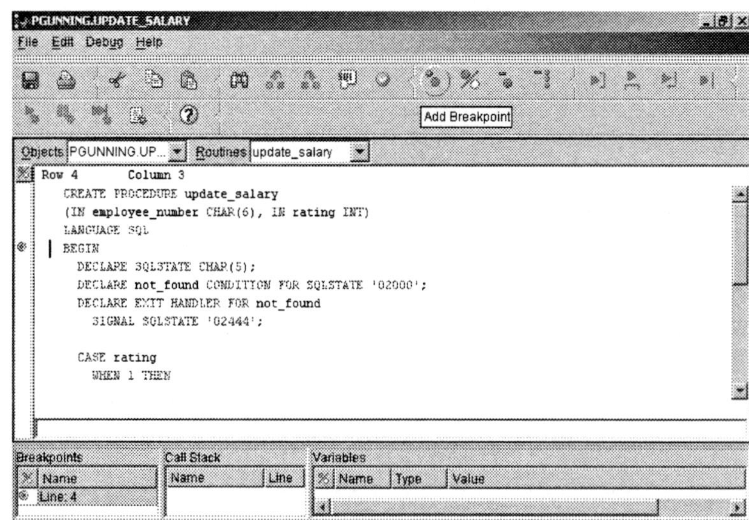

Figure 4.21
Adding breakpoints.

We added a breakpoint to our UPDATE_SALARY procedure by placing the cursor in the location where we want the breakpoint inserted, and clicking on the Add Breakpoint button from the toolbar. You can use breakpoints to step through the procedure to the breakpoint specified.

Procedures and UDFs can be deployed via the Development Center to server platforms throughout the DB2 family. After you have successfully created and built a procedure or UDF, the next time you enter the Development Center you can select existing projects instead of creating a new one, as shown in Figure 4.22.

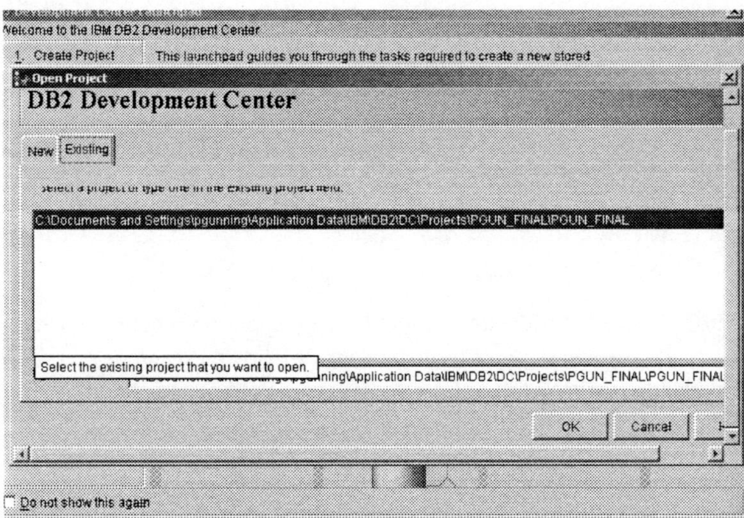

Figure 4.22
Launching Development Center using an existing project.

Although I have highlighted the creation of SQL procedures, the Development Center supports the development of Java stored procedures and structured types. A new Execute Privilege has been included to control who can invoke routines (stored procedures, UDFs, and methods).

> **NOTE**
> IN v8, SQL procedures are now automatically registered as NOT FENCED. NOT FENCED routines now support nesting and recursion and NOT FENCED procedures can return result sets.

JAVA THREAD-SAFE ROUTINES

Java stored procedures support recursion in v8 and Java routines can invoke routines written in other languages and vice versa. The new threading of Java UDFs and stored procedures has resulted in significant performance improvements for Java-based routines. Instead of creating a

JVM for each routine, which was done in previous versions of DB2 prior to v8, routines that run as thread-safe now share a single fenced process. The resulting performance improvement is gained by not having to go through the overhead of creating a JVM for each routine.

Java Common Client

The DB2 internal protocol has been totally rearchitected in v8. The new architecture results in a much more streamlined interface. Layers of code have been removed and unnecessary memory movements have been eliminated. Significant performance improvements have been realized with the new architecture.

A new type-4 JDBC driver is provided with the new architecture. It is designed to replace the type-3 driver in the area of usability and performance. Support for DATALINK as a data type has been added. Unnecessary code page conversion between a DB2 client and DB2 server when previously connecting to a UNICODE database has been eliminated. `OUTPUT LOB` parameter support for `CallableStatement` had been added. The performance of `PreparedStatements` is improved and `FetchSize` for `ResultSets` is supported by the type-3 driver.

The type-2 driver is now J2EE certified. It is the driver of choice for application servers such as Websphere Application Server. The new SQLJ profile customizer supports the `java.sql.Blob` and `java.sql.Clob` types of JDBC 2.0, as well as host variable expressions.

SQL Enhancements

DB2 v8 contains many SQL enhancements to enable DB2 to meet the business demands of today's 24 × 7 × 365 operating environment. Declared Global Temporary Tables now support the addition of indexes and the ability to run `RUNSTATS` on Temporary Table objects. Several new SQL enhancements have been made and will be addressed later in the chapter. User-Maintained Materialized Query Tables provide users with the ability to load precomputed data, and they can maintain the refresh of this based on business rules.

Declared Global Temporary Table (DGTT) Enhancements

Significant enhancements have been made to DGTTs. You can create indexes on DGTTs. Logging support has been added and rollback of table changes is now supported. `RUNSTATS` can now be run against DGTTs.

SQL Assist

Previously only available in the Data Warehouse Center, SQL Assist is now part of the base product. SQL Assist is launched from the Command Center. It enables you to create `SELECT`, `INSERT`, `UPDATE`, and `DELETE` statements with expert advice. Outcome and detail panels are available to help you write the SQL statement. Assistance is also provided for writing joins and syntax checking is built in. You can copy and paste SQL statements and use SQL Assist to format them.

SQL Enhancements

As with all previous releases of DB2, v8 contains several SQL enhancements that will help you to develop business applications. Version 8 is compliant with ANSI and ISO standards.

Instead Of Triggers

Instead Of triggers can simplify application programming by allowing developers to code inserts, updates, and deletes against views, while the actual update operation is redirected to the underlying table.

New Built-in Functions

Twelve new trigonometric functions have been added to the `SYSIBM` schema. The `FETCH FIRST` and `ORDER BY` statements are supported in subqueries.

Informational Constraints

DB2 can use new informational constraints to perform query optimization. When informational constraints are defined, you indicate to DB2 whether or not they can be used for query optimization. If enabled, the DB2 optimizer can use the values in the informational constraint to better optimize the access plan. Not enforcing constraints in the database requires that the application enforce the constraint with application logic.

Insert Through Union All Views

The SQL Insert statement is now supported for views that use a `UNION ALL` construction, in addition to the `UPDATE` and `DELETE` capabilities provided in previous releases.

Insert Through Union All Views can be used to accomplish range partitioning via a combination of check constraints and use of separate table spaces. This provides a flexible solution to the 64 GB per table limit by allowing you to break up a large table into smaller tables and by placing each table into a separate table space. Through the use of a check contraint on a data ranger, the DB2 optimizer can determine which table to access.

Summary Tables

A summary table is a table whose definition is based on the result of a query and whose data is in the form of precompleted results that are taken from one or more tables on which the summary table definition is based.

Since summary tables contain precomputed results, they can be used to significantly improve the performance of queries running against data that is not summarized. For example, instead of scanning a large daily sales table to procedure a monthly sales summary report, a summary table could be defined to summarize sales and DB2 could use the summary table to get the results instead of scanning a very large table to first get the data and then summarize it. The DB2 optimizer will determine at run time whether or not to use a summary table. If it decides a query will benefit from using a summary table, the optimizer will develop an access strategy using its query rewrite capability.

A table definition whose fullselect contains a `GROUP BY` clause is summarizing data from tables referenced in the fullselect. This type of summary table, is a special type of Materialized Query Table (MQT), new in v8.

A summary table is created using a `CREATE TABLE` statement. The following is an example of a `CREATE TABLE` statement to create a summary table:

```
CREATE SUMMARY TABLE SALES SKU AS (SELECT sku.
    SUM(qty) as QTY,
    SUM9class) as CLASS
  From Daily_Sales Group by sku)
  Data Initially Deferred
  Refresh Deferred
```

In the above example, the keyword summary is used to indicate that this is a summary table. If it is omitted, DB2 will still recognize this as a summary table as a result of the `AS` keyword.

> **NOTE**
> Summary tables can only be accessed when using Dynamic SQL.

There are two ways to update the data in the summary table: Refresh Deferred or Refresh Immediate. This option is specified on the `CREATE TABLE` statement using one of the refresh options:

- **Refresh Deferred**—the data in the table is refreshed when a `REFRESH TABLE` statement is executed.
- **Refresh Immediate**—the changes made to the underlying tables as part of a `DELETE`, `INSERT`, or `UPDATE` statement are cascaded to the summary table immediately.

The `DATA INITIALLY DEFERRED` clause means that the data is not inserted at Create Table time, but when the `REFRESH TABLE` statement is executed.

> **NOTE**
> System maintained summary tables cannot be directly modified by the `INSERT`, `UPDATE`, or `DELETE` statement.

Current Refresh Age Special Register

The CURRENT REFRESH AGE special register specifies a timestamp duration value with a data type of (20, 6). This duration represents the maximum duration since a REFRESH DEFERRED.

It is used by the optimizer to determine if the summary table can be used to optimize the query. Use SET CURRENT REFRESH AGE to change the value of the Current Refresh Age special register.

> **NOTE**
> Summary tables are represented by type S in the DB2 catalog.

- Zero (0) means that only summary tables defined with REFRESH IMMEDIATE may be used to optimize the query.
- 99999999999999 (9,999 years, 99 months, 99 days, 99 hours, 99 minutes, and 99 seconds) or ANY means any summary tables defined with REFRESH.
- DEFERRED or REFRESH IMMEDIATE may be used to optimize the processing of a query.

The initial value of the Current Refresh Age is 0. To enable the optimizer to consider using the deferred refresh summary tables, you have to set the CURRENT REFRESH AGE Special Register to ANY. This can be done using the SET CURRENT REFRESH AGE ANY statement.

There are several limitations on using Summary Tables. Refer to the *DB2 SQL Reference* for further information.

Materialized Query Table (MQT)

The definition of an MQT is a table whose definition is based on the result of a query, and whose data is in the form of precomputed results that are taken from one or more tables on which the MQT definition is based. The definition of an MQT contains joins, functions, and other SQL statements that are not allowed in summary tables.

The following is an example of an MQT:

```
CREATE SUMMARY TABLE  POAMT
  AS  (SELECT VENDOR, CODE, CLASS, SKU
       FROM VENDOR V, SKU S
         WHERE V.CODE = S.CLASS)
  DATA INITIALLY DEFERRED
REFRESH DEFERRED;
```

The MQT can be used to prejoin tables together. This allows the optimizer to bypass the join if the MQT contains the columns and rows that it needs.

USER-MAINTAINED MQTS

New in v8, user-maintained MQTs enable you to load precomputed data into a user-defined summary table.

> **NOTE**
> User-maintained summary tables make it easier for Oracle users to migrate to DB2.

The primary difference between a system-maintained summary table and a user-maintained MQT is that with a user-maintained MQT, the creation and loading of the table is under user control.

Since the data is generated by the user, it is not refreshed by DB2. It is the user's responsibility to periodically update the table based on your particular business rules. Use the `MAINTAINED BY USER` option on the `CREATE SUMMARY TABLE` statement to create a user-maintained summary table. The following is an example of how to load a user-maintained summary table:

```
INSERT INTO UMST_INVOICE
  SELECT * FROM
    (SELECT VENDOR, COUNT(*)  SUM (INV_AMT)
     FROM INVOICE
     GROUP BY VENDOR  )
AS V;
```

To prevent other summary tables from being used while loading the table, you can issue the following command:

```
SET CURRENT MAINTAINED TABLE TYPES FOR OPTIMIZATION = NONE;
```

Set this register back to `ALL` when you have completed loading the user-maintained summary table. Also, don't forget to set the `CURRENT REFRESH AGE` special register to `ANY` so that the optimizer will consider the summary table for optimization.

> **NOTE**
> `Insert`, `Update`, and `Delete` statements can be used to modify and delete data in a user-maintained MQT.

EXTENSIBLE MARKUP LANGUAGE (XML)

The XML Extender is provided with DB2 and allows you to store XML documents as a new column data type. DB2 also has the ability to decompose and store XML in its component parts as columns in multiple tables. Indexes can be defined on XML columns for fast retrieval. Furthermore, text search and section searches can be done on the XML column or its decomposed part via the DB2 Net Search Extender. XML documents can be formulated from existing DB2 tables to enable business-to-business (B2B) transactions.

With these capabilities and DB2's support of Web Services Object Framework (WORF), DB2 can serve as both a provider and consumer of Web services.

SUMMARY

The DB2 Development Center is an integrated development environment that offers developers a standard platform from which to develop applications for DB2. Visual Explain, used in conjunction with Design Advisor, enables you to develop top performing applications. Summary tables, MQTs, and user-maintained MQTs offer you opportunities with which to obtain significant performance improvements. DB2, through its strong support of XML, enables DB2 to serve as a provider or consumer of Web services.

CHAPTER 5

Type-2 Indexes and Multidimensional Clustering

New in v8, type-2 indexes have been designed to significantly reduce next key share locking for DELETE and UPDATE transactions, and to enable many new availability and performance features in v8. These features are explained in more detail in this chapter. Multidimensional clustering (MDC) is a significant new clustering capability introduced in v8 that enables tables to be continuously and automatically clustered along multiple dimensions. MDC tables don't require regular reorganization and provide for significant performance and availability enhancements for v8 databases.

Benefits of Type-2 Indexes

Type-2 indexes enable an index to be created on columns whose length is greater than 255 bytes (this available in DB2 UDB v7.2 via a registry variable). Type-2 indexes eliminate most next key share index locking, which reduced concurrency in prior releases of DB2. With type-2 indexes, index entries are pseudodeleted instead of being physically removed from the page.

> **NOTE**
> DB2 uses the one-byte ridFlag byte stored for each row identifier (RID) on the leaf page of a type-2 index to mark the RID as logically deleted so that it can be physically removed later.

If possible, these pseudodeleted index entries are then cleaned up during a lull in database activity. However, if you have a database that is always busy, you can run the REORGCHK utility to identify candidates for a cleanup via the REORG utility. Additional ways that pseudodeleted entries can be cleaned up are as follows:

- During subsequent insert, update, or delete activity

- During key insertion, keys that are marked deleted and are known to be committed are cleaned up if such a cleanup might avoid the need to perform a page split and prevent the index from increasing in size.
- If there is an X lock on the table when a key is deleted, the key is physically deleted instead of just being marked deleted. During this physical deletion, any deleted keys on the same page are also removed if they are marked deleted and known to be committed.
- By executing the `REORG INDEXES` command with `CLEANUP` options specified. Refer to the definition of the `REORG` utility in Chapter 7 for further details.
- Any rebuild of an index by one of the following utilities:
  - `REORG INDEXES` when not using one of the `CLEANUP` options
  - `REORG TABLE` when not using the `INPLACE` option
  - `IMPORT` with the `REPLACE` option
  - `LOAD` with the `INDEXING MODE REBUILD` option

Type-2 Indexes and Next-Key Locking

Next-key locking for type-2 indexes occurs when a key is inserted into an index. During insertion of a key into an index the row that corresponds to the key that will follow the new key in the index is locked only if that row is currently locked by an RR scan. The lock mode used for the next-key lock is NW (Next Key Weak Exclusive). The next-key lock is released before the key insertion is actually performed. Key insertion occurs when a row is inserted into a table.

Next-key locking with type-2 indexes can also occur when updates to columns in a row change the value of the index key. When this happens, DB2 marks the original key value as deleted and the new key value is inserted into the index.

This is a significant improvement over type-1 indexes, where index key deletion requires an X lock on the next key and the lock is held until commit time.

Migration Considerations for Type-2 Indexes

All new indexes are created as type-2 indexes. The only exception to this is when you try and create a type-2 index on a table that already has type-1 indexes. The new index will also be a type-1 index.

You can use the `INSPECT` command to find out what kind of indexes exist on a table. Refer to Chapter 7, Commands and Utilities for detailed information on the `INSPECT COMMAND`. Type-1 indexes can be converted to type-2 indexes by executing the `REORG INDEXES` command.

Type-2 indexes are required in order for you to use the following new features in v8:

- `ONLINE` Table Reorganization
- `ONLINE` Index Reorganization
- `ONLINE LOAD`
- MDC Clustering
- For elimination of most Next-Key locking problems

SUGGESTED MIGRATION STRATEGY FOR TYPE-2 INDEXES

You should prioritize your migration to type-2 indexes based on your business rules and priorities. Important tables that you need to `REORG ONLINE` or `LOAD ONLINE` should be done first during your normal maintenance window or you may need to schedule a maintenance window for these tables. The strategy you use depends on your environment and operational procedures. The remaining indexes can be converted to type-2 as part of ongoing maintenance via utilities that cause a rebuild of the index. Of course, you need to develop a strategy that works for you in your environment and within your operational and business constraints.

MULTIDIMENSIONAL CLUSTERING

MDC enables tables to be physically clustered on more than one dimension (key) simultaneously. To understand how MDC works, it's helpful to understand the following definitions:

- A Dimension block index is an index that is automatically created for each dimension specified.
- A Composite block index is an index automatically created that contains all dimension key columns and will be used to maintain the clustering of data over insert and update activity. This index will only be created if a single dimension does not already contain all the dimension key columns. The optimizer can use both dimension block indexes and composite block indexes to efficiently retrieve data.
- A Cell is made up of unique combinations of dimension values composed of blocks of pages, where a block is a set of consecutive pages on disk.
- A Slice is a set of blocks containing pages having a certain key value of one of the dimension block indexes.

Every page of an MDC table is *part* of exactly one block, and all blocks of an MDC table consist of the same number of pages. This is known as the Blocking Factor. The Blocking Factor is equal to the extent size so that block boundaries line up with extent boundaries.

If you are using SMS table spaces for MDC tables, the SMS file (directory) is extended one page at a time. Since MDC tables are extended by a block, you should run the `db2empfa` utility to enable multipage file allocation. With multipage file allocation enabled, the SMS file will be extended by exactly the size required. This will significantly improve performance of MDC tables using SMS table spaces.

Dimension block indexes are structured like traditional index structures except at the leaf level. Instead of using RID as traditional indexes do, dimension block indexes at the index-leaf level use a Block Identifier (BID) instead. Because BIDs point to blocks that can contain many pages, BID entries are much smaller than traditional RID index entries.

Here is a sample command to create an MDC table :

```
CREATE TABLE REGION
( Region           INT  NOT NULL,
  YearAndMonth     DATE
  Region_Cde       INT NOT NULL,
  Region_Cat       INT NOT NULL,
  Region_Sales     INT NOT NULL,
  Region_Perf      INT NOT NULL
                                 )
ORGANIZE BY DIMENSIONS (REGION, YearAndMonth);
```

The `ORGANIZE BY DIMENSION` statement is what indicates this is an MDC table.

A typical implementation of an MDC table might be a table that stores sales data for a retailer. The table is clustered along the dimensions `YearAndMonth` and Region. Records in the table are stored in blocks, which contain extents worth of consecutive pages on disk. See Figure 5.1 for an example of an MDC table.

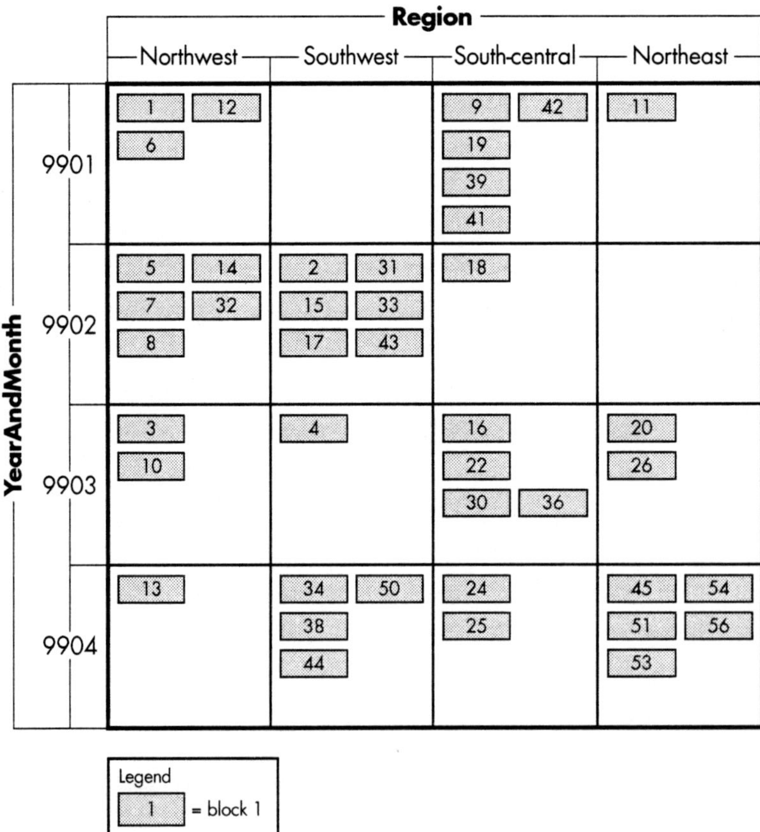

Figure 5.1
MDC table with dimensions of `REGION` and `YearAndMonth`.

A block in Figure 5.1 is represented by a rectangle, and is numbered according to the logical order of allocated extents in the table. The grid in the diagram represents the logical partitioning of these blocks, and each square represents a logical cell. A column or row in the grid represents a slice for a particular dimension. Furthermore, all records containing the value "South-central" in the region column are found in the blocks contained in the slice defined by the "South-central" column in the grid. In fact, each block in this slice also only contains records having "South-central" in the region field. Therefore, a block is contained in this slice or column of the grid if and only if it contains records having 'South-central' in the region field.

To provide for the indentification of which blocks comprise a slice, or which blocks contain all records having a particular dimension key value, a *dimension block index* is *automatically* created for each dimension when the table is created. See Figure 5.2 for an example of dimensions and dimension block indexes.

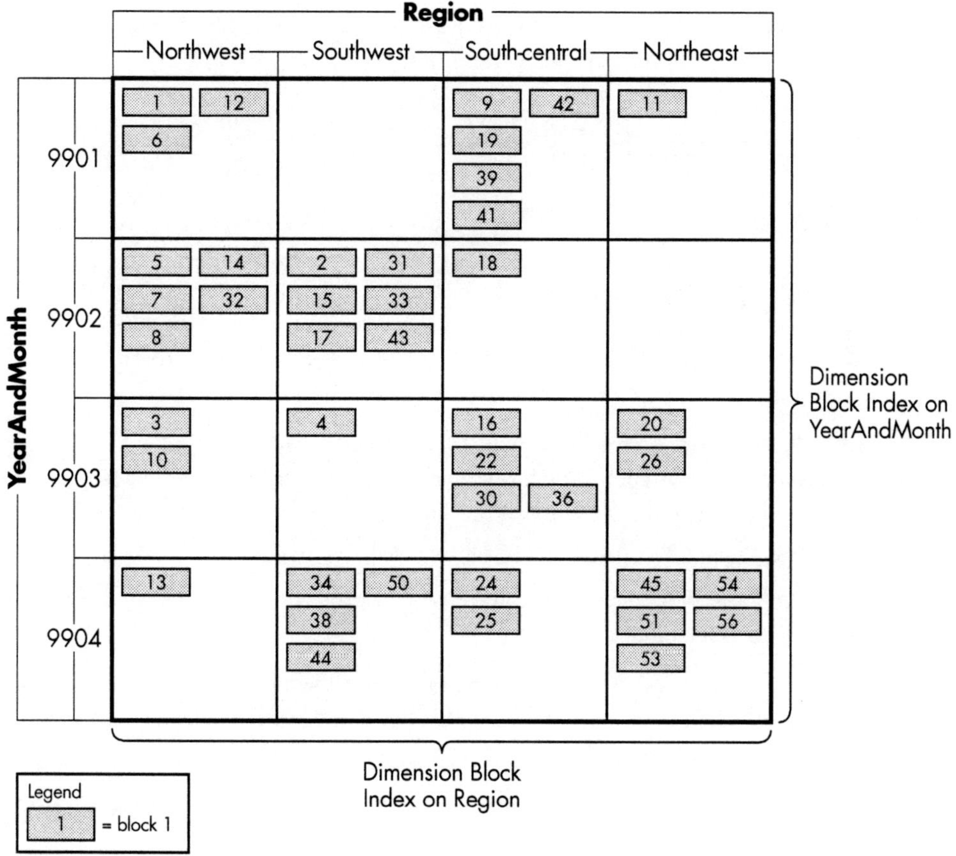

Figure 5.2
MDC table with dimension block indexes on `REGION` and `YearAndMonth`.

In Figure 5.2, a dimension block index is created for each dimension: one for `YearAndMonth` and one for `REGION`. A slice, or the set of blocks containing pages with all records having a particular key value in a dimension, will be represented in the associated dimension block index by a BID list for that key value. Figure 5.3 is an example of how a dimension block index on `REGION` would appear.

South-central | 9 | 16 | 18 | 19 | 22 | 24 | 25 | 30 | 36 | 39 | 41 | 42

Key Value **BID List**

Figure 5.3
Dimension block index key on `REGION`.

The key is comprised of a key value, in our example "South-central," and a list of BIDs. Each BID contains a block location. In our example the block numbers listed are the same that are found in the "South-central" slice found in the grid for our Sales table. See Figure 5.4 for an example of the dimension block index on `YearAndMonth`.

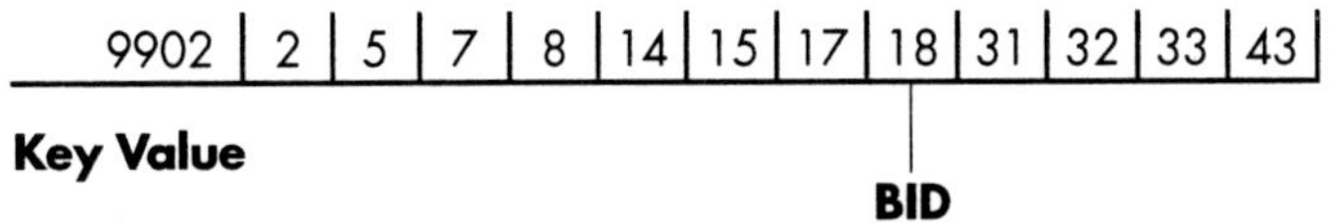

Figure 5.4
Key for dimension block index on `YearAndMonth`.

To find the list of blocks containing all records having "9902" for the `YearAndMonth` dimension, we would look up this value in the `YearAndMonth` dimension block index.

Now that we have discussed dimension block indexes, we need to discuss another type of index, called a *composite block index*. A composite block index is *automatically* created when multiple dimensions have been defined and it contains all the dimension key columns and will be used to maintain the clustering of data over insert and update activity.

In our example, a composite block index is created on `YearAndMonth`, `REGION`. See Figure 5.5 for an example composite block index structure.

In our example, if you want to find all records in the sales table having `REGION` of "Southwest" and `YearAndMonth` of "9902," DB2 would look up the key value 9902, Southwest in the composite block index, as shown in Figure 5.6.

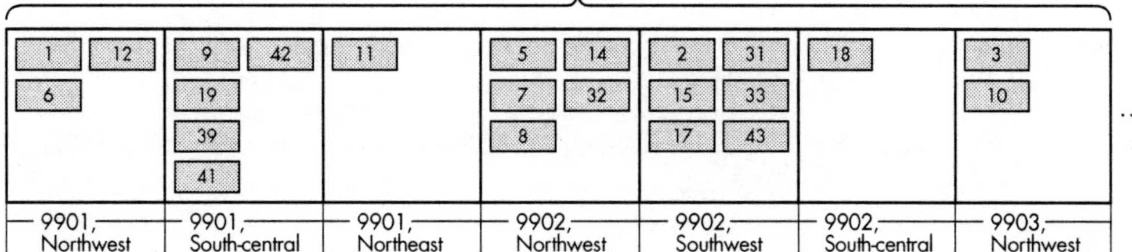

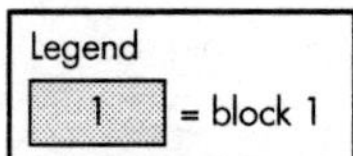

Figure 5.5
Composite block index structure.

9902 Southwest	2	15	17	31	33	43

Key Value **BID List**

Figure 5.6
Key from composite block index on `YearAndMonth`, `REGION`.

In this case we have six BIDs listed.

MDC Table Consideratoins

For MDC tables, DB2 can find the intersection of slices using index ANDing on BID lists. DB2 can also do a mini-relational scan of each block while scanning a list of blocks. This only involves one I/O per block as each block is stored as an extent and can be read into the bufferpool as a unit. DB2 only has to reapply the predicates on one record in the block as all records in the block are guaranteed to have the same dimension key values. If other predicates are present, DB2 only needs to check these on the remaining records in the block.

MDC tables can also have regular RID-based indexes defined. Also, RID and block indexes can be combined by index ANDing and ORing. MDC tables can also be used with database partitioning.

Queries involving columns with equality and range queries and columns with low cardinalities are good candidates for MDC tables. MDC benchmark tests have shown that MDC can speed up certain queries by over 50%. An MDC table can also take advantage of the LOAD utility. The loader understands the structure of an MDC table and so it will generate the appropriate blocks. MDC will also take advantage of the free extents that may be created during delete activity. MDC tables reclaim space after a delete by releasing the extent back to the tablespace for future use. And MDC tables do not require reorganization.

Since MDC tables do not require reorganization and reclaim space, MDC tables offer significant availability improvements over non-MDC tables. MDC offers significant performance improvements for range queries or when selecting a group of records. These queries are typical of BI/DW environments, but can also benefit OLTP queries with improved insert times.

MDC tables can also have traditional indexes, triggers, and referential integrity defined on them.

SUMMARY

Type-2 indexes offer improved performance through the elimination of most next key-locking. Type-2 indexes are also key to facilitating many of the new availability enhancements in v8. Specifically, type-2 indexes are required for `ONLINE REORG` of tables and indexes, MDC, and `ONLINE LOAD`.

Type-2 index migration considerations were discussed and a strategy provided.

MDC tables were introduced and examples provided. MDC tables can significantly improve performance and increase availability by reclaiming deleted space and eliminate the requirement for frequent reorganization.

Type-2 indexes and MDC tables are key enablers for superior DB2 performance and availability.

CHAPTER 6

High Performance Tablespace Design and I/O Strategies

The physical layout of tablespaces over various types of disk topologies is a rather complex task and has been identified as one of the areas where DBAs can make significant performance improvements if the complexities and technology involved are understood. Along with that, DBAs are constantly trying to decide which type of tablespace is best; Database Managed Space (DMS) or System Managed Space (SMS). Which type of RAID should be used? RAID 1, RAID 5, or the new RAID 0+1, or RAID 10 as it is referred to. Furthermore, when using RAID, we are faced with additional questions such as, How do I stripe the tablespace? Or should I let the hardware take care of that for me? In that respect, you then ask, "How does the use of the AIX Logical Volume Manager striping work with hardware RAID striping?

In conjunction with all these questions, you then ask, How does DB2 use striping, and what effect does the `DB2_PARALLEL_IO` registry variable have with RAID devices? And what about new technology that is just on the horizon like InfiniBand?

My goal in this chapter is to answer all these questions and provide you with a framework to use when designing your tablespaces and disk strategies for high performance. Additionally, we will take a look at existing I/O technologies, as well as emerging I/O technology that you will be able to take advantage of to provide a competitive advantage to your company.

TABLESPACES

A *tablespace* is an object used to specify the physical location of data in a database. You can think of it as a layer between the database and the actual container that holds table data. A container is assigned to a tablespace. This assignment lets you specify the number and types of containers associated with a tablespace and allows you to control the physical placement of data on disks during the physical design process. This capability ambles you to create containers on faster disks for higher priority work, and create them on slower disks for lower priority work. Business requirements should be taken into consideration when prioritizing container location. Tables exist within tablespaces. A tablespace can contain one or many tables. There are three types of tablespaces in DB2 that can be specified when creating tablespaces. They are defined as follows:

- `REGULAR TABLESPACE`—used to store user data, *Long Data*, or indexes. `REGULAR` is the default tablespace type. By default a tablespace called `USERSPACE1` is created when the `CREATE DATABASE` command is executed.
- `LARGE TABLESPACE`—used to store *Long Field* data or *Long Object* data, which may be spread over multiple, long tablespaces. In v8, indexes can also be created in large tablespaces. Note that `LARGE` tablespaces must be DMS. The maximum size of a large tablespace is 2 TB.

There are two commands that we can use to list the characteristics and details regarding tablespaces. The first command, `LIST TABLESPACES SHOW DETAIL`, returns a list of all tablespaces defined and includes the following detailed information, as shown in Example 6.1.

```
Tablespace configuration for PXXPRD
Taken on 2002.08.01 @ 00:01:02
------------------------------------------------------------------
------------------------------------------------------------------
SYSCATSPACE
------------------------------------------------------------------
 Tablespace ID                                 = 0
 Name                                          = SYSCATSPACE
 Type                                          = Database managed space
 Contents                                      = Any data
 State                                         = 0x0000
   Detailed explanation:
     Normal
 Total pages                                   = 262144
 Useable pages                                 = 262128
 Used pages                                    = 103984
 Free pages                                    = 158144
 High water mark (pages)                       = 126640
 Page size (bytes)                             = 4096
 Extent size (pages)                           = 8
 Prefetch size (pages)                         = 16
 Number of containers                          = 2
 Minimum recovery time                         = 2002-06-07-12.20.08.000000
```

Example 6.1
Output from `LIST TABLESPACES SHOW DETAIL` command.

For DMS tablespaces the output of this command can be used to determine the type of space management being used, how full a tablespace is becoming, and how many containers are defined, as well as PAGESIZE, PREFETCHSIZE, and EXTENTSIZE information that can be used in analyzing tablespace performance. You can use file system commands for the appropriate operating system to monitor SMS tablespace usage.

You can use the LIST TABLESPACE CONTAINERS FOR 0 command to display the details associated with the tablespace with an ID of 0 (see Example 6.2). The number and types of containers associated with the tablespace with an ID of 0 are displayed.

```
Tablespace Containers for Tablespace 0

 Container ID                         = 0
 Name                                 = /dev/rPXXPRD_cat01
 Type                                 = Disk

 Container ID                         = 1
 Name                                 = /dev/rPXXPRD_cat02
 Type                                 = Disk
```

Example 6.2
Output of LIST TABLESPACE CONTAINERS FOR 0 command.

You can use the output of this command to find the names of the containers associated with the tablespace with an ID of 0, and we can tell what kind of container is being used: a file, a path (directory), or a device. In this example, an AIX Raw Logical volume (DMS device container) is being used.

Tables

Tables in DB2 contain rows of data that are organized into blocks called *pages*. Pages can be 4, 8, 16, or 32 KB in size. Groups of pages are stored as *extents* and are used by DB2 when writing data to and prefetching from containers. DB2 uses extents to stripe data across multiple containers. Tables are created within tablespaces. There can be one or many tables per tablespace.

We will discuss the advantages and disadvantages of single and multiple tablespaces later in the chapter.

Storage Models

There are two types of tablespace storage models in DB2: System Managed Space (SMS) and Database Managed Space (DMS).

System Managed Space

SMS containers are created as directories by the target operating system (OS). SMS containers are allocated one page at a time, as needed (unless you have multipage file allocation enabled). This makes efficient use of disk storage but incurs a performance penalty as a result of the time and resources used to allocate pages as needed. SMS tablespaces are generally chosen according to the following criteria:

- Good performance is required
- Only small to moderate growth is expected
- Few or no DBAs available to administer the database

Page-at-a-time allocation can be changed so that extents are allocated instead of pages. This can be enabled by issuing the `db2empfa` command from a command line. This causes SMS tablespaces to have extents at a time allocated and the `multipage_alloc` informational DB CFG parameter set to `YES` to reflect the fact that the default behavior has been changed. Note that once enabled, it cannot be reversed (`db2empfa` does not change the way temporary space is allocated in System Temporary space).

By default, `SYSCATSPACE` and system temporary space (`TEMPSPACE1`) are created as SMS tablespaces. Since the DB2 catalog is relatively small and is infrequently updated, SMS is normally the right choice. The default system temporary space, `TEMPSPACE1`, is used for storing intermediate result sets and work tables when sorts or hash joins overflow from `SORTHEAP`. System temporary space is also used when reorganizing tables in SMS tablespaces or using "classic" reorg with temporary tablespace specified.

By default, an SMS system temporary tablespace called `TEMPSPACE1` is created at database creation. A system temporary tablespace is required for DB2 to operate. The system temporary tablespace can be DMS or SMS. SMS is generally adequate for most workloads. When absolute top performance is required, system temporary space may be created as DMS. If you don't want to use `TEMPSPACE1`, you can create a new system temporary tablespace with a different name and then drop `TEMPSPACE1`.

> **HINT**
> Create system temporary tablespaces with multiple containers across multiple physical disks to exploit opportunities for parallel I/O. *Do not* create more than one system temporary tablespace per page size.

> **NOTE**
> The maximum size of a regular tablespace depends on the page size being used. For 4 KB pages the maximum is 64 GB and for 8 KB pages, 128 GB.

Database Managed Space

In DMS tablespaces, DB2 can use either DMS file containers or DMS devices (raw logical volumes). DMS file containers are allocated in extents over physical disk storage and make use of file system and database manager buffering. This is known as "double buffering." DMS file containers allocate all specified space at container creation. A DMS tablespace can have one or many containers associated with it. On the other hand, DMS device containers are managed by the database manager, do not use file system buffering, and generally outperform all other types of tablespaces.

Criteria for Choosing DMS

DMS tablespaces should generally be used when your requirements meet the following criteria:

- ALWAYS, when top performance is required
- For separation of data and indexes over multiple physical disks
- Data is expected to grow on a regular basis
- To use RAW devices for performance gain
- Separation of regular and long data is desired
- Sufficient DBA resources are available

When in doubt and performance is the overriding factor, use DMS tablespace raw logical volumes. Table 6.1 lists the container types for SMS and DMS tablespaces.

Table 6.1 SMS and DMS Container Types

Type of Container	SMS	DMS
Directory	X	
File		X
Device		X

Extents

Tablespace Pages are allocated in *extents*. The `EXTENTSIZE` is specified on the `CREATE TABLESPACE` command. If not specified the `EXTENTSIZE` is controlled by the `DFT_EXTENT_SZ` DB CFG parameter. The `EXTENTSIZE` is the unit of allocation in DB2 and extents are comprised of pages. Extents are used by DB2 when writing data to and from containers.

> **NOTE**
> Once the `EXTENTSIZE` is defined for a tablespace it cannot be altered.

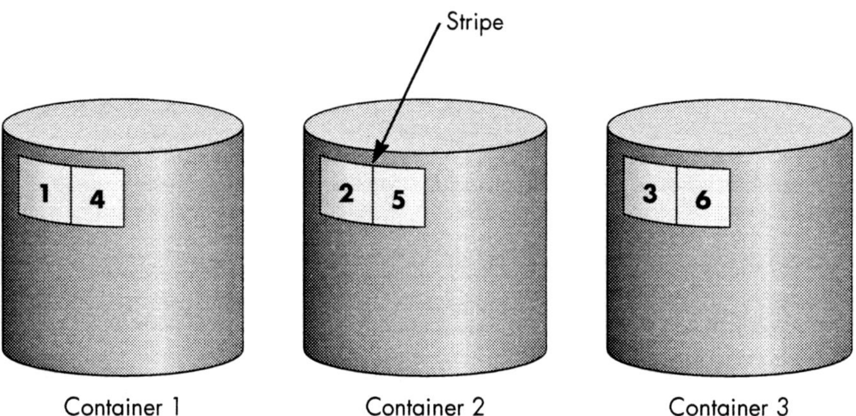

Figure 6.1
Example of DB2 using round.robin striping.

When multiple containers are defined, DB2 writes extents to each container in a round-robin fashion. DB2 implements striping by writing extents to each container defined. See Figure 6.1 for an example of how extents are written to multiple containers.

Figure 6.1 depicts how DB2 writes extent 1 to Container 1, then extent 2 to Container 2 and extent 3 to Container 3, and then extent 4 back to Container 1 in a round-robin fashion.

> **NOTE**
> In an SMS tablespace, if any container becomes full, then the entire tablespace is considered full, and no more data can be added.

> **NOTE**
> The maximum size of a temporary tablespace is 2TB.

Choosing an Extent Size

Several factors need to be taken into consideration when choosing the extent size for a tablespace. DB2 allocates two extents for each object defined for a DMS tablespace. If you are using many small tables, then this two extent overhead can use a significant amount of space. In this case, an SMS tablespace that allocates a page at a time is a better choice.

However, if you have large tables where data is constantly being added and the tablespace is DMS, then if you use a small `EXTENTSIZE`, many extents would now be needed that would require additional overhead to retrieve the frequently needed new extents.

How the table will be accessed is another primary concern when determining the EXTENTSIZE. If large amounts of data will be accessed in a sequential manner, as with data warehousing, then a larger EXTENTSIZE would be appropriate. This would improve the performance of sequential prefetch as larger extents would enable more data to be processed per I/O request.

On the other hand, in an OLTP environment, queries typically only return a small amount of data in a random manner. Here, a smaller EXTENTSIZE would bring fewer pages into the bufferpool. Since OLTP typically processes data randomly, only retrieving a row or so at a time, a large EXTENTSIZE would result in too many pages being fetched into the bufferpool that are not needed by the application.

> **NOTE**
> Specifying proper EXTENTSIZE is critical to the performance of your DB2 applications. In conjunction with PREFETCHSIZE, DB2 issues multiple EXTENTSIZE I/O requests.

PREFETCHING

DB2 uses a technique called *sequential prefetch* when accessing data in a sequential manner. DB2 issues asynchronous sequential prefetch requests to bring data into the bufferpool in advance of the application needing it. Thus, DB2 anticipates that the application is accessing data that is sequential, similar to a table scan, and provides improved application performance as the application does not have to wait for data. DB2 recognizes this at bind (Static SQL) or prepare time (Dynamic SQL) and incorporates sequential prefetch into the access plan developed.

DB2 can also detect that data is being accessed in a sequential manner at run time. This is called "sequential detection." This behavior is controlled by the seqdetect DB CFG parameter. By default it is enabled. In most cases, this should not be changed.

> **WARNING**
> If the DB CFG parameter intra_parallel is enabled, DB2 will perform more aggressive prefetching as the prefetching algorithm tolerates wider gaps between pages. Make sure you have sufficient I/O bandwidth and additional physical disks if you enable this parameter.

Prefetching Performance

The EXTENTSIZE, PREFETCHSIZE, and container layout on a disk are important factors in determining prefetch performance and therefore, to a large extent, the overall performance of the database. When developing a prefetch request, DB2 considers the EXTENTSIZE, PREFETCHSIZE, and number of containers and develops appropriate I/O requests. If tablespace containers are allocated over separate physical disks (disk actuators or arms), DB2 can issue parallel read requests, resulting in improved performance. Note that the Database Manager Bufferpool Services component may reject prefetch requests if it determines that pages that are currently or likely to be used by executing applications would be invalidated by the pages coming in. Thus, prefetching that is too aggressive can hurt performance, not help it. An EXTENTSIZE of 32 is generally a good starting point for most applications. For Data Warehouses, a larger extentsize can be beneficial due to the large amount of data processed sequentially.

The number of EXTENTSIZE prefetch requests that DB2 may issue can be determined using the following formula:

PREFETCHSIZE ÷ EXTENTSIZE = number of EXTENTSIZE prefetch requests

For example, for a three container tablespace with an PREFETCHSIZE of 96, then

96 ÷ 32 = 3 EXTENTSIZE prefetch requests will be issued.

If the three containers are allocated over separate physical disks or ranks in the case of ESS, parallel I/O will be used using multiple prefetchers. As a rule of thumb, set the PREFETCHSIZE to a multiple of the EXTENTSIZE times the number of containers defined for the tablespace.

> **NOTE**
> The number of pages prefetched per request into the bufferpool should be close to or equal to the extent size.

If the number of pages prefetched per request are less than the extent size, the following conditions may exist:

- bufferpool overheated
- bufferpool is too small or can't be increased due to resource constraints
- extent size too large
- prefetch size too large

In Chapter 8, "Tuning Bufferpools," we will see how to determine if these conditions exist.

Tables and Tablespace Considerations

One of the most often asked questions is, "How many tables per tablespace should I use?" or "Should I use one table per tablespace for a particular application?"

I'll point out the advantages and disadvantages of single or multitable tablespaces.

Most ERP and CRM independent software vendor (ISV) packages for DB2 use the multitable-per-tablespace approach. This approach is used for the following reasons:

- Ease of administration for companies without DBAs
- Ease of administration by DBAs
- Easier packaging of DDL and scripts
- Ease of installation

Also, most ISVs are now providing separate tablespaces for indexes so that they can be placed on different physical disks and assigned to different bufferpools. However, there are some potential disadvantages of using multiple tables per tablespace:

- Potential performance degradation when multiple tables in the same tablespace on the same physical disks are being accessed concurrently
- Recovery considerations
  - While a tablespace is being recovered, all tables in the tablespace are inaccessible until the recovery and copy is complete.

> **NOTE**
> DB2 v8 online load only locks the table being loaded. Prior to v8, the tablespace was locked and all tables in the tablespace were inaccessible until the load completed.

Potential disadvantages of using a single table-per-tablespace strategy:

- Backup and recovery considerations
  - Tables with Referential Integrity involved will need to be backed up together
  - Requires additional administration to manage
- Numbers of tablespaces
  - Several thousand tablespaces could present an administrative challenge

A good solution is to use a strategy that includes a mix of single and multiple tables-per-tablespace so that business objectives are accomplished. To that end, high priority tables should be placed in separate tablespaces as well as on separate disks and bufferpools.

The Life of an I/O Request

DB2 issues I/O requests via the OS Kernel routines. If SMS or DMS file containers are being used, these requests go through the OS file system code. If DMS device containers are used, DB2 issues I/O requests that are passed to the appropriate device drivers by the OS Kernel. The file system is not used in this case. In either case, the actual request is transferred to the host adapter. Figure 6.2 is an example of an I/O request using the Small Computer System Interface (SCSI).

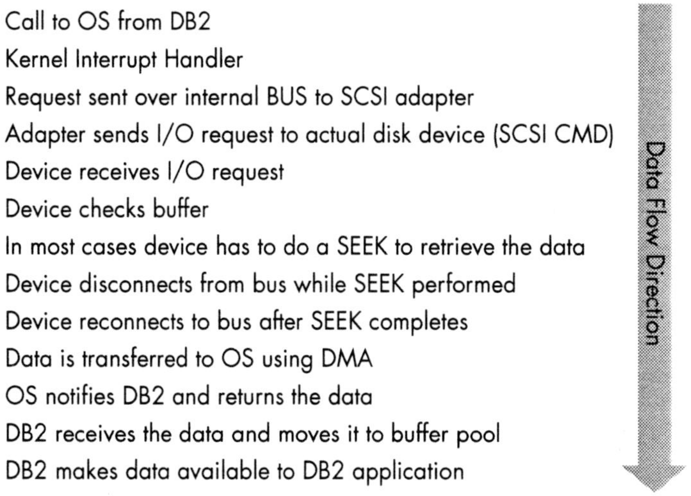

Call to OS from DB2
Kernel Interrupt Handler
Request sent over internal BUS to SCSI adapter
Adapter sends I/O request to actual disk device (SCSI CMD)
Device receives I/O request
Device checks buffer
In most cases device has to do a SEEK to retrieve the data
Device disconnects from bus while SEEK performed
Device reconnects to bus after SEEK completes
Data is transferred to OS using DMA
OS notifies DB2 and returns the data
DB2 receives the data and moves it to buffer pool
DB2 makes data available to DB2 application

Data Flow Direction

Figure 6.2
The life of an I/O.

In Figure 6.2, DB2 issues a call (I/O request) to the OS. The OS Kernel routine passes the request to either the OS file system, or in the case of DMS devices, directly to the SCSI device driver. The SCSI device driver sends the appropriate SCSI command to the target device. The target device receives the request and immediately checks its own internal buffers for the data; if not found, the device must perform a disk seek operation to retrieve the requested data. The device issues the seek and disconnects from the bus to wait for the seek to complete. In the meantime another request can be sent by the adapter over the bus to a different disk. The second disk device receives the request, checks its own buffer, and starts the seek to retrieve the data and disconnect from the bus. In the meantime, the seek to the first device completes and this device gains control of the bus and transfers the data. The I/O operation is thus complete.

It is important to note that Figure 6.2 illustrates a single request; however the process works the same way for multiple requests. Multiple requests can be processed if containers are on separate physical disks. DB2 will use a separate prefetcher per container.

In that case, while the first disk is seeking and has given up control of the bus, the next request from the queue is processed, for example, to Disk2. Disk2 checks its buffer and has to do a seek, causing it to give up control of the bus. Meanwhile, the I/O on Disk1 completes so Disk1 can now transfer the data while Disk2 seeks, and so on. See Figure 6.3 for a sample tablespace disk layout.

In the example, three physical disks enable multiple disk seek operations to occur. And, having the data spread over three host adapters ensures that required throughput and high availability can be attained. These disks are configured in a RAID-1 configuration. However, the second copy of the data is not shown. In the next section, we show an example that illustrates how to design and configure tablespaces in a RAID-5 ESS environment.

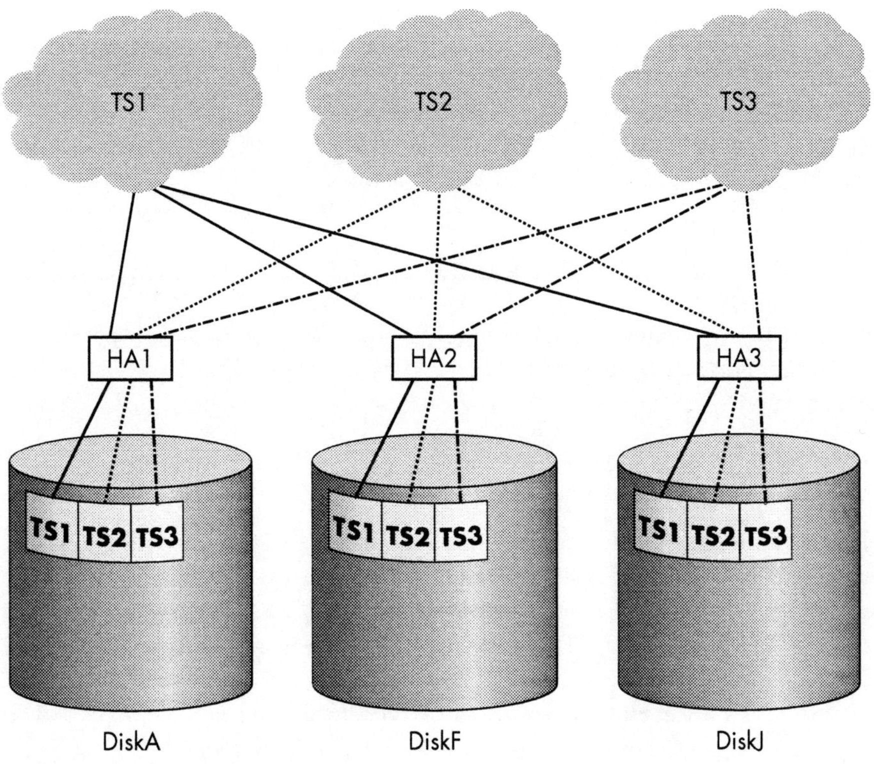

Figure 6.3
Sample disk layout.

REDUNDANT ARRAY OF INDEPENDENT DISKS (RAID)

The term "RAID" was first coined by researchers at UC-Berkeley. Since then it has been implemented in various levels by many storage vendors. There are various "types" or "levels" of RAID implementations, some vendors even developing their own "levels." It is in widespread use for enterprise database applications. However, its various levels and implementations are somewhat misunderstood by IT professionals. Further complicating its implementation are the myriad of various vendor storage "black box" solutions in use today, and the lack of documentation regarding how to lay out DB2 tablespaces on these devices.

The RAID Advisory Board (RAB) is an industry organization comprised of major hardware and software vendors. The RAB coordinates and influences industry directions and standards and promulgates RAID terminology and concepts throughout the IT industry.

In Table 6.2, I have included the most common attributes for the well-known RAID levels.

Table 6.2 RAID Levels

RAID Type	Striping	Mirroring	Parity	Performance	Data Protection
RAID-0	X				
RAID-1		X		X (Read)	X
RAID-5	X		X	X (Read)	X
RAID-10 (0+1)	X	X		X (Read & Write)	X

The most common RAID types used with DB2 are RAID-1 and RAID-5. RAID-0+1, or RAID-10 as it is also known, provides the performance of RAID-0, the mirroring of RAID-1, and is becoming fairly common.

I'll discuss the details of the most popular implementations in use today, RAID-1, RAID-5, and RAID-10 (0+1).

RAID-1 implements mirroring. Two identical copies of the data are stored on two drives. If one drive fails, the other is used. This provides a level of fault tolerance and data integrity. However, it requires twice as many disks to implement than just a bunch of disks (JOBDS) to store the second copy of the data. When using RAID-1 with AIX there are three important AIX LVM parameters that need to be considered: `Write_Scheduling_Policy` and *Mirror Write Consistency.* `Write_Scheduling_Policy` controls how writes are written to disk. It can be set to parallel or sequential. The default, parallel, should be used so that writes to both disks will be done in parallel and DB2 doesn't have to wait for the second write to complete. If set to sequential, the write is not considered complete until the write to the last copy completes. This would cause DB2 to wait, which is not desirable. The `Write Verify` parameter controls whether or not the AIX LVM verifies whether a write was successful. If enabled, the LVM would perform a READ for every write that was performed. This unnecessarily impacts writes, is not enabled by default, and should not be used.

Mirror Write Consistency (MWC) ensures that the data is consistent (the same) across ALL mirrored copies. In the event of a system crash or improper shutdown, MWC is used by AIX to identify copies that are inconsistent. These copies are marked as "stale" at boot time and the MWC is used to make copies consistent. If disabled, the volume groups containing such logical volumes need to have their autovaryon capability disabled and then after the system comes back up, each mirrored logical volume would need to be resynchronized by running the `syncvq -f -l` command. It is enabled by default and the default should be used with the exception of volumes containing DB2 logs. MWC requires that every write consist of two operations, one to write the data and one to update the MWC cache record, which is located on the outer edge of the disk.

Logical volumes with MWC enabled should be created on the outer edge of the disk, as that is where the MWC cache is stored. This will minimize disk head movement when performing writes.

RAID-5

RAID-5 is by far the most popular RAID level in use today. RAID-5 uses block level stripping with distributed parity and provides a high level of fault tolerance and high availability. Unlike RAID-3, RAID-5 writes data and parity across all the drives. This prevents one disk from becoming a bottleneck when writing parity information. However, the parity information still has to be calculated, so there is overhead involved. Fault tolerance is maintained by keeping the parity block separated from the data block. That way if one drive fails, all the data on that drive can be rebuilt from the parity information stored across the array. When a disk in the array fails, the data and parity are automatically rebuilt by the RAID controller. Note that an application slowdown may occur during the rebuild period, but improvements in the size of controller cache and controller improvements have continued to reduce the effects of the performance degradation during rebuild time. RAID-5 requires a minimum of three disks to implement.

While offering high availability and a good price/performance ratio, RAID-5 does have a "write penalty" associated with it. Each write to the array requires four I/O operations:

1. Read old data
2. Record old parity
3. Write new data
4. Write new parity

However, *fast write cache* (FWC), which is now fairly common with RAID adaptors, can reduce the effects of the write penalty. FWC enables parity information for writes to be calculated without reading old parity data from disks in many cases. Therefore, the effects of the write penalty are not as significant as it used to be.

Since a RAID-5 array is comprised of some number of physical disks, top priority tablespaces should be allocated to only one such array. This enables parallel I/O to be used as the data is spread over multiple physical disks in the array. Set the `DB2_Parallel_IO` registry variable to * or include a list of TS IDs to enable parallel I/O against single container tablespaces on RAID-5. If you allocate multiple tablespace containers to the same array and the data from one or more tables in these tablespaces is needed at the same time, IO delays will occur as I/O requests will be distributed to the same physical disks. Now you say, "We just don't have the luxury of dedicating space like this." If that is the case, then at least allocate TS containers over the same array that have dissimilar access characteristics and that are not accessed at the same time. This will reduce contention and improve performance. This applies to containers on RAID-1 and RAID-5.

The `DB2_STRIPED_CONTAINERS` *registry variable is obsolete in DB2 v8.* Instead, the former `DB2_STRIPED_CONTAINERS = YES` behavior is now the default behavior used in creating tablespace containers. The container page tag is now allocated by default in a full extent instead of just a page. The new v8 `DB2_USE_PAGE_CONTAINER_TAG` registry variable can be used to revert to the pre-v8 behavior where the container page tag uses only a partial extent. However, this is not recommended. When the EXTENTSIZE is lined up with the RAID stripe size, DB2 can use parallel I/O and save I/O operations as the tablespace EXTENTSIZE is aligned with the RAID stripe size, which causes DB2 data to be striped across RAID arrays with extents aligned with the RAID stripe size. If the EXTENTSIZE is not equal to or a multiple of the RAID stripe size, additional I/O may be required.

> **NOTE**
> DB2 v8 allocates page container tags in the first extent of each DMS container. Before v8, the container tag was stored in a single page, and did not line up with RAID stripes, which caused more I/O than was necessary. *Do not* change the setting of the DB2_USE_PAGE_CONTAINER_TAG registry variable!

See Figures 6.4 and 6.5 for an example of the performance benefits gained by DB2 v8 allocating the container tag in a full extent versus the previous default behavior, which caused extents to not line up with the RAID stripe size.

As indicated in Figure 6.4, since the tablespace EXTENTSIZE is not equal to or a multiple of the RAID stripe size, additional I/Os will be required as DB2 retrieves data by extent. In Figure 6.5, we can observe the improvement in I/O by aligning the EXTENTSIZE with the RAID STRIPE size, which enables DB2 to retrieve the data much more efficiently, driving six parallel EXTENTSIZE prefetch requests at a time.

RAID-5 (6+1) Example

Single prefetch drives all 6 drives simultaneously but can require two I/Os from each instead of one. This was the former default behavior when extents were not aligned with the RAID stripe size.

```
DB2 create tablespace TSP1_INV
Managed by database
Using (Device 'prdrhdl' 9000)
Pagesize 4k
Extentsize 16 Prefetchsize 96
DB2SET DB2_PARALELL_IO = *
```

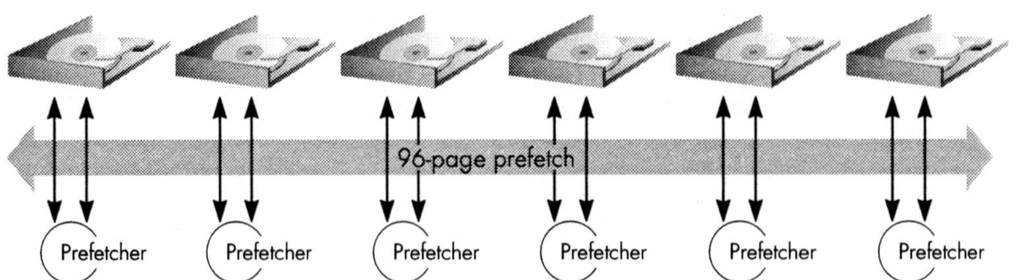

Figure 6.4
Pre-DB2 v8 default behavior without DB2_STRIPED_CONTAINERS enabled.

RAID-5 (6+1) Example

Physical Disk Striping

- Each extent aligned on an internal raid stripe boundary on RAID-5
- Single prefetch drives all six drives simultaneously
- Each disk must handle one I/O

```
DB2 create tablespace TSP1_INV
Managed by database
Using (Device 'prdrhdl' 9000)
Pagesize 4k
Extentsize 16 Prefetchsize 96
DB2SET DB2_PARALELL_IO = *
```

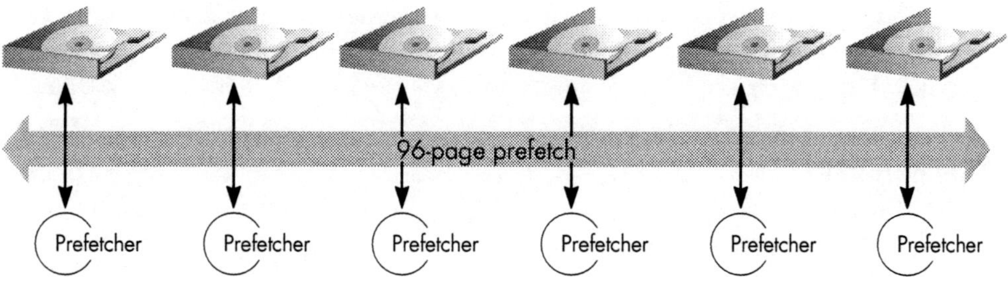

Figure 6.5
New DB2 v8 default behavior.

Aligning the container tag in a full extent benefits DMS raw devices the most as DB2 ensures that pages are contiguous on the device. With DMS file containers, DB2 will use a complete extent for the container tag, but since DB2 is using the OS file system, DB2 cannot ensure that the pages are contiguous. This is controlled by the OS file system and is subject to fragmentation.

Tablespace Container Management

Although we as DBAs attempt to obtain accurate tablespace sizing information as part of the physical design process, oftentimes the data is not available and we have to take an educated guess. Sometimes our educated guess is incorrect or we may have been given erroneous data, or the data is just growing a lot faster than anticipated. In these cases we need the ability to add containers, resize, or drop containers to support the changing data requirements. For SMS Managed Space, the only change that can be made is through a redirected restore. During a redirected restore, additional directory containers can be added or removed.

For DMS Managed Space, we have more options and flexibility with which to deal with space problems.

> **NOTE**
> DB2 v8 offers the ability to add DMS container(s) so that a rebalance does not occur. Using the command `BEGIN NEW STRIPE SET` we can add a new container above the high water mark so that a rebalance does not occur.

DB2 and IBM Enterprise Storage System (ESS SHARK)

IBM first shipped the SHARK, as ESS is known, in 1999. If you were one of those lucky first customers, then your SHARK may have even had a SHARK fin on top of it!

The ESS uses RAID-5 (prior to Model 800) and consists of arrays containing physical disks. The examples in this chapter are based on an F20 ESS. To AIX, these disks appear as *hdisks*. There are many ways that ranks, arrays, and disks can be configured. I'll cover the main points you need to know to be able to properly lay out your tablespaces with performance in mind. My goal in this section is not to make you an ESS expert, but to provide you with enough information to help you get good performance in environments where you are using ESS in support of DB2.

ESS Terminology

When discussing how to lay out tablespace containers on ESS, it's helpful to understand the terminology used. I'll identify and discuss the key terms you need to know as a DBA.

- **STRIP**—in storage terminology, a "STRIP" is a stripe that exists on a single device. We can think of this as an extent in DB2.
- **STRIPE WIDTH**—the number of DB2 containers spread across multiple physical disks.
- **ESS LOGICAL DISK**—an array comprised of 7+P array (7+P means 7 disks + 1 parity make up the array). So, for example, four DB2 containers residing on four ESS logical disks would have data spread across 32 physical disks. This arrangement would result in DB2 being able to drive 32 I/O operations at once.
- **VPATH**—an entity built by SDD to represent an ESS logical disk to the OS. Vpaths enable SDD to balance I/O across multiple paths and to reroute traffic to good paths in the event of path failure.

Cache Management

In ESS, each cluster manages cluster cache and nonvolatile storage (NVS). With the latest ESS Model 800 supporting up to 64 GB of cache, database performance will benefit more as more data will be found in the cache and less access to physical disks will be required.

Whenever reads from or writes to an ESS occur, a copy of the data is stored in cluster cache. This is in anticipation of the data being re-referenced from the cache. Data in the cache ages and is subsequently removed from the cache when the caching algorithm determines it is unlikely to be referenced again during a predetermined time interval. Modified data is destaged from the cluster cache to the RAID arrays and changes to the data are made permanent.

The ESS cache management algorithms take into consideration data access patterns. For random reads, ESS will use a record-caching strategy, which means a DB2 page will be read into the cache. When nearby physical records are also accessed, this will be detected and the ESS sequential access algorithms will use a "track-caching" strategy, which results in ESS staging additional data into the cache, corresponding to an ESS logical track.

> **NOTE**
> An ESS logical track is the same as the physical stripe size, approximately 32 KB for SCSI and Fibre-Channel attached hosts.

Since DB2 accesses data sequentially for table scans, and more so in a DW environment, ESS has been designed to detect and optimize sequential access patterns by detecting this activity and prestaging the data into ESS cache. So with ESS, we have DB2-sequential prefetch on top of ESS asynchronous prefetching into ESS cache. Simply stated, DB2 detects and recognizes sequential access and invokes sequential prefetch as part of the access plan or uses sequential detection in anticipation that the application is accessing data sequentially. At the same time, ESS is prefetching data in advance into ESS cache. This DB2 and ESS working together provides substantial performance improvements for applications that process large amounts of data sequentially.

ESS manages the cache so a balanced efficiency is achieved between sequential and random access requests, preventing just one or two sequential applications from monopolizing the cache.

ESS manages sequential writes by converting RAID-5 sequential writes into RAID-3 operations. This is accomplished by the ESS cache manager and disk adapter writing the data from NVS and cluster cache to the disks in parallel, while at the same time internally calculating parity and sending it to a disk. This technique eliminates the RAID-5 write penalty previously discussed.

Nonvolatile Storage

NVS provides protection for modified data in case of a cluster failure. The NVS for each cluster is physically maintained within the other cluster. In this way, the surviving cluster contains all of the cache-modified data. When DB2 writes a record, ESS stores two copies of the record in cache (one in cluster cache and the other in NVS) and immediately indicates that the write is complete when both copies are stored safely. The record is doubly protected at this point. When the data is destaged from cache to disk (and thereby doubly protected by RAID-5), the storage in the NVS is available for reuse by another application.

To AIX without ESS, each individual fixed-disk drive is called a physical volume (PV) and has a name. These PVs correspond to specific *hdisks.* With ESS using Subsystem DeviceDriver (SDD), which enables *virtual pathing,* each *hdisk* represents one path to an ESS logical disk. The PV is represented by the *vpath* name.

So in an AIX, ESS implementation, PVs identifying ESS storage are not physical devices. They represent logical devices that are striped across multiple disk drives.

At the simplest level, a logical disk consists of a 7+P+S RAID array. The +S signifies a "spare" disk. In ESS, this disk is free-floating between arrays. A SCSI ID is assigned to each array. A logical unit (LUN) is a subdivision under a SCSI ID. Each SCSI ID can have up to eight LUNs assigned to it; that's why a logical disk has eight disks associated with it. DB2 data is striped across all disks in the array and all the disks in the array can be used for parallel I/O by using a SCSI technique called *command-tag queueing.*

Internally, ESS uses Serial Storage Architecture (SSA) for performing disk I/O. SSA disks are configured to provide redundancy and use a loop configuration with multiple adapters. In ESS, almost all RAID functions are performed by the SSA disk adapters. Parity generation, disk rebuild, and sparing are all done at the SSA adapter level. This provides improved performance by offloading these functions from the CPU and cache.

ESS uses clustering to tie two clusters together. In ESS, a cluster is a collection of processors, cache, NVS, and SSA disk adapters. Each ESS contains two clusters. Each cluster controls one half of the storage within the ESS, but can assume control of the other half if its partner should fail. Each cluster owns separate cache, disk adapters, and arrays, so under normal conditions does not affect the performance of the other cluster. The clusters even run separate kernels and communicate via an internal network connection. The ESS Web interface tool, ESS Specialist, is used to manage clusters.

Configuring DB2 for Optimal Performance on ESS

There are five general rules to follow when defining DB2 tablespaces on ESS:

- Know where your data resides and understand how DB2 containers map to ESS logical disks. *Spread data across as many RAID arrays as possible.*
- Balance the workload across ESS resources. Establish a method with which to control the allocation of containers, based on business priorities.
- Use the inherent striping of DB2, placing containers for tablespaces on separate ESS logical disks, *which reside on separate ESS RAID arrays.* This will eliminate the need for using underlying OS logical volume manager striping.
- Select an ESS logical disk size that allows for granularity and growth without proliferating the number of logical disks. Eight logical disks is a good number for most environments.
- Use ESS multipathing along with DB2 striping to help balance use of Fibre Channel or SCSI paths.

Let us take a look at the cardinal rule, knowing where your data resides. The key to this is balancing the I/O workload across available resources. Keep these tips in mind to help balance activity across ESS storage:

1. Span ESS cabinets
2. Span clusters within a cabinet

3. Span disk adapters
4. Use as many arrays as possible (maximizes parallelism)

See Figure 6.6, which illustrates the implementation of the above tips.

In Figure 6.6, we have a tablespace with eight containers that has been spread across multiple physical disks, adapters, and ESS systems. This container strategy provides multiple paths and disks for high performance, and multiple host adapters, paths, and even ESS systems for very high availability. Today's demanding business applications require similar configurations to provide true 24 × 7 availability.

IBM ESS tests have shown that data, indexes, and System Temporary Tablespace can be intermixed across logical disks. This results in I/O activity evenly spread across all the components involved, which inherently makes more disk arms available to each of these objects. However, do not place tablespace containers that have multiple tables per tablespace and that are accessed in the same SQL statement on the same logical disk. This would cause contention on the underlying disk drives.

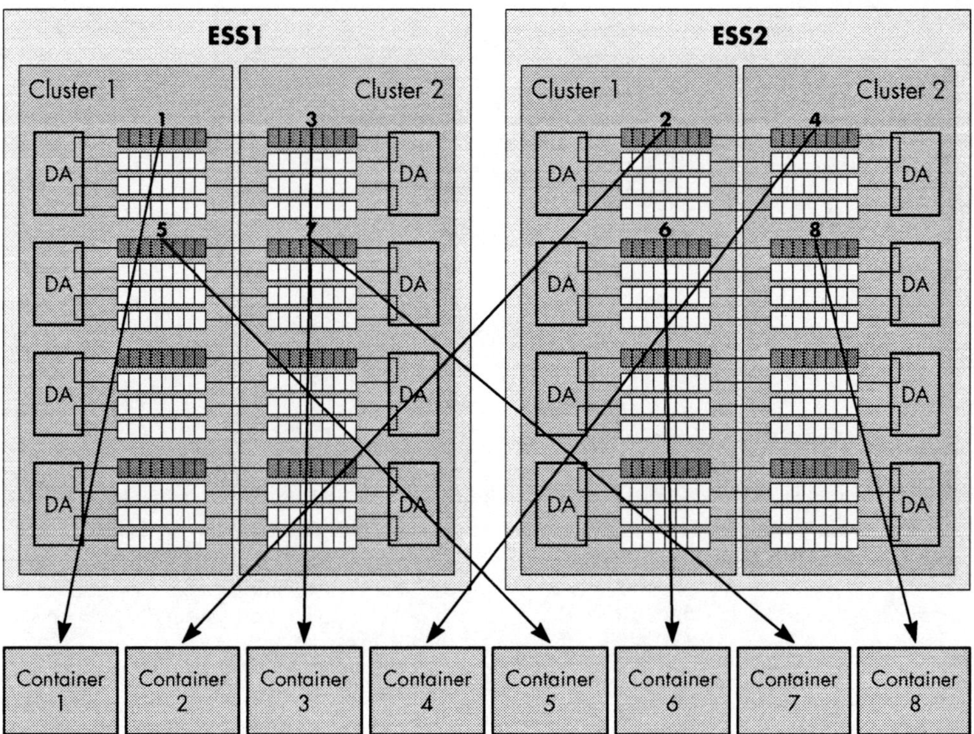

Figure 6.6
How to layout tablespace containers over multiple ESS resources.

Tying It All Together

Since ESS elements appear to the OS as if they are PVs, but really aren't, some tools are provided with ESS that allow you to tie together the underlying ESS structure and OS level structure. Additionally, SDD provides a view into the underlying storage structure that will help you to associate AIX resources and terms with the underlying ESS structure.

ESS Storwatch Specialist

StorWatch Specialist enables you to configure and review your logical disk layout. See Figure 6.7 for an example StorWatch Specialist view.

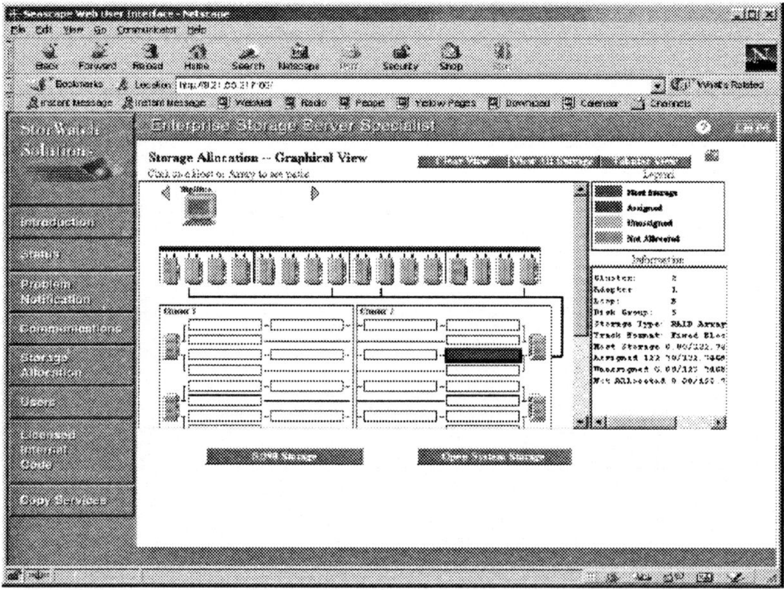

Figure 6.7
ESS StorWatch Specialist.

StorWatch Specialist can show you how much space has been set aside for a logical disk and show, `vpath`, and volume information that will enable you and your storage specialist to map from AIX to the ESS and back.

Figure 6.8 is an example that shows how AIX resources are mapped to `vpaths` and logical disks.

In Figure 6.8, you can see how `hdisks` (from `iostat`) translate into a `vpath` and then how that `vpath` is tied to an ESS logical disk.

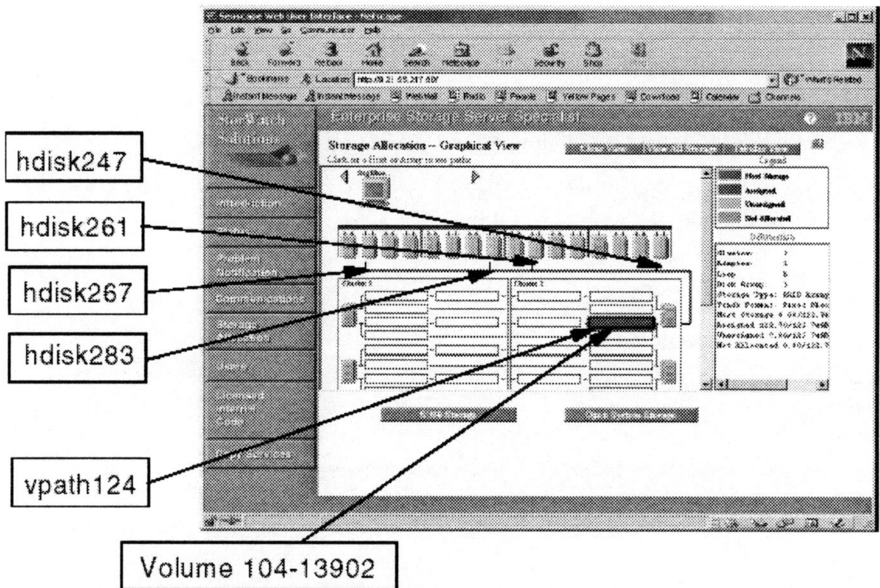

Figure 6.8
Example of mapping hdisks to virtual paths.

KEEPING A MAP OF YOUR DATABASE

You should always have a current map of how your tablespaces are laid out on your storage devices. Such a map will help you map from DB2 through AIX and the AIX LVM, the SDD software, and the ESS support software. Table 6.3 lists where and how to get and record information for such a map.

Table 6.3 ESS/AIX Storage Layout Map

Source	Command	Description
DB2	List tablespace containers	Provides a listing of the OS device name used as the DB2 container.
AIX	Mount or cat/etc/filesystems	Provides a listing of mounted devices.
AIX	ls /dev	Provides a listing of all devices mounted or not.
ESS Specialist	Tabular view of storage saved as a .txt file	Provides a listing of each ESS logical disk, its identification, size, and adapter connections.
SDD (AIX command line)	lsvpcfg	Maps AIX hdisks to their virtual paths.
ESSutil	lsess	Maps AIX hdisks to ESS logical volumes.

ESS Storage Expert

ESS Storage Expert is a separately priced software package used to collect statistics on ESS performance. It is an extension to the ESS Storage Specialist, is Web based, and interaces with Storage Specialist. See Figure 6.9 for an example of the Storage Expert Interface.

Figure 6.9 is an example of using Storage Expert to configure and schedule a data collection. Storage Expert produces predefined reports as follows:

- Disk utilization
- Disk cache
- Cluster and disk adapters
- Disk arrays
- Logical disks

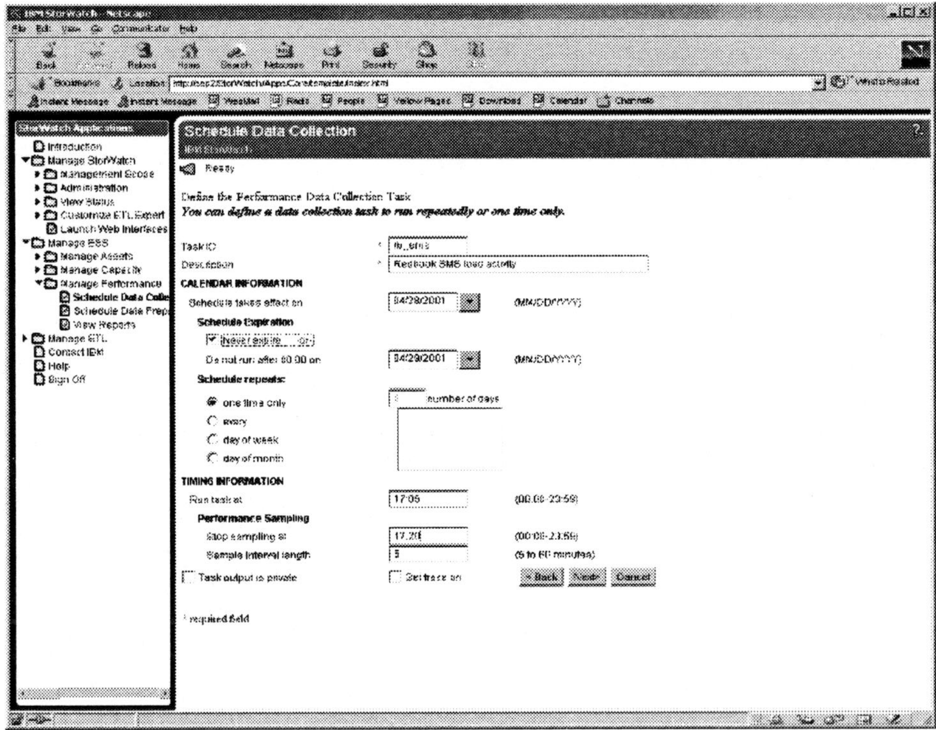

Figure 6.9
ESS Storage Expert Data Collection Setup.

The I/O Bottleneck

Database workloads have caused the PCI bus to become saturated in many cases, while CPUs have continued to scale in accordance with Moore's Law. I/O improvements have lagged behind, thus we have the "I/O bottleneck." Disks are becoming more dense and thus are bigger (72 GB disks are the norm with 146 GB disks on the horizon) and able to store more data. However, even though disk speed (RPMs) has increased from 15,000 to 20,000 RPMs, the time it takes a disk actuator to seek has remained steady. Thus, larger disks with moderate increases in RPMs equals slow seek times. *Disk access is getting slower, not faster.*

PCI Bus

The predominant bus used in most PCs and servers today is also contributing to the I/O bottleneck. PCI (peripheral component interconnect) is a bus-based system that allows the transfer of data between exactly two devices at a time. PCI was developed by Intel in 1992 as a local bus for PC and server platforms.

In DB2 as well as other enterprise-level RDBMS implementations, PCI is a bottleneck to the CPU. Originally, PCI had a transfer rate of 133 MB/sec (Megabytes per second). It has been enhanced several times over the past 10 years and the latest PCI-X 1.0 specification has up to a 1066 MB/sec transfer rate. While these transfer rates may be acceptable for the average PC and small- to mid-tier server, they have fallen way behind processor speeds and Internet and database applications are saturating the bus, while the processors sit idle. Industry users, vendors, and the PCI Special Interest Group (PCI-SIG), the proponent for PCI, have recognized the problem and have developed the faster PCI-X and PCI-Express specifications.

CPU speed doubles every 18 months and with the rapid drop in memory prices, main memory sizes have grown faster than CPU speeds. All along disk transfer rates have only increased 7%.

So what does all this mean? It means a revolutionary change has to take place to develop an I/O fabric capable of supporting today's data transfer rates and data transfer requirements well into the future.

PCI Express (Arapahoe, 3GIO)

PCI Express was formerly code named *Arapahoe* and 3GIO. The names were officially changed to PCI Express. PCI Express will be the upgrade path for the existing PCI bus on PCs, and will eventually replace PCI, but it will take many years due to the proliferation of PCI over the past 10 years. PCI Express is software backward-compatible with PCI, but not hardware-compatible. PCI Express can operate at data transfer speeds of 2.1 GB/sec. It is scalable and uses serial I/O. It will see widespread use in late 2003 or early 2004.

PCI-X

PCI-X will provide data transfer rates of up to 4.2 GB/sec, and is designed primarily for server implementations. PCI-X is designed primarily to compete at the server level in the enterprise, on the lower to middle end. It is fully backward-compatible with PCI. It is being positioned as an alternative to InfiniBand for the low-end server market. PCI-X is a local bus.

InfiniBand Comes to the Rescue

InfiniBand Architecture (IBA) is promulgated by the InfiniBand Trade Association (IBTA). The IBTA, formed in August 1999, is an outgrowth of the Intel/Microsoft-led NGIO, and IBM, COMPAQ, and SUN FUTURE IO effort. InfiniBand is an industry standard, channel-based, switched fabric interconnect architecture for servers.

InfiniBand is not a replacement for the PCI or PCI Express local bus. Instead, it is a new IO fabric for servers within a data center while PCI is a point-to-point architecture.

IBA is an emerging technology that defines a whole new I/O paradigm and way for I/O to take place. Instead of being buss-based like PCI, IBA is point to point, avoids bus arbitration, and overcomes PCI local bus limitations by using an interface to communicate with CPUs via messages (commands and data), which do not involve memory operations and associated CPU overhead. In fact, one such IBM test without IBA drove CPU to 100%. The same test using IBA only drove the CPU to 15%. A significant reduction!

See Figure 6.10 for a high-level view of the IBA.

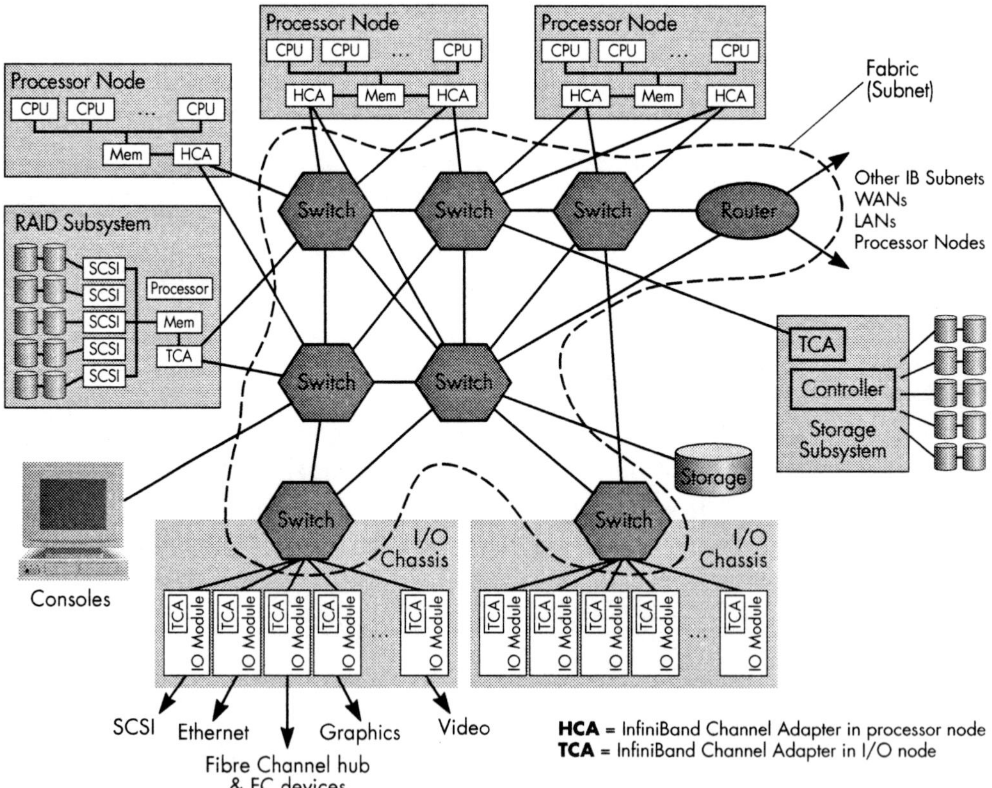

Figure 6.10
IBA high-level overview. (Used with permission of InfiniBand Trade Association)

IBA can be thought of as existing outside the server, unlike PCI, which is a local, in-the-box interconnect.

The name InfiniBand means "infinite bands," which describes the high degree of scalability built into InfiniBand. It can scale to thousands of devices with parallel communications between each node.

> **NOTE**
> DB2 v8 is the first Relational Database Management System (RDBMS) to provide built-in support for InfiniBand.

IBA consists of four main types of devices: Host Channel Adapters (HCAs), Target Channel Adapters (TCAs), switches, and routers. See Figure 6.11 which is an example of the main devices making up the InfiniBand fabric.

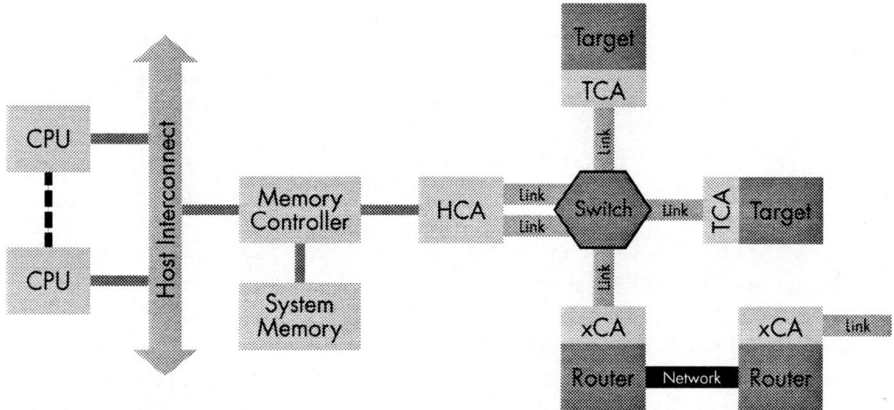

Figure 6.11
InfiniBand component close-up. (Used with permission of InfiniBand Trade Association)

Figure 6.11 lists the primary components of IBA. These components and their functions are as follows:

- **Host Channel Adapter** (HCA). HCAs are the interface to the CPU through messaging semantics (for legacy systems, this is a PCI adapter). As part of the InfiniBand fabric, HCAs manage connections between links.
- **Target Channel Adapter**(TCA). TCAs are simple devices that deliver requested data. A TCA can be a disk interface to a physical hard drive that replaces existing SCSI or FC interfaces.
- **InfiniBand Switch**.The InfiniBand switch links multiple HCAs and TCAs together to form a network. These switches can manage translation and bandwidth and are the

backbone of the InfiniBand fabric. They allow the integration of existing network or I/O components for a smooth migration path and integration and interoperability with existing systems.

- **Router.** The IBA router enables interfacing with other networks and for the translation of legacy components and networks.

> **NOTE**
> The smallest complete IBA unit is a subnet. Multiple subnets joined by routers create large IBA networks. HCAs and TCAs are endnodes in the fabric that send messages over links to other endnodes.

And finally, each subnet has a subnet manager that performs routing and subnet discovery.

IBA Link Speeds

IBA links come in the following speeds:

- 1x—500 MB/sec. (full duplex)
- 4x—2 GB/sec. (full duplex)
- 12x—6 GB/sec. (full duplex)

Of course, what is so exciting about IBA are the data transfer speeds. The throughput of the 12x link is 50 times higher than the theoretical limit of Gigabit Ethernet.

While InfiniBand offers significant performance benefits through increased I/O bandwidth, the industry has been hesitant to replace PCI and thus PCI-Express and PCI-X have been developed. There is an emerging industry interest in Remote Direct Memory Access (RDMA) which offers a partial solution to the I/O bottleneck. RDMA enables remote processes to transfer data directly to host process memory with minimal demands on the memory bus and CPU. Refer to the Remote Direct Memory Access Consortium at *www.RDMAConsortium.org* for additional details.

SUMMARY

In this chapter we have discussed tablespace parameters that are critical for DB2 performance. The storage models were discussed and samples and recommendations provided for you to follow to achieve high performance with DB2. The various RAID levels and attributes were discussed. The concept of spreading your tablespace containers over multiple logical disks on ESS was covered and an example was provided. The life of an I/O in DB2 was presented. Emerging technologies that benefit DB2 were identified and discussed. Based on the information in this chapter, you should be more informed on I/O performance and what information you should get from your storage specialist.

CHAPTER 7

Utilities and Commands

This chapter focuses on new utilities and commands introduced in v8. IBM has enhanced several utilities to provide us with very high availability and serviceability. Online Reorganization of Tables and Indexes and Online Load are highlighted. Several new commands have been introduced to allow DB2 to provide the continuous availability demanded by businesses, in today's demanding, $24 \times 7 \times 365$ environment.

Additionally, I have included 18 utilities and commands that are critical to successful DB2 operation such as Backup Database, Roll-Forward, and Restore Database, along with several others. Also, several new DB2 commands that will help you in administering and supporting DB2 have been included.

I have sequenced related utilities and commands in this chapter to make it easier for you to perform related tasks. There are a number of new wizards in v8. I have included examples of them in this chapter where appropriate. See Figure 7.1, which shows how the wizards can be launched from the Control Center.

As Figure 7.1 indicates, all wizards can be launched from the Control Center. Simply by clicking on the "Tools" menu item on the Control Center toolbar, and then selecting "Wizards," you can view a drop-down list of wizards, as shown in Figure 7.2.

For information on all DB2 utilities and commands, refer to the *DB2 UDB Command Reference.*

> **NOTE**
> The term *utility* and *command* are used interchangeably throughout the book.

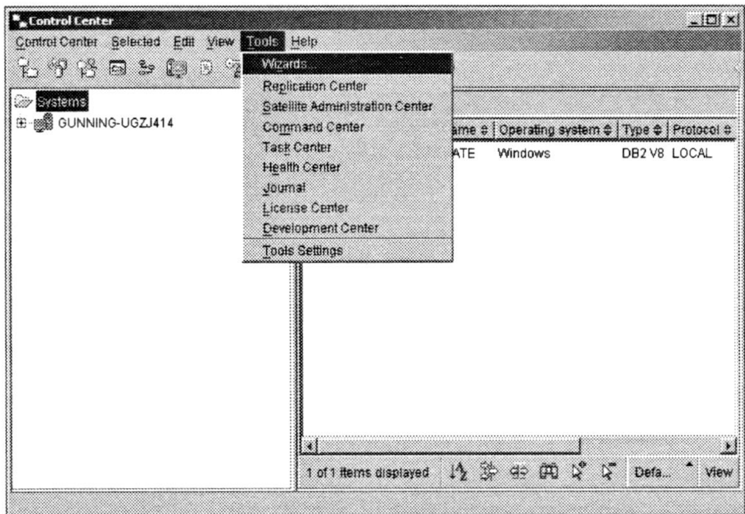

Figure 7.1
Control Center Tools menu.

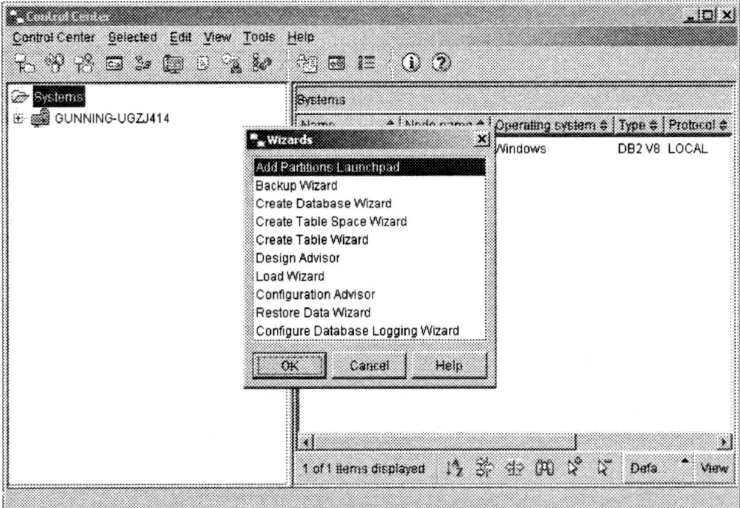

Figure 7.2
Drop-Down list of v8 Wizards.

Reorganizing Indexes/Tables

The REORG utility has been significantly enhanced in v8. Tables can now be reorganized online with almost full access to the table allowed. Indexes can now be reorganized online.

> **NOTE**
> The `REORG` utility has been significantly enhanced in v8. Over 20 new command options have been added to support online reorganization of tables and indexes, along with support for stopping, pausing, and resuming a reorganization.

Other improvements are the capability to pause a `reorg` and restart it later. This is new in v8 and is an enhancement that gives you, the DBA, more flexibility. Prior to v8, a `reorg` could not be paused and restarted and had to run to completion. These enhancements enable DB2 to support the demanding business requirements of today's business environment. The `REORG` utility, along with detailed description of each option, follows.

> **NOTE**
> For syntax diagrams, refer to the *DB2 UDB Command Reference.*

The reorganization utility reorganizes an index or a table.

The index option reorganizes all indexes defined on a table by rebuilding the index data into unfragmented, physically contiguous pages. If you specify the `CLEANUP ONLY` option of the index option, cleanup is performed without rebuilding the indexes.

Scope This command cannot be used against indexes on declared temporary tables and will return an `SQLSTATE` of 42995 if attempted.

Authorization The table option reorganizes a table by reconstructing the rows to eliminate fragmented data, and by compacting information. This command affects all database partitions in the database group. One of the following authorizations is required to run the reorg utility:

- `Sysadm`
- `Sysctrl`
- `Sysmaint`
- `Dbadm`
- `CONTROL` privilege on the table

Required Connection A connection to the database is required.

Command Parameters

`INDEXES ALL FOR TABLE` *`table-name`*

Specifies the table whose indexes are to be reorganized. The table can be in a local or a remote database.

`ALLOW NO ACCESS`—Specifies that no other users can access the table while the indexes are being reorganized. This is the default.

`ALLOW READ ACCESS`—Specifies that other users can have read-only access to the table while the indexes are being reorganized.

`ALLOW WRITE ACCESS`—Specifies that other users can read from and write to the table while the indexes are being reorganized.

`CLEANUP ONLY`—When `CLEANUP ONLY` is requested, a cleanup rather than a full reorganization will be done. The indexes will not be rebuilt and any pages freed up will be available for reuse by indexes defined on this table only.

The `CLEANUP ONLY PAGES` option will search for and free committed pseudo-empty pages. A committed pseudo-empty page is one where all the keys on the page are marked as deleted and all these deletions are known to be committed. The number of pseudo-empty pages in an index can be determined by running runstats and looking at the `NUM EMPTY LEAFS` if they are determined to be committed.

The `CLEANUP ONLY ALL` option will free committed pseudo-empty pages, as well as remove committed pseudo deleted keys from pages that are not pseudo empty. This option will also try to merge adjacent leaf pages if doing so will result in a merged leaf page, where `PCTFREE` is 10%. If two pages can be merged, one of the pages will be freed. The number of pseudo-deleted keys in an index, excluding those on pseudo-empty pages, can be determined by running runstats and then selecting the `NUMRIDS DELETED` from `SYSCAT.INDEXES`. The `ALL` option will clean the `NUMRIDS DELETED` and the `NUM EMPTY LEAFS` if they are determined to be committed.

`ALL`—Specifies that indexes should be cleaned up by removing committed pseudo-deleted keys and committed pseudo-empty pages.

`PAGES`—Specifies that committed pseudo-empty pages should be removed from the index tree. This will not clean up pseudo-deleted keys on pages that are not pseudo-empty. Since it is only checking the pseudo empty leaf pages, it is considerably faster than using the `ALL` option in most cases.

`CONVERT`—If you are not sure whether the table on which you are operating has a type-1 or type-2 index, but want type-2 indexes, you can use the `CONVERT` option. *If the index is type-1, this option will convert it into type-2. If the index is already type-2, this option has no effect.* All indexes created by DB2 prior to Version 8 are type-1 indexes. All indexes created by Version 8 are type-2 indexes, except when you create an index on a table that already has a type-1 index. In this case the new index will also be of type-1. `REORG INDEXES` will always convert type-1 indexes to type-2 indexes unless you use the `CLEANUP` option.

Using the `INSPECT` command to determine the index type can be slow.

NOTE

`CONVERT` allows you to ensure that the new index will be type-2 without your needing to determine its original type.

Use the `ALLOW READ ACCESS` or `ALLOW WRITE ACCESS` option to allow other transactions either read-only or read-write access to the table while the indexes are being reorganized.

> **NOTE**
> While `ALLOW READ ACCESS` and `ALLOW WRITE ACCESS` allow access to the table, during the period in which the reorganized copies of the indexes are made available, no access to the table is allowed.

`TABLE` *`table-name`*

Specifies the table to reorganize. The table can be in a local or a remote database. The name or alias in the form *schema.table-name* may be used. The *schema* is the user name under which the table was created. If you omit the schema name, the default schema is assumed. For typed tables, the specified table name must be the name of the hierarchy's root table.

> **NOTE**
> You cannot specify an index for the reorganization of a multidimensional clustering (MDC) table.

> **NOTE**
> In-place reorganization of tables cannot be used for MDC tables.

`INDEX` *`index-name`*

Specifies the index to use when reorganizing the table. If you do not specify the fully qualified name in the form *schema.index-name,* the default schema is assumed. The *schema* is the user name under which the index was created. The database manager uses the index to physically reorder the records in the table it is reorganizing.

> **NOTE**
> For an inplace table reorganization, if a clustering index is defined on the table and an index is specified, it must be the clustering index.

If the inplace option is not specified, any index specified will be used. If you do not specify the name of an index, the records are reorganized without regard to order. If the table has a clustering index defined, however, and no index is specified, then the clustering index is used to cluster the table. *You cannot specify an index if you are reorganizing an MDC table.*

`INPLACE`

Reorganizes the table while permitting user access. In-place table reorganization is allowed only on tables with type-2 indexes and without extended indexes.

> `ALLOW READ ACCESS`—Allows only read access to the table during reorganization.

> **NOTE**
> `ALLOW WRITE ACCESS`—Allows write access to the table during reorganization. This is the default behavior.

> `NOTRUNCATE TABLE`—Do not truncate the table after inplace reorganization. During truncation, the table is S-locked.
>
> `START`—Start the inplace `REORG` processing. Because this is the default, this keyword is optional.
>
> `STOP`—Stop the in-place `REORG` processing at its current point.
>
> `PAUSE`—Suspend or pause inplace `REORG` for the time being.
>
> `RESUME`—Continue or resume a previously paused in-place table reorganization.

`USE` *`tablespace-name`*

Specifies the name of a system temporary tablespace in which to store a temporary copy of the table being reorganized. If you do not provide a tablespace name, the database manager stores a working copy of the table in the tablespaces that contain the table being reorganized.

For an 8 KB, 16 KB, or 32 KB table object, the page size of any system temporary tablespace that you specify must match the page size of the tablespaces in which the table data resides, including any `LONG` or `LOB` column data.

`INDEXSCAN`

For a clustering `REORG`, an index scan will be used to reorder table records. Reorganize table rows by accessing the table through an index. The default method is to scan the table and sort the result to reorganize the table, using temporary tablespaces as necessary. Even though the index keys are in sort order, scanning and sorting is typically faster than fetching rows by first reading the row identifier from an index.

`LONGLOBDATA`

Long field and LOB data are to be reorganized. This is not required even if the table contains long or LOB columns. The default is to avoid reorganizing these objects because it is time consuming and does not improve clustering.

Examples

For a classic `REORTG TABLE` like the default in DB2, Version 7, enter the following command:

```
db2 reorg table employee index empid allow no access indexscan
longlobdata
```

Note that the defaults are different in v8.

To reorganize a table to reclaim space and use the temporary table space mytemp 1, enter the following command:

```
db2 reorg table homer.employee use mytemp1
```

To reorganize tables in a partitiongroup consisting of nodes 1, 2, 3, and 4 of a four-node system, you can enter either of the following commands:

```
db2 reorg table employee index empid on dbpartitionnum (1,3,4)
db2 reorg tab homer.employee index gprod.empid on all
dbpartitionnums except dbpartitionnu (2)
```

To clean up the pseudo-empty pages in all the indexes on the `EMPLOYEE` table while allowing other transactions to read and update the table, enter:

```
db2 reorg indexes all for table .employee allow write access cleanup
only pages
```

To reorganize the employee table using the system temporary tablespace `TEMPSPACE1` as a work area, enter:

```
db2 reorg table homer.employee using tempspace1
```

To start, pause, and resume an in-place reorganization of the `EMPLOYEE` table with the default schema `GPROD`, which is specified explicitly in previous examples, enter the following commands:

```
db2 reorg table employee index empid inplace start
db2 reorg table employee inplace pause
db2 reorg table homer.employee inplace allow read access notruncate
table resume
```

NOTE

Note that the command to `resume` the reorganization contains additional keywords to specify read access only and to skip the truncation step, which share-locks the table.

Utility Guidelines and Exceptions

Information about the current progress of table reorganization is written to the history file for database activity. The history file contains a record for each reorganization event. To view this file, execute the `db2 list history` command for the database that contains the table you are reorganizing.

You can also use table snapshots to monitor the progress of table reorganization. Table reorganization monitoring data is recorded regardless of the Database Monitor Table Switch setting.

If an error occurs, an SQLCA dump is written to the history file. For an in-place table reorganization, the status is recorded as `PAUSED`.

When an indexed table has been modified many times, the data in the indexes may become fragmented. If the table is clustered with respect to an index, the table and index can get out of cluster order. Both of these factors can adversely affect the performance of scans using the index, and can impact the effectiveness of index page prefetching. `REORG INDEXES` can be used to reorganize all of the indexes on a table, remove any fragmentation, and restore physical clustering to the leaf pages. Use `REORGCHK` to help determine if an index needs reorganizing.

> **NOTE**
> The `REORG TABLE` command is not supported for declared temporary tables.

Indexes may not be optimal following an in-place `REORG TABLE` operation, since only the data object and not the indexes are reorganized. It is recommended that you perform a `REORG INDEXES` after an in-place `REORG TABLE` operation. Indexes are completely rebuilt during the last phase of a classic `REORG TABLE`, however, so reorganizing indexes is not necessary.

Tables that have been modified so many times that data is fragmented and access performance is noticeably slow are candidates for the `REORG TABLE` command. You should also invoke this utility after altering the inline length of a structured type column in order to benefit from the altered inline length. Use `REORGCHK` to determine whether a table needs reorganizing. After reorganizing a table, use `RUNSTATS` to update the table statistics, and `REBIND` to rebind the packages that use this table. The reorganize utility will implicitly close all the cursors.

If the table contains a mixed row format because the table value compression has been activated or deactivated, an offline table reorganization can convert all the existing rows into the target row format.

If the table is partitioned onto several database partitions, and the table reorganization fails on any of the affected database partitions, *only the failing database partitions will have the table reorganization rolled back.*

> **NOTE**
> If the reorganization is not successful, temporary files should not be deleted. These files are created on the database path. The database manager uses these files to roll back the failed reorganization.

If the name of an index is specified, the database manager reorganizes the data according to the order of the index.

> **NOTE**
> To maximize performance, specify an index that is often used in SQL queries. If the name of an index is not specified, and if a clustering index exists, the data will be ordered according to the clustering index.

The PCTFREE value of a table determines the amount of free space designated per page. If the value has not been set, the utility will fill up as much space as possible on each page.

This utility does not support the use of nicknames.

To complete a table space roll-forward recovery following a table reorganization, both data and LONG table spaces must be roll-forward enabled.

If the table contains LOB columns that do not use the COMPACT option, the LOB DATA storage object can be significantly larger following table reorganization. This can be a result of the order in which the rows were reorganized and the types of tablespaces used (SMS/DMS).

REORG TABLE cannot use an index that is based on an index extension.

> **NOTE**
> Reorganizing data is one of the most important performance-improving actions you can take.

REORGCHK UTILITY

Calculates statistics on the database to determine if tables or indexes, or both, need to be reorganized or cleaned up. The REORGCHK utility should be run on a weekly basis or more often, if necessary. The output of the utility will indicate if a reorganization is required. *The* REORGCHK *utility has been enhanced in v8 to report on pseduo-deleted index entries that require cleanup. Also, the* ON SCHEMA *option has been added in v8.* This allows you to specify the object schema for which you want to run the REORGCHK utility.

Scope This command can be issued from any database partition in the *db2nodes.cfg* file. It can be used to update table and index statistics in the catalogs.

Authorization One of the following:

- `sysadm` or `dbadm` authority
- `CONTROL` privilege on the table.

Required Connection Database.

Command Parameters

`UPDATE STATISTICS`

Calls the `RUNSTATS` routine to update table statistics, and then uses the updated statistics to determine if table organization is required.

If a table partition exists on the node where `REORGCHK` has been issued, `RUNSTATS` executes on this node. If a table partition does not exist on this node, the request is sent to the first node in the database partition group that holds a partition for the table. `RUNSTATS` then executes on that node.

`CURRENT STATISTICS`

Uses the current table statistics to determine if table reorganization is required.

`ON SCHEMA` *`schema-name`*

Checks all the tables created under the specified schema.

`ON TABLE`

`USER`—Checks the tables that are owned by the run-time authorization ID.
`SYSTEM`—Checks the system tables.
`ALL`—Checks all users and system tables.
`table-name`—Specifies the table to check. The fully qualified name or alias in the form *schema.table-name* must be used. The *schema* is the user name under which the table was created. If the table specified is a system table catalog, the *schema* is `SYSIBM`.

> **NOTE**
> For typed tables, the specified table name must be the name of the hierarchy's root table.

See Example 7.1 for an example of `REORGCHK` output.

```
Doing RUNSTATS ....

Table statistics:

F1: 100 * OVERFLOW / CARD < 5

F2: 100 * (Effective Space Utilization of Data Pages) > 70

F3: 100 * (Required Pages / Total Pages) > 80

SCHEMA     NAME                  CARD    OV    NP    FP  ACTBLK    TSIZE   F1   F2   F3  REORG
----------------------------------------------------------------------------------------------
PGUNNING   CL_SCHED                 -     -     -     -       -        -    -    -    -    ---
PGUNNING   CONNHEADER_STATEM>     131     0     7     7       -    23973    0   98  100    ---
PGUNNING   CONTROL_STATEMENTS      14     0     1     1       -      700    0    -  100    ---
PGUNNING   DEADLOCK_STATEMEN>       -     -     -     -       -        -    -    -    -    ---
PGUNNING   DEPARTMENT               9     0     1     1       -      549    0    -  100    ---
PGUNNING   DLCONN_STATEMENTS        -     -     -     -       -        -    -    -    -    ---
PGUNNING   DLLOCK_STATEMENTS        -     -     -     -       -        -    -    -    -    ---
PGUNNING   EMP_ACT                 75     0     1     1       -     2850    0    -  100    ---
PGUNNING   EMP_PHOTO               12     0     1     1       -     2028    0    -  100    ---
PGUNNING   EMP_RESUME               8     0     1     1       -      984    0    -  100    ---
PGUNNING   EMPLOYEE                32     0     2     2       -     2784    0   68  100    -*-
PGUNNING   EXPLAIN_ARGUMENT        12     0     1     1       -     3180    0    -  100    ---
PGUNNING   EXPLAIN_INSTANCE         1     0     1     1       -      127    0    -  100    ---
PGUNNING   EXPLAIN_OBJECT           2     0     1     1       -      662    0    -  100    ---
```

Example 7.1
Sample enhanced v8 REORGCHK output.

```
PGUNNING  EXPLAIN_OPERATOR      3    0    1    1     -      525    0   -  100   ---
PGUNNING  EXPLAIN_PREDICATE     2    0    1    1     -      530    0   -  100   ---
PGUNNING  EXPLAIN_STATEMENT     2    0    1    1     -      956    0   -  100   ---
PGUNNING  EXPLAIN_STREAM        4    0    1    1     -     1844    0   -  100   ---
PGUNNING  IN_TRAY               -    -    -    -     -        -    -   -    -   ---
PGUNNING  ORG                   8    0    1    1     -      440    0   -  100   ---
PGUNNING  PROJECT              20    0    1    1     -     1340    0   -  100   ---
PGUNNING  SALES                41    0    1    1     -     1845    0   -  100   ---
PGUNNING  STAFF                35    0    1    1     -     1575    0   -  100   ---
PGUNNING  STMT_STATEMENTS    8128    0  937  937     -  4096512    0 100  100   ---

-------------------------------------------------------------------------------------

Index statistics:

F4: CLUSTERRATIO or normalized CLUSTERFACTOR > 80

F5: 100 * (KEYS * (ISIZE + 9) + (CARD - KEYS) * 5) / ((NLEAF - NUM EMPTY LEAFS) * INDEXPAGESIZE) > 50

F6: (100 - PCTFREE) * ((INDEXPAGESIZE - 96) / (ISIZE + 12)) ** (NLEVELS - 2) * (INDEXPAGESIZE -
96) / (KEYS * (ISIZE + 9) + (CARD - KEYS) * 5) < 100

F7: 100 * (NUMRIDS DELETED / (NUMRIDS DELETED + CARD)) < 20

F8: 100 * (NUM EMPTY LEAFS / NLEAF) < 20
```

Example 7.1
Sample enhanced v8 REORGCHK output. (Continued)

```
SCHEMA    NAME                     CARD LEAF ELEAF LVLS ISIZE NDEL KEYS   F4  F5  F6  F7  F8   REORG
-------------------------------------------------------------------------------------------------


Table:  PGUNNING.EMP_PHOTO
SYSIBM    SQL030107194346850         12    1     0    1    14    0   12  100   -   -   0   0   -----

Table:  PGUNNING.EMP_RESUME
SYSIBM  SQL030107194349680            8    1     0    1    16    0    8  100   -   -   0   0   -----

Table:  PGUNNING.EXPLAIN_INSTANCE
SYSIBM    SQL030107195634000          1    1     0    1    50    0    1  100   -   -   0   0   -----

Table:  PGUNNING.EXPLAIN_STATEMENT
SYSIBM    SQL030107195635030          2    1     0    1    59    0    2  100   -   -   0   0   -----


-------------------------------------------------------------------------------------------------

CLUSTERRATIO or normalized CLUSTERFACTOR (F4) will indicate REORG is necessary for indexes that
are not in the same sequence as the base table. When multiple indexes are defined on a table, one
or more indexes may be flagged as needing REORG. Specify the most important index for REORG
sequencing.

Tables defined using the ORGANIZE BY clause and the corresponding dimension indexes have a '*'
suffix to their names. The cardinality of a dimension index is equal to the Active blocks
statistic of the table.
```

Example 7.1
Sample enhanced v8 REORGCHK output. (Continued)

Note that two new formulas have been added in v8 to address pseudo-deleted RID entries and MDC tables. New fields are ELEAF and NDEL and are defined as follows:

- ELEAF—The number of pseudo-empty index leaf pages (NUM_EMPTY_LEAFS). (A pseudo-empty index leaf page is a page on which all the RIDS are marked as deleted, but have not been physically removed.)
- NDEL—The number of pseudo-deleted RIDS (NUMRIDS_DELETED). (A pseudo-deleted RID is a RID that is marked deleted. This statistic reports pseudo-deleted RIDS on leaf pages that are not pseudo-empty. It does not include RIDS marked as deleted on leaf pages where all the RIDS are marked deleted.)

Formula F7

100 * (NUMRIDS_DELETED / (NUMRIDS_DELETED + CARD)) < 20

The number of pseudo-deleted RIDs on non-pseudo-empty pages should be less than 20%.

Formula F8

100 * (NUM_EMPTY_LEAFS/NLEAF) < 20

The number of pseudo-empty leaf pages should be less than 20% of the total number of leaf pages.

If only the results of the calculations for Formula 7 exceed the bounds set, then cleanup of the indexes using the CLEANUP ONLY option of REORG INDEXES is recommended. When the CLEANUP ONLY option is used, a cleanup, rather than a full reorganization, is done. The indexes are not rebuilt and any pages freed up will be available for reuse by indexes defined only on the involved table.

If only the results of the calculations for Formula 8 are exceeded, then a cleanup of the pseudo-empty pages of the indexes using the CLEANUP ONLY PAGES option of REORG INDEXES is recommended. When the CLEANUP ONLY PAGES option is used, the utility will search for and free committed pseudo-empty pages. Committed pseudo-empty pages will be removed from the index tree. This will not clean up pseudo-deleted keys on pages that are not pseudo-empty. This option will run much faster than using the ALL option because it is only checking the pseudo-empty leaf pages.

DATABASE LOGGING

Key to any relational database, database logging is the ability to log database changes and undo any changes that are not committed to the database. Also, the ability to undo inflight transactions, which occur when a database crashes as a result of a server crash or power failure, is an inherent function that a relational database must provide.

Crash Recovery

After such an occurrence, DB2 invokes crash recovery (by default), which uses the DB2 logs to bring the database to a consistent state. DB2 provides this capability by default. A database configured in this way is referred to as being nonrecoverable because the only recovery ability is crash recovery and version recovery. Roll-forward recovery is not supported when using a database configured as nonrecoverable.

Version Recovery

Version recovery is when a database backup is used to restore the database to a previous point using a backup of the database. In version recovery, roll-forward is not possible with a database using circular logging.

Circular Logging

Circular logging enables version recovery and the backout of uncommitted transactions. Circular logging uses primary logs to record changes to the database. When a primary log fills up, a secondary log file may be used. Circular logging uses only active logs and works in a circular manner.

In circular logging, as one primary log becomes full, the next primary log is used. After a log file has had all of its transactions committed or rolled back, it is eligible for reuse. In circular logging, DB2 will reuse active logs as they become available and are needed. If all primary logs are in use, DB2 will allocate secondary logs until primary active logs become available again.

NOTE

The default value of `LOGFILSIZE` is 1,000 4K pages for Linux and UNIX and 250 4K pages for Windows. These values should be adjusted via system testing or benchmark testing.

In circular logging, logs are not archived and forward recovery is not possible. This type of logging is good for applications that are read only or relatively few changes to the data are made. In most Enterprise OLTP or e-commerce environments, archival logging is used to fully protect the firm's data. Figure 7.3 is an example of the Configure Database Logging Wizard that can be used to assist you in configuring the type of logging appropriate for your environment.

Archival Logging

Archival logging enables a DB2 database to be fully recoverable. That is, all the previous recovery methods mentioned apply, plus archival logging provides for forward recovery. Forward recovery enables a database or tablespace to be recovered just prior to the point of failure. Hence, only inflight transactions at the time of failure are nonrecoverable.

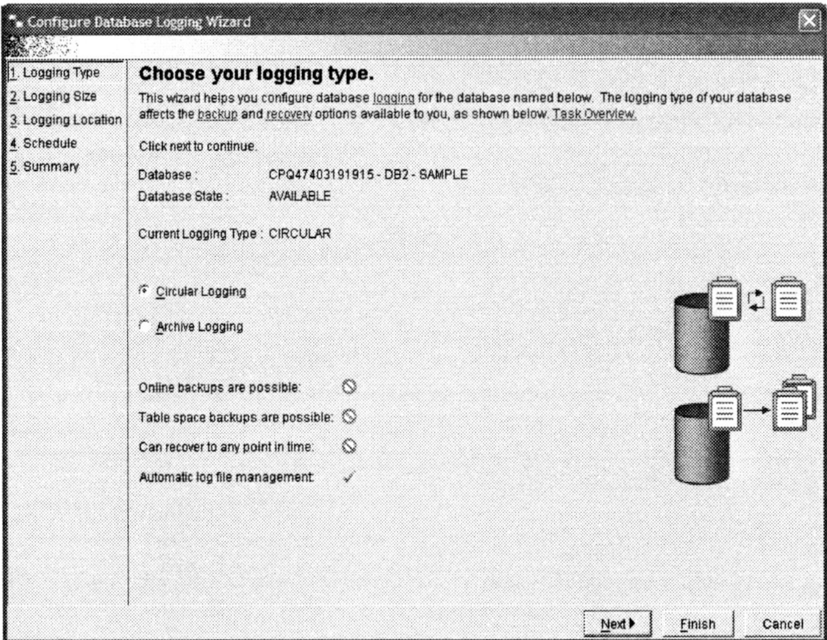

Figure 7.3
Configure Database Logging Wizard.

> **NOTE**
> Archival logging is not enabled by default. If either database configuration parameters `LOGRETAIN` or `USEREXIT` are enabled, then the database is enabled for archival logging and forward recovery.

DB2 uses three types of log files when configured for archival logging:

- Active logs, which contain information for current units of work that have not yet been committed or rolled back. They also contain information about transactions that have been committed but whose changes have not yet been written to the database files.
  As discussed earlier, active logs are used for crash recovery and additionally for rollforward to a point in time or to the end of logs.
- Online archived—Active logs become online archived logs when all changes in the active log are no longer needed for normal processing. The log is then closed and becomes an archived log. Online archive logs contain information regarding completed transactions no longer needed for restart recovery. They are called *online* beside they still reside in the same subdirectory as the active log files.

> **NOTE**
> DB2 supports dual logging at the database level. The `MIRROR_LOGPATH DB CFG` parameter enables this capability, and when enabled, DB2 can write a copy of the log to a different path.

- Offline archived—Log files that are moved from the active log file directory become *offline archived*. These files can be moved via the sample userexit provided with DB2. They can also be managed by an external storage manager such as IBM's TSM, or some other third-party vendor product.

Roll-forward Recovery

Roll-forward recovery can use archived logs, offline archived logs, and active logs to rebuild a database or tablespace to the end of the logs or to a specific point in time.

> **NOTE**
> With the `USEREXIT` enabled, the `ARCHIVE LOG COMMAND` can be used to force an archive of the log. Note that it can also be used to test the userexit if enabling it for the first time.

> **NOTE**
> When restoring a database using archived logs, the `DB CFG NEW LOGPATH` parameter can be used to change the log file location so archived logs that are needed for recovery can be placed there.

Important Facts Regarding Logs

If an active log is erased, lost, or destroyed, the database becomes unusable and a restore must be done before it can be used again.

If an archive log file is erased, you will only be able to roll forward changes up to the first log erased.

You must take the necessary steps to secure and protect log files.

For top performance, log files can be placed on *raw devices* on all supported platforms. Some consideration when using RAW devices are:

- Only the primary log file extents are used
- The amount of space must be at least (`LOGPRIMARY` * (`LOGFILSZ` +2)) +1) 4 KB pages.

Since secondary log files are not used on raw devices, you will have to take this into consideration when sizing your logs and determining how many you need.

NOTE

The maximum amount of log space has increased from 32 GB to 256 GB. *Infinite logging* is now available and allows an active unit of work to span primary logs and archive logs, ostensibly enabling a transaction to use an infinite number of logs.

Backup Database Utility

Backing up your company's data is one of the most important functions you can perform as a DBA. Companies entrust DBAs with enormous responsibility and rely on them to safeguard the corporate data. Some companies that have lost corporate data due to databases not being backed up have lost sizable amounts of revenue, declared bankruptcy, or gone completely out of business.

As DBAs, we have all had our tense moments when we had difficulty restoring or recovering data due to inadequate backups, lack of knowledge of the backup utility, or lack of detailed backup and recovery procedures. In v8, we can use the Backup Wizard to assist us in developing an appropriate backup strategy for our environment. See Figure 7.4 for an example of the Backup Wizard.

NOTE

Backup and recovery procedures should be documented, tested, and practiced. Don't wait until you need to do a recovery to figure out how to do it. Have documented and tested procedures in place.

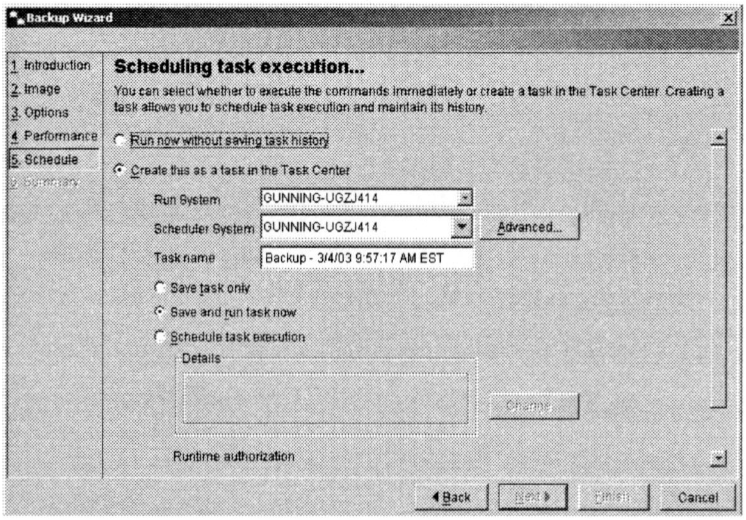

Figure 7.4
Backup Wizard.

Types of Backup

The recovery history file is updated automatically with summary information whenever you carry out a backup of a database. It is useful for tracking the backup history of a database.

Offline

An offline backup records the complete contents of the database. During an offline backup, only the backup utility itself can be connected to the database. While the backup runs, no other utilities or applications can connect to the database. This type of backup is used when there are no business requirements driving the need to enable the database for full access $24 \times 7 \times 365$. It is used when the load files that were used to populate the database have been retained and the database can be reloaded, if necessary. You might use offline backups in a DW environment where the data is mostly read-only. Or when you have a nightly or weekly window when you can force off all application connections from the database and take an offline backup. With offline backups, only *crash* and *version* recovery are possible.

You may recall that the `AUTORESTART DB CFG` parameter enables crash recovery at DB2 to start by default.

Scope This command only affects the database partition on which it is executed.

Authorization One of the following:

- `Sysadm`
- `Sysctrl`
- `Sysmaint`

Required connection Database. This command automatically establishes a connection to the specified database.

> **NOTE**
> If a connection to the specified database already exists, that connection will be terminated and a new connection established specifically for the backup operation. The connection is terminated at the completion of the backup operation.

Command Parameters

`DATABASE` *`database-alias`*

Specifies the alias of the database to back up.

`USER` *`username`*

Identifies the user name under which to back up the database.

`USING` *`password`*

The password used to authenticate the user name. If the password is omitted, the user is prompted to enter it.

`TABLESPACE` *`tablespace-name`*

A list of names used to specify the table spaces to be backed up.

`ONLINE`

Specifies online backup. The default is offline backup. Online backups are only available for databases configured with *logretain* or *userexit* enabled. If this option is used, the database must be enabled for forward recovery. Online backups use archived logs to enable fully recoverable databases using roll-forward recovery.

> **NOTE**
> An online backup operation may time out if there is an IX lock on sysibm.systables, because the DB2 backup utility requires an S lock on objects containing LOBs.

`INCREMENTAL`

Specifies a cumulative (incremental) backup image. An incremental backup image is a copy of all database data that has changed since the most recent, successful full backup operation.

`DELTA`

Specifies a noncumulative (delta) backup image. A delta backup is a copy of all database data that has changed since the most recent, successful backup operation of any type.

`USE TSM`

Specifies that the backup is to use Tivoli Storage Manager output.

`OPEN` *`num-sessions`* `SESSIONS`

The number of I/O sessions to be created between DB2 and TSM or another backup vendor product.

> **NOTE**
> This parameter has no effect when backing up to tape, disk, or other local devices.

`USE XBSA`

Specifies that the XBSA interface is to be used. Backup Services APIs (XBSA) are an open application programming interface for applications or facilities needing data storage management for backup or archiving purposes. Legato NetWorker is storage manager that currently supports the XBSA interface.

`TO` *`dir/dev`*

A list of directory or tape device names. The full path on which the directory resides must be specified. If `USE`, `TSM`, `TO`, and `LOAD` are omitted, the default target directory for the backup image is the current working directory of the client computer. This target directory or device must exist on the database server. This parameter may be repeated to specify the target directories and devices that the backup image will span. If more than one target is specified (e.g., target1, target2, and target3), target1 will be opened first. The media header and special files (including the configuration file, tablespace table, and history file) are placed in target1. All remaining targets are opened, and are then used in parallel during the backup operation, because there is no general tape device that requires a unique device driver. To back up to the FAT file system on Windows operating systems, users must conform to the 8.3 naming restriction.

Use of tape devices or floppy disks may generate messages and prompts for user input. Valid response options are:

- **c** Continue. Continue using the device that generated the warning message (e.g., when a new tape has been mounted).
- **d** Device terminate. Stop using only the device that generated the warning message (e.g., when there are no more tapes).
- **t** Terminate. Abort the backup operation.

If the tape system does not support the ability to uniquely reference a backup image, it is recommended that multiple backup copies of the same database not be kept on the same tape.

`LOAD` *`library-name`*

The name of the shared library (DLL on Windows operating systems) containing the vendor backup and restore I/O functions to be used. It can contain the full path. If the full path is not given, it will default to the path on which the user exit program resides.

`WITH` *`num-buffers`* `BUFFERS`

The number of buffers to be used. The default is 2. However, when creating a backup to multiple locations, a larger number of buffers may be used to improve performance.

`BUFFER` *`buffer-size`*

The size in 4 KB pages of the buffer used when building the backup image. The minimum value for this parameter is 8 pages; the default value is 1,024 pages.

If using tape with variable block size, reduce the buffer size to within the range that the tape device supports. Otherwise, the backup operation may succeed, but the resulting image may not be recoverable.

When using tape devices on SCO UnixWare 7, specify a buffer size of 16.

With most versions of Linux, using DB2's default buffer size for backup operations to a SCSI tape device results in error SQL2025N, reason code 75. To prevent the overflow of Linux internal SCSI buffers, use this formula:

Bufferpages <= `ST_MAX_BUFFERS` * `ST_BUFFER_BLOCKS` / $

Where *bufferpages* is the value you want to use with the `BUFFER` parameter, and `ST_MAX_BUFFERS` and `ST_BUFFER_BLOCKS` are defined in the Linux kernel under the drivers/scsi directory.

`PARALLELISM` *n*

Determines the number of table spaces that can be read in parallel by the backup utility. The default value is 1.

`WITHOUT PROMPTING`

Specifies that the backup will run unattended, and that any actions that normally require user intervention will return an error message.

Examples

In the following example, the database WSDB is defined on all four partitions, numbered 0 through 3. The path /dev3/ backup is accessible from all partitions. Partition 0 is the catalog partition, and needs to be backed up separately since this is an offline backup. To perform an offline backup of all the WSDB database partitions to /dev3/backup, issue the following commands from one of the database partitions:

```
db2_all '<<+0< db2 BACKUP DATABASE wsdb TO /dev3/backup'
db2_all '<<<-0< db2 BACKUP DATABASE wsdb TO /dev3/backup'
```

In the second command, the `db2_all` utility will issue the same backup command to each database partition in turn (except partition 0). All four database partition backup images will be stored in the /dev3/backup directory.

In the following example, database SAMPLE is backed up to a TSM server using two concurrent TSM client sessions. The backup utility will use four buffers, which are the default buffer size (1024 × 4 K pages).

```
db2 backup database sample use tsm open 2 sessions with 4 buffers
```

In the next example, a table space-level backup of table spaces (syscatspace, uerspace1) of database payroll is done to tapes.

```
db2 backup database payroll tablespace (syscatspace, userspace1) to /
dev/rmt0, /dev/rmt1 with 8 buffers without prompting
```

Following is a sample weekly incremental backup strategy for a recoverable database. It includes a weekly full database backup operation, a daily noncumulative (delta) backup operation, and a mid-week cumulative (incremental) backup operation:

```
(Sun)  db2 backup db sample use tsm
(Mon)  db2 backup db sample online incremental delta use tsm
(Tues) db2 backup db sample online incremental delta use tsm
(Wed)  db2 backup db sample online incremental use tsm
(Thu)  db2 backup db sample online incremental delta use tsm
(Fri)  db2 backup db sample online incremental delta use tsm
(Sat)  db2 backup db sample online incremental use tsm
```

RESTORE DATABASE UTILITY

Rebuilds a damaged or corrupted database that has been backed up using the DB2 backup utility. The restore database utility can also be invoked using the Restore Data Wizard, as shown in Figures 7.5 and 7.6.

The Restore Data Wizard initially displays the Introduction tab, which allows you to select the type of restore desired. Figure 7.6 displays a list of the backup images that are recorded in the recovery history file. In Figure 7.6, the Restore Data Wizard Available Backup Image tab allows you to select the backup image to be used.

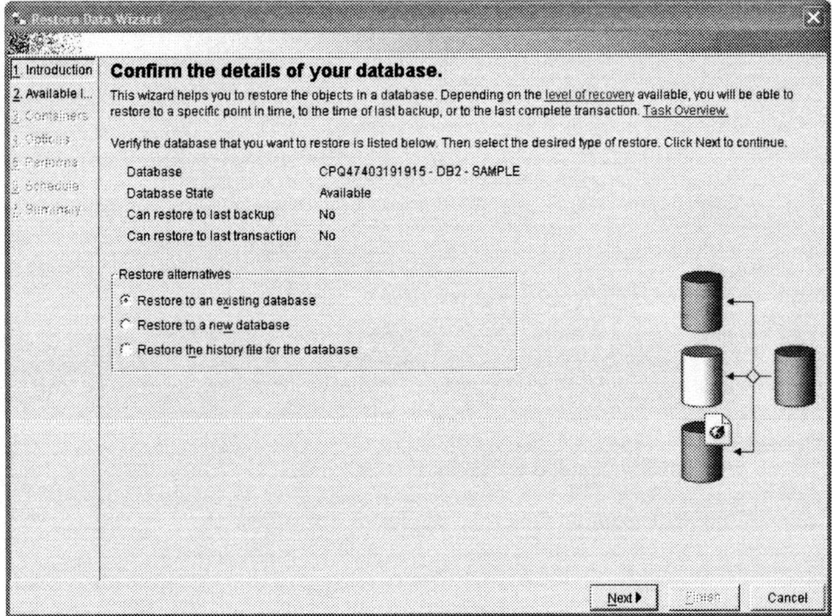

Figure 7.5
Restore Data Wizard Confirm Details tab.

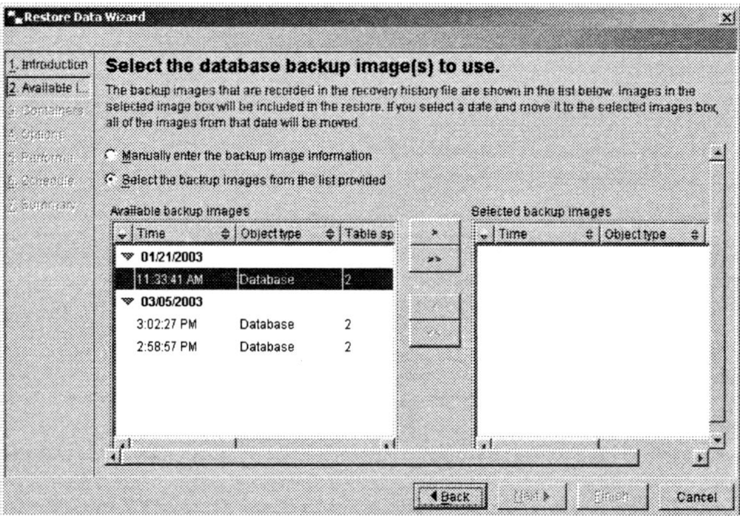

Figure 7.6
Restore Data Wizard Available Images Data tab.

The restored database is in the same state it was in when the backup copy was made. This utility can also restore to a database with a name different from the database name in the backup image (in addition to being able to restore to a new database).

This utility can also be used to restore backup images that were produced by the previous two versions of DB2. *If a migration is required, it will be invoked automatically at the end of the restore operation.*

If, at the time of the backup operation, the database was enabled for roll-forward recovery, the database can be brought to the state it was in prior to the occurrence of the damage or corruption by invoking the roll-forward utility after successful completion of a restore operation.

This utility can also restore from a tablespace-level backup.

To restore a database that was backed up on a different workstation platform, use the db2move utility. You can restore databases created in one version of Windows from another version. *Databases created on AIX, HP, and Sun platforms may also be restored from each other's system.*

Scope The command only affects the node on which it is executed.

Authorization To restore to an existing database, use one of the following:

- `Sysadm`
- `Sysctrl`
- `Sysmaint`

To restore to a new database, use one of the following:

- Sysadm
- Sysctrl

Required connections Database, to restore to an existing database. This command automatically establishes a connection to the specified database.

Instance and database, to restore to a new database. The instance attachment is required to create the database.

To restore to a new database at an instance different from the current instance (as defined by the value of the DB2INSTANCE environment variable), it is necessary to first attach to the instance where the new database will reside.

To restore to a new *remote* database, it is necessary to attach to the instance where the new database will reside.

Command Parameters

DATABASE *source-database-alias*

Alias of the source database from which the backup was taken.

CONTINUE

Specifies that the containers have been redefined, and that the final step in a redirected restore operation should be performed.

ABORT

This parameter:

- Stops a redirected restore operation. This is useful when an error has occurred that requires one or more steps to be repeated. After RESTORE DATABASE with the ABORT option has been issued, each step of a redirected restore operation must be repeated, including RESTORE DATABASE with the REDIRECT option.
- Terminates an incremental restore operation before completion.

USER *username*

Identifies the user name under which the database is to be restored.

USING *password*

The password used to authenticate the user name. If the password is omitted, the user is prompted to enter it.

TABLESPACE *tablespace-name*

A list of names used to specify the table spaces that are to be restored.

`ONLINE`

This keyword, applicable only when performing a table space-level restore operation, is specified to allow a backup image to be restored online. This means that other agents can connect to the database while the backup image is being restored, and that the data in other tablespaces will be available while the specified tablespaces are being restored.

`HISTORY FILE`

The keyword is specified to restore only the history file from the backup image.

`INCREMENTAL`

Without additional parameters, `INCREMENTAL` specifies a manual cumulative restore operation. During manual restore the user must issue each restore command manually for each image involved in the restore. Do so according to the following order: last, first, second, third, and so on, up to and including the last image.

`INCREMENTAL AUTOMATIC/AUTO`

Specifies an automatic cumulative restore operation.

`INCREMENTAL ABORT`

Specifies abortion of an in-progress manual cumulative restore operation.

`USE TSM`

Specifies that the database is to be restored from TSM-managed output.

`OPEN` *`num-sessions`* `SESSIONS`

Specifies the number of I/O sessions that are to be used with TSM or the vendor product.

`USE XBSA`

Specifies that the XBSA interface is to be used. Backup Services APIs (XBSA) are omitted, the default value is the current working directory of the client machine. This target directory or device must exist on the database server.

On Windows operating systems, the specified directory must not be a DB2-generated directory. For example, given the following commands:

```
db2 backup database sample to c:\backup
db2 restore database sample from c:\backup
```

DB2 generates subdirectories under the c:\backup directory that should be ignored. To specify precisely which backup image to restore, use the `TAKEN AT` parameter. There may be several backup images stored on the same path.

If several items are specified, and the last item is a tape device, the user is prompted for another tape. Valid response options are:

- **c** Continue. Continue using the device that generated the warning message (e.g., continue when a new tape has been mounted).
- **d** Device terminate. Stop using *only* the device that generated the warning message (e.g., terminate when there are no more tapes).
- **t** Terminate. Abort the restore operation after the user has failed to perform some action requested by the utility.

`LOAD` *`shared-library`*

The name of the shared library (DLL on Windows operating systems) containing the vendor backup and restore I/O functions to be used. The name can contain a full path. If the full path is not given, the value defaults to the path on which the user exit program resides.

`TAKEN AT` *`date-time`*

The time stamp of the database backup image. The time stamp is displayed after successful completion of a backup operation, and is part of the path name for the backup image. It is specified in the form *yyyymmddhhmmss.* A partial time stamp can also be specified. For example, if two different backup images with time stamps 19971001010101 and 19971002010101 exist, specifying 19971002 causes the image with time stamp 19971002010101 to be used. If a value for this parameter is not specified, there must be only one backup image on the source media.

`TO` *`target-directory`*

The target database directory. This parameter is ignored if the utility is restoring to an existing database. The drive and directory that you specify must be local.

> **NOTE**
> On Windows operating systems, when using this parameter specify the drive letter. For example, you might specify x:\path_name to restore to a specific path, or x: if you do not need to specify a path. If the path name is too long, an error is returned.

`INTO` *`target-database-alias`*

The target database alias. If the target database does not exist, it is created.

When you restore a database backup to an existing database, the restored database inherits the alias and database name of the existing database. When you restore a database backup to a nonexistent database, the new database is created with the alias and database name that you specify. This new database name must be unique on the system where you restore it.

NEWLOGPATH *directory*

The absolute pathname of a directory that will be used for active log files after the restore operation. This parameter has the same function as the newlogpath database configuration in which it is specified. The parameter can be used when the log path in the backup image is not suitable for use after the restore operations (e.g., when the path is no longer valid or is being used by a different database).

WITH *num-buffers* BUFFERS

The number of buffers to be used. The default value is 2. However, a larger number of buffers can be used to improve performance when multiple sources are being read from, or if the value of PARALLELISM has been increased.

BUFFER *buffer-size*

The size, in pages, of the buffer used for the restore operation. The minimum value for this parameter is 8 pages; the default value is 1,024 pages.

The restore buffer size must be a positive integer multiple of the backup buffer size specified during the backup operation. If an incorrect buffer size is specified, the buffers are allocated to be of the smallest acceptable size.

When using tape devices on SCO UnixWare 7, specify a buffer size of 16.

DLREPORT *filename*

The file name, if specified, must be specified as an absolute path. Reports the files that become unlinked, as a result of a fast reconcile, during a restore operation. This option is only to be used if the table being restored has a DATALINK column type and linked files.

REPLACE EXISTING

If a database with the same alias as the targeted database alias already exists, this parameter specifies that the restore utility is to replace the existing database with the restored database. This is useful for scripts that invoke the restore utility, because the command line processor will not prompt the user to verify deletion of an existing database. If the WITHOUT PROMPTING parameter is specified, it is not necessary to specify REPLACE EXISTING, but in this case, the operation will fail if events occur that normally require user intervention.

REDIRECT

Specifies a redirected restore operation. To complete a redirected restore operation, this command should be followed by one or more SET TABLESPACE CONTAINERS commands, and then by a RESTORE DATABASE command with the CONTINUE option.

WITHOUT ROLLING FORWARD

Specifies that the database is not to be put in roll-forward pending state after it has been successfully restored.

If, following a successful restore operation, the database is in roll-forward pending state, the ROLLFORWARD command must be invoked before the database can be used again.

WITHOUT DATALINK

Specifies that any tables with DATALINK columns are to be put in Datalink_Reconcile_Pending (DRP) state, and that no reconciliation of linked files is to be performed.

PARALLELISM *n*

Specifies the number of buffer manipulators that are to be spawned during the restore operation. The default value is 1.

WITHOUT PROMPTING

Specifies that the restore operation is to run unattended. Actions that normally require user intervention will return an error message. When using a removable media device, such as a tape or diskette, the user is prompted when the device ends, even if this option is specified.

Examples

In the following example, the database WSDB is defined on all four partitions, numbered 0 through 3. The path /dev3/backup is accessible from all partitions. The following offline backup images are available from /dev3/backup:

```
wsdb.0.db2inst1.NODE0000.CATN0000.20020331234149.001
wsdb.0.db2inst1.NODE0001.CATN0000.20020331234427.001
wsdb.0.db2inst1.NODE0002.CATN0000.20020331234828.001
wsdb.0.db2inst1.NODE0003.CATN0000.20020331235235.001
```

To restore the catalog partition first, then all other database partitions of the WSDB database from the /dev3/backup directory, issue the following commands from one of the database partitions:

```
db2_all '<<+0< db2 RESTORE DATABASE wsdb FROM /dev3/backup
TAKEN AT 20020331234149
  INTO wsdb REPLACE EXISTING '
db2_all '<<+1< db2 RESTORE DATABASE wsdb FROM /dev3/backup
TAKEN AT 20020331234427
  INTO wsdb REPLACE EXISTING '
db2_all '<<+2< db2 RESTORE DATABASE wsdb FROM /dev3/backup
TAKEN AT 20020331234828
  INTO wsdb REPLACE EXISTING '
```

```
db2_all '<<+3< db2 RESTORE DATABASE wsdb FROM /dev3/backup
TAKEN AT 20020331235235
  INTO wsdb REPLACE EXISTING '
```

The db2_all utility issues the restore command to each specified database partition.

Following is a typical redirected restore scenario for a database whose alias is MYDB:

1. Issue a `RESTORE DATABASE` command with the `REDIRECT` option.

   ```
   db2 restore db mydb replace existing redirect
   ```

   After successful completion of step 1, and before completing step 3, the restore operation can be aborted by issuing:

   ```
   db2 restore db mydb abort
   ```

2. Issue a `SET TABLESPACE CONTAINERS` command for each tablespace whose containers must be redefined. For example:

   ```
   db2 set tablespace containers for 5 using
      (file `f:\ts3con1` 20000, file `f:\ts3con2` 20000)
   ```

   To verify that the containers of the restored database are the ones specified in this step, issue the `LIST TABLESPACE CONTAINERS` command.

3. After successful completion of steps 1 and 2, issue:

   ```
   db2 restore db mydb continue
   ```

   This is the final step of the redirected restore operation.

4. If step 3 fails, or if the restore operation has been aborted, the redirected restore can be restarted, beginning at step 1.

Following is a sample weekly incremental backup strategy for a recoverable database. It includes a weekly full database backup operation, a daily noncumulative (delta) backup operation, and a mid-week cumulative (incremental) backup operation:

```
(Sun) backup db mydb use tsm
(Mon) backup db mydb online incremental delta use tsm
(Tue) backup db mydb online incremental delta use tsm
(Wed) backup db mydb online incremental use tsm
(Thu) backup db mydb online incremental delta use tsm
(Fri) backup db mydb online incremental delta use tsm
(Sat) backup db mydb online incremental use tsm
```

For an automatic database restore of the images created on Friday morning, issue:

```
restore db mydb incremental automatic taken at (Fri)
```

For a manual database restore of the images created on Friday morning, issue:

```
restore db mydb incremental taken at (Fri)
restore db mydb incremental taken at (Sun)
restore db mydb incremental taken at (Wed)
```

```
restore db mydb incremental taken at (Thu)
restore db mydb incremental taken at (Fri)
```

Utility Guidelines and Exceptions

Any `RESTORE DATABASE` command of the form `db2 restore db <name>` will perform a full database restore, regardless of whether the image being restored is a database image or a tablespace image. Any `RESTORE DATABASE` command of the form `db2 restore db <name>` tablespace will perform a tablespace restore of the tablespaces found in the image. Any `RESTORE DATABASE` command in which a list of tablespaces is provided will perform a restore of whatever tablespaces are explicitly listed.

> **NOTE**
> Following the restore of an online backup, you must perform a roll-forward recovery.

ROLL-FORWARD DATABASE

Roll-forward database recovers a database by applying transactions recorded in the database log files. It is invoked after a database or a tablespace backup image has been restored, or if any tablespaces have been taken offline by the database due to a media error. The database must be recoverable (i.e., either `logretain`, `userexit`, or both of these database configuration parameters must be enabled) before the database can be roll-forward recovered.

Scope In a partitioned database environment, this command can only be invoked from the catalog partition. A database or tablespace roll-forward operation to a specified point in time affects all partitions that are listed in the *db2nodes.cfg* file. A database or tablespace roll-forward operation to the end of logs affects the partitions that are specified. If no partitions are specified, it affects all partitions that are listed in the *db2nodes.cfg* file; if roll-forward recovery is not needed on a particular partition, that partition is ignored.

Authorization One of the following:

- `Sysadm`
- `Sysctrl`
- `Sysmaint`

Required connection None. This command establishes a database connection.

Command Parameters

`DATABASE` *`database-alias`*

The alias of the database that is to be roll-forward recovered.

`USER` *`username`*

The user name under which the database is to be roll-forward recovered.

`USING` *`password`*

The password used to authenticate the user name. If the password is omitted, the user is prompted to enter it.

`TO` *`isotime`*

The point in time to which all committed transactions are to be rolled forward (including the transaction committed precisely at that time, as well as all transactions committed previously).

This value is specified as a time stamp, a seven-part character string that identifies a combined date and time. The format is *yyyy-mm-dd-hh.mm.ss.nnnnnn* (year, month, day, hour, minutes, seconds, microseconds), expressed in coordinated universal time (UTC). UTC helps to avoid having the same time stamp associated with different logs (because of a change in time associated with daylight savings time, for example). The time stamp in a backup image is based on the local time at which the backup operation started. The `CURRENT TIMEZONE` special register specifies the difference between UTC and local time at the application server. The difference is represented by a time duration (a decimal number in which the first two digits represent the number of hours, the next two digits represent the number of minutes, and the last two digits represent the number of seconds). Subtracting `CURRENT TIMEZONE` from a local time converts that local time to UTC.

`USING LOCAL TIME`

Allows the user to roll forward to a point in time that is the user's local time rather than GMT time. This makes it easier for users to roll forward to a specific point in time on their local machines, and eliminates potential user errors due to the translation of local to GMT time.

Notes

1. If the user specifies a local time for roll-forward, all messages returned to the server will also be in local time. Note that all times are converted on the server, and if MPP, on the catalog database partition.
2. The timestamp string is converted to GMT on the server, so the time is local to the server's time zone, not the client's. If the client is in one time zone and the server in another, the server's local time should be used. This is different from the local time option from the Control Center, which is local to the client.
3. If the timestamp string is close to the time change of the clock due to daylight savings, it is important to know if the stop time is before or after the clock change, and specify it correctly.

`END OF LOGS`

Specifies that all committed transactions from all online archive log files listed in the database configuration parameter *logpath* are to be applied.

`ALL DBPARTITIONNUMS`

Specifies that transactions are to be rolled forward on all partitions specified in the db2node.cfg file. This is the default if a database partition clause is not specified.

`EXCEPT`

Specifies that transactions are to be rolled forward on all partitions specified in the db2nodes.cfg file, except those specified in the database partition list.

`ON DBPARTITIONNUM/ON DBPARTITIONNUMS`

Roll the database forward on a set of database partitions.

`db-partition-number1`

Specifies a database partition number in the database partition list.

`db-partition-number2`

Specifies the second database partition number, so that all partitions from *db-partition-number1* up to and including *db-partition-number2* are included in the database partition list.

`COMPLETE/STOP`

Stops the rolling forward of log records, and completes the roll-forward recovery process by rolling back any incomplete transactions and turning off the roll-forward pending state of the database. This allows access to the database or tablespaces that are being rolled forward. These keywords are equivalent; specify one or the other, but not both. The keyword AND permits specification of multiple operations at once; for example, db2 rollforward db sample to end of logs and complete.

> **NOTE**
> When rolling tablespaces forward to a point in time, the tablespaces are placed in backup pending state.

`CANCEL`

Cancels the roll-forward recovery operation. This puts the database or one or more tablespaces on all partitions on which forward recovery has been started in restore pending state:

- If a *database* roll-forward operation is not in process (i.e., the database is in roll-forward pending state), this option puts the database in restore pending state.

- If a *tablespace* roll-forward operation is not in progress (i.e., the tablespaces are in roll-forward pending state), a tablespace list must be specified. All tablespaces in the list are put in restore pending state.
- If a tablespace roll-forward operation *is* in progress (i.e., at least one tablespace is in roll-forward in progress state), all tablespaces that are in roll-forward in progress state are put in restore pending state. If a tablespace list is specified, it must include all tablespaces that are in roll-forward in progress state. All tablespaces on the list are put in restore pending state.
- If rolling forward to a point in time, any tablespace name that is passed in is ignored, and all tablespaces that are in roll-forward in progress state are put in restore pending state.
- If rolling forward to the end of the logs with a tablespace list, only the tablespaces listed are put in restore pending state.

This option cannot be used to cancel a roll-forward operation *that is actually running*. It can only be used to cancel a roll-forward operation that is in progress but not actually running at the time. A roll-forward operation can be in progress but not running if:

- It terminated abnormally.
- The `STOP` option was not specified.
- An error caused it to fail. Some errors, such as rolling forward through a nonrecoverable load operation, can put a tablespace into restore pending state.

> **NOTE**
> Use the `CANCEL` option with caution, and only if the roll-forward operation that is in progress cannot be completed because some of the tablespaces have been put in roll-forward pending state or in restore pending state. When in doubt, use the `LIST TABLESPACES` command to identify the tablespaces that are in roll-forward in progress state, or in roll-forward pending state.

QUERY STATUS

Lists the log files that the database manager has rolled forward, the next archive file required, and time stamp (in CUT) of the last committed transaction since roll-forward processing began. In a partitioned database environment, this status information is returned for each partition. The information returned contains the following fields:

Database Partition Number

Roll-forward Status

Status can be: database or tablespace roll-forward pending, database or tablespace roll-forward in progress, database or tablespace roll-forward processing STOP, or not pending.

Next Log File to be Read

A string containing the name of the next required log file. In a partitioned database environment, use this information if the roll-forward utility fails with a return code indicating that a log file is missing or that a log information mismatch has occurred.

Log Files Processed

A string containing the names of proceeded log files that are no longer needed for recovery, and that can be removed from the directory. If, for example, the oldest uncommitted transaction starts in log file *x*; the range of obsolete log files will not include *x;* the range ends at *x* –1.

Last Committed Transaction

A string containing a time stamp in ISO format (*yyyy-mm-dd-hh.mm.ss*). This time stamp marks the last transaction committed after the completion of roll-forward recovery. The time stamp applies to the database. For tablespace roll-forward recovery, it is the time stamp of the last transaction committed to the database.

> **NOTE**
> `QUERY STATUS` is the default value if the `TO`, `STOP`, `COMPLETE`, or `CANCEL` clauses are omitted. If `TO`, `STOP`, or `COMPLETE` was specified, status information is displayed if the command has completed successfully. If the individual tablespaces are specified, they are ignored; the status request does not apply only to specified tablespaces.

Tablespace

This keyword is specified for tablespace-level roll-forward recovery.

`Tablespace-name`

Mandatory for tablespace-level roll-forward recovery to a point in time. Allows a subset of tablespaces to be specified for roll-forward recovery to the end of the logs. In a partitioned database environment, each tablespace in the list does not have to exist at each partition that is rolling forward. If it does exist, it must be in the correct state.

ONLINE

This keyword is specified to allow tablespace-level roll-forward recovery to be done online. This means that other agents are allowed to connect while roll-forward recovery is in progress.

OVERFLOW FOG PATH *log-directory*

Specifies an alternate log path to be searched for archived logs during recovery. Use this parameter if log files were moved to a location other than that specified by the *logpath* database configuration parameter. In a partitioned database environment, this is the (fully qualified) default overflow log path *for all partitions.* A relative overflow log path can be specified for single-partition database.

> **NOTE**
> The OVERFLOW LOG PATH command parameter will overwrite the value (if any) of the database configuration parameter OVERFLOW-LOGPATH.

Log-directory ON DBPARTITIONNUM

In a partitioned database environment, allows a different log path to override the default overflow log path for a specific partition.

NORETRIEVE

Allows the user to control which log files to be rolled forward on the standby machine by allowing the user to disable the retrieval of archive logs. The benefits of this are:

- By controlling the logfiles to be rolled forward, one can ensure that the standby machine is X hours behind the production machine, to prevent the user affecting both systems.
- If the standby system does not have access to archive (e.g., if TSM is the archive, it only allows the original machine to retrieve the files).
- It might also be possible that while the production system is archiving a file, the standby system is retrieving the same file, and it might then get an incomplete log file. NORETRIEVE would solve this problem.

RECOVER DROPPED TABLE *drop-table-id*

Recovers a dropped table during the roll-forward operation. The table ID can be obtained using the LIST HISTORY command.

TO *export-directory*

Specifies a directory to which files containing the table data are to be written. The directory must be accessible to all database partitions.

Examples

Example 1

The ROLLFORWARD DATABASE command permits specifications of multiple operations at once, each being separated with the keyword AND. For example, to roll forward to the end of logs and complete the separate commands:

```
db2 rollforward db sample to end of logs
db2 rollforward db sample complete
```

can be combined as follows:

```
db2 rollforward db sample to end of logs and complete
```

Although the two are equivalent, it is recommended that such operations be done in two steps. It is important to verify that the roll-forward operation has progressed as expected, before stopping it and possibly missing logs. This is especially important if a bad log is found during roll-forward recovery, and the bad log is interpreted to mean the "end of logs." In such cases, an undamaged backup copy of that log could be used to continue the roll-forward operation through more logs.

Example 2

Roll forward to the end of the logs (two tablespaces have been restored):

```
db2 rollforward db sample to end of logs
db2 rollforward db sample to end of logs and stop
```

These two statements are equivalent. Neither AND STOP or AND COMPLETE is needed for tablespace roll-forward recovery to the end of the logs. Tablespace names are not required. If not specified, all tablespaces requiring roll-forward recovery will be included. If only a subset of these tablespaces is to be rolled forward, their names must be specified.

Example 3

After three tablespaces have been restored, roll one forward to the end of the logs, and the other two to a point in time, both to be done online:

```
db2 rollforward db sample to end of logs tablespace (TBS1) online
db2 rollforward db sample to 1998-04-03-14.21.56.245378 and stop
tablespace (TBS2, TBS3) online
```

Note that two roll-forward operations cannot be run concurrently. The second command can only be invoked after the first roll-forward operation completes successfully.

Example 4

After restoring the database, roll forward to a point in time, using OVERFLOW LOG PATH to specify the directory where the user exit saves archived logs:

```
db2 rollforward db sample to 1998-04-03-14.21.56.245378 and stop
overflow log path (/logs)
```

Example 5

There are three database partitions: 0, 1, and 2. Tablespace TBS1 is defined on all partitions, and tablespace TBS2 is defined on partitions 0 and 2. After restoring the database on database partition 1, and TBS1 on database partitions 0 and 2, roll the database forward on database partition 1:

```
db2 rollforward db sample to end of logs and stop
```

This returns warning SQL1271 ("Database is recovered but one or more tablespaces are offline on database partition(s) 0 and 2.")

```
db2 rollforward db sample to end of logs
```

This rolls TBS1 forward on database partitions 0 and 2. The clause `TABLESPACE` (TBS1) is optional in this case.

Example 6 (MPP)

After restoring tablespace TBS1 on database partitions 0 and 2 only, roll TBS1 forward on database partitions 0 and 2:

```
db2 rollforward db sample to end of logs
```

Database partition 1 is ignored.

```
db2 rollforward db sample to end of logs tablespace (TBS1)
```

This fails, because TBS1 is not ready for roll-forward recovery on database partition 1. Reports SQL4906N.

```
db2 rollforward db sample to end of logs on dbpartitionnums (0,2)
tablespace (TBS1)
```

This completes successfully.

```
db2 rollforward db sample to 1998-04-03-14.21.56.245378 and stop and
tablespace (TBS1)
```

This fails, because TBS1 is not ready for roll-forward recovery on database partition 1; all pieces must be rolled forward together.

> **NOTE**
> With tablespace roll-forward to a point in time, the database partition clause is not accepted. The roll-forward operation must take place on all the database partitions on which the tablespace resides.

After restoring TBS1 on database partition 1:

```
db2 rollforward db sample to 1998-04-03-14.21.56.245378 and stop
tablespace (TBS1)
```

This completes succcessfully.

Example 7 (Partitioned Database Environment)

After restoring a tablespace on all database partitions, roll forward to PIT2 but do not specify AND STOP. The roll-forward operation is still in progress. Cancel and roll forward to PIT1:

```
db2 rollforward db sample to pit2 tablespace(TBS1)
db2 rollforward db sample cancel tablespace(TBS1)
**restore TBS1 on all database partitions**
db2 rollforward db sample to pit1 tablespace (TBS1)
db2 rollforward db sample stop tablespace(TBS1)
```

Example 8 (MPP)

Roll-forward recovers a tablespace that resides on eight database partitions (3 to 10) listed in the *db2nodes.cfg* file:

```
db2 rollforward database dwtest to end of logs tablespace (tssprodt)
```

This operation to the end of logs (not point in time) completes successfully. The database partitions on which the tablespace resides do not have to be specified. The utility defaults to the *db2nodes.cfg* file.

Example 9 (Partitioned Database Environment)

Roll-forward recovers six small tablespaces that reside on a single-partition database partition group (on database partition 6):

```
db2 rollforward database dwtest to end of logs on dbpartitionnum (6)
tablespace(tsstore, tssbuyer, tsstime, tsslscat, tssvendor)
```

This operation to the end of logs (not point in time) completes successfully.

Utility Guidelines and Exceptions

If restoring from an image that was created during an online backup operation, the specified point in time for the roll-forward operation must be later than the time at which the online backup operation completed. If the roll-forward operation is stopped before it passes this point, the database is left in roll-forward in progress state.

If one or more tablespaces is being rolled forward to a point in time, the roll-forward operation must continue at least to the minimum recovery time, which is the last update to the system catalogs for this tablespace or tables. The minimum recovery time (in UTC) for a tablespace can be retrieved using the `LIST TABLESPACES SHOW DETAIL` command.

Rolling databases forward may require a load recovery using tape devices. If prompted for another tape, the user can respond with one of the following:

- **c** Continue. Continue using the device that generated the warning message (e.g., when a new tape has been mounted).
- **d** Device terminate. Stop using the device that generated the warning message (e.g., when there are no more tapes).
- **t** Terminate. Terminate all devices.

IF the roll-forward utility cannot find the next log that it needs, the log name is returned in the SQLCA, and roll-forward recovery stops. If no more logs are available, use the STOP option to terminate roll-forward recovery. Incomplete transactions are rolled back to ensure that the database or tablespace is left in a consistent state.

ARCHIVE LOG COMMAND

Closes and truncates the active log file for a recoverable database. If user exit is enabled, an archive request is issued. As previously mentioned, this command can be used to test the archive log userexit, as it will force an active log to be archived.

Authorization One of the following:

- `sysadm`
- `sysctrl`
- `sysmaint`
- `sbadm`

Required connection None. This command establishes a database connection for the duration of the command.

Command Parameters

`DATABASE` *`database-alias`*

Specifies the alias of the database whose active log is to be archived.

`USER` *`username`*

Identifies the user name under which a connection will be attempted.

`USING` *`password`*

Specifies the password to authenticate the user name.

`ON ALL DBPARTITIONNUMS`

Specifies that the command should be issued on all database partitions in the *db2nodes.cfg* file. This is the default if a database partition number clause is not specified.

`EXCEPT`

Specifies that the command should be issued on all database partitions in the db2nodes.cfg file, except those specified in the database partition number list.

`ON DBPARTITIONNUM/ON DBPARTITIONNUMS`

Specifies that the logs should be archived for the specified database on a set of database partitions.

`db-partition-number`

Specifies a database partition number in the database partition number list.

`TO` *`db-partition-number`*

Used when specifying a range of database partitions for which the logs should be archived. All database partitions from the first database partition number specified up to and including the second database partition number specified are included in the database partition number list.

Utility Guidelines and Exceptions

This command can be used to collect a complete set of log files up to a known point. The log files can then be used to update a standby database.

This command can only be executed when the invoking application or shell does not have a database connection to the specified database. This prevents a user from executing the command with uncommitted transactions. As such, the `ARCHIVE LOG` command will not forcibly commit the user's incomplete transactions. If the invoking application or shell already has a database connection to the specified database, the command will terminate and return an error. If another application has transactions in progress with the specified database when this command is executed, there will be a slight performance degradation since the command flushes the log buffer to disk. Any other transactions attempting to write log records to the buffer will have to wait until the flush is complete.

> **NOTE**
> If used in a partitioned database environment, a subset of database partitions may be specified by using a database partition number clause. If the database partition number clause is not specified, the default behavior for this command is to close and archive the active log on all database partitions.

Using this command will use up a portion of the active log space due to the truncation of the active log file. The active log space will resume its previous size when the truncated log becomes inactive. Frequent use of this command may drastically reduce the amount of the active log space available for transactions.

Compatibilities

For compatibility with versions earlier than version 8:

- The keyword `NODE` can be substituted for `DBPARTITIONNUM`.
- The keyword `NODES` can be substituted for `DBPARTITIONNUMS`.

LIST HISTORY

Lists entries in the history file. The history file contains a record of recovery and administrative events. Recovery events include full database- and tablespace-level backup, incremental backup, restore, and roll-forward operations. Additional logged events include create, alter, drop or rename tablespace, reorganize table, drop table, and load.

Authorization None.

Required connection Instance. You must attach to any remote database in order to run this command against it. For a local database, an explicit attachment is not required.

Command Parameters

`HISTORY`

Lists all events that are currently logged in the history file.

`BACKUP`

Lists backup and restore operations.

`ROLLFORWARD`

Lists roll-forward operations.

`DROPPED TABLE`

Lists dropped table records.

`LOAD`

Lists load operations.

`CREATE TABLESPACE`

Lists tablespace create and drop operations.

`RENAME TABLESPACE`

Lists tablespace renaming operations.

`REORG`

Lists reorganization operations.

`ALTER TABLESPACE`

Lists alter tablespace operations.

`ALL`

Lists all entries of the specifies type in the history file.

`SINCE` *`timestamp`*

A complete time stamp (format *yyyymmddhhnnss*) or initial prefix (minumum *yyyy*) can be specified. All entries with time stamps equal to or greater than the time stamps equal to or greater than the time stamp provided are listed.

`CONTAINING` *`schema1.object_name`*

This qualified name uniquely identifies a table.

`CONTAINING` *`object_name`*

This unqualified name uniquely identifies a tablespace.

`FOR DATABASE` *`database-alias`*

Used to identify the database whose recovery history file is to be listed.

Examples

```
db2 list history since 19980201 for sample
db2 list history backup containing userspace1 for sample
db2 list history dropped table all for db sample
```

Utility and Guidelines and Exceptions

The report generated by this command contains the following symbols:

Operation

- `A-` Create tablespace
- `B-` Backup
- `C-` Load copy
- `D-` Dropped table

`F-` Roll forward
`G-` Reorganize table
`L-` Load
`N-` Rename tablespace
`O-` Drop tablespace
`Q-` Quiesce
`R-` Restore
`T-` Alter tablespace
`U-` Unload

Type

Backup types:

`F-` Offline
`N-` Online
`I-` Incremental offline
`O-` Incremental online
`D-` Delta offline
`E-` Delta online

Roll-forward types:

`E-` End of logs
`P-` Point in time

Alter tablespace types:

`C-` Add containers
`R-` Rebalance

Quiesce types:

`S-` Quiesce share
`U-` Quiesce update
`X-` Quiesce exclusive
`Z-` Quiesce reset

LIST TABLESPACES

Lists tablespaces for the current database.

> **NOTE**
> Information displayed by this command is also available in the tablespace snapshot.

Scope This command returns information only for the node on which it is executed.

Authorization One of the following:

- `sysadm`
- `sysctrl`
- `sysmaint`
- `dbadm`
- `load`

Required Connection Database

Command Parameters

`SHOW DETAIL`

If this option is not specified, only the following basic information about each tablespace is provided:

- Table space ID
- Name
- Type (system managed space or database managed space)
- Contents (any data, long, or index data or temporary data)
- State, a hexadecimal value indicating the current tablespace state. The externally visible state of a tablespace is composed of the hexadecimal sum of certain state values. For example, if the state is "quiesced: EXCLUSIVE" and "Load pending," the value is 0x004 + 0x0008, which is 0x000c. The `db2tbst` (Get Tablespace State) command can be used to obtain the tablespace state associated with a given hexadecimal value. Following are the bit definitions listed in *sqlutil.h*:

0x0	Normal
0x1	Quiesced: SHARE
0x2	Quiesced: UPDATE
0x4	Quiesced: EXCLUSIVE
0x8	Load pending
0x10	Delete pending
0x20	Backup pending

0x40	Roll forward in progress
0x80	Roll forward pending
0x100	Restore pending
0x100	Recovery pending (not used)
0x200	Disable pending
0x400	Reorg in process
0x800	Backup in progress
0x1000	Storage must be defined
0x2000	Restore in progress
0x4000	Offline and not accessible
0x8000	Drop pending
0x2000000	Storage may be defined
0x4000000	StorDef is in 'final' state
0x8000000	StorDef was changed prior to rollforward
0x10000000	DMS rebalancer is active
0x20000000	TBS deletion in progress
0x40000000	TBS creation in progress
0x8	For service use only

Set Tablespace Containers Command

A *redirected restore* is a restore in which the set of tablespace containers for the restored database is different from the set of containers for the original database at the time the backup was done. This command permits the addition, change, or removal of tablespace containers for a database that is to be restored. If, for example, one or more containers become inaccessible for any reason, the restore fails if it is not redirected to different containers.

> **NOTE**
> A redirected restore is not allowed when a user exit program is used to perform the restore.

Authorization One of the following:

- `sysadm`
- `sysctrl`

Required connection Database

Command Parameters

`FOR` *`tablespace-id`*

An integer that uniquely represents a tablespace used by the database being restored.

`REPLAY ROLLFORWARD CONTAINER OPERATIONS`

Specifies that any `ALTER TABLESPACE` operation issued against this tablespace since the database was backed up is to be redone during a subsequent roll-forward of the database.

`IGNORE ROLLFORWARD CONTAINER OPERATIONS`

Specifies that `ALTER TABLESPACE` operations in the log are to be ignored when performing a roll forward.

`USING PATH` *`"container-string"`*

For an SMS tablespace, identifies one or more containers that will belong to the tablespace and into which the tablespace data will be stored. It is an absolute or relative directory name. If the directory name is not absolute, it is relative to the database directory. The string cannot exceed 240 bytes in length.

`USING PATH` *`"container-string" number-of-pages`*

For a DMS tablespace, identified one or more containers that will belong to the tablespace and into which the tablespace data will be stored. The container type (either `FILE` or `DEVICE`) and its size (in 4 KB pages) are specified. A mixture of file and device containers can be specified. The string cannot exceed 254 bytes in length.

For a file container, the string must be an absolute or relative file name. If the file name is not absolute, it is relative to the database directory.

For a device container, the string must be a device name. The device must already exist.

Examples

See the example in `RESTORE DATABASE`

Utility Guidelines and Exceptions

A backup of a database, or one or more tablespaces, keeps a record of all the tablespace containers in use by the tablespaces being backed up. During a restore, all containers listed in the backup are checked to see if they currently exist and are accessible. If one or more of the containers is inaccessible for any reason, the restore will fail. In order to allow a restore in such a case, the redirecting of tablespace containers is supported during the restore. This support includes adding, changing, or removing of tablespace containers. It is this command that allows the user to add, change, or remove those containers.

DB2TBST—GET TABLESPACE STATE COMMAND

This new v8 command accepts a hexadecimal tablespace state value, and returns the state. The state value is part of the output from `LIST TABLESPACES`.

Authorization None

Required connection None

Command Parameters

`tablespace-stat`

A hexadecimal tablespace state value

Examples

The request `db2tbst 0x0000` produces the following output:

```
State = Normal
```

RUNSTATS UTILITY

Updates statistics about the physical characteristics of a table and the associated indexes. These characteristics include number of records, number of pages, and average record length. The optimizer uses these statistics when determining access paths to the data.

This utility should be called when a table has had many updates, or after reorganizing a table.

Scope This command can be issued from any database partition in the *db2nodes.cfg* file. It can be used to update the catalogs on the catalog database partition.

The command collects statistics for a table on the database partition from which it is invoked. If the table does not exist on the database partition, the first database partition in the database partition group is selected.

Authorization One of the following:

- sysadm
- sysctrl
- sysmaint
- dbabm
- CONTROL privilege on the table
- LOAD authority

A user does not need any explicit privilege to use this command on any declared global temporary table that exists within its connection.

Required connection Database

Command Parameters

table-name

Identifies the table on which statistics are to be collected. It must be a table described in the catalog and must not be a view of a hierarchy table. For types tables, table-name must be the name of the root table of the table hierarchy. The fully qualified name or alias in the form schema.table-name must be used. The schema is the user name under which the table was created.

index-name

Identifies an existing index defined on the table. The fully qualified name in the form *schema.index.name* must be used.

FOR INDEXES

Identifies an existing index defined on the table. The fully qualified name in the form *schema.index-name* must be used.

AND INDEXES

Collects and updates statistics for both the table and the indexes.

DETAILED

Calculates extended index statistics. These are the CLUSTERFACTOR and PAGE_FETCH_PAIRS statistics that are gathered for relatively large indexes.

SAMPLED

This option, when used with the DETAILED option, allows RUNSTATS to employ a CPU sampling technique when compiling the extended index statistics. If the option is not specified, every entry in the index is examined to compute the extended index statistics.

ON ALL COLUMNS

Statistics collection can be done on some columns and not on others. Columns such as LONG VARCHAR or CLOB columns are ineligible. If it is desired to collect statistics on all eligible columns, one can use the ON ALL COLUMNS clause. Columns can be specified either for basic statistics collection (on-cols-clause) or in conjunction with the WITH DISTRIBUTION clause (on-dist-cols-clause). The ON ALL COLUMNS specification is the default option if neither of the column specific clauses are specified.

If it is specified in the on-cols-clause, all columns will have only basic column statistics collected unless specific columns are chosen as part of the WITH DISTRIBUTION clause. Those columns specified as part of the WITH DISTRIBUTION clause will also have basic and distribution statistics collected.

If the WITH DISTIRIBUTION ON ALL COLUMNS is specified, both basic statistics and distribution statistics are collected for all eligible columns. Anything specified in the on-cols-clause is redundant and therefore not necessary.

ON COLUMNS

This clause allows the user to specify a list of columns for which to collect statistics. If you specify a group of columns, the number of distinct values for the group will be collected. Statistics for columns that you do not list will be cleared. This clause can be used in the on-cols-clause and the on-dist-cols-clause.

> **NOTE**
> Collecting distribution statistics for a group of columns is not currently supported in v8 but planned for as a future capability.

ON KEY COLUMNS

Instead of listing specific columns, one can choose to collect statistics on columns that make up all the indexes defined on the table. It is assumed here that critical columns in queries are also those used to create indexes on the table. If there are no indexes on the table, it is as good as an empty list and no column statistics will be collected. It can be used in the on-cols-clause or the on-dist-cols-clause. It is redundant in the on-cols-clause if specified in both clauses since the WITH DISTRIBUTION clause is used to specify collection of both basic and distribution statistics.

column-name

column-name must be the name of a column in the table. If you specify the name of an ineligible column for statistics collection, such as a nonexistent column or a mistyped column name, error (-205) is returned. Two lists of columns can be specified, one without distribution and one with distribution. If the column is specified in the list that is not associated with the WITH DIS-

TRIBUTION clause, only basic column statistics will be collected. If the column appears in both lists, distribution statistics will be collected (unless NUM_FREQVALUES and NUM_QUANTILES are set to zero).

NUM_FREQVALUES

Defines the maximum number of frequency values to collect. It can be specified for an individual column in the ON COLUMNS clause. If the value is not specified for an individual column, the frequency limit value will be picked up from that specified in the DEFAULT clause. If it is not specified there either, the maximum number of frequency values to be collected will be what is set in the NUM_FREQVALUES database configuration parameter.

NUM_QUANTILES

Defines the maximum number of distribution quantile values to collect. It can be specified for an individual column in the ON COLUMNS clause. If the value is not specified for any individual column, the quantile limit value will be picked up from that specified in the DEFAULT clause. If it is not specified there either, the maximum number of quantile values to be collected will be what is set in the NUM_QUANTILES database configuration parameter.

WITH DISTRIBUTION

This clause specifies that both basic statistics and distribution statistics are to be collected on the columns. If the ON COLUMNS clause is not specified, distribution statistics are collected on all the columns of the table (excluding columns that are ineligible such as CLOB and LONG VARCHAR). If the ON COLUMNS clause is specified, distribution statistics are collected only on the column list provided (excluding those ineligible for statistics collection). If the clause is not specified, only basic statistics are collected.

> **NOTE**
> Collection of distribution statistics on column groups is not currently supported. In v8, distribution statistics will not be collected when column groups are specified in the WITH DISTRIBUTION ON COLUMNS clause. This is planned as a future enhancement.

DEFAULT

If the DEFAULT NUM_FREQVALUES and/or NUM_QUANTILES limited are specified, these will be used to determine how many frequency and/or quantile statistics are attempted to be collected for the columns if these are not specified for the individual column in the ON COLUMNS clause. If the DEFAULT clause is not specified, the values used will be those in the corresponding database configuration parameters.

LIKE STATISTICS

When this option is specified, additional column statistics are collected. These statistics are the SUB_COUNT and the SUB_DELIM_LENGTH statistics in SYSSTAT.COLUMNS. They are collected for string columns only and they are used by the query optimizer to improve the selectivity estimates for predicates of the type "column like '%xyz'" and "column like '%xyz%'"

ALLOW WRITE ACCESS

Specifies that other users can read from and write to the table while statistics are calculated.

ALLOW READ ACCESS

Specifies that other users can have read-only access to the table while statistics are calculated.

> **NOTE**
> In a partitioned database, the RUNSTATS command collects the statistics on only a single node. If the database partition from which the RUNSTATS command is executed has a partition of the table, then the command executes on that database partition. Otherwise, the command executes on the first database partition in the database partition group across which the table is partitioned.

Utility Guidelines and Exceptions

1. It is recommended to run the RUNSTATS command:
   - On tables that have been modified considerably (e.g., if a large number of updates have been made, or if a significant amount of data has been inserted or deleted or if LOAD has been done without the statistics option during LOAD).
   - On tables that have been reorganized (using REORG, REDISTRIBUTE DATABASE PARTITION GROUP).
   - When a new index has been created.
   - Before binding applications whose performance is critical.
   - When the prefetch quantity is changed.
2. The options chosen must depend on the specific table and the application. In general:
   - If the table is a very critical table in critical queries, is relatively small, or does not change too much and there is not too much activity on the system itself, it may be worth spending the effort on collecting statistics in as much detail as possible.
   - If the time to collect statistics is limited, the table is relatively large, and/or the table changes a lot, it might be beneficial to execute RUNSTATS limited to the set of columns that are used in predicates. This way, one will be able to execute the RUNSTATS command more often.

- If time to collect statistics is very limited and the effort to tailor the `RUNSTATS` command on a table-by-table basis is a major issue, consider collecting statistics for the "KEY" columns only. It is assumed that the index contains the set of columns that are critical to the table and most likely appear in predicates.
- If there are many indexes on the table and DETAILED (extended) information on the indexes might improve access plans, consider the `SAMPLED` option to reduce the time it takes to collect statistics. Regardless of whether you use the `SAMPLED` option, collecting detailed statistics on indexes is time consuming. Do not collect these statistics unless you are sure that they will be useful for your queries.
- If there is skew in certain columns and predicates of the type "column= constant," it may be beneficial to specify a larger `NUM_FREQVALUES` value for that column.
- Collect distribution statistics for all columns that are used in equality predicates and for which the distribution of values might be skewed.
- For columns that have range predicates (e.g., "column >= constant," "column BETWEEN constant1 AND constant2") or of the type "column LIKE '%xyz'," it may be beneficial to specify a larger `NUM_QUALITIES` values for columns that are not used in predicates.
- If storage space is a concern and one cannot afford too much time on collecting statistics, do not specify high `NUM_FREQVALUES` or `NUM_QUANTILES` values for columns that are not used in predicates.
- Note that if index statistics are requested, and statistics have never been run on the table containing the index, statistics on both the table and indexes are calculated.

3. After the command is run, note the following:

- A `COMMIT` should be issued to release the locks.
- To allow new access plans to be generated, the packages that reference the target table must be rebound.
- Executing the command on portions of the table could result in inconsistencies as a result of activity on the table since the command was last issued. In this case a warning message is returned. Issuing `RUNSTATS` on the table only might make table- and index-level statistics inconsistent. For example, you might collect index-level statistics on a table and later delete a significant number of rows from the table. If you then issue `RUNSTATS` on the table only, the table cardinality might be less then `FIRSTKEYCARD`, which is an inconsistency. In the same way, if you collect statistics on a new index when you create it, the table-level statistics might be inconsistent.

4. In the "On Dist Cols" clause of the command syntax, the "Frequency Option" and "Quantile Options" parameters are not currently supported for Column `GROUPS`. This will be supported in a future enhancement. These options are supported for single columns.

Examples

Collect statistics on the table only, on all columns without distribution statistics:

```
RUNSTATS ON TABLE db2user.employee
```

Collect statistics on the table only, on columns empid and empnmae with distribution statistics:

```
RUNSTATS ON TABLE db2user.employee
    WITH DISTRIBUTION ON COLUMNS (empid, empname)
```

Collect statistics on the table only, on all columns with distribution statistics using a specified number of frequency limit for the table while picking the `NUM_QUANTILES` from the configuration setting:

```
RUNSTATS ON TABLE db2.employee for indexed db2user.empl1, db2user.empl2
```

Collect basic statistics on all indexes only:

```
RUNSTATS ON TABLE db2user.employee FOR INDEXES ALL
```

Collect basic statistics on the table and all indexes using sampling for the detailed index statistics collection:

```
RUNSTATS ON TABLE db2user.employee AND SAMPLED DETAILED INDEXES ALL
```

Collect statistics on table, with distribution statistics on columns empid, empname, and empdept and the two indexed Xempid and Xempname. Distribution statistics limited are set individually for empdept, while the other two columns use a common default:

```
RUNSTATS ON TABLE db2user.employee
  WITH DISTRIBUTION ON COLUMNS (empid, empname, empdept
NUM_FREQVALUES 50 NUM_QUANTILES 100)
DEFAULT NUM_FREQVALUES 5 NUM_QUANTILES 10
AND INDEXES Xempid, Xempname
```

Collect statistics on all columns used in indexes and on all indexes:

```
RUNSTATS ON TABLE db2user.employee ON KEY COLUMNS AND INDEXES ALL
```

Collect statistics on all indexes and all columns without distribution except for one column. Consider T1 containing columns c1, c2,..., c8

```
RUNSTATS ON TABLE db2user.T1
WITH DISTRIBUTION ON COLUMNS (c1, c2, c3, NUM_FREQVALUES 20
NUM_QUANTILES 40, c4, c5, c6, c7, c8)
DEFAULT NUM_FREQVALUES 0, NUM_QUANTILES 0
AND INDEXES ALL
RUNSTATS ON TABLE db2user.T1
WITH DISTRIBUTION ON COLUMNS (c3 NUM_FREQVALUES 20 NUM_QUANTILES 40)
```

Collect statistics on table T1 for the individual columns c1 and c5 as well as on the column combinations (c2, c3) and (c2, c4). Multicolumn cardinality is very useful to the query optimizer when it estimates filter factors for predicates on columns in which the data is correlated.

```
RUNSTATS ON TABLE db2user.T1 ON COLUMNS (c1, (c2, c3), (c2, c4), c5)
```

Collect statistics on table T1 for the individual columns c1 and c2. For column c1 also collect the `LIKE` predicate statistics.

```
RUNSTATS ON TABLE db2user.T1 ON COLUMNS (c1 LIKE STASTICS, c2)
```

LOAD UTILITY

The `LOAD UTILITY` is used to load data into a DB2 table. Data residing on the server may be in the form of a file, tape, or named pipe. Data residing on a remotely connected client may be in the form of a fully qualified file or named pipe. New in v8, data can also be loaded from a user-defined cursor. The load utility does not support loading data at the hierarchy level. As indicated in Figure 7.7, the Load Wizard can assist you in quickly loading data into tables.

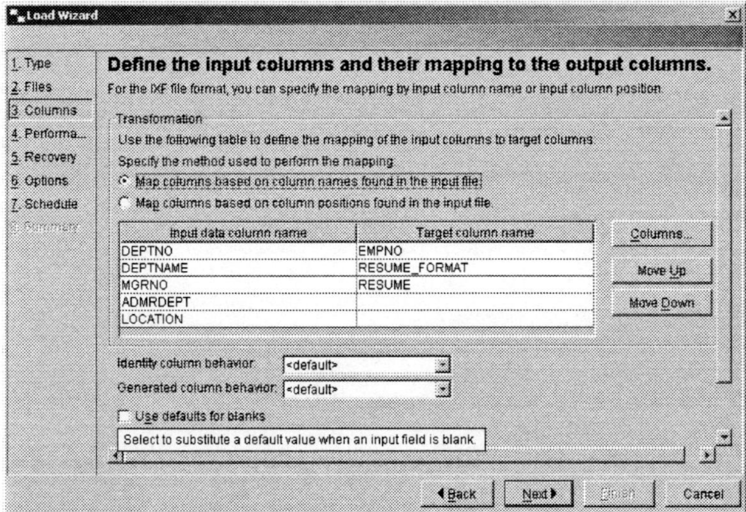

Figure 7.7
Load Wizard example.

As with all of the DB2 wizards, the Load Wizard can help you to load data quickly and seamlessly, resulting in improved productivity.

Scope This command may be issued against multiple database partitions in a single request.

Authorization One of the following:

- `sysadm`
- `dbadm`
- `load` authority on the database and
  - `INSERT` privilege on the table when the load utility is invoked in `INSERT` mode, `TERMINATE` mode (to terminate a previous load replace operation), or `RESTART` mode (to restart a previous load replace operation)
  - `INSERT` and `DELETE` privilege on the table when the load utility is invoked in `REPLACE` mode, `TERMINATE` mode (to terminate a previous load replace operation), or `RESTART` mode (to restart a previous load replace operation)
  - `INSERT` privilege on the exception table, if such a table is used as part of the load operation.

NOTE

Since all load process (and all DB2 server processes, in general) are owned by the instance owner, and all of these processes use the identification of the instance owner to access needed files, the instance owner must have read access to input data files. These input data files must be readable by the instance owner, regardless of who invokes the command.

Required connection *Database:* If implicit connect is enabled, a connection to the default database is established. *Instance:* An explicit attachment is not required. If a connection to the database has been established, an implicit attachment to the local instance is attempted.

NOTE

In v8, the `LOAD UTILITY` now operates at the table level instead of the tablespace level. This enhancement enables DB2 to deliver higher degrees of availability than ever before and is a welcomed enhancement in the field.

Command Parameters

`ALLOW NO ACCESS`

Load will lock the target table for exclusive access during the load. The table state will be set to `LOAD IN PROGRESS` during the load. `ALLOW NO ACCESS` is the default behavior. It is the only valid option for `LOAD REPLACE`.

When there are constraints on the table, the table state will be set to `CHECK PENDING` as well as `LOAD IN PROGRESS`. The `SET INTEGRITY` command must be used to take the table out of `CHECK PENDING`.

ALLOW READ ACCESS

Load will lock the target table in a share mode. The table state will be set to both LOAD IN PROGRESS and READ ACCESS. Readers may access the nondelta portion of the data while the table is being loaded. In other words, data that existed before the start of the load will be accessible by readers to the table; data that is being loaded is not available until the load is complete. LOAD TERMINATE or LOAD RESTART of an ALLOW READ ACCESS load may use this option; LOAD TERMINATE or LOAD RESTART of an ALLOW NO ACCESS load may not use this option. Furthermore, this option is not valid if the indexes on the target table are marked as requiring a rebuild.

When there are constraints on the table, the table state will be set to CHECK PENDING as well as LOAD IN PROGRESS and READ ACCESS. At the end of the load the table state LOAD IN PROGRESS will be removed but the table states CHECK PENDING and READ ACCESS will remain. The SET INTEGRITY command must be used to take the table out of CHECK PENDING. While the table is in CHECK PENDING and READ ACCESS, the nondelta portion of the data is still accessible to readers, the new (delta) portion of the data will remain inaccessible until the SET INTEGRITY command has completed. A user may perform multiple loads on the same table without issuing a SET INTEGRITY command. Only the original (checked) data will remain visible, however, until the SET INTEGRITY command is issued.

ALLOW READ ACCESS also supports the following modifiers:

> USE *tablespace-name*—If the indexes are being rebuilt, a shadow copy of the index is built in tablespace *tablespace-name* and copied over to the original tablespace at the end of the load during an INDEX COPY PHASE. Only system-temporary tablespaces can be used with this option. If not specified, then the shadow index will be created in the same tablespace as the index object. If the shadow copy is created in the same tablespace as the index object, the copy of the shadow index object over the old index object is instantaneous. If the shadow copy is in a different tablespace from the index object, a physical copy is performed. This could involve considerable I/O and time. The copy happens while the table is offline at the end of a load during the INDEX COPY PHASE.
>
> Without this option the shadow index is built in the same tablespace as the original. Since both the original index and shadow index by default reside in the same tablespace simultaneously, there may be insufficient space to hold both indexes within one tablespace. Using this option ensures that you retain enough tablespace for the indexes.
>
> This option is ignored if the user does not specify INDEXING MODE REBUILD or INDEXING MODE AUTOSELECT. This option will also be ignored if INDEXING MODE AUTOSELECT is chosen and load chooses to incrementally update the index.

CHECK PENDING CASCADE

If LOAD puts the table into a check pending state, the CHECK PENDING CASCADE option allows the user to specify whether or not the check pending state of the loaded table is immediately cascaded to all descendents (including descendent foreign key tables, and immediate staging tables).

`IMMEDIATE`

Indicates that the check pending state (read or no access mode) for foreign key constraints is immediately extended to all descendent foreign key tables. If the table has descendent immediate materialized query tables or descendent immediate staging tables, the check pending state is extended immediately to the materialized query tables and the staging tables. Note that for a `LOAD INSERT` operation, the check pending state is not extended to descendent foreign key tables even if the `IMMEDIATE` option is specified.

When the loaded table is later checked for constraint violations (using the `IMMEDIATE CHECKED` option of the `SET INTEGRITY` statement), descendent foreign key tables that were placed in check, pending a read state, will be put into check pending no access state.

`DEFERRED`

Indicates that only the loaded table will be placed in the check pending state (read or no access mode). The states of the descendent foreign key tables, descendent immediate materialized query tables, and descendent immediate staging tables will remain unchanged.

Descendent foreign key tables may later be implicitly placed in the check pending no access state when their parent tables are checked for constraint violations (using the `IMMEDIATE CHECKED` option of the `SET INTEGRITY` statement). Descendent immediate materialized query tables and descendent immediate staging tables will be implicitly placed in the check pending no access state when one of its underlying tables is checked for integrity violations. A warning (SQLSTATE 01586) will be issued to indicate that dependent tables have been placed in the check pending state. See the Notes section of the `SET INTEGRITY` statement in the SQL Reference for when these descendents tables will be put into the check pending state.

If the `CHECK PENDING CASCADE` option is not specified:

- Only the loaded table will be placed in the check pending state. The state of descendent foreign key tables, descendent immediate materialized query tables, and descendent immediate staging tables will remain unchanged, and may later be implicitly put into the check pending state when the loaded table is checked for constraint violations.
- If `LOAD` does not put the target table into check pending state, the `CHECK PENDING CASCADE` option is ignored.

`CLIENT`

Specifies that the data to be loaded resides on a remotely connected client. This option is ignored if the load operation is not being invoked from a remote client. This option is not supported in conjunction with the `CURSOR` filetype.

Notes

1. The DUMPFILE and LOBSINFILE modifier refer to files on the server even when the CLIENT keyword is specified.
2. Code page conversion is not performed during a remote load operation. If the code page of the data is different from that of the server, the data code page should be specified using the CODEPAGE modifier.

In the following example, a data file (/u/user/data.del) residing on a remotely connected client is to be loaded into MYTABLE on the server database:

```
db2 load client from /u/user/data.del
modified by codepage = 850 insert into mytable
```

COPY NO

Specifies that the tablespace in which the table resides will be placed in backup pending state if forward recovery is enabled (i.e., *logretain* or *userexit* is on). Copy no will also put the tablespace state into the Load in Progress tablespace state. This is a transient state that will disappear when the load completes or aborts. The data in any table in the tablespace cannot be updated or deleted until a tablespace backup or a full database backup is made. However, it is possible to access the data in any table by using the SELECT statement.

COPY YES

Specifies that a copy of the loaded data will be saved. This option is invalid if forward recovery is disabled (both *logretain* and *userexit* are off). The option is not supported for tables with DATALINK columns.

> USE TSM—Specifies that the copy will be stored using Tivoli Storage Manager (TSM).
>
> OPEN *num-sess* SESSIONS—The number of I/O sessions to be used with TSM or the vendor product. The default value is 1.
>
> TO *device/directory*—Specifies the device or directory on which the copy image will be created.
>
> LOAD *lib-name*—The name of the shared library (DLL on Windows operating systems) containing the vendor backup and restore I/O functions to be used. It may contain the full path. If the full path is not given, it will default to the path where the user exit programs reside.

CPU_PARALLELISM *n*

Specifies the number of processes or threads that the load utility will spawn for parsing, converting, and formatting records when building table objects. This parameter is designed to exploit intrapartition parallelism. It is particularly useful when loading presorted data, because record order in the source data is preserved. If the value of this parameter is zero, or has not been specified, the load utility uses an intelligent default value (usually based on the number of CPUs available) at run time.

Notes

1. If this parameter is used with tables containing either `LOB` or `LONG VARCHAR` fields, its value becomes one, regardless of the number of system CPUs or the value specified by the user.
2. Specifying a small value for the `SAVECOUNT` parameter causes the loader to perform many more I/O operations to flush both data and table metadata. When `CPU_PARALLELISM` is greater than one, the flushing operations are asynchronous, permitting the loader to exploit the CPU. When `CPU_PARALLELISM` is set to 1, the loader waits on I/O during consistency points. A load operation with `CPU_PARALLELISM` set to 2, and `SAVECOUNT` set to 10,000, completes faster than the same operation with `CPU_PARALLELISM` set to 1, even though there is only one CPU.

`DATA BUFFER` *`buffer-size`*

Specifies the number of 4 KB pages (regardless of the degree of parallelism) to use as buffered space for transferring data within the utility. If the value specified is less than the algorithmic minimum, the minimum required resource is used, and no warning is returned.

This memory is allocated directly from the utility heap, whose size can be modified through the `util_heap_sz` database configuration parameter.

If a value is not specified, an intelligent default is calculated by the utility at run time. The default is based on a percentage of the free space available in the utility heap at the instantiation time of the loader, as well as some characteristics of the table.

`DISK_PARALLELISM` *`n`*

Specifies the number of processes or threads that the load utility will spawn for writing data to the tablespace containers. If a value is not specified, the utility selects an intelligent default based on the number of tablespace containers and the characteristics of the table.

`FOR EXCEPTION` *`table-name`*

Specifies the exception table into which rows in error will be copied. Any row that is in violation of a unique index or a primary key index is copied. `DATALINK` exceptions are also captured in the exception table. If an unqualified table name is specified, the table will be qualified with the `CURRENT SCHEMA`.

Information that is written to the exception table is *not* written to the dump file. In a partitioned database environment, an exception table is defined for those partitions on which the loading table is defined. The dump file, on the other hand, contains rows that cannot be loaded because they are invalid or have syntax errors.

FROM *filename/pipename/device/cursorname*

Specifies the file, pipe, device, or cursor referring to an SQL statement that contains the data being loaded. If the input source is a file, pipe, or device, it must reside on the database partition where the database resides, unless the CLIENT option is specified. If several names are specified, they will be processed in sequence. If the last item specified is a tape device, the user is prompted for another tape. Valid response options are

- **c** Continue. Continue using the device that generated the warning message (e.g., when a new tape has been mounted).
- **d** Device terminate. Stop using the device that generated the warning message (e.g., when there are no more tapes).
- **t** Terminate. Terminate all devices.

Notes

1. It is recommended that the fully qualified file name be used. If the server is remote, the fully qualified file name must be used. If the database resides on the same database partition as the caller, relative paths may be used.
2. Loading data from multiple IXF files is supported if the files are physically separate, but logically one file. It is *not* supported if the files are both logically and physically separate. (Multiple physical files would be considered logically one if they were all created with one invocation of the EXPORT command.)
3. If loading data that resides on a client machine, the data must be in the form of either a fully qualified file or a named pipe.

INDEXING MODE

Specifies whether the load utility is to rebuild indexes or to extend them incrementally. Valid values are:

AUTOSELECT—The load utility will automatically decide between REBUILD or INCREMENTAL mode.

REBUILD—All indexes will be rebuilt. The utility must have sufficient resources to sort all index key parts for both old and appended table data.

INCREMENTAL—Indexes will be extended with new data. This approach consumes index free space. It only requires enough sort space to append index keys for the inserted records. This method is only supported in cases where the index object is valid and accessible at the start of a load operation (it is, for example, not valid immediately following a load operation in which the DEFERRED mode was specified). If this mode is specified, but not supported due to the state of the index, a warning is returned, and the load operation continues in `REBUILD` mode. Similarly, if a load restart operation is begun in the load build phase, `INCREMENTAL` mode is not supported.

Incremental indexing is not supported when all of the following conditions are true:

- The `LOAD COPY` option is specified (*logretain* or *userexit* is enabled).
- The table resides in a DMS tablespace.
- The index object resides in a tablespace that is shared by other table objects belonging to the table being loaded.

To bypass this restriction, it is recommended that indexes be placed in a separate tablespace.

`DEFERRED`—The load utility will not attempt index creation if this mode is specified. Indexes will be marked as needing a refresh. The first access to such indexes that is unrelated to a load operation may force a rebuild, or indexes may be rebuilt when the database is restarted. This approach requires enough sort space for all key parts for the largest index. The total time subsequently taken for index construction is longer than that required in `REBUILD` mode. Therefore, when performing multiple load operations with deferred indexing, it is advisable (from a performance viewpoint) to let the last load operation in the sequence perform an index rebuild rather than allow indexes to be rebuilt at first nonload access.

Deferred indexing is only supported for tables with nonunique indexes, so that duplicate keys inserted during the load phase are not persistent after the load operation.

NOTE
Deferred indexing is not supported for tables that have DATALINK columns.

`INSERT`—One of four modes under which the load utility can execute. Adds the loaded data to the table without changing the existing table data.

`insert-column`—Specifies the table column into which the data is to be inserted.

The load utility cannot parse columns whose names contain one or more spaces. For example,

```
db2 load from delfile1 of del modified by noeofchar noheader
method P (1, 2, 3, 4, 5, 6, 7, 8, 9)
insert into table1 (BLOB1, S2, I3, Int 4, I5, I6, DT7, I8, TM9)
```

`INTO` *`table-name`*—Specifies the database table into which the data is to be loaded. This table cannot be a system table or a declared temporary table. An alias or the fully qualified or unqualified table name can be specified. A qualified table name is in the form *schema.tablename*. If an unqualified table name is specified, the table will be qualified with the CURRENT SCHEMA.

LOCK WITH FORCE

The utility acquired various locks, including table locks, in the process of loading. Rather than wait, and possibly timeout, when acquiring a lock, this option allows the load to force off other applications that hold conflicting locks. Forced applications will roll back and release the locks the load utility needs. The load utility can then proceed. This option requires the same authority as the FORCE APPLICATIONS command (SYSADM or SYSCTRL).

> **NOTE**
> The new LOCK WTH FORCE option enables a load utility to force applications holding locks that are preventing a load from completing.

ALLOW NO ACCESS loads may force applications holding conflicting locks at the start of the load operation. At the start of the load the utility may force applications that are attempting to either query or modify the table.

ALLOW READ ACCESS loads may force applications holding conflicting locks at the start or end of the load operation. At the start of the load the load utility may force applications that are attempting to modify the table. At the end of the load the load utility may force applications that are attempting to either query or modify the table.

MESSAGES *message-file*

Specifies the destination for warning and error messages that occur during the load operation. If a message file is not specified, messages are written to standard output. If the complete path to the file is not specified, the load utility uses the current directory and the default drive as the destination. If the name of a file that already exists is specified, the utility appends the information.

The message file is usually populated with messages at the end of the load operation and, as such, is not suitable for monitoring the progress of the operation.

METHOD

L Specifies the start and end column numbers from which to load data. A column number is a byte offset from the beginning of a row of data. It is numbered starting from 1.

> **NOTE**
> This method can only be used with ASC files, and is the only valid method for that file type.

N Specifies the names of the columns in the data file to be loaded. The case of these column names must match the case of the corresponding names in the system catalogs. Each table column that is not nullable should have a corresponding entry in the METHOD N list. For example, given data fields F1, F2, F3, F4, F5, and F6, and table columns C1 INT, C2 INT NOT NULL, C3 INT NOT NULL, and C4 INT, method N (F2, F1, F4, F3) is a valid request, while method N (F2, F1) is not valid.

> **NOTE**
> This method can only be used with file types IXF or CURSOR.

P Specifies the field numbers (numbered from 1) of the input data fields to be loaded. Each table column that is not nullable should have a corresponding entry in the METHOD P list. For example, given data fields F1, F2, F3, F4, F5, and F6, and table columns C1 INT, C2 INT NOT NULL, C3 INT NOT NULL, and C4 INT, method P (2, 1, 4, 3) is a valid request, while method P (2, 1) is not valid.

> **NOTE**
> This method can only be used with file types IXF, DEL, or CURSOR, and is the only valid method for the DEL file type.

MODIFIED BY *filetype-mod*

Specifies additional options.

NONRECOVERABLE

Specifies that the load transaction is to be marked as nonrecoverable and that it will not be possible to recover it by subsequent roll-forward action. The roll-forward utility will skip the transaction and will mark the table into which data was being loaded as "invalid." The utility will also ignore any subsequent transactions against that table. After the roll-forward operation is completed, such a table can only be dropped or restored from a backup (full or tablespace) taken after a commit point following the completion of the nonrecoverable load operation.

With this option, tablespaces are not put in backup pending state following the load operation, and a copy of the loaded data does not have to be made during the load operation.

This option should not be used when DATALINK columns with the FILE LINK CONTROL attribute are present in, or being added to, the table.

NULL INDICATORS *null-indicate-list*

This option can only be used when the METHOD L parameter is specified; that is, the input file is an ASC file. The null indicator list is a comma-separated list of positive integers specifying the column number of each null indicator field. The column number is the byte offset of the null indicator field from the beginning of a row of data. There must be one entry in the null indicator list for each data field defined in the `METHOD L` parameter. A column number of zero indicates that the corresponding data field always contains data.

A value of `Y` in the `NULL` indicator column specifies that the column data is `NULL`. Any character *other than* `Y` in the `NULL` indicator column specifies that the column data is not `NULL`, and that column data specified by the `METHOD L` option will be loaded.

The `NULL` indicator character can be changed using the `MODIFIED BY` option.

`OF` *`filetype`*

Specifies the format of the data:

- `ASC` (nondelimited ASCII format)
- `DEL` (delimited ASCII format)
- `IXF` (integrated exchange format, PC version), exported from the same or from another DB2 table
- `CURSOR` (a cursor declared against a `SELECT` or `VALUES` statement)

`REPLACE`

One of four modes under which the load utility can execute. Deletes all existing data from the table and inserts the loaded data. The table definition and index definitions are not changed. If this option is used when moving data between hierarchies, only the data for an entire hierarchy, not individual subtables, can be replaced.

This option is not supported for tables with `DATALINK` columns.

`RESTART`

One of four modes under which the load utility can execute. Restarts a previously interrupted load operation. The load operation will automatically continue from the last consistency point in the load, build, or delete phase.

`RESTARTCOUNT`

Reserved.

`ROWCOUNT` *`n`*

Specifies the number of *n* physical records in the file to be loaded. Allows a user to load only the first *n* rows in a file.

`SAVECOUNT` *`n`*

Specifies that the load utility is to establish consistency points after every *n* rows. This value is converted to a page count, and rounded up to intervals of the extent size. Since a message is issued at each consistency point, this option should be selected if the load operation will be monitored using `LOAD QUERY`. If the value of *n* is not sufficiently high, the synchronization of the activities performed at each consistency point will impact performance.

The default value is zero, meaning that no consistency points will be established, unless necessary.

This option is not supported in conjunction with the `CURSOR` filetype.

`SORT BUFFER` *`buffer-size`*

This option specifies a value that overrides the `SORTHEAP` database configuration parameter during a load operation. It is relevant only when loading tables with indexes and only when the `INDEXING MODE` parameter is not specified as `DEFERRED`. The value that is specified cannot exceed the value of `SORTHEAP`. This parameter is useful for throttling the sort memory that is used when loading tables with many indexes without changing the value of `SORTHEAP`, which would also affect general query processing.

`STATISTICS NO`

Specifies that no statistics are to be collected, and that the statistics in the catalogs are not to be altered. This is the default.

`STATISTICS YES`

Specifies that statistics are to be collected for the table and for any existing indexes. This option is supported only if the load operation is in `REPLACE` mode.

> `WITH DISTRIBUTION`—Specifies that distribution statistics are to be collected.
> `AND INDEXES ALL`—Specifies that both table and index statistics are to be collected.
> `FOR INDEXES ALL`—Specifies that only index statistics are to be collected.
> `DETAILED`—Specifies that extended index statistics are to be collected.

`TEMPFILES PATH` *`temp-pathname`*

Specifies the name of the path to be used when creating temporary files during a load operation, and should be fully qualified according to the server database partition.

Temporary files take up file system space. Sometimes this space requirement is quite substantial. Following is an estimate of how much file system space should be allocated for all temporary files:

- 4 bytes for each duplicate or rejected row containing `DATALINK` values
- 136 bytes for each message that the load utility generates
- 15 KB overhead if the data file contains long field data or LOBs. This quantity can grow significantly if the `INSERT` option is specified, and there is a large amount of long field or LOB data already in the table.

TERMINATE

One of four modes under which the load utility can execute. Terminates a previously interrupted load operation to the point in time at which it started, even if consistency points were passed. The states of any tablespaces involved in the operation return to normal, and all table objects are made consistent (index objects may be marked as invalid, in which case index rebuild will automatically take place at next access). If the load operation being terminated is a load REPLACE, the table will be truncated to an empty table after the load TERMINATE operation. If the load operation being terminated is a load INSERT, the table will retain all of its original records after the load TERMINATE operation.

The load terminate option will not remove a backup pending state from tablespaces.

> **NOTE**
> This option is not supported for tables with DATALINK columns.

USING *directory*

This option has been reserved for future use.

WARNINGCOUNT *n*

Stops the load operation after *n* warnings. Set this parameter if no warnings are expected, but verification that the correct file and table are being used is desired. If *n* is zero, or this option is not specified, the load operation will continue regardless of the number of warnings issued. If the load operation is stopped because the threshold of warnings was encountered, another load operation can be started in RESTART mode. The load operation will automatically continue from the last consistency point. Alternatively, another load operation can be initiated in REPLACE mode, starting at the beginning of the input file.

WITHOUT PROMPTING

Specifies that the list of data files contains all the files that are to be loaded, and that the devices or directories listed are sufficient for the entire load operation. If a continuation input file is not found, or the copy targets are filled before the load operation finishes, the load operation will fail, and the table will remain in load pending state.

If this option is not specified, and the tape device encounters as end of tape for the copy image, or the last item listed is a tape device, the user is prompted for a new tape on that device.

LOAD QUERY COMMAND

Checks the status of a load operation during processing and returns for the table state. New in v8, if a load is not processing, then the table state alone is returned. A connection to the same database, and a separate CLP session are also required to successfully invoke this command. It can be used either by local or remote users.

Authorization None

Required connection Database

Command Parameters

NOSUMMARY

Specifies that no load summary information (rows read, rows skipped, rows loaded, rows rejected, rows committed, and number of warnings) is to be reported.

SHOWDELTA

Specifies that only new information (pertaining to load events that have occurred since the last invocation of the LOAD QUERY command) is to be reported.

SUMMARYONLY

Specifies that only load summary information is to be reported.

TABLE *table-name*

Specifies the name of the table into which data is currently being loaded. If an unqualified table name is specified, the table will be qualified with the CURRENT SCHEMA.

TO *local-message-file*

Specifies the destination for warning and error messages that occur during the load operation. This file cannot be the *message-file* specified for the LOAD command. If the file already exists, all messages that the load utility has generated are appended to it.

Examples

A user loading a large amount of data into the STAFF table wants to check the status of the load operation. The user can specify:

```
db2 connect to <database>
db2 load query table staff to /u/mydir/staff.tempmsg
```

The output file */u/mydir/staff.tempmsg* might look like the following:

```
SQL3501W    The table space(s) in which the table resides will not be
            placed in backup pending state since forward recovery is
            disabled for the database.
SQL3109N    The utility is beginning to load data from file "/u/mydir/
            data/staffbig.del"
```

```
SQL3500W   The utility is beginning the "LOAD" phase at time "03-21-
           2002 11:31:16.597045."
SQL3519W   Begin Load Consistency Point. Input record count = "0"
SQL3520W   Load Consistency Point was successful.
SQL3519W   Begin Load Consistency Point. Input record count = "104416"
SQL3520W   Load Consistency Point was successful.
SQL3519W   Begin Load Consistency Point. Input record count = "205757"
SQL3520W   Load Consistency Point was successful.
SQL3519W   Begin Load Consistency Point. Input record count = "307098"
SQL3520W   Load Consistency Point was successful.
SQL3519W   Begin Load Consistency Point. Input record count = "408439"
SQL3520W   Load Consistency Point was successful.
SQL35321   The Load utility is currently in the "LOAD" phase.
Number of rows read = 453376
Number of rows skipped = 0
Number of rows loaded = 453376
Number of rows rejected = 0
Number of rows deleted = 0
Number of rows committed = 408439
Number of warnings = 0
Tablestate: Load in Progress
```

Utility Guidelines and Exceptions

In addition to locks, the load utility used table states to control access to the table. The LOAD QUERY command can be used to determine the table state; LOAD QUERY may be used on tables that are not currently being loaded. The table states described by LOAD QUERY are as follows:

Normal

No table states affecting the table.

Check Pending

The table has constraints and the constraints have yet to be verified. Use the SET INTEGRITY command to take the table out of Check Pending. The load utility puts a table into the Check Pending state when it begins a load on a table with constraints.

Load in Progress

There is a load actively in progress on this table.

Load Pending

A load has been active on this table but has been aborted before the load could commit. Issue a load terminate, a load restart, or a load replace to bring the table out of the Load Pending state.

Read Access Only

The table data is available for read access queries. Loads using the `ALLOW READ ACCESS` option put the table into Read Access Only state.

Unavailable

The table is unavailable. The table may only be dropped or it may be restored from a backup. Roll forward through a nonrecoverable load will put a table into the unavailable state.

Not Load Restartable

The table is in a partially loaded state that will not allow a load restart. The table will also be in the Load Pending state. Issue a load terminate or a load replace to bring the table out of the Not Load Restartable state. The table can be placed in the not load restartable table state during a roll-forward operation. This can occur if you roll forward to a point in time that is prior to the end of a load operation, or if you roll forward through an aborted load operation but do not roll forward to the end of the load terminate or load restart operation.

Unknown

Load query is unable to determine a table state.

QUIESCE COMMAND

Forces all users off the specified instance and database and puts it into a quiesced mode. In quiesced mode, users cannot connect from outside of the database engine. While the database instance or database is in quiesced mode, you can perform administrative tasks on it. After administrative tasks are complete, use the `UNQUIESCE` command to activate the instance and database and allow other users to connect to the database but avoid having to shut down and perform another database start.

In this mode only users with the authority in this restricted mode are allowed to attach or connect to the instance/database. Users with `sysadm`, `sysmaint`, and `sysctrl` authority always have access to an instance while it is quiesced, and users with `sysadm` authority always have access to a database while it is quiesced.

Scope `QUIESCE DATABASE` *database-name* results in all objects in the database database-name being in the quiesced mode. Only the allowed user/group and `sysadm`, `sysmaint`, `dbadm`, or `sysctrl` will be able to access the database or its objects.

`QUIESCE INSTANCE` *instance-name* means the instance and the database in the instance *instance-name* will be in quiesced mode. The instance will be accessible just for `sysadm`, `sysmaint`, and `sysctrl` and allowed user/group.

If an instance is in quiesced mode, a database in the instance cannot be put in quiesced mode.

Authorization One of the following:

- For database-level quiesce:
  - `sysadm`
  - `dbadm`
- For instance-level quiesce:
  - `sysadm`
  - `sysctrl`

Required connection Database. (Database connection is not required for an instance quiesce)

Command Parameters

`DEFER`

Wait for the applications until they commit the current unit of work. This parameter is not currently functional.

`IMMEDIATE`

Do not wait for the transactions to be committed, immediately roll back the transactions.

`FORCE CONNECTIONS`

Force the connections off.

`DATABASE` *`database-names`*

Quiesce the database *database-name*. All objects in the database will be placed in quiesced mode. Only specified users in specified groups and users with `sysadm`, `sysmaint`, and `sysctrl` authority will be able to access to the database or its objects.

`INSTANCE` *`instance-name`*

The instance *instance-name* and the databases in the instance will be placed in quiesced mode. The instance will be accessible only to users with `sysadm`, `sysmaint`, and `sysctrl` authority and specified users in specified groups.

> `FOR USER` *`user-id`*—Specifies the name of a user who will be allowed access to the instance while it is quiesced.
> `FOR GROUP` *`group-id`*—Specifies the name of a group that will be allowed access to the instance while the instance is quiesced.

Examples

In the following example, the default behavior is to force connections, so it does not need to be explicitly stated and can be removed from this example.

```
db2 quiesce instance crankarm immediate
    for user frank
```

The following example does not require you to attach to the database before you execute the command. The command is executed in `IMMEDIATE` mode:

```
db2 quiesce db employees force connections
```

- The first example will quiesce the instance `crankarm`, while allowing user `frank` to continue using the database.
  The second example will quiesce the specified database, employees, preventing access by all users except `sysadm`, `sysmaint`, and `sysctrl`.
- This command will force all users off the database or instance if `FORCE CONNECTION` option is supplied. `FORCE CONNECTION` is the default behavior; the parameter is allowed in the command for compatibility reasons.
- The command will be synchronized with the `FORCE` and will only complete once the `FORCE` has completed.

Utility Guidelines and Exceptions

- If the database is in I/O suspend mode neither quiesce or unquiesce will be allowed.
- After `QUIESCE INSTANCE`, only users with `sysadm`, `sysmaint`, and `sysctrl` authority or a user ID and group name provided as parameters to the command can connect to the instance.
- After `QUIESCE DATABASE`, users with `sysadm`, `sysmaint`, `sysctrl`, `dbadm`, and `GRANT/REVOKE DataControlLang` authority can designate who will be able to connect. This information will be stored permanently in the database catalog tables.

`UNQUIESCE` COMMAND

Restore user access to instances or databases that have been quiesced for maintenance or other reasons. `UNQUIESCE` restores user access without necessitating a shutdown and database restart.

Unless specifically designated, no user except `sysadm`, `sysmaint`, and `sysctrl` has access to a database while it is quiesced. Therefore, an `UNQUIESCE` is required to restore general access to a quiesced database.

Scope `UNQUIESCE DB` *`database-name`* restores user access to all objects in the quiesced database database-name.

`UNQUIESCE INSTANCE` *`instance-name`* restores user access to the instance and the databases in the instance *instance-name.*

To stop the instance and unquiesce it and all its databases, issue the `db2stop` command. Stopping and restarting DB2 will unquiesce all instances and databases.

Authorization One of the following:

- `sysadm`
- `sysctrl`
- `CONTROL` privilege on the table

Required connection Database

Command Parameters

`DB` *`db-name`*

Unquiesce the database db-name. User access will be restored to all objects in the database.

`INSTANCE` *`instance-name`*

Access is restored to the instance *instance-name* and the databases in the instance.

Examples

Unquiescing a database

```
db2 unquiesce db dbname
```

This command will unquiesce the database that had previously been quiesced.

MIGRATE DATABASE UTILITY

Converts pervious versions of DB2 databases to current formats.

> **WARNING**
> The database premigration tool must be run prior to DB2 Version 8 installation (on Windows operating systems), or before instance migration (on UNIX-based systems), because it cannot be executed on DB2 Version 8. On Windows the premigration tool is `db2ckmig`. On UNIX systems, `db2imigr` performs similar tasks. Back up all databases prior to migration, and prior to DB2 Version 8 installation on Windows operating systems.

Authorization `sysadm`

Required connection This command establishes a database connection.

Command Parameters

`DATABASE` *`database-alias`*

Specifies the alias of the database to be migrated to the currently installed version of the database manager.

`USER` *`username`*

Identifies the user name under which the database is to be migrated.

`USING` *`password`*

The password used to authenticate the user name. If the password is omitted, but a user name was specified, the user is prompted to enter it.

Examples

The following example migrates the database cataloged under the database alias sales:

```
db2 migrate database sales
```

Utility Guidelines and Exceptions

This command will only migrate a database to a newer version, and cannot be used to convert a migrated database to its pervious version.

The database must be cataloged before migration.

If an error occurs during migration, it may be necessary to issue the `TERMINATE` command before attempting the suggested user response. For example, if a log full error occurs during migration (SQL1704: Database migration failed. Reason code "3".), it will be necessary to issue the `TERMINATE` command before increasing the values of the database configuration parameters `LOGPRIMARY` and `LOGFILSIZ`. The CLP must refresh its database directory cache if the migration failure occurs after the database has already been relocated (which is likely to be the case when a "log full" error returns).

INSPECT UTILITY

Inspects the database for architectural integrity, checking the pages of the database for page consistency. The inspection checks that the structures of table objects and structures of tablespaces are valid. `INSPECT` will also identify type-1 and type-2 indexes defined.

Scope In a single-partition system, the scope is that single partition only. In a partitioned database system, it is the collection of all logical partitions defined in *db2nodes.cfg*.

Authorization For `INSPECT CHECK`, one of the following:

- sysadm
- dbadm
- sysctrl
- sysmaint
- CONTROL privilege if single table.

Required Connection Database

Command Parameters

CHECK

Specifies check processing.

DATABASE

Specifies whole database.

BEGIN TBSPACEID *n*

Specifies processing to begin from tablespace with given tablespace ID number.

BEGIN TBSPACEID *n* OBJECTID *n*

Specifies processing to begin from table with given tablespace ID number and object ID number.

TABLESPACE

NAME *tablespace-name*—Specifies single tablespace with given tablespace name.

TBSPACEID *n*—Specifies single tablespace with given tablespace ID number.

BEGIN OBJECTID *n*—Specifies processing to begin from table with given object ID number.

TABLE

NAME *table-name*—Specifies table with given table name.

SCHEMA *schema-name*—Specifies schema name for specified table name for single table operation.

TBSPACEID *n* OBJECTID *n*—Specifies table with given tablespace ID number and object ID number.

CATALOG TO TABLESPACE CONSISTENCY

Specifies the processing to include checking for the consistency of physical tables listed in the catalog.

FOR ERROR STATE ALL

For table object with internal state already indicating error state, the check will just report this status and not scan through the object. Specifying this option will have the processing scan through the object even if internal state already lists error state.

LIMIT ERROR TO *n*

Number of pages in error for an object to limit reporting for. When this limit of the number of pages in error for an object is reached, the processing will discontinue the check on the rest of the object.

LIMIT ERROR TO ALL

No limit on number of pages in error reported.

EXTENTMAP

NORMAL—Specifies processing level is normal for extent map. Default.
NONE—Specifies processing level is none for extent map.
LOW—Specifies processing level is low for extent map.

DATA

NORMAL—Specifies processing level is normal for data object. Default.
NONE—Specifies processing level is none for data object.
LOW—Specifies processing level is low for data object.

BLOCKMAP

NORMAL—Specifies processing level is normal for block map object. Default.
NONE—Specifies processing level is none for block map object.
LOW—Specifies processing level is low for block map object.

INDEX

NORMAL—Specifies processing level is normal for index object. Default.
NONE—Specifies processing level is none for index object.
LOW—Specifies processing level is low for index object.

LONG

NORMAL—Specifies processing level is normal for long object. Default.
NONE—Specifies processing level is none for long object.
LOW—Specifies processing level is low for long object.

LOB

NORMAL—Specifies processing level is normal for LOB object. Default.
NONE—Specifies processing level is none for LOB object.
LOW—Specifies processing level is low for LOB object.

RESULTS

Specifies the result output file. The file will be written out to the diagnostic data directory path. If there is no error found by the check processing, this result output file will be erased at the end of the INSPECT operation. If there are errors found by the check processing, this result output file will not be erased at the end of the INSPECT operation.

KEEP—Specifies to always keep the result output file.
file-name—Specifies the name for the result output file.
ALL DBPARTITIONNUMS—Specifies that operation is to be done on all database partitions specified in the *db2nodes.cfg* file. This is the default if a node clause is not specified.
EXCEPT—Specifies that operation is to be done on all database partitions specified in the *db2nodes.cfg* file, except those specified in the node list.
ON DBPARTITIONNUM/ON DBPARTITIONNUM—Performs operation on a set of database partitions.
db-partition-number1—Specifies a database partition number in the database partition list.
db-partition-number2—Specifies the second database partition number, so that all database partitions from db-partition-number1 up to and including db-partition-number2 are included in the database partition list.

Utility Guidelines and Exceptions

1. For check operations on table objects, the level of processing can be specified for the objects. The default is NORMAL level; specifying NONE for an object excludes it. Specifying LOW will do a subset of checks that are done for NORMAL.
2. The check database can be specified to start from a specific tablespace or from a specific table by specifying the ID value to identify the tablespace or the table.
3. The check tablespace can be specified to start from a specific table by specifying the ID value to identify the table.
4. The processing of tablespaces will affect only the objects that reside in the tablespace.
5. The online inspect processing will access database objects using isolation level uncommitted read. COMMIT processing will be done during INSPECT processing. It is advisable to end the unit of work by issuing a COMMIT or ROLLBACK before invoking INSPECT.
6. The online inspect check processing will write out unformatted inspection data results to the results file specified. The file will be written out to the diagnostic data directory

path. If there is no error found by the check processing, this result output file will be erased at the end of the INSPECT operation. If there are errors found by the check processing, this result output file will not be erased at the end of the INSPECT operation. To see inspection details after check processing completes, the inspection result data will require to be formatted out with the *db2inspf* utility. The results file will have file extension of the database partition number. In a partitioned database environment, each database partition will generate its own results output file with an extension corresponding to its database partition number. The output location for the results output file will be the database manager diagnostic data directory path. If the name of a file that already exists is specified, the operation will not be processed and the file will have to be removed before that file name can be specified.

SUMMARY

In this chapter we have covered 18 primary utilities and commands that every DBA must have in their toolbox. I have highlighted the numerous enhancements IBM has made to these utilities in the area of 24×7×365 availability. IBM has strengthened DB2's already robust availability capabilities with the addition of ONLINE LOAD, ONLINE REORGANIZATION of tables and indexes, and the ability to pause and resume an ONLINE TABLE REORGANIZATION. The LOCK WITH FORCE option of the LOAD utility enables loads to be run when needed. With the new capability to run LOAD at the table level, previous barriers to complete 24×7 operations have been eliminated. And finally, several new wizards have been provided or enhanced to enable utilities to be built and run using the assistance of a wizard. IBM has leaped over the competition with these utility enhancements, and look for more to come!

C H A P T E R 8

Tuning Bufferpools

INTRODUCTION

DB2 uses computer areas of memory called bufferpools for the purpose of minimizing disk I/O to the computer's disk storage devices. When DB2 executes SQL statements, the DB2 optimizer will control access to certain index and data pages. Often, especially in OLTP systems, indexes are accessed first to locate actual table data (the RID, or Row ID, list), then the tablespace data pages are accessed to retrieve the data. DB2 first attempts to locate the required index and data pages in its bufferpool memory by performing "logical reads." If the required data is not found to be already present in bufferpool memory, then a "physical read" is issued to obtain the required data from disk storage. Accessing memory is extremely fast, as most commercially available memory chips deliver performance that is measured in nanoseconds, often 70 ns or faster. Contrast this to the time typically required to access disk storage devices, which is commonly measured in milliseconds. Good disk performance is typically measured in the 3 ms to 7 ms range, suggesting that accessing memory for data is about 1,000 times faster than accessing disk storage. It logically follows, then, that the more data that is stored in DB2 bufferpool memory, the faster the database will perform because physical reads of disk storage devices can be avoided. However, be cautioned that extremely large bufferpools cannot be successfully used to offset poor performance of an application with improper physical design. If indexes are missing, or suboptimally defined, DB2 will have to perform hundreds, if not thousands, of logical reads (which may require physical reads) to search memory and find appropriate results for SQL statements. Large memory scans consume a great deal of CPU resources, and this is why so many of today's business applications are CPU constrained and fail to scale as new users and data are added. Tuning will be discussed in detail later in this chapter.

MAINTAINING BUFFERPOOLS

Creating Bufferpools

Bufferpools can be defined in 4 K, 8 K, 16 K, or 32 K page sizes. The page size used depends on the page size(s) of the tablespace(s) assigned to the bufferpool. Larger page sizes will be used when table row widths (number of bytes) exceed the capacity of the smaller page sizes. It is good and common practice to limit any given database to using either one or two different page sizes; 4 K and 8 K pages are the most popular.

The amount of memory allocated to bufferpools will be primarily limited to the amount of real memory installed in the machine, less reserves for operating system functions, application programs, and other DB2 memory heaps and caches. As a rule of thumb, 50–75% of real memory is often dedicated to DB2 bufferpools on a DB2 server machine.

Bufferpools should have an intended I/O purpose or strategy. If the I/O performed within a bufferpool will be predominately asynchronous prefetch I/O, this will dictate the certain use of some bufferpool features that optimize prefetch I/O. If I/O will be predominantly synchronous (random), other attributes will be important to a bufferpool's definition.

To create a bufferpool with an 8 K page size that is intended for random I/O in an OLTP database, consider the following sample create bufferpool command:

```
CREATE BUFFERPOOL randombuffpool IMMEDIATE SIZE 61440 NUMBLOCKPAGES 0
PAGESIZE 8192;
```

This bufferpool would be (61440 × 8192 / 1048576) 480 megabytes in size with zero pages reserved for prefetch block I/O.

To create a bufferpool with a 4 K page size that is intended for sequential I/O in a BI/DW database, consider the following sample create bufferpool command:

```
CREATE BUFFERPOOL seqbuffpool IMMEDIATE SIZE 81920
NUMBLOCKPAGES 80256 BLOCKSIZE 64 PAGESIZE 4K;
```

This bufferpool would be (81920 × 4096 / 1048576) 320 megabytes in size with 80,256 pages reserved for prefetch block I/O. The `NUMBLOCKPAGES` value cannot exceed 98% of the bufferpool size, and it should be a multiple of the `BLOCKSIZE` (which, by default, is 32). The `BLOCKSIZE` should ideally match the `EXTENTSIZE` of the tablespace(s) assigned to the bufferpool.

To find the largest possible `NUMBLOCKPAGES` value, use the formula:

$$\text{NUMBLOCKPAGES} = (\text{Floor}(\text{Floor}(\text{BP \#Pages} \times 98 / 100)/\text{Blocksize \#Pages})) \times \text{Blocksize \#Pages}$$

Since not all I/O in a BI/DW database is sequential (some random I/O may occur via nested loop joins or other DB2 data accesses), consider reserving 60% of the bufferpool size for sequential I/O with the formula:

NUMBLOCKPAGES =
(Floor(Floor(BP #Pages × **60** / 100)/Blocksize #Pages)) × Blocksize #Pages

Tuning bufferpools for OLTP versus BI/DW databases will be covered in greater detail later in this chapter.

Altering Bufferpools

The definition of a bufferpool can be changed with an `ALTER` command. Use `ALTER BUFFERPOOL` to change the `SIZE` of a bufferpool, change the `NUMBLOCKPAGES`, or change the `BLOCKSIZE`. A change to the size of the bufferpool will take effect immediately, unless the `DEFERRED` option is used. `NUMBLOCKPAGES` and `BLOCKSIZE` are discussed in depth later in this chapter.

Here is an example of an `ALTER BUFFERPOOL` command:

```
ALTER BUFFERPOOL bufferpoolname SIZE 81920;
```

Where 81920 is the updated number of pages for the bufferpool to use.

Prior to v8, the `DBHEAP` memory required one page of memory for each 30 pages of bufferpool memory. Beginning with v8, the bufferpool descriptor pages are now stored in database shared memory, so `DBHEAP` is no longer a concern with respect to bufferpool sizes.

> **NOTE**
> DB2 v8 uses internal hidden bufferpools at DB2 startup if memory cannot be obtained in the amount requested. This enables DB2 to start and then you can alter the bufferpool effected to the appropriate size. To ensure that an appropriate bufferpool is available in all circumstances, DB2 creates small bufferpools, one for each page size. The size of these bufferpools are 16 pages.

Dropping Bufferpools

Bufferpools can be removed from a database by dropping them with the `DROP BUFFERPOOL` command. Before a bufferpool can be dropped, the DBA must ensure that there are no tablespaces currently assigned to the bufferpool or the `DROP` will fail. Once a bufferpool is dropped, the real memory used by the bufferpool becomes immediately available to the operating system for other purposes, including allocation or assignment to other DB2 caches, heaps, or bufferpools.

Drop Bufferpool Command example:

```
DROP BUFFERPOOL bufferpoolname;
```

Monitoring Bufferpool Performance

Monitor Switches

In order to obtain DB2 bufferpool performance data, the `BUFFERPOOL` monitor switch must be turned `ON`. To check the status of the DB2 monitor switches, use the command:

```
GET MONITOR SWITCHES;
```

To turn the bufferpool monitor switch on, use the command:

```
update monitor switches using bufferpool ON;
```

The command above will turn the bufferpool monitor switch on for the current connection to DB2. To have bufferpool monitor performance information available for all connections at all times, update the database manager configuration and set the default monitor switch to `ON` using the command:

```
Update dbm cfg using dft_mon_bufpool ON;
```

Snapshot Commands

Once the bufferpool monitor switch has been turned on, bufferpool performance information can be obtained by issuing DB2 Snapshot commands. Snapshots for `DATABASE`, `BUFFERPOOLS`, and `TABLESPACES` each provide bufferpool performance information that is aggregated to the named object level, with `DATABASE` snapshots providing summaries of all bufferpools, `BUFFERPOOLS` snapshot providing summaries for each bufferpool, and `TABLESPACES` snapshots providing the greatest level of detail for I/O performance at the tablespace level.

To get bufferpool performance summarized at the overall database level, issue the command:

```
GET SNAPSHOT FOR DATABASE ON DBNAME;
```

To obtain bufferpool performance for each bufferpool individually, issue the command:

```
GET SNAPSHOT FOR BUFFERPOOLS ON DBNAME;
```

See Example 8.1 for sample output from a "get snapshot for bufferpools" command.

To obtain bufferpool performance I/O details for each tablespace individually, issue the command:

```
GET SNAPSHOT FOR TABLESPACES ON DBNAME;
```

See Example 8.2 for sample output from a "get snapshot for tablespaces" command.

Interpretation of these various numbers, along with additional formulas, will be discussed in great detail later in this chapter; see "Formulas for Determining Bufferpool Efficiency and Effectiveness."

DB2 Event Monitors

Bufferpool performance information can also be obtained from DB2 Event Monitors. Database, Bufferpool, Tablespace, and Connection Events all provide detailed bufferpool I/O numbers similar to the DB2 Snapshot commands. Again, the performance metrics are aggregrated at the corresponding DB2 object level, with Database Events summarizing bufferpool performance across all bufferpools for the entire database, Bufferpool Events detailing performance for each individual bufferpool, Tablespace Events detailing bufferpool I/O performance at the individual tablespace level, and Connection Events detailing bufferpool I/O performance for each individual connection to the database.

Database, Bufferpool, and Tablespace event records are only written by DB2 when the database is stopped or the `FLUSH` command is issued. For purposes of evaluating bufferpool performance, the DB2 Snapshot commands are usually the best choice because the data is easy to obtain and interpret. Connection event records, however, are very interesting to analyze because this data can help the DBA answer such questions as:

- Which users or applications experience the best I/O performance? And worst?
- Which users or applications perform the most physical read or write I/O? Direct I/O?
- Are there applications or users that experience I/O times that are substantially better or worse than the norm; that is, the overall average for the database?
- Some companies may choose to implement cost center charge-back systems based on the CPU times and bufferpool I/O counts reported by the Connection Event Monitor.

Event monitors can write their data to raw binary format files, to pipes, and, beginning with v8, directly to DB2 tables. Since a pipe is merely a memory address, this output method uses the least overhead, but carries with it the burden of needing a program or process that continuously reads and processes the piped data. Writing the Event data directly to files usually uses very little disk space (the flat files have an efficient, compact, internal binary format) and captures the information at very low overhead cost to the database. Raw Event files must be subsequently processed and formatted for human interpretation; most DBAs may want to use the IBM-supplied sample program `db2evmon` for formatting raw Event data. Writing Event data directly to tables is the most convenient for interpreting the data, but carries with it the highest monitoring cost since DB2 must insert the event records into a table that is local to the monitored database.

Formulas for Determining Bufferpool Efficiency and Effectiveness

The next several paragraphs describe formulas that are applicable to both tablespaces and bufferpools. Once these formulas have been described, we explore how to use them in order to make effective bufferpool assignments. Example 8.1 shows information from a sample bufferpool snapshot. Example 8.2 shows information from a sample tablespace snapshot. You should note that the performance variables provided by both the bufferpool and tablespace snapshots are essentially the same. The following formulas will use sample data taken from these examples.

```
Bufferpool Snapshot

Bufferpool name                              = IBMDEFAULTBP
Database name                                = SAMPLE
Database path                                = E:\DB2\NODE0000\SQL00002\
Input database alias                         = SAMPLE
Bufferpool data logical reads                = 13872
Bufferpool data physical reads               = 515
Bufferpool data writes                       = 74
Bufferpool index logical reads               = 14345
Bufferpool index physical reads              = 616
Total bufferpool read time (ms)              = 663
Total bufferpool write time (ms)             = 9232
Asynchronous pool data page reads            = 108
Asynchronous pool data page writes           = 56
Bufferpool index writes                      = 0
Asynchronous pool index page reads           = 21
Asynchronous pool index page writes          = 0
Total elapsed asynchronous read time         = 168
Total elapsed asynchronous write time        = 9034
Asynchronous read requests                   = 17
Direct reads                                 = 676
Direct writes                                = 1666
Direct read requests                         = 116
Direct write requests                        = 121
Direct reads elapsed time (ms)               = 930
Direct write elapsed time (ms)               = 1207
Database files closed                        = 184
Data pages copied to extended storage        = 0
Index pages copied to extended storage       = 0
Data pages copied from extended storage      = 0
Index pages copied from extended storage     = 0
Unread prefetch pages                        = 6
Vectored IOs                                 = 22
Pages from vectored IOs                      = 129
Block IOs                                    = 0
Pages from block IOs                         = 0
Physical page maps                           = 0
```

Example 8.1
Bufferpool snapshot.

```
Node number                              = 0
Tablespaces using bufferpool             = 0
Alter bufferpool information:
  Pages left to remove                   = 0
  Current size                           = 0
  Post-alter size                        = 0
```

Example 8.1
Bufferpool snapshot. (Continued)

Index Hit Ratio (IHR)

IHR FORMULA

```
(Bufferpool index logical reads * 100) /
(Bufferpool index logical reads + Bufferpool index physical reads)
```

Using the values found in Example 8.1,

$$IHR = ((14345 \times 100)/(14345 + 616)) = 96\%$$

A page that was already in the bufferpool satisfied 96 out of 100 logical read requests. The higher the hit ratio, the less frequently DB2 needs to access disk devices to bring pages into the bufferpool. A high index hit ratio is especially important to transactional OLTP applications, including e-commerce web sites.

Overall Hit Ratio (OHR)

OHR FORMULA

```
((Bufferpool data logical reads + Bufferpool index logical reads) *
100)/(Bufferpool index logical reads +
Bufferpool index physical reads + Bufferpool data logical reads +
Bufferpool data physical reads)
```

Using the values found in Example 8.1,

$$OHR = ((13872 + 14345) \times 100) / (14345 + 616 + 13872 + 515) = 96\%$$

Again, the higher the hit ratio, the less frequently DB2 needs to access disk devices to bring pages into bufferpools. Because there are usually many times more data pages than index pages, the OHR is often less than the IHR for most applications. High OHR numbers can be observed when tables are small or an application performs application joins.

Physical Pages Read per Minute (PRPM)

PRPM FORMULA

```
(Bufferpool data physical reads + Bufferpool index physical reads) /
Number of elapsed minutes since monitor switches activated or reset
```

Given a reasonably steady workload, PRPM provides a measure of bufferpool effectiveness. As bufferpool hit ratios increase, physical I/O rates should conversely decrease, yielding quicker elapsed times for SQL statements.

By computing PRPM for each tablespace, the DBA can quickly determine the tablespaces with the heaviest physical I/O workloads by ranking tablespaces by PRPM. For the tablespaces with the highest PRPM rates, performance can be optimized by ensuring tablespaces have their containers distributed across as many disk devices as possible. This increases the number of disk arms and improves opportunities to do parallel I/O, thus generally lowering disk read times.

Asynchronous Pages Read per Request (APPR)

APPR FORMULA

```
(Asynchronous pool data page reads + Asynchronous pool index page reads)
/ (Asynchronous read requests)
```

Using the values found in Example 8.1,

$$APPR = (108 + 21) / 17 = 7.6$$

APPR provides the DBA with a measure of *prefetch effectiveness*. Each tablespace has a `PREFETCHSIZE` assigned to it. The `PREFETCHSIZE` is supposed to determine how many pages are asynchronously delivered to the bufferpool in anticipation of the application SQL statement's desire for large quantities of data.

By way of example, consider the following scenario: Along comes an SQL statement with an access strategy of `TBSCAN`. DB2 issues prefetch requests (called prefetches and controlled by the `NUM.IOSERVERS DB CFG PARAMETER`) and these prefetchers will fetch data measuring approximately one `PREFETCHSIZE` worth of data. The `NUM_IOSERVER` agents go out to disk, retrieve `PREFETCHSIZE` number of pages, and are returned to the bufferpool manager. One of two things now happens:

1. The pages are accepted by the bufferpool manager and placed into the designated bufferpool. (This is good.) APPR is equal, or nearly equal, to the `EXTENTSIZE`(s) of the tablespace(s) assigned to the bufferpool.

2. The bufferpool manager assesses the current state of activity within the target destination bufferpool and decides that there just isn't enough room for all those PREFETCHed pages. In this case, the bufferpool manager may accept only a few pages and then issue additional. Now, please go get prefetch requests. (This is not good.) The NUM_IOSERVER agents return to the disk drives and continue to process prefetch requests the contents of which cannot be fully accepted by the bufferpool manager. In this case, APPR is less than the EXTENTSIZE(s) of the tablespace(s) assigned to the bufferpool.

This discussion brings us to the first golden rule regarding the sizing of bufferpools.

Sizing Rule #1: *Asynchronous bufferpools should be sized at least large enough to accommodate the prefetch demands placed upon them.* APPR should be at least 90–95% of the average EXTENTSIZE of tablespaces assigned to a given bufferpool.

Asynchronous and Synchronous Read Percentages (ARP and SRP)

ARP FORMULA

```
((Asynchronous pool data page reads +
Asynchronous pool index page reads) * 100) /
(Bufferpool data physical reads + Bufferpool index physical reads)
```

```
Tablespace Snapshot

First database connect timestamp           = 11-11-2002 07:11:35.641366
Last reset timestamp                       =
Snapshot timestamp                         = 11-11-2002 07:15:42.109578
Database name                              = SAMPLE
Database path                              = E:\DB2\NODE0000\SQL00002\
Input database alias                       = SAMPLE
Number of accessed tablespaces             = 3

Tablespace name                            = SYSCATSPACE
  Tablespace ID                            = 0
  Tablespace Type                          = System managed space
  Tablespace Content Type                  = Any data
  Tablespace Page size (bytes)             = 4096
  Tablespace Extent size (pages)           = 32
  Tablespace Prefetch size (pages)         = 16
  Bufferpool ID currently in use           = 1
  Bufferpool ID next startup               = 1
  Tablespace State                         = 0x'00000000'
   Detailed explanation:
     Normal
  Total number of pages                    = 2677
```

Example 8.2
Tablespace snapshot.

```
   Number of usable pages                    = 2677
   Number of used pages                      = 2677
   Minimum Recovery Time                     =
   Number of quiescers                       = 0
   Number of containers                      = 1

... ... ( container information deleted) ... ...

   Bufferpool data logical reads             = 13593
   Bufferpool data physical reads            = 501
   Asynchronous pool data page reads         = 108
   Bufferpool data writes                    = 74
   Asynchronous pool data page writes        = 56
   Bufferpool index logical reads            = 14333
   Bufferpool index physical reads           = 610
   Asynchronous pool index page reads        = 21
   Bufferpool index writes                   = 0
   Asynchronous pool index page writes       = 0
   Total bufferpool read time (ms)           = 662
   Total bufferpool write time (ms)          = 9232
   Total elapsed asynchronous read time      = 168
   Total elapsed asynchronous write time     = 9034
   Asynchronous read requests                = 17
   Direct reads                              = 676
   Direct writes                             = 1666
   Direct read requests                      = 116
   Direct write requests                     = 121
   Direct reads elapsed time (ms)            = 930
   Direct write elapsed time (ms)            = 1207
   Number of files closed                    = 184
   Data pages copied to extended storage     = 0
   Index pages copied to extended storage    = 0
   Data pages copied from extended storage   = 0
   Index pages copied from extended storage  = 0
```

Example 8.2
Tablespace snapshot. (Continued)

Using the values found in Example 8.2 for tablespace `SYSCATSPACE`,

$$ARP = ((108 + 21) \times 100)/(501+ 610)) = 12\%$$

Asynchronous Read Percentage (ARP), together with Synchronous Read Percentage (SRP = 100 – ARP), indicates whether an object, bufferpool, or tablespace is predominantly randomly read or asynchronously read (prefetched). Simply stated, the ARP and SRP will effectively help you assign tablespace objects to appropriate bufferpool "clubs." Tablespaces that are randomly read (high SRP) should be assigned to bufferpools with random objectives. Tablespaces that are asynchronously read (high ARP) should be assigned to bufferpools with asynchronous objectives.

I/O Performance Measurements: ORMS, ARMS, SRMS

Overall Read Milliseconds (ORMS)

ORMS FORMULA

```
(Total bufferpool read time (ms)) /
(Bufferpool data physical reads + Bufferpool index physical reads)
```

Using the values found in Example 8.2 for tablespace SYSCATSPACE,

ORMS = 662 / (501 + 610) = 0.60 ms

For each tablespace, compute the overall read millisecond time then create an ordered list of tablespaces by ORMS. Is there a tablespace with a much higher than average ORMS? If so, find out why. Tablespaces with higher ORMS numbers (slower I/O) may have containers of unequal size, multiple containers accidentally placed on the same physical devices, and/or one super-sized container on a single disk. It's also possible that tablespaces with slower physical I/O performance may be placed on disk devices or controllers with above-average activity rates. Improving I/O response time by a few milliseconds may seem trivial, but the gain becomes significant when millions of physical I/Os are involved.

Asynchronous Read Milliseconds (ARMS) and Synchronous Read Milliseconds (SRMS)

ARMS FORMULA

```
(Total elapsed asynchronous read time (ms)) /
(Asynchronous pool data page reads + Asynchronous pool index page reads)
```

Using the values found in Example 8.2 for tablespace SYSCATSPACE,

ARMS = 168 / (108 + 21) = 1.302 ms

Average asynchronous read time (ms) provides the DBA with the average time to complete an asynchronous I/O. Like ORMS, ARMS values can be computed for and compared against all tablespaces to discover tablespaces with slower response times.

SRMS FORMULA

```
(Total bufferpool read time (ms) - Total elapsed asynchronous read time) /
((Bufferpool data physical reads + Bufferpool index physical reads) -
(Asynchronous pool data page reads + Asynchronous pool index page reads))
```

Using the values found in Example 8.2 for tablespace SYSCATSPACE,

SRMS = (662 – 168) / ((501 + 610) – (108 + 21)) = .503 ms

These particular snapshot examples (as found in Examples 8.1 and 8.2) were taken on a very fast laptop running Windows NT. We commonly see ARMS numbers of 1–3 ms, SRMS of 8–25 ms, and ORMS of 3–10 ms. Of course, actual results will depend on many factors, some of which include: the number and types of devices in use, numbers of containers on devices, processor speeds, and more.

Monitoring and Tuning Tables, Bufferpools, and Tablespaces

Bufferpools, and memory allocations in general, can have a profound performance impact on DB2 Universal Database regardless of platform. Ever since multiple bufferpools became available in DB2/MVS V3.1, strategies for configuring multiple bufferpools became a widely discussed and often-written-about topic. Today, many articles can be found on the Internet. While opinions and circumstances vary, it seems most experts agree that between 6 and 10 bufferpools provide optimized performance.

Table Activity

Begin your bufferpool analysis by determining which tables in your database are the most frequently read, for there is little value in dedicating bufferpool memory to tables that are rarely referenced. The DB2 Control Center can provide this information, or you can use the command line interface:

```
db2 "get snapshot for tables on DBNAME"
```

Sort the results of the snapshot in descending sequence by `ROWS READ`, and now you have your list of "heavy hitters," or tables that could benefit the most from focused bufferpool tuning. Of course, this list could also include tables that are victims of excessive table scans due to missing or suboptimal indexes.

The trouble, however, with the tables snapshot is that it does not provide the low-level I/O numbers as found in the tablespace or bufferpool snapshots. So, even though it is relatively easy to determine the most heavily read tables, it is difficult, if not impossible, to know if the reads are random (synchronous) or prefetch (asynchronous). Therefore, once you have your list of the "Top 10 Most Frequently Read Tables," you next need to take steps to ensure these tables are placed into their own tablespaces so that the type of I/O can be accurately determined. As a rule of thumb, each frequently read table should be assigned to its own tablespace.

Speaking of private table placements, if you are using Materialized Query Tables (formerly called Automatic Summary Tables in DB2 v7 and prior), you should be sure to define each MQT in its own tablespace. By doing so, you will be able to effectively measure whether or not the AST is being used in a manner that is consistent with its objectives. You could also assign your AST tablespaces to AST tablespace if the frequency of access warrants the dedication of resources.

Table Space Activity

Once you have the database's "important" tables isolated into their own tablespaces, you should compute performance metrics for each tablespace on a regular basis and save the results of your calculations in a tablespace performance history table or spreadsheet. Of particular importance, be sure to compute I/O performance times (ORMS, ARMS, SRMS), APPR, PRPM, and ARP and SRP. If you also track and save Used Pages on a periodic basis, you may be able to infer a growth rate, or Pages used Per Day (PPD).

Assigning Table Spaces to Bufferpools: General Concepts

In one sense, bufferpools are like a private club. They work best when the majority of the members share the same beliefs, principles, and behaviors. The DBA should try to organize a number of bufferpool "clubs" within his or her database so that the bufferpool will be more effective.

In society, there are certain clubs or organizations whose objectives and behaviors clash. In DB2, the central controversy lies between random and sequential I/O. When assigning objects to DB2 UDB bufferpools, it is very important, first and foremost, to keep objects with random I/O patterns (high SRP values) separated from objects with sequential I/O patterns (low SRP values). Within these two broad groupings, it can also be beneficial to create special-purpose bufferpools that have very specific and well-defined objectives.

Given these premises, I suggest the following general guidelines for defining bufferpools in an OLTP database (individual circumstances and results may vary):

- `TEMPBP`—A bufferpool dedicated to `TEMPSPACE` tablespace I/O, which tends to be predominantly sequential (low SRP value) and can be substantial when occasional decision support queries are executed.
- `RANDOMBP`—A bufferpool for objects whose access patterns are highly random in nature; that is, rarely exhibit prefetch or asynchronous I/O behaviors (high SRP value).
- `ASYNCBP`—A bufferpool for objects whose access patterns are predominantly asynchronous; that is, prefetch I/O occurs more often than not (low SRP value).
- `HOTINDEXBP`—A bufferpool for indexes of tables that are very frequently read via index access. Access should be predominantly random (high SRP value).
- `HOTDATABP`—A bufferpool for tables that are very frequently read, especially those at the heart of an OLTP system (high SRP value).
- `ASTBP`—A bufferpool for tablespaces containing Automatic Summary Tables.
- `SYSCATBP_R`—Randomly read bufferpool for the `SYSCATSPACE` tablespace.

The first three bufferpools defined above can have broad object membership. The latter four are bufferpools with special causes and specific agendas.

For a BI/DW database, I suggest using one large bufferpool for all tablespaces of a given page size. Thus, if the database has both 4 K and 8 K page size tablespaces, your BI/DW database should have two large bufferpools, one for each page size.

Optimum Bufferpool Assignments

Armed with the knowledge of the Asynchronous and Synchronous Read Percentages for each tablespace, you will be able to prudently assign tablespaces that are predominantly read asynchronously to bufferpools designed for asynchronous (sequential) I/O, and tablespaces that are mostly randomly read to bufferpools designed for random I/O. If the SRP for a tablespace is greater than 80%, assign the table space to a random I/O bufferpool. If the SRP for a tablespace is less than or equal to 80%, then assign the tablespace to a sequential I/O (prefetch) bufferpool. Tables with very high random read activity may have their tablespaces assigned to a special `HOT` bufferpool. Tablespaces that are assigned to a asynchronous (highly sequential/prefetch) bufferpool should have their APPR carefully monitored. Asynchronous bufferpools should be large enough to accommodate the prefetch demand that is placed on them, but not excessively large since improving hit ratios and reducing physical I/Os is unlikely (some exceptions apply). The key point is to remove prefetch I/O from your random tablespace so that the random bufferpool memory can be effectively used toward reducing physical I/O rates.

In an OLTP database, the `TEMPSPACE` tablespace should be assigned its own bufferpool. Access tends to be highly asynchronous, although some synchronous access may also be observed, especially when Nested Loop Joins are performed. If your database is OLTP, the bufferpool for `TEMPSPACE` need not be very large, maybe 4–8 MB. A Decision Support database, on the other hand, should use one large bufferpool for both data and `TEMPSPACE`.

Sizing Bufferpools

In a BI/DW database environment, one large bufferpool is ideal. Since I/O will be predominantly asynchronous sequential, the primary objective is to ensure that prefetching is effective. Compute and monitor APPR for each tablespace, and validate that the APPR is not less than 80% of the tablespace's `EXTENTSIZE`. If APPRs are less than 80% of a tablespace's `EXTENTSIZE`, then the bufferpool is too small to accommodate prefetch I/O demands (requests) placed upon it. As a rule of thumb, a 512 MB bufferpool is a good start.

In an OLTP database environment, a strategy of using multiple bufferpools that separates random I/O from sequential I/O should be used (as discussed in the previous sections). The sequential I/O bufferpool again should be sufficiently large enough to satisfy the prefetch request demands placed upon them, and this should be measured and verified by computing the APPR for each tablespace assigned to a sequential I/O bufferpool. If the APPR is less than 80% of the tablespace's `EXTENTSIZE`, then the size of the sequential I/O bufferpool needs to be increased. For tablespaces with mostly random I/O, the DBA should determine the optimum bufferpool size as the size that is not too small (results in unnecessary physical I/O and slows transactions) nor too large (may cause operating system paging and consumes excessive CPU to manage all the pages in the pool). The size that is "just right" is the point of diminishing returns—the point where a larger bufferpool size does not provide improved performance results (as measured by the IHR, OHR, and PRPM) and a smaller bufferpool size results in measurably poorer performance results (as measured by IHR, OHR, and PRPM). The optimum size can often be determined by sampling performance at varying bufferpool sizes until the point of diminishing returns is discovered.

Block Prefetch I/O, Special Considerations

As I previously discussed, new in DB2 v8 is the ability to reserve portions of a bufferpool's pages for sequential I/O. This new capability makes optimum use of memory for block prefetch I/O, and should result in faster query times for SQL that performs table scans. To reserve a portion of DB2 bufferpool memory for prefetch I/O, use the new `NUMBLOCKPAGES` parameter with the `CREATE` or `ALTER BUFFERPOOL` statement.

Summary

Most database administrators are handed an application or a database and instructed to make it go faster. There's no documentation, no SQL activity rates, nothing. The DBA needs to use the monitoring facilities available to discover the tuning opportunities. Learn which tables are most frequently read and assign them to their own tablespaces. Pair synchronously read tablespaces with bufferpools that are intended to have random access, and tablespaces that are heavily asynchronously read with bufferpools that are intended to have prefetch access. Prefetch bufferpools need to be large enough to accommodate the demand, while random bufferpools should seek to minimize physical I/O rates via size increases until either (1) system paging occurs, or (2) the point of diminishing returns is reached.

In this chapter, bufferpools were introduced and their purpose described. Creating, altering, dropping, and monitoring bufferpools was discussed, in conjunction with monitoring tables and tablespaces. Several important formulas for evaluating tablespace and bufferpool performance were presented, and techniques for tuning tablespaces were discussed.

C H A P T E R 9

Tuning Configuration Parameters

DB2 Database Manager (DBM) and Database Configuration (DB CFG) parameters control how memory and resources are used by DB2. How they are set affects the overall performance of DB2. DBAs that have worked on DB2 for z/OS are used to setting ZPARMS that control subsystem performance. These ZPARMS are relatively few in number compared to the number of DBM and DB CFG parameters. However, in DB2 for Linux, UNIX, and Windows, there are a multitude of configuration parameters and many are interrelated. In order to tune DBM and DB CFG parameters, you must understand how memory is allocated and used, and what parameters control the use and allocation of these associated memory areas.

There have been many changes to DBM and DB CFG parameters in DB2 v8. Some are no longer valid, some can be set to automatic, and many can be changed online.

The following list of DBM and DB CFG parameters are obsolete in DB2 v8:

- `backbufsz`—In version 8, `backbufsz` must be explicitly specified on the backup command.
- `dft_client_adpt`, `dft_client_comm`, `dir_obj_name`, `dir_path_name`, `dir_type`, and `route_obj_name`—These all have been removed as DCE directory services are no longer supported.
- `dos_rqrioblk`—This parameter is obsolete.
- `fcm_num_anchors`, `fcm_num_connect`, `fcm_num_rqb`—These all have been removed as DB2 will now manage these FCM resources automatically.
- `fileserver`, `ipx_socket`, `objectname`—IPX/SPX is no longer supported as a communication protocol.
- `initdari_jvm`—Java-stored procedures now use threading by default and will each get a separate Java Virtual Machine (JVM) environment established, so this protection is no longer needed.

- keepdari—This has been replaced by the keepfenced parameter.
- max_logicagents—This has been replaced by the max_connections parameter, which is used to enable connection concentration.
- maxdari—This has been replaced by the fenced_pool parameter.
- num_initdaris—This has been replaced by the num_initfenced parameter.
- restbufsz—Like the backfufsz parameter, restbufsz must now be explicitly specified on the restore command.
- ss_logon—Previously applied to OS/2, which is no longer supported.
- udf_mem_sz—UDFs now pass data in shared memory so udf_mem_sz is no longer required.

DB CFG parameters:

- buffpage—This parameter provided the default bufferpool size in pages if not explicitly stated on the create bufferpool command in prior releases; in v8 it must be explicitly specified on the create bufferpool command.
- copyprotect—An old parameter used for copy protection on non-UNIX platforms.
- indexsort—Previously, this parameter specified whether or not DB2 would sort index entries during index creation; in v8, DB2 will only use sort during index creation if intra_parallel is enabled on an SMP server.

> **NOTE**
> DBM and DB CFG files should not be directly edited. They should be updated through the Control Center or from a command line. Direct editing may render your database inoperable.

My experience, feedback from DBAs during consulting engagements, and from presentations I've given at local DB2 user groups indicates that additional information is needed in the field on setting and tuning configuration parameters. This chapter concentrates on tuning key DBM and DB CFG parameters. For a complete list of all parameters, refer to the *DB2 UDB v8 Administration Guide: Performance.*

Autonomic Computing

With the advent of Autonomic Computing, IBM is helping DBAs to be more productive in this era of "do more with less."

Autonomic computing is a term coined from the body's nervous system where body processes such as breathing, blood flow, and body temperature are automatically managed.

In v8, several DBM and DB CFG parameters can be set to automatic and DB2 will monitor and adjust values for these parameters automatically. These parameters will be identified later in this chapter.

IBM has developed the SMART initiative, which stands for "Self Managing and Resource Tuning." SMART consists of built-in automation, wizards and tools, and expert advice. The goal of the SMART is to:

- Automate configuration of parameters
- Expand wizards and tools
- Provide automated expert advice

Additionally, SMART will help to reduce the number and skill level of DBAs required to support and maintain DB2. Typically, the average IT budget is devoted to 60% people costs and SMART will help to reduce that cost. The intent of SMART is not to replace DBAs, but to automate tasks and parameters that don't require DBA intervention.

ONLINE CONFIGURATION PARAMETERS

New to v8 is the ability to dynamically configure over 50 online configuration parameters. Online configurable parameters are associated with one of the propagation classes that control when the change takes effect. The classes and definitions are:

- Immediate—Causes the parameter change to have immediate effect. For example, changing the *notify* level has an immediate effect.
- Statement Boundary—Change takes effect on SQL statement and statement-like boundaries. For example, if you change the `stmtheap`, all-new SQL requests will use the new value.
- Transaction Boundary—Parameter changes take effect on the next `COMMIT`. For example, changing *avg_appls* would take effect on the next commit.

For a complete list of the propagation classes for DBM or DB CFG parameter, and whether or not they can be changed online, refer to the parameter definitions in the *DB2 UDB v8 Administration Guide: Performance*.

Online parameter changes can be made immediately (depending on the propagation class) and/or deferred to the next `db2start`. The default behavior for the `UPDATE DBM CFG` command is to apply the change immediately. To display the current value of configuration parameters, use the `GET DBM CFG` or `GET DB CFG FOR` *`database`* command. To see deferred values, use the `SHOW DETAIL` option of these commands. See Figure 9.1.

In this example `sortheap` has been changed to the value 256 from 512. You can see the in-memory and deferred values in this example.

> **NOTE**
> Changes to *immediate* online configuration parameters may not take effect until memory can be allocated or transactions complete.

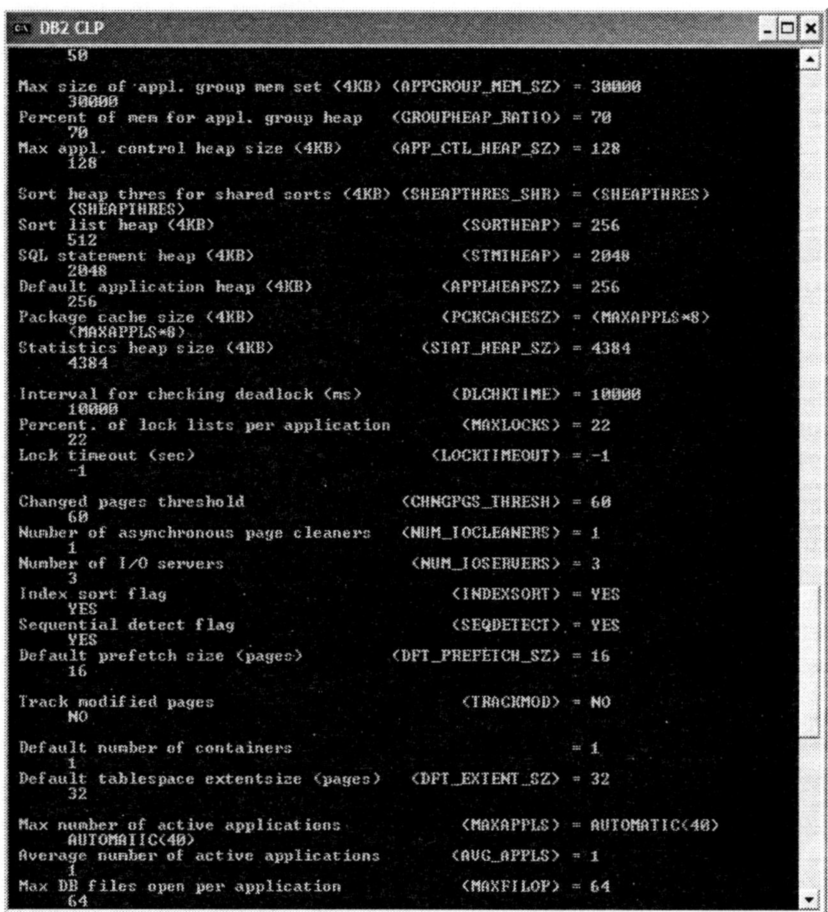

Figure 9.1
Deferred DB CFG `sortheap` values.

DB2 Memory Areas

The DB2 memory model (Figure 9.2) consists of Database Manager Shared Memory, Database Global Memory, Application Global Memory, and Agent Private Memory. Database Manager shared memory is used across the instance for various heaps and for storing control information regarding databases defined. Database Global Memory is allocated per database and is used to store memory areas related to a particular database. Database Global Memory is allocated for each database defined. Application Global Memory is used in a partitioned database environment to pass messages between agents and subagents. It is allocated per node in a partitioned database environment. It is not used in an ESE nonpartitioned environment.

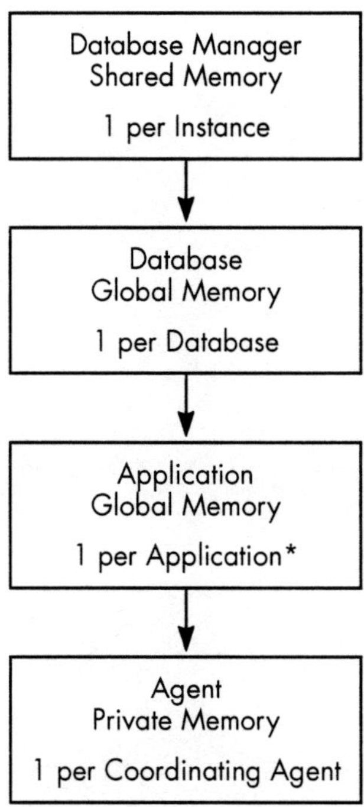

Figure 9.2
DB2 memory model.

DATABASE MANAGER SHARED MEMORY

Database Manager shared memory is allocated at the instance level. It is shared across all databases within the instance. All other memory used by DB2 is chained off shared memory. Shared memory is allocated at `db2start` and deallocated at `db2stop`.

Database Manager shared memory consists of control structures as outlined in Figure 9.3. Database Manager shared memory is used to store and manage activity across all databases. It is allocated at `db2start` and freed at `db2stop`. The Fast Communication Manager (FCM) is the DB2 component that manages communication (messages) between multiple logical nodes in a partitioned environment and parallel subagents in an ESE environment with the `intra_parallel` configuration parameter enabled. When specifying FCM DBM CFG parameters, keep in mind that the higher the `maxagent` DB CFG setting, the higher the potential for Database Manager Shared Memory to grow rather large. In a partitioned environment, Database Manager Shared Memory is used differently and is outlined in Chapter 13.

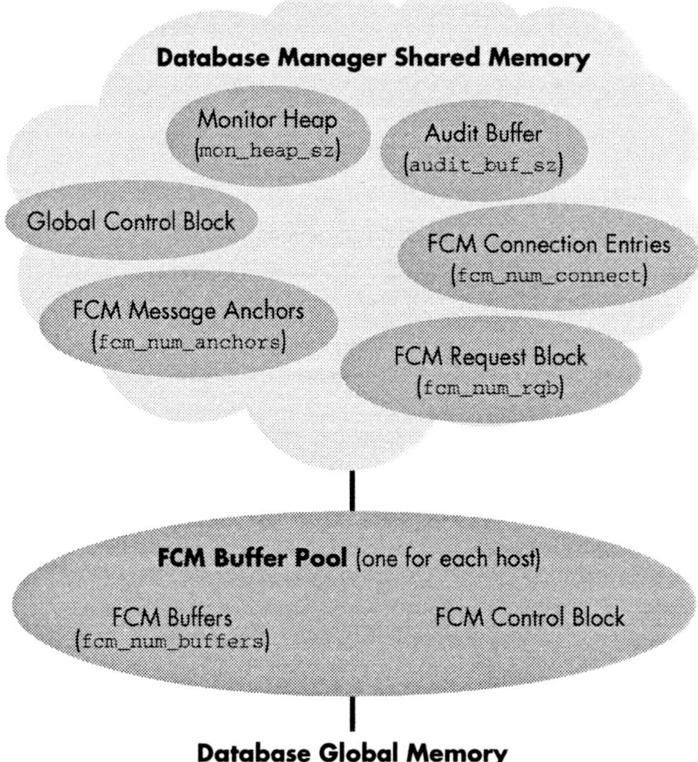

Figure 9.3
Database Manager Shared Memory (ESE nonpartitioned environment).

Instance Memory (`instance_memory`)

Instance memory, also referred to as Database Shared Memory, can now be automatically managed by DB2. I recommend that the default of automatic be used. Care should be taken if you decide to specify this value instead of using the default. Remember, monitor heap, FCM resources, Java heap, and control blocks are allocated out of `instance_memory`.

Group Heap Ratio (`group_heap_ratio`)

This new parameter specifies the percentage of memory allowed for the shared heap. Setting this too low limits the size of caches. Setting it too high could cause applications to get an SQL0973 error, which indicates that you are running out of application control heap. The default of 70% should be used unless you experience performance problems, then you should make adjustments based on stress testing.

Sort Heap Threshold for Shared Sorts

This new parameter specifies a hard limit for shared sorts. When this limit is reached, applications will fail with SQL0955C SQL message. If set to 0, the threshold for shared sort memory will be equal to the value of the `sheapthres` DBM CFG setting. `sheapthres_shr` only applies when `intra-parallel` is set to `YES`, connection concentration is enabled, or when using the cursor `WITH HOLD` option. When using cursor `WITH HOLD`, sort heap will be allocated from `sheapthres_shr` memory.

Global Control Block

Contains instance and database control information for all databases defined to the instance.

Monitor Heap (`mon_heap_sz`)

Monitor heap is used across all databases to store monitoring information for all logical views of system monitor data. The amount of monitor heap allocated is controlled by the `mon_heap_sz` parameter. The amount of memory used depends on the number of monitoring applications, database activity, monitoring switches enabled, and use of event monitors. It is allocated at `db2start` and freed when DB2 is shut down. If `mon_heap_sz` is set to 0, monitoring is disabled. If you receive a –973 SQLCODE while monitoring, you may need to increase the size of *monitor heap*.

Audit Buffer (`audit_buf_sz`)

The audit buffer is used for buffering audit records asynchronously when written by the audit facility with auditing enabled. If `audit_buf_sz` is set to 0 and auditing is used, records are written synchronously, causing the application to wait for the disk write to complete.

HINT

FCM resources are fully committed at `db2start` so you should monitor them closely and make sure they are not overallocated.

NOTE

FCM performance information can be captured through DB2 database-level snapshot monitoring. When FCM resources are exceeded, communication is degraded and error messages are returned to applications and are written to the *db2diag.log* file.

FCM Connection Entries (`fcm_num_connect`)

FCM connection entries are used by FCM to pass data between agents. This is set in conjunction with `fcm_num_rqdb` and other FCM parameters.

FCM Message Anchors (fcm_num_anchors)

FCM message anchors are used by FCM to pass messages between agents. This is set in conjunction with fcm_num_rqdb and other FCM parameters.

FCM Request Block (fcm_num_rqdb)

FCM request blocks are used by FCM as the mechanism by which information is passed between an FCM daemon and an agent, or to facilitate passing information between agents.

FCM Bufferpool

The FCM bufferpool contains FCM buffers and control blocks that are used to enable rapid communication between parallel subagents in a parallel environment.

FCM Buffers (fcm_num_buffers)

fcm_num_buffers *are only used in ESE when partitioning is enabled or when intrapartition parallelism is enabled* and specifies the number of 4 KB buffers that are used for internal communication between subagents in a partitioned database environment. This parameter is critical to database performance and, in a future release, may be adjusted automatically by the database manager. The more logical nodes, the more buffers you will need.

FCM Control Block

FCM control blocks are used as control mechanisms to manage the allocation and use of FCM buffers.

> **NOTE**
> FCM communication is used when using partitioned databases or when using ESE with the DBM CFG parameter intra_parallel enabled.

Java Heap Size (java_heap_sz)

This new parameter controls the amount of heap that the Java interpreter uses to service Java-stored procedures and UDFs. On UNIX there is one heap for each DB2 process (one for each agent or subagent on UNIX-based platforms, and one for each instance on other platforms). There is one heap per fenced UDF and fenced SP process. Each db2famp process uses one heap. For multithreaded db2famp processes, there is only one heap used. Java heap is only allocated by processes that run Java UDFs or SPs. For partitioned databases, the same value is used at each database partition. Start with the default and monitor to ensure you have it set correctly in your environment.

Database Memory (`database_memory`)

This parameter sets the minimum size of database global memory. These areas are shown in Figure 9.3. The default setting for this parameter is automatic. This allows DB2 to dynamically adjust areas such as bufferpools, catalog cache, and other database global memory areas. This parameter allows DB2 to take advantage of 64-bit addressing on AIX and increase the size of this memory as needed. Use the default and monitor and adjust if necessary.

DATABASE GLOBAL MEMORY

Database Global Memory is allocated at the database level, one per database up to the value of `numdb`.

> **NOTE**
> Shared sort memory is allocated out of Database Global Memory when partitioning is used or ESE with parallelism enabled.

Database Global Memory contains memory that is allocated at "first connect." It is used across all applications that connect to the database and contains many important memory areas (see Figure 9.4).

> **NOTE**
> DBM and DB CFG parameters should be set using formulas, benchmarking, or stress testing in the affected environment.

Database Manager Shared Memory
↓
Database Global Memory

Utility Heap (`util_heap_sz`)	Buffer Pools	Database Heap (`dbheap`)
Backup Buffer* (`backbufsz`)	Extended Memory Cache	Log Buffer (`logbufsz`)
Restore Buffer* (`restbufsz`)	Lock List (`locklist`)	Catalog Cache (`catalogcache_sz`)
Package Cache (`pckcachesz`)	Sort Heap—Shared Sort (`sortheap`)	

* obsolete

Figure 9.4
Database Global Memory.

Utility Heap (`util_heap_sz`)

Utility heap specifies the maximum amount of memory that can be concurrently used by the backup, restore, recovery, and load utility. It is allocated when needed by a utility and freed when no longer needed by the utility. This parameter generally has a low effect on performance.

Backup Buffer (`backbufsz`)

This parameter is now obsolete in DB2 v8. Backup buffers are now explicitly specified as part of the backup command.

Restore Buffer (`restbufsz`)

This parameter is now obsolete in DB2 v8. Restore buffers are now explicitly specified on the restore command.

Package Cache Size (`pckcachesz`)

Package cache size specifies the amount of memory allocated for caching dynamic and static SQL. Allocated at database startup and freed at shutdown. DB2 uses package cache to eliminate the need to access the DB2 catalog to load a package for static SQL or eliminate a prepare for dynamic SQL. SQL statements are stored in the cache (in memory) if the amount of cache available is greater than that needed to store concurrently executing SQL. If not, DB2 will not cache SQL. Package sections remain cached until the database is shut down, the statement becomes invalidated, the cache fills up, or the new v8 `FLUSH PACKAGE CACHE` command is issued.

TIP
DB2 uses direct IO to load a package from the catalog if it isn't found in package cache, which bypasses the bufferpool and is much slower than reading packages from the package cache. So to have a well performing database it's important to make maximum use of the package cache.

HINT
DB2 matches cached SQL byte by byte. Dynamic SQL should use parameter markers instead of literals, which will result in DB2 getting a match in the cache (cache hit) and improved performance.

Package cache is more important in OLTP implementations than in business intelligence or data warehousing implementations as OLTP transactions tend to be executed repetitively versus BI transactions, which tend to be more ad-hoc and executed less frequently.

The amount of memory specified for package cache is a *soft-limit* and can be exceeded if enough memory is available to the database manager. If this occurs, this is called a "package cache overflow" and can be monitored using the monitor element `pkg_cache_num_overflows` and `pkg_cache_size_top`. If *package cache* overflows, DB2 will temporarily borrow memory from `locklist`, `dbheap`, or other Database Shared Memory. This could result in a reduction in overall database concurrency through additional `locklist` usage or a shortage of `dbheap`. See the *DB2 System Monitor Guide and Reference* for additional monitor elements relating to package cache.

If you set package cache too large, memory is wasted and not available for use. Carefully set and monitor package cache usage and if it is too large, reduce the amount used and allocate it to other important areas, like bufferpools. Use benchmarking techniques to determine proper package cache size.

Bufferpool Size (`buffpage`)

This parameter is obsolete in DB2 v8.1.

Extended Memory Cache

Extended Memory Cache can be used when the amount of physical memory available exceeds the addressable virtual memory on 32-bit operating systems, which is usually 2 or 4 GB depending on the operating system. Extended memory cache is associated with one or more bufferpools.

Extended memory cache serves as a "second-level cache" for bufferpools and can benefit applications that do lots of reads versus updates. Pages are moved to extended memory cache and are reused when referenced by an application. Because there is a CPU cost associated with managing extended storage cache, it should only be used if your database has an I/O bottleneck and is not CPU constrained.

Lock List (`locklist`)

The `locklist` DB CFG parameter specifies the amount of global memory that should be reserved for storing locks by the lock manager. There is one `locklist` per database. It is allocated at startup and freed when the last application disconnects from the database. `locklist` works in conjunction with the `maxlocks` database configuration parameter. `maxlocks` specifies the maximum percentage of `locklist` that can be used by a single application, after which lock escalation will occur. Lock escalation only occurs for the application exceeding the `maxlocks` parameter. Since row level locking is the default isolation level in DB2, escalation will cause a table lock to be taken on the table and the row level locks will be released. This frees up `locklist` memory for use by other applications. Lock escalation can also take place if the `locklist` memory becomes full. Lock escalation reduces the amount of concurrency and should generally be avoided.

Database Heap (dbheap)

The dbheap parameter specifies the amount of global memory that is allocated for storing control blocks for tablespaces, tables, and indexes. There is one dbheap per database and it is allocated when the first application connects to the database and it is freed when the last application disconnects from the database. The log buffer and catalog cache are also allocated out of dbheap. The dbheap parameter should be set through benchmarking techniques. If the size of the log buffer or catalog cache changes, dbheap should be changed accordingly. dbheap usage should be monitored on a continuous basis using either snapshot monitoring or a third-party vendor monitoring tool. Monitoring element db_heap_top can be used to monitor dbheap high water mark usage. Additional dbheap monitoring elements can be obtained by issuing a snapshot on the Database Manager.

Log Buffer (logbufsz)

logbufsz specifies the size of the log buffer. It is allocated and deallocated as part of dbheap. The log buffer is used to hold log records before they are written to disk. logbufsz should be set in conjunction with database configuration parameter mincommit. While logbufsz controls the size of the log buffer, mincommit is used to group commits and controls how often log records are written to disk. Log records are written to disk when one of the following occurs:

- A transaction commits or a group of transactions commit as defined by mincommit
- The log buffer is full
- As a result of some other internal database manager event

The log buffer should be sized as large as possible given available memory and so that it is large enough so that it doesn't fill up during a period of normal activity, causing unnecessary commits. Use the below formula to set mincommit in an OLTP environment:

$$\frac{\text{Number of Transactions per second}}{10}$$

For example:

$$\frac{95}{10} = 9.5 \text{ (rounded to 10)}$$

Use the following command to set mincommit to 10:

```
db2 update DB CFG using mincommit 10
```

This grouping of commits enables DB2 to make efficient use of the log buffer, which can significantly affect performance.

Catalog Cache (catalogcache_sz)

catalogcache_sz specifies the total amount of memory that can be allocated for storing table descriptor information. It is allocated and de-allocated as part of dbheap.

> **NOTE**
> DB2 does not use the bufferpool when accessing the catalog, instead it performs direct reads from disk if information is not found in the catalog cache.

The catalog cache stores table descriptor information that is used when a table, view, or alias is referenced during compilation of an SQL statement. Use of cache helps improve performance of SQL statements when the same tables, views, or aliases have been referenced in previous statements. Descriptor information for declared temporary tables is not stored in catalog cache; it is stored in application control heap. Running DDL against a table will purge that table's entry from the cache. Otherwise, it is kept in the cache until room is needed for another table, but not until all units of work have been completed. Start with the default and monitor it by using the following monitoring elements:

- `cat_cache_lookups`
- `cat_cache_inserts`
- `cat_cache_overflows`
- `cat_cache_heap_full`

New in v8, catalogue cache elements can be obtained by issuing a snapshot on the Database Manager.

Application Group Memory (`appgroup_mem_sz`)

This parameter determines the maximum size of the application group shared memory segment. This memory is only used in a partitioned database environment, when intrapartition paralellism is enabled or connection concentration is being used. Each application has its own application control heap, allocated out of application group memory and all applications share one application group shared heap. The size of each application control heap is calculated as follows:

`App_ctl_heap_sz` * (100-groupheap_ratio)/100

Start with using the default and monitor and adjust if performance problems are observed.

Application Global Memory (`app_ctl_heap_sz`)

Application global memory is allocated if using DB2 ESE with `intra_parallelism` enabled or if using partitioned databases (see Figure 9.5). For nonpartitioned databases its use is minimal.

Application Global Memory specifies how much application control heap is allocated for each application at the database where the application is active (in the case of partitioned databases, heap is allocated at each database partition where the application is active). The heap is allocated during connect processing by the first agent to receive a request for the application at the database (or database partition). The heap is used by agents working for the application to share information

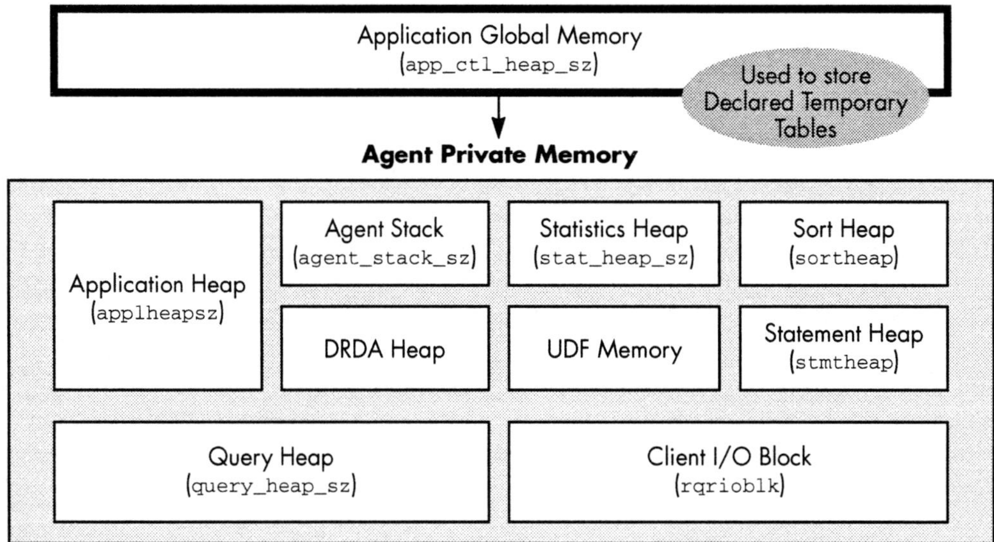

Figure 9.5
Application Global Memory

(in a partitioned database, sharing occurs at the database partition level). The heap is also used to store descriptor information for declared temporary tables, which is kept until the declared temporary table is explicitly dropped. In a partitioned database environment, heap is used to store executing copies of SQL statements for agents and subagents. Note that SMP subagents use `applheapsz` instead. Allocation only occurs if `intra_parallel` is set on and the `CURRENT DEGREE` special register is set greater than 1. Start with the default value and increase it if you use lots of declared temporary tables, run complex SQL, or have many database partitions.

Agent Private Memory

Agent private memory is allocated per application. As applications connect and complete processing, agent private memory is allocated and deallocated as necessary. The amount of agent private memory that can be allocated can be controlled by setting agent private memory parameters or by setting `maxagents` or `maxappls` to the number of applications that available resources can support. Of course, knowing what the available resources can support is often difficult to determine. Benchmarking should be conducted using a normal and worst-case workload to assist you in setting agent parameters correctly and to provide information on proper server hardware and memory requirements. Failure to do so can result in surprises when the application is moved to production! See Figure 9.6.

Application Heap (`applheapsz`)

`applheapsz` specifies the amount of private memory to be used by the database manager on behalf of a specific agent or subagent. Application heap is allocated at agent initialization and when the agent completes the work to be done for an application. The initial amount allocated

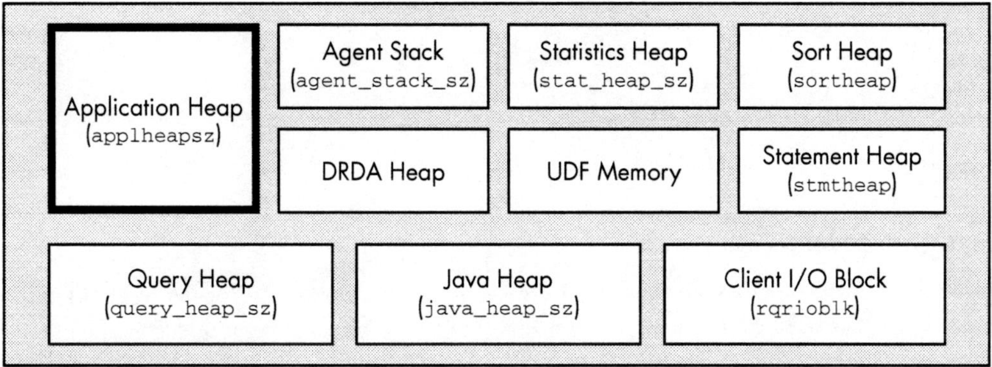

Figure 9.6
Agent Private Memory.

will be the minimum amount required for the work. As more heap space is needed, it will be allocated by the database manager as needed, up to the maximum amount specified. Start with the default setting and monitor. Increase if errors are received indicating a shortage in heap.

Agent Stack Size (`agent_stack_sz`)

`agent_stack_sz` specifies the amount of virtual memory allocated per agent. This parameter is not applicable for DB2 running on UNIX platforms. Agent stack size is used when needed to process an SQL statement. The more complex the query, the more stack space is required. You should start with the default and only increase if you run out of space or receive error messages. Error messages will be written to the *db2diag.log*. Large `agent_stack_sz` settings could affect concurrency, as you will probably run out of address space before you reach `maxagents` on 32-bit operating systems.

Statistics Heap (`stat_heap_sz`)

`stat_heap_sz` specifies the maximum amount of heap allocated when running `RUNSTATS`. It is allocated when needed and freed when the utility completes. The default may not be adequate for wide tables or when running `RUNSTATS` with distribution statistics being gathered.

Sort Heap (`sortheap`)

`sortheap` specifies the amount of sort memory allocated for each agent (private sort). It is allocated when needed and freed when no longer needed. One exception to this is when a piped sort is used and a cursor is still open, in this case the `sortheap` is not freed until the cursor is closed. This should be taken into consideration when designing applications. See Chapter 12 for a complete description of private and shared sort configuration parameters and tuning recommendations.

DRDA Heap (drda_heap_sz)

drda_heap_sz is obsolete in DB2 v8.

UDF Memory (udf_mem_sz)

Udf_mem_sz is obsolete in DB2 v8.

Statement Heap (stmtheap)

stmtheap specifies the amount of memory to be used as a workspace for the SQL compiler when compiling an SQL statement. For dynamic SQL this heap will be used during the execution of the dynamic SQL statement, whereas for static SQL it is only used during the bind process. It is allocated for each statement during precompiling or binding. It is freed when precompiling or binding of each statement is complete. The default should be adequate. If not, an error will be returned indicating the statement is "too complex." Increase the size in regular increments until the problem is resolved. In EEE, the app_ctl_heap_sz is used instead.

Query Heap Size (query_heap_sz)

query_heap_sz specifies the maximum amount of what can be allocated for the query heap. A query heap is used to store each query in the agent's private memory. Information stored for each query consists of the SQLDA, statement, SQLCA, package name, creator, section number, and consistency token. Memory for blocking cursors is also allocated from query heap along with cursor control blocks and fully resolved output SQLDA. Query heap size defaults to the size of the Application Support Layer Heap Size (aslheapsz).

Client IO Block (rqrioblk)

rqrioblk specifies the size of the communication buffer between the remote applications and the database and their local client and the database server. It is allocated when a remote client application issues a connection request for a server database, and when a blocking cursor is opened, additional blocks are opened at the client. It is freed when the remote application disconnects from the server database and when the blocking cursor is closed. When a remote client requests a connection to remote database, this communication buffer is allocated on the client. On the database server, a communication buffer of 32,767 is initially allocated until a connection is established and the database server can determine the value of rqrioblk at the client. Once the server knows this value it will reallocate its buffer if the client is not 32,767. rqrioblk is also used to determine the size of the I/O block at the database client when a blocking cursor is opened. The default is generally sufficient. If more fetch requests are generated than required by the application, OPTIMIZE FOR N ROWS can be used to influence the access path and to control the number of rows returned in a block.

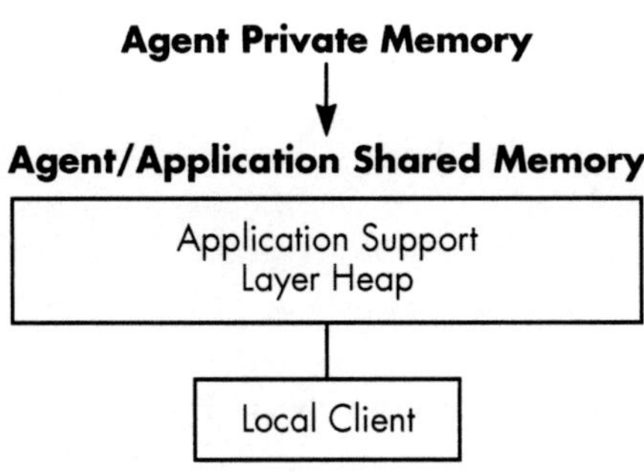

Figure 9.7
Application Support Layer Heap size.

Application Support Layer Heap (aslheapsz)

The application support layer heap is used by local clients when communicating with local databases. It serves as a communication buffer between the client and the database. It serves the same purpose as the `rqrioblk` parameter for remote applications. See Figure 9.7.

AGENT PARAMETERS

DB2 uses a client-server based processing model. Clients or applications use agents to accomplish work within the database. DB2 uses several types of agents as follows.

Coordinating Agents

Coordinating agents are created for each application and manage work on behalf of applications. Coordinating agents also distribute work to subagents in a database with intra-partition parallelism enabled. The DBM CFG parameter `MAX_COORDAGENTS` is used to define the number of coordinating agents available to process application requests. If a coordinating agent is not available for an application, the requesting application will receive a negative SQL code. You should set `MAX_COORDAGENTS` such that this situation does not occur. The default for `MAX_COORDAGENTS` is the setting of the `MAXAGENTS` DBM CFG parameter. This setting is a good starting point. In an ESE environment without partitioning enabled or `intra_parallel` set to `YES`, `MAX_COORDAGENTS` must equal `MAXAGENTS`.

MAXAGENTS

The `MAXAGENTS` DBM CFG parameter specifies the maximum number of database manager agents, whether coordinating or subagents available at any given time to accept application requests. In memory constrained environments, `MAXAGENTS` can be set low so as to limit the total memory usage of the database manager as each additional agent requires additional memory. If you use this to limit resources, remember it is only a temporary solution. You will need to reduce resource consumption or acquire additional capacity to support your business requirements.

MAXCAGENTS

MAXCAGENTS defines the Maximum Number of Concurrent Agents that can be executing in the database manager. Before an agent can do work for an application it must obtain a token from the database manager. If a token is not available, the agent will wait. MAXCAGENTS controls the number of tokens available. The default is that MAXCAGENTS is equal to MAX_COORDAGENTS. Start with the default and adjust through benchmark testing. Generally, you don't want agents waiting for a token. You can monitor this with a DBM snapshot. If agents waiting for tokens occurs frequently then MAXCAGENTS and other related agent parameters should be increased until agents waiting for tokens is 0, or occurs very infrequently.

MAXAPPLS

MAXAPPLS defines the maximum number of concurrent applications that can be connected to the database. If MAXAPPLS is reached, an error will be returned to any application attempting to connect to the database and a connection will not be established. In v8, MAXAPPLS can be set to automatic which will allow any number of connected applications. If resources are not a concern, set MAXAPPLS to automatic. If resources are constrained (due to CPU or memory constraints), then set MAXAPPLS equal to or greater than the sum of the connected applications, plus the number of these same applications that may be concurrently completing a two-phase commit or rollback; plus the sum of the anticipated number of in-doubt transactions that might occur at any time.

MAXAPPLS is also governed by MAXAGENTS. An application can only connect to the database if there is an available connection (MAXAPPLS) as well as an available agent (MAXAGENTS). Additionally, no new applications (coordinating agents) can be started if MAX_COORDAGENTS has been reached.

AGENT MONITORING

A database manager snapshot will provide you with monitoring elements regarding agent activity. Refer to chapter 2 for an example database manager snapshot. Elements of interest are as follows:

- High water mark for agents registered
- High water mark for agents waiting for a token
- Agents registered
- Agents waiting for a token
- Agents stolen from another application
- High water mark for coordinating agents
- Max agents overflow

These elements will indicate whether or not agent settings are adequate or require adjustment. Generally, any time when 80% of agent resources are used (High water mark) you should increase the associated parameter until less than 80% of the setting for the resource are in use. Monitor over time to make sure that changes are working as desired.

CONFIGURATION ADVISOR

Now that we have discussed various database manager and database configuration parameters, it is time to introduce the Configuration Advisor. The Configuration Advisor is designed to configure database manager and database configuration parameters based on inputs from the DBA. It helps to get you started and helps you set a performance baseline for your database. After monitoring your database in a typical production environment, the parameter settings should be reviewed and adjusted as necessary. The Configuration Advisor consists of a 10-step process, as depicted in Figures 9.8–9.17.

> **NOTE**
> The Configuration Advisor is an example of IBM's SMART program. The SMART program is designed to improve DBA productivity by providing tools and wizards to perform self-tuning, monitoring, and analysis of DB2 databases.

1. Introduction—Calculate new values or restore saved values. See Figure 9.8.

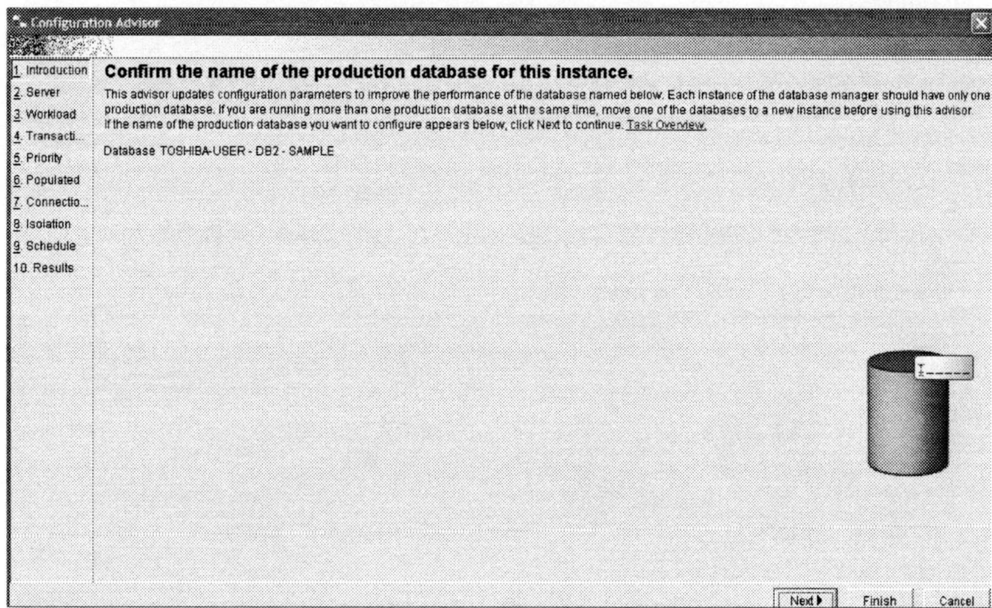

Figure 9.8
Configuration Advisor Wizard—Introduction.

2. Server—Set target values for database server real memory. See Figure 9.9.

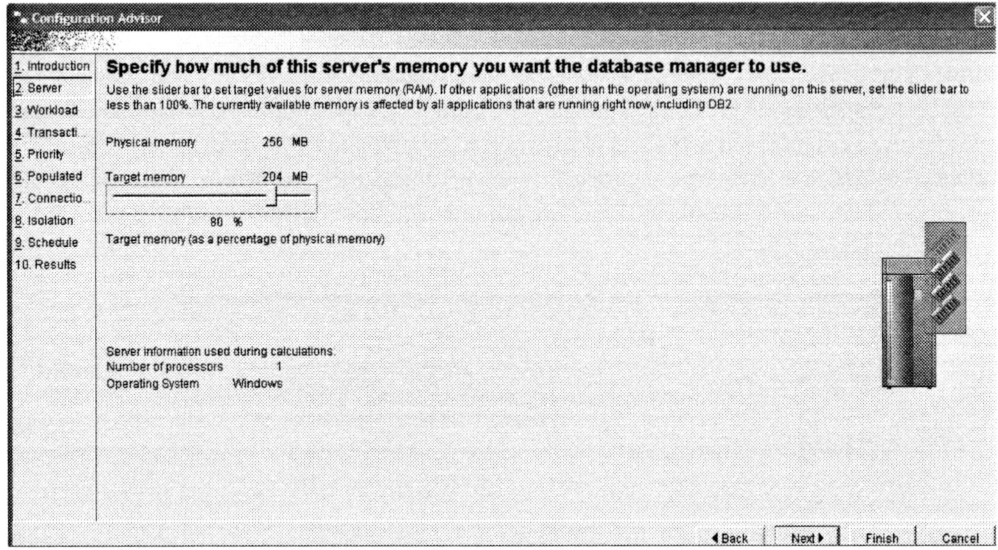

Figure 9.9
Set server values.

If you have a dedicated database server, then set the slider bar to 80%. If other applications are running on the server, set this to a lower value.

3. Set the type of workload. See Figure 9.10.

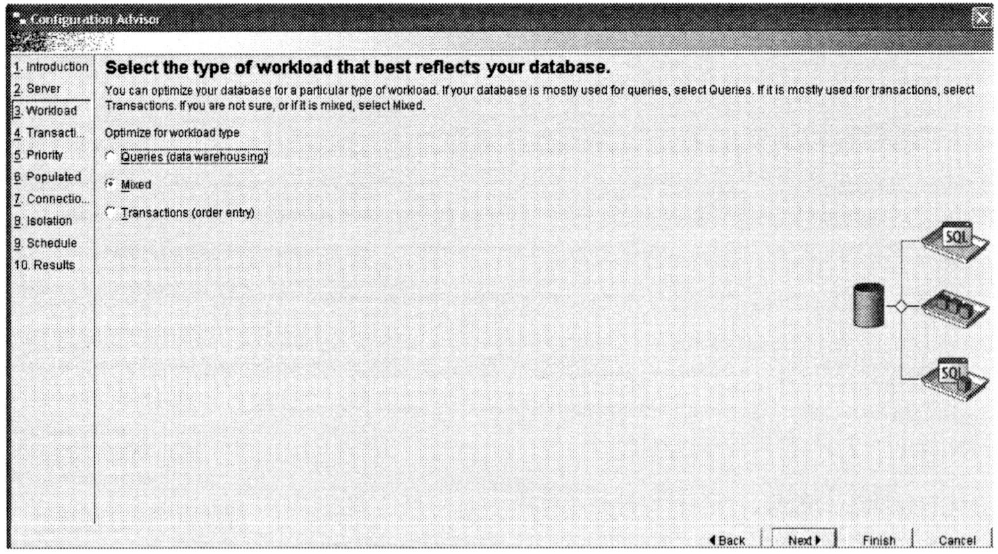

Figure 9.10
Set the type of workload.

By setting the type of workload, we are telling the Configuration Advisor to optimize DB2 memory for your particular workload. In a data warehousing environment, queries tend to run longer, use more `sortheap`, and differ in use of package cache and bufferpool efficiency. Queries in a data warehouse environment tend to be "ad-hoc" and dissimilar, which mean the package cache hit rate will usually be low and table objects too large to fit in the bufferpool, resulting in physical reads from disk for the data. However, bufferpools in this environment tend to support keeping all or part of index pages in the bufferpool, resulting in reading indexes from the bufferpool.

4. Specify a typical database transaction. See Figure 9.11.

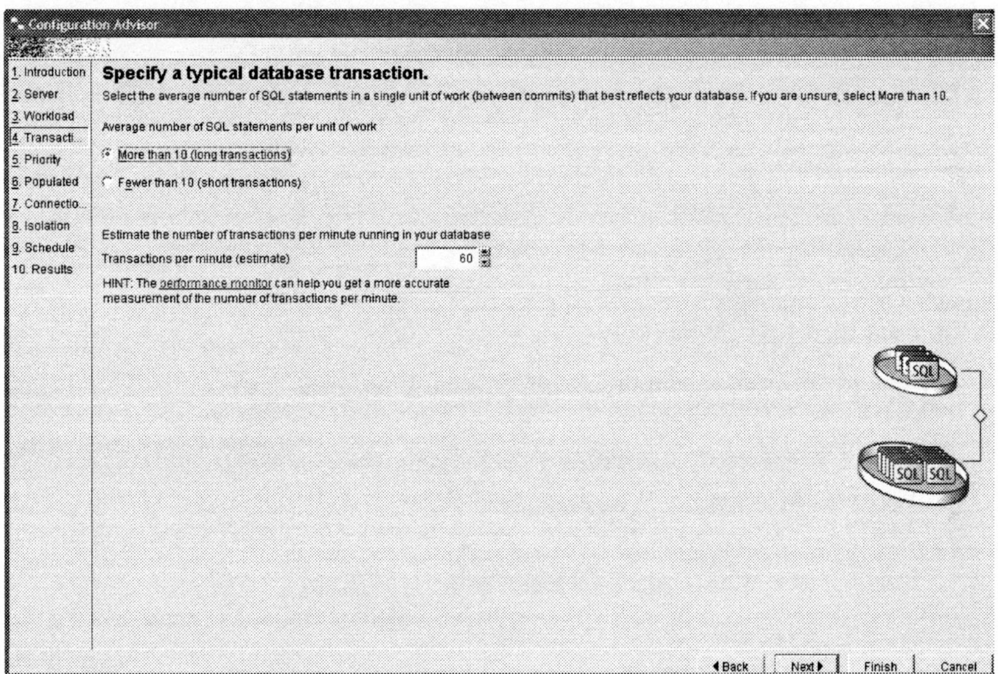

Figure 9.11
Specify a typical database transaction.

By specifying a typical database transaction number, the Configuration Advisor uses this number to calculate the size of `locklist`, `maxlocks`, and other configuration parameters.

5. Specify a database administration priority. See Figure 9.12.

By setting a database administration priority, the Configuration Advisor will determine whether or not to optimize the database configurations settings for performance or fast recovery, or both depending on the option selected. This option will calculate configuration settings such as `num_iocleaners`, `min_commit`, and other parameters that affect logging activity.

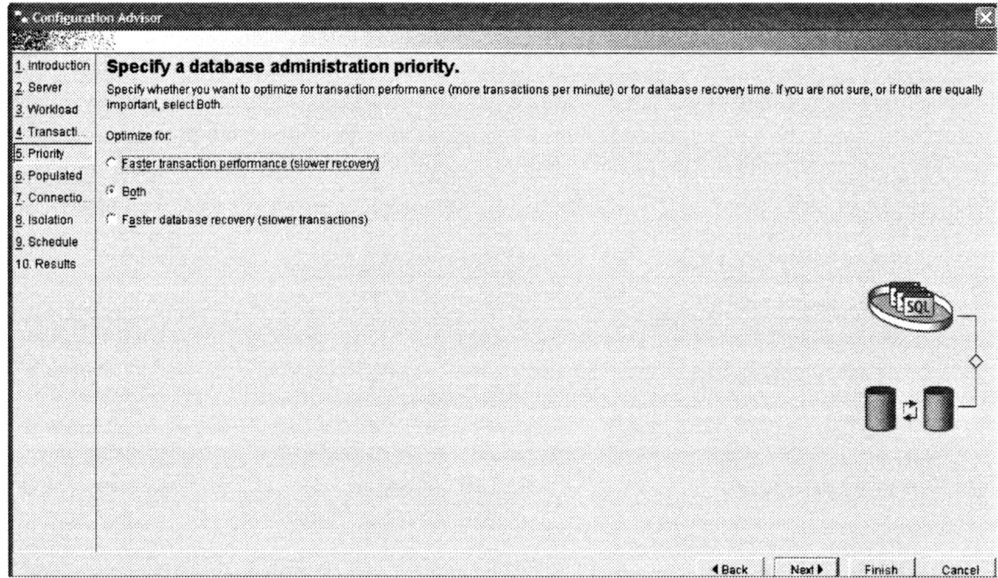

Figure 9.12
Specify a database administration priority.

6. Specify whether or not the database is populated. See Figure 9.13.

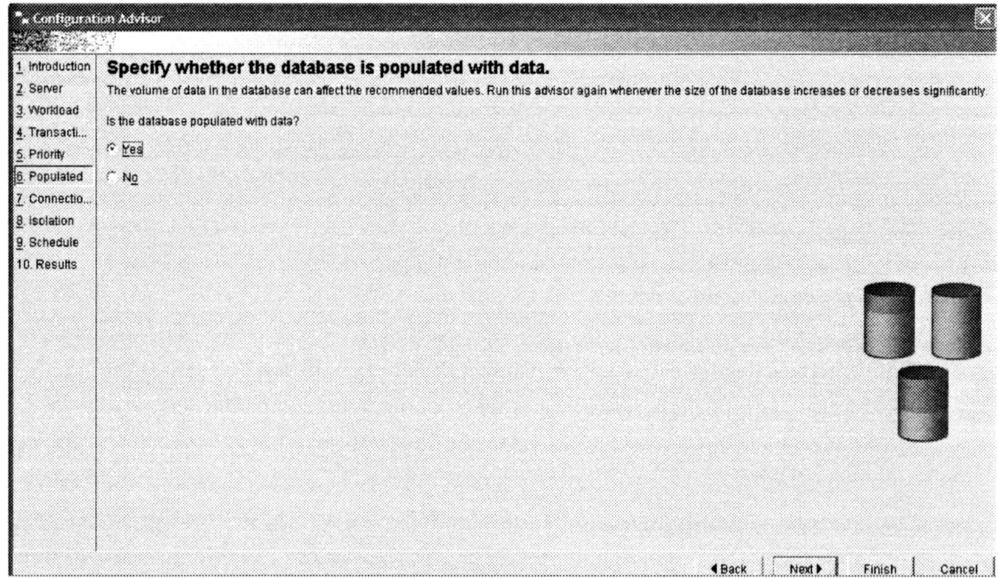

Figure 9.13
Specify whether or not the database is populated.

By specifying whether or not the database is populated, we are telling DB2 to size *bufferpools* and `num_ioservers` and other configuration parameters appropriately.

7. Estimate the number of applications connected to the database. See Figure 9.14.

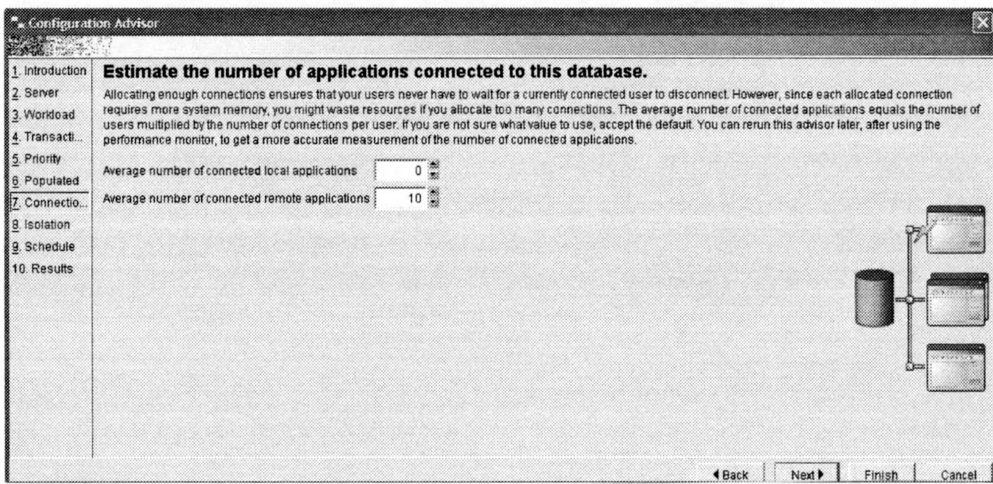

Figure 9.14
Estimate the number of connections connected to the database.

DB2 uses this information to help arrive at recommended configuration settings for `rqrioblk`, `maxappls`, `aslheapsz`, `maxagents`, and other configuration parameters.

8. Specify an isolation level. See Figure 9.15.

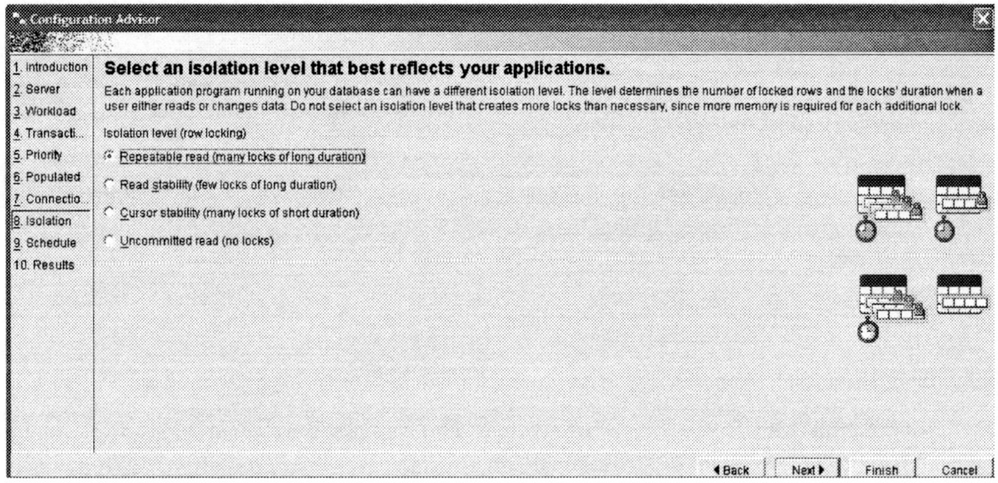

Figure 9.15
Specify the isolation level.

By specifying an isolation level, we are providing DB2 with information on how to size `locklist`, `maxlocks`, and other configuration parameters.

9. Schedule. See Figure 9.16.

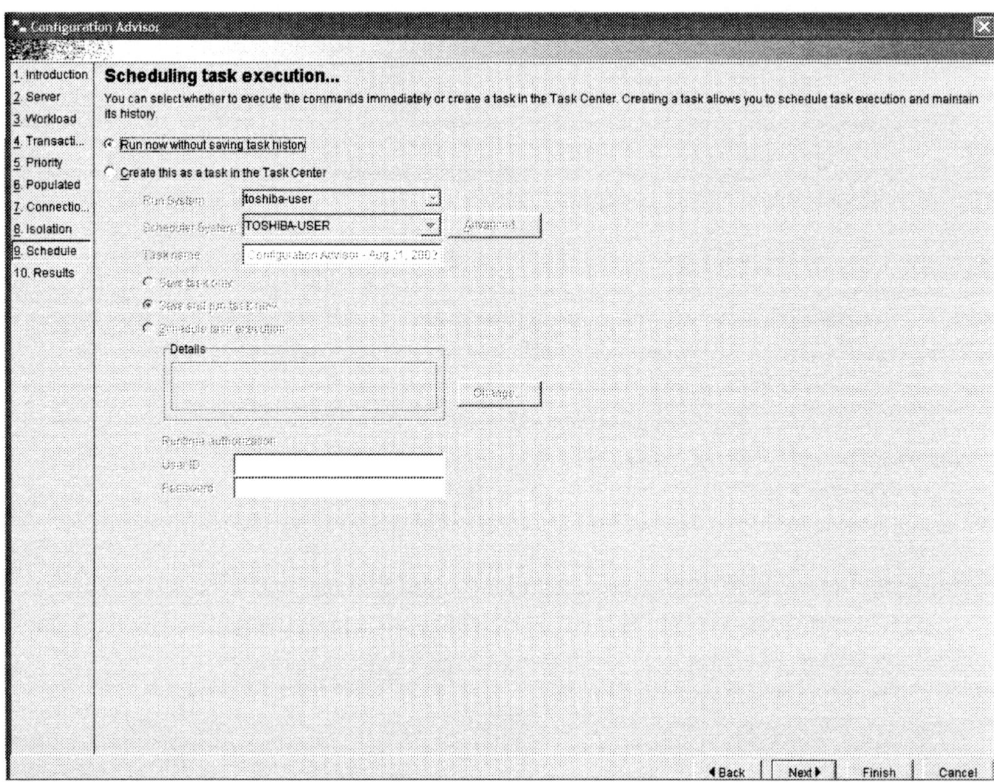

Figure 9.16
Configuration advisor scheduling.

The results of the Configuration Advisor session can be scheduled or executed immediately. Recommendations can be saved to the Task Center by checking the appropriate checkbox and run at a later date.

10. Results. See Figure 9.17.

Recommendations can be applied by selecting the Finish button.

The Configuration Advisor was formerly known as the Configure Performance Wizard in previous releases. In a recent benchmark, a comparison of a database configured by an expert and one configured by the Configuration Advisor resulted in almost equivalent database performance, so the Configuration Advisor is definitely a good starting point for configuring your database. What

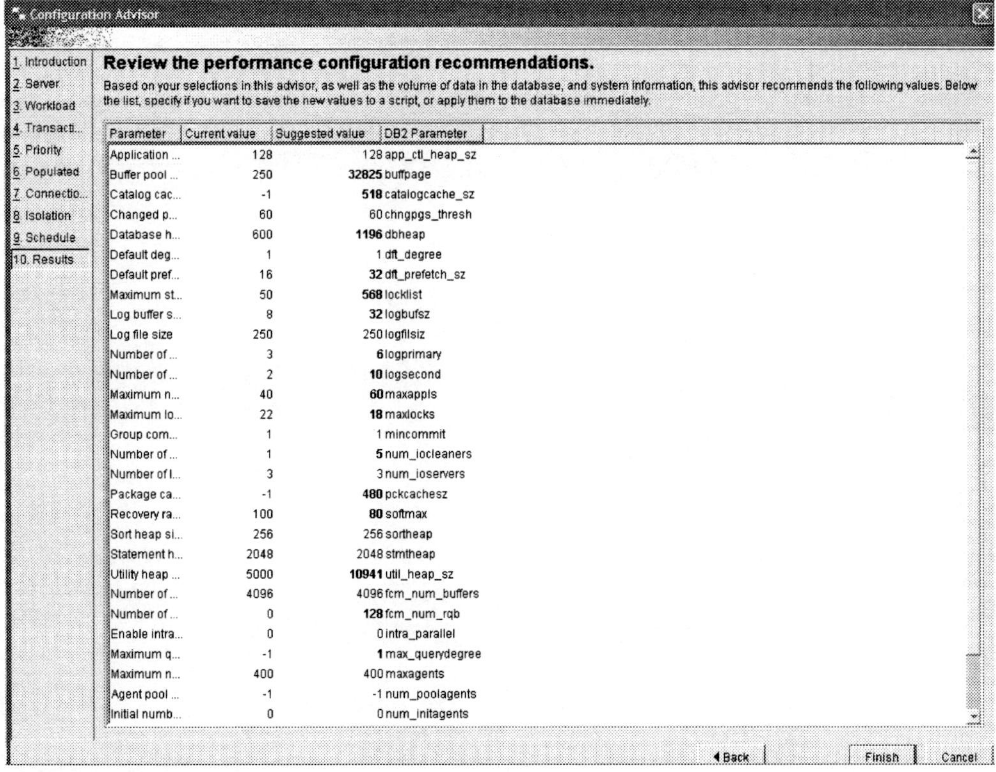

Parameter	Current value	Suggested value	DB2 Parameter
Application ...	128	128	app_ctl_heap_sz
Buffer pool ...	250	**32825**	buffpage
Catalog cac...	-1	**518**	catalogcache_sz
Changed p...	60	60	chngpgs_thresh
Database h...	600	**1196**	dbheap
Default deg...	1	1	dft_degree
Default pref...	16	**32**	dft_prefetch_sz
Maximum st...	50	**568**	locklist
Log buffer s...	8	**32**	logbufsz
Log file size	250	250	logfilsiz
Number of ...	3	**6**	logprimary
Number of ...	2	**10**	logsecond
Maximum n...	40	**60**	maxappls
Maximum lo...	22	**18**	maxlocks
Group com...	1	1	mincommit
Number of ...	1	**5**	num_iocleaners
Number of I...	3	3	num_ioservers
Package ca...	-1	**480**	pckcachesz
Recovery ra...	100	**80**	softmax
Sort heap si...	256	256	sortheap
Statement h...	2048	2048	stmtheap
Utility heap ...	5000	**10941**	util_heap_sz
Number of ...	4096	4096	fcm_num_buffers
Number of ...	0	**128**	fcm_num_rqb
Enable intra...	0	0	intra_parallel
Maximum q...	-1	**1**	max_querydegree
Maximum n...	400	400	maxagents
Agent pool ...	-1	-1	num_poolagents
Initial numb...	0	0	num_initagents

Figure 9.17
Configuration Advisor results.

it also pointed out was that the majority of default parameter values should only be used as a starting point and should not be used for production databases.

> **NOTE**
> The Configuration Advisor is not currently available for partitioned databases.

SUMMARY

In this chapter you have learned about parameters that are obsolete in v8 and about new parameters in v8 along with recommended settings. The DB2 memory model was discussed and definitions and recommendations provided for setting memory related parameters.

The new v8 capability to change configurations online was discussed and propagation classes identified. A method was discussed for identifying deferred changes. Some parameters can be set to automatic and recommendations were provided regarding these settings.

Agent parameters were discussed, and definitions and recommended settings were provided along with pertinent monitoring elements with which to determine the adequacy of agent and agent-related parameters.

And lastly, the Configuration Advisor was discussed and its capability to accurately configure DBM and DB CFG parameters, along with identifying a backup and logging strategy, was highlighted.

CHAPTER 10

Monitoring

Regardless of how well a RDBMS performs, the monitoring of SQL statements and resources is required to ensure continued good performance and to identify problem areas. Using the information gathered, adjustments can be made to instance and database configuration parameters, physical design, or SQL to improve performance. The nature of RDBMSs and their implementation, may lead to frequent occurences of events like lock escalation, low bufferpool hit ratios, disk I/O activity, and out-of-space conditions. A DBA group must have a well-established monitoring program to ensure that the database is performing to expectations and that the database will continue to meet performance expectations. This includes having DBA standards and procedures that address monitoring and outline how the DBA organization should conduct monitoring activities.

DB2 provides built-in monitoring capability through the use of snapshot monitoring and event monitoring.

ENABLING MONITORING

Before we go into the details of *snapshot monitoring*, you need to understand how to display and set *Database Manager* monitor switches. We can see the current settings of monitor switches by issuing either the `GET DBM MONITOR SWITCHES` or `GET MONITOR SWITCHES` command and reviewing the output. See Example 10.1.

The output of the `GET MONITOR SWITCHES` command shows the status of the seven monitor switches at the database level. When DB2 is installed all switches are turned off. The `dft_monswitches` DBM parameters can be changed to enable monitoring switches at the instance level. A switch that is on at this level has been turned on by a monitoring application. The date and time that the monitoring switch was enabled is also shown. Monitor switches can be turned on by a DBA with the appropriate authority by issuing the appropriate command from a command line, or through a

```
                    Monitor Recording Switches

Switch list for db partition number 0
Bufferpool Activity Information  (BUFFERPOOL)  = ON  03-17-2003
15:02:57.169849
Lock Information                       (LOCK)  = ON  03-17-2003
15:02:57.169849
Sorting Information                    (SORT)  = ON  03-17-2003
15:02:57.169849
SQL Statement Information         (STATEMENT)  = ON  03-17-2003
15:02:57.169849
Table Activity Information            (TABLE)  = ON  03-17-2003
15:02:57.169849
Take Timestamp Information        (TIMESTAMP)  = ON  03-17-2003
15:02:57.169849
Unit of Work Information                (UOW)  = ON  03-17-2003
15:02:57.169849
```

Example 10.1
Database Monitor switches.

program using the DB2 Administrative Application Programming Interface (API), or by a vendor tool. When a switch is on it indicates that the database system monitor component of DB2 is collecting data for any monitoring application. Furthermore, each person or application monitoring DB2 has its own logical view of monitor switches. While snapshot monitoring adds overhead to the database monitored, it is difficult to understand what is happening without monitoring. In most cases this overhead is acceptable. The frequency of snapshots will vary from environment to environment and you should be conscious of the effects of very frequent snapshots on the database. A reasonable snapshot frequency is 60 seconds between snapshots. Five minute frequencies are also commonly used for well-tuned databases. I have had to take snapshots every 5 seconds in a high volume OLTP environment to identify problem SQL. So the frequency will vary depending on your environment. Only use frequencies less than 60 seconds, if you must, to help solve severe performance problems.

Monitor switches can be turned on and off at the instance level or at the application level. Setting the instance configuration parameter for monitor switches affects all databases within the instance. Every application connecting to a database inherits the default switches set at the instance level. Snapshot monitor switches can be turned on and off as needed. Use the `UPDATE DBM CONFIGURATION USING DFT_ON_TABLE ON` or `UPDATE MONITOR SWITCHES USING TABLE ON` command. The `UPDATE MONITOR SWITCHES` command will only capture information for the application that activated the switch. See Table 10.1 for a complete description of Database Manager and application level monitor switches.

When a monitor switch is turned on, the monitor data starts being collected and a `GET SNAPSHOT` command can be used to collect the data. There is a minor performance degradation when

Table 10.1 Database Manager and Database Level Monitor Switches

Database Manager Switch	Monitor Switch	Information of Interest
`DFT_MON_BUFFERPOOL`	Bufferpool	Logical and physical reads, Asynchronous I/O activity, Information with which to compute hit ratios. Number of reads and writes, time taken
`DFT_MON_LOCK`	Lock	Locks held by applications, lock waits, escalations, deadlocks
`DFT_MON_SORT`	Sort	Amount of `sortheap` used, sort overflows, number of sorts, sort time
`DFT_MON_STMT`	Statement	`APPLID`, connect time, sorts, DML activity, locks held, bufferpool activity
`DFT_MON_TABLE`	Table	Read and write activity
`DFT_MON_UOW`	UOW	Completion status, start and end times.
`*DFT_MON_TIMESTAMP`	Timestamp	Timestamp for time dependent functions

* New in v8

the data is recorded and taking snapshots incur additional performance overhead, as previously discussed. It is important to note that monitor switches must be enabled before issuing a snapshot command. If the appropriate monitor switches are not enabled at either the instance or database level, no snapshot information will be returned.

There are eight snapshot levels available:

- Database Manager—Records information at the instance level
- Database—Records information at the database level
- Application—Records application information
- Bufferpools—Records bufferpool activity
- Tablespace—Records tablespace activity
- Table—Records table activity
- Lock—Records lock information for locks held by applications
- Dynamic SQL cache—Records point-in-time statement information from the SQL statement cache

> **NOTE**
> DB2 v8 introduced a new `TIMESTAMP` monitor switch. By default this switch is enabled. If timestamp information is not required, this switch can be turned off, resulting in improved database performance. This switch was introduced to reduce the number of context switches taking place. See Table 10.2 for a list of snapshot commands.

Table 10.2 Frequently Used Snapshot Commands

Snapshot Type	Command
Snapshot for locks	`db2 get snapshot for locks on sample`
Database Manager Snapshot	`db2 get snapshot for DBM`
Database Snapshot	`db2 get snapshot for database on SAMPLE`
Tablespace Snapshot	`db2 get snapshot for tablespaces on SAMPLE`
Tables	`db2 get snapshot for tables on SAMPLE`
Bufferpool Snapshot	`db2 get snapshot for bufferpools on SAMPLE`
Applications	`db2 get snapshot for applications on SAMPLE`
Dynamic SQL	`db2 get snapshot for dynamic sql on SAMPLE`

The snapshot commands in Table 10.2 are the basic snapshot monitoring commands you should know. For additional options and information refer to the *DB2 UDB v8.1 Command Reference.*

See Example 10.2 for sample output from the following command issued from the CLP:

```
db2 get snapshot for database manager
```

Database Manager Snapshot

```
                    Database Manager Snapshot
Node name                                     =
Node type                                     = Enterprise Server
                                                Edition with local
                                                and remote clients
Instance name                                 = DB2
Number of database partitions in DB2 instance = 1
Database manager status                       = Active

Product name                                  = DB2 v8.1.0.36
Service level                                 = s021023

Private Sort heap allocated                   = 0
Private Sort heap high water mark             = 277
Post threshold sorts                          = 0
Piped sorts requested                         = 9
Piped sorts accepted                          = 9

Start Database Manager timestamp              = 03-17-2003 15:02:57.169849
Last reset timestamp                          =
Snapshot timestamp                            = 03-17-2003 20:36:31.584122
```

Example 10.2
Database Manager snapshot.

```
Remote connections to db manager                    = 0
Remote connections executing in db manager          = 0
Local connections                                   = 3
Local connections executing in db manager           = 0
Active local databases                              = 2

High water mark for agents registered               = 9
High water mark for agents waiting for a token = 0
Agents registered                                   = 9
Agents waiting for a token                          = 0
Idle agents                                         = 0

Committed private Memory (Bytes)                    = 16809984

Switch list for db partition number 0
Bufferpool Activity Information  (BUFFERPOOL)  = ON  03-17-2003
                                                    15:02:57.169849
Lock Information                           (LOCK) = ON  03-17-2003
                                                    15:02:57.169849
Sorting Information                        (SORT) = ON  03-17-2003
                                                    15:02:57.169849
SQL Statement Information             (STATEMENT) = ON  03-17-2003
                                                    15:02:57.169849
Table Activity Information                (TABLE) = ON  03-17-2003
                                                    15:02:57.169849
Take Timestamp Information            (TIMESTAMP) = ON  03-17-2003
                                                    15:02:57.169849
Unit of Work Information                    (UOW) = ON  03-17-2003
                                                    15:02:57.169849

Agents assigned from pool                           = 133
Agents created from empty pool                      = 11
Agents stolen from another application              = 0
High water mark for coordinating agents             = 8
Max agents overflow                                 = 0
Hash joins after heap threshold exceeded            = 0

Total number of gateway connections                 = 0
Current number of gateway connections               = 0
Gateway connections waiting for host reply          = 0
Gateway connections waiting for client request = 0
Gateway connection pool agents stolen               = 0

Memory usage for database manager:

    Memory Pool Type                                = Backup/Restore/Util Heap
       Current size (bytes)                         = 16384
```

Example 10.2
Database Manager snapshot. (Continued)

```
      High water mark (bytes)                    = 16384
      Maximum size allowed (bytes)               = 20660224

   Memory Pool Type                              = Package Cache Heap
      Current size (bytes)                       = 327680
      High water mark (bytes)                    = 327680
      Maximum size allowed (bytes)               = 265289728

   Memory Pool Type                              = Catalog Cache Heap
      Current size (bytes)                       = 81920
      High water mark (bytes)                    = 81920
      Maximum size allowed (bytes)               = 265289728

   Memory Pool Type                              = Bufferpool Heap
      Current size (bytes)                       = 1179648
      High water mark (bytes)                    = 1179648
      Maximum size allowed (bytes)               = 265289728

   Memory Pool Type                              = Bufferpool Heap
      Current size (bytes)                       = 655360
      High water mark (bytes)                    = 655360
      Maximum size allowed (bytes)               = 265289728

   Memory Pool Type                              = Bufferpool Heap
      Current size (bytes)                       = 393216
      High water mark (bytes)                    = 393216
      Maximum size allowed (bytes)               = 265289728

   Memory Pool Type                              = Bufferpool Heap
      Current size (bytes)                       = 262144
      High water mark (bytes)                    = 262144
      Maximum size allowed (bytes)               = 265289728

   Memory Pool Type                              = Bufferpool Heap
      Current size (bytes)                       = 196608
      High water mark (bytes)                    = 196608
      Maximum size allowed (bytes)               = 265289728

   Memory Pool Type                              = Lock Manager Heap
      Current size (bytes)                       = 262144
      High water mark (bytes)                    = 262144
      Maximum size allowed (bytes)               = 442368

   Memory Pool Type                              = Database Heap
      Current size (bytes)                       = 1376256
      High water mark (bytes)                    = 1376256
      Maximum size allowed (bytes)               = 3588096
```

Example 10.2
Database Manager snapshot. (Continued)

```
Memory Pool Type                              = Backup/Restore/Util Heap
   Current size (bytes)                       = 16384
   High water mark (bytes)                    = 16384
   Maximum size allowed (bytes)               = 20660224

Memory Pool Type                              = Package Cache Heap
   Current size (bytes)                       = 327680
   High water mark (bytes)                    = 327680
   Maximum size allowed (bytes)               = 265289728

Memory Pool Type                              = Catalog Cache Heap
   Current size (bytes)                       = 163840
   High water mark (bytes)                    = 163840
   Maximum size allowed (bytes)               = 265289728

Memory Pool Type                              = Bufferpool Heap
   Current size (bytes)                       = 8339456
   High water mark (bytes)                    = 8339456
   Maximum size allowed (bytes)               = 265289728

Memory Pool Type                              = Bufferpool Heap
   Current size (bytes)                       = 1179648
   High water mark (bytes)                    = 1179648
   Maximum size allowed (bytes)               = 265289728

Memory Pool Type                              = Bufferpool Heap
   Current size (bytes)                       = 655360
   High water mark (bytes)                    = 655360
   Maximum size allowed (bytes)               = 265289728

Memory Pool Type                              = Bufferpool Heap
   Current size (bytes)                       = 393216
   High water mark (bytes)                    = 393216
   Maximum size allowed (bytes)               = 265289728

Memory Pool Type                              = Bufferpool Heap
   Current size (bytes)                       = 262144
   High water mark (bytes)                    = 262144
   Maximum size allowed (bytes)               = 265289728

Memory Pool Type                              = Bufferpool Heap
   Current size (bytes)                       = 196608
   High water mark (bytes)                    = 196608
   Maximum size allowed (bytes)               = 265289728

Memory Pool Type                              = Lock Manager Heap
   Current size (bytes)                       = 262144
```

Example 10.2
Database Manager snapshot. (Continued)

```
      High water mark (bytes)                        = 262144
      Maximum size allowed (bytes)                   = 442368

   Memory Pool Type                                  = Database Heap
      Current size (bytes)                           = 1376256
      High water mark (bytes)                        = 1376256
      Maximum size allowed (bytes)                   = 3588096

   Memory Pool Type                                  = Database Monitor Heap
      Current size (bytes)                           = 409600
      High water mark (bytes)                        = 409600
      Maximum size allowed (bytes)                   = 4259840

   Memory Pool Type                                  = Other Memory
      Current size (bytes)                           = 6127616
      High water mark (bytes)                        = 6144000
      Maximum size allowed (bytes)                   = 265289728
```

Example 10.2
Database Manager snapshot. (Continued)

NOTE
The Database Manager Snapshot output has changed significantly in v8. Heap memory areas are now separately reported for the various heaps. These are identified by the element "Memory Pool Type" followed by the heap being reported. They are illustrated in Example 10.2.

Key Database Manager snapshot elements to review and to monitor on a regular basis and tuning tips are listed in Table 10.3.

Table 10.3 Key Database Manager Snapshot Elements

Monitor Element	Tuning Tips
Post threshold sorts	If > 0 then sorts are degraded; tune SQL, reduce `sortheap`, increase `sheapthres` in that order.
Pipe sort accepted requested	If these aren't equal, piped sorts are being rejected resulting in degraded performance. Occurs when post threshold sorts are occurring.
Agents waiting for a token	Agents are waiting for token from the Database manager, increase maxcagents.
Agents stolen from another application	This should be 0. Idle agents are stolen and used to do work for another application. This creates unnecessary overhead.

Table 10.3 Key Database Manager Snapshot Elements (Continued)

Monitor Element	Tuning Tips
Maxagents overflow	Occurs when `maxagents` is reached. If it occurs frequently, increase `maxagents` along with related parameters.
Hash joins after heap threshold exceeded	Consider moderate increases in `sortheap` until none are observed.
Package cache hwm and max size allowed	Used to monitor package cache memory growth. Increase if overflows occur. Do not over-allocate. Memory better used for bufferpools if high hit ratio cannot be obtained.
Catalog cache hwm and max size allowed	Increase when hwm > 80% of max size allowed. Keep hit ratio above 90%.
Lock manager heap hwm and max size allowed	Increase `locklist` when hwm > 50% of max size allowed.
Database heap hwm and max size allowed	A soft limit. Monitor and increase as necessary.
Hwm for agents registered	Hwm of all agents (coordinating and subagents) registered. Use this element when evaluating maxagent setting.
Hwm for coordinating agents	Maximum number of coordinating agents working at one time. Tune in conjunction with `maxagents`.

Database Snapshot

```
                          Database Snapshot

Database name                                 = SAMPLE
Database path                                 = C:\DB2\NODE0000\SQL00002\
Input database alias                          = SAMPLE
Database status                               = Active
Catalog database partition number             = 0
Catalog network node name                     =
Operating system running at database server = NT
Location of the database                      = Local
First database connect timestamp              = 03-17-2003 20:29:54.280691
Last reset timestamp                          =
Last backup timestamp                         = 03-05-2003 15:02:46.982272
Snapshot timestamp                            = 03-17-2003 20:36:09.196630
```

Example 10.3
Database snapshot.

```
High water mark for connections              = 3
Application connects                         = 3
Secondary connects total                     = 1
Applications connected currently             = 2
Appls. executing in db manager currently     = 0
Agents associated with applications          = 1
Maximum agents associated with applications = 3
Maximum coordinating agents                  = 3

Locks held currently                         = 6
Lock waits                                   = 0
Time database waited on locks (ms)           = 0
Lock list memory in use (Bytes)              = 1008
Deadlocks detected                           = 0
Lock escalations                             = 0
Exclusive lock escalations                   = 0
Agents currently waiting on locks            = 0
Lock Timeouts                                = 0

Total Private Sort heap allocated            = 0
Total Shared Sort heap allocated             = 0
Shared Sort heap high water mark             = 0
Total sorts                                  = 0
Total sort time (ms)                         = 0
Sort overflows                               = 0
Active sorts                                 = 0

Bufferpool data logical reads                = 38
Bufferpool data physical reads               = 11
Asynchronous pool data page reads            = 0
Bufferpool data writes                       = 0
Asynchronous pool data page writes           = 0
Bufferpool index logical reads               = 55
Bufferpool index physical reads              = 28
Asynchronous pool index page reads           = 0
Bufferpool index writes                      = 0
Asynchronous pool index page writes          = 0
Total bufferpool read time (ms)              = 295
Total bufferpool write time (ms)             = 0
Total elapsed asynchronous read time         = 0
Total elapsed asynchronous write time        = 0
Asynchronous read requests                   = 0
LSN Gap cleaner triggers                     = 0
Dirty page steal cleaner triggers            = 0
Dirty page threshold cleaner triggers        = 0
Time waited for prefetch (ms)                = 0
Unread prefetch pages                        = 0
```

Example 10.3
Database snapshot. (Continued)

```
Direct reads                                   = 40
Direct writes                                  = 0
Direct read requests                           = 6
Direct write requests                          = 0
Direct reads elapsed time (ms)                 = 63
Direct write elapsed time (ms)                 = 0
Database files closed                          = 0
Data pages copied to extended storage          = 0
Index pages copied to extended storage         = 0
Data pages copied from extended storage        = 0
Index pages copied from extended storage       = 0

Host execution elapsed time                    = 0.000154

Commit statements attempted                    = 0
Rollback statements attempted                  = 2
Dynamic statements attempted                   = 2
Static statements attempted                    = 2
Failed statement operations                    = 1
Select SQL statements executed                 = 0
Update/Insert/Delete statements executed       = 0
DDL statements executed                        = 0

Internal automatic rebinds                     = 0
Internal rows deleted                          = 0
Internal rows inserted                         = 0
Internal rows updated                          = 0
Internal commits                               = 3
Internal rollbacks                             = 0
Internal rollbacks due to deadlock             = 0

Rows deleted                                   = 0
Rows inserted                                  = 0
Rows updated                                   = 0
Rows selected                                  = 0
Rows read                                      = 18
Binds/precompiles attempted                    = 0

Log space available to the database (Bytes)   = 5100000
Log space used by the database (Bytes)         = 0
Maximum secondary log space used (Bytes)       = 0
Maximum total log space used (Bytes)           = 8351
Secondary logs allocated currently             = 0
Log pages read                                 = 0
Log pages written                              = 3

Package cache lookups                          = 2
```

Example 10.3
Database snapshot. (Continued)

```
Package cache inserts                          = 0
Package cache overflows                        = 0
Package cache high water mark (Bytes)          = 165384
Application section lookups                    = 2
Application section inserts                    = 0

Catalog cache lookups                          = 6
Catalog cache inserts                          = 2
Catalog cache overflows                        = 0
Catalog cache high water mark                  = 0

Workspace Information

 Shared high water mark                        = 0
 Corresponding shared overflows                = 0
 Total shared section inserts                  = 0
 Total shared section lookups                  = 0
 Private high water mark                       = 0
 Corresponding private overflows               = 0
 Total private section inserts                 = 0
 Total private section lookups                 = 0

Number of hash joins                           = 0
Number of hash loops                           = 0
Number of hash join overflows                  = 0
Number of small hash join overflows            = 0
```

Example 10.3
Database snapshot. (Continued)

Key Database snapshot elements to review, monitor, and track on a regular basis along with tuning tips are listed in Table 10.4.

Table 10.4 Key Database Snapshot Elements

Monitoring Element	Tuning Tips
Lock waits	The total time an application waited for locks. Use with time database waited on locks to compute average time waiting for a lock. This should be < 10 ms. Look for application sequencing problems, packages bound with RR, and lock escalations to X table locks. Get snapshot on application and locks and find all locks associated with application holding the most locks.
Time database waited on locks	The total amount of elapsed time that applications were waiting for locks. Use last reset time and compute average time applications waited for locks. If lock wait and this parameter are high, you have concurrency issues.

Table 10.4 Key Database Snapshot Elements (Continued)

Monitoring Element	Tuning Tips
Deadlocks detected	Monitor and find application sequencing problems if deadlocks occur frequently.
Lock escalations	Not necessarily a problem but if occurs constantly, investigate application problems, review size of `locklist` and `maxlocks`.
Lock timeouts	Set `locktimeout` to 10–30 seconds and monitor. If too many lock timeouts occur, review applications running during this time, review reasons they are timing out and correct application problem, then and only then consider increasing `locktimeout`.
Sort Overflows	Sort overflows should be < 3% in OLTP. This is difficult to achieve in DW/BI environments. Eliminate sorts through proper indexing and clustering. Since we can't eliminate sorts in DW/BI environments, then tune temporary tablespace container placement and create multiple containers on separate disks to maximize opportunity for parallel I/O.
Bufferpool data physical reads	In OLTP seek to minimize. In DW/BI, sort overflow tuning I/O tip should be used.
Bufferpool data writes	Bufferpool data writes occur to free a page in the bufferpool so another page can be read, and to flush the bufferpool. Consider increasing the size of the bufferpool if bufferpool data writes is high in proportion to asynchronous page writes.
Bufferpool index physical reads	Same as bufferpool data physical reads.
Dirty page cleaner triggers	Consider increasing size of bufferpool and number of I/O cleaners. Consider decreasing `chngpgs_thres` if you cannot increase size of bufferpool.
Dirty page threshold cleaner triggers	Indicates number of times `chngpgs_thres` has been reached and dirty pages written asynchronously to disk. Start with the default and decrease to 40% in OLTP environment.
Database files closed	Try to keep this at 0. Unnecessary closing and opening of files incurs unneeded overhead.
Failed statement operations	Can be an indicator of application problems. Investigate with application staff and resolve. Not necessarily a problem but if high frequency is a possible indicator of locking, application, or other problems.
Package cache overflows	Package cache overflows to utility heap, `locklist`, and other `dbheap` memory. Increase package cache until no overflows occur, but do not over allocate.

Table 10.4 Key Database Snapshot Elements (Continued)

Monitoring Element	Tuning Tips
Catalog cache overflows	Catalog cache overflows cause table descriptors, etc. to be flushed as needed resulting in I/O if descriptors need to be brought back in. Set `catalogcache_sz` so that at least 90% hit ratios are observed.
Number of hash join overflows	Hash joins overflow from `sortheap` through bufferpool to temporary space. Increase `sortheap` and eliminate unnecessary sorts via elimination and through clustering techniques described in Chapter 12.

Application Snapshot

```
                         Application Snapshot

Application handle                            = 156
Application status                            = Connect Completed
Status change time                            = 03-17-2003 20:56:52.943184
Application code page                         = 1208
Application country/region code               = 0
DUOW correlation token                        = *LOCAL.DB2.00CD48015655
Application name                              = javaw.exe
Application ID                                = *LOCAL.DB2.00CD48015655
Sequence number                               = 0001
TP Monitor client user ID                     =
TP Monitor client workstation name            =
TP Monitor client application name            =
TP Monitor client accounting string           =

Connection request start timestamp            = 03-17-2003 20:56:52.940767
Connect request completion timestamp          = 03-17-2003 20:56:52.943182
Application idle time                         = 0
Authorization ID                              = PGUNNING
Client login ID                               = PGUNNING
Configuration NNAME of client                 =
Client database manager product ID            = SQL08010
Process ID of client application              = 1588
Platform of client application                = NT
Communication protocol of client              = Local Client

Inbound communication address                 = *LOCAL.DB2
```

Example 10.4
Application snapshot.

```
Database name                               = SAMPLE
Database path                               = C:\DB2\NODE0000\SQL00002\
Client database alias                       = SAMPLE
Input database alias                        = SAMPLE
Last reset timestamp                        =
Snapshot timestamp                          = 03-17-2003 20:58:27.133782
The highest authority level granted         =
        Direct DBADM authority
        Direct CREATETAB authority
        Direct BINDADD authority
        Direct CONNECT authority
        Direct CREATE_NOT_FENC authority
        Direct LOAD authority
        Direct IMPLICIT_SCHEMA authority
        Indirect SYSADM authority
        Indirect CREATETAB authority
        Indirect BINDADD authority
        Indirect CONNECT authority
        Indirect IMPLICIT_SCHEMA authority
Coordinating database partition number      = 0
Current database partition number           = 0
Coordinator agent process or thread ID      = 1680
Agents stolen                               = 0
Agents waiting on locks                     = 0
Maximum associated agents                   = 1
Priority at which application agents work   = 0
Priority type                               = Dynamic

Locks held by application                   = 0
Lock waits since connect                    = 0
Time application waited on locks (ms)       = 0
Deadlocks detected                          = 0
Lock escalations                            = 0
Exclusive lock escalations                  = 0
Number of Lock Timeouts since connected     = 0
Total time UOW waited on locks (ms)         = 0

Total sorts                                 = 0
Total sort time (ms)                        = 0
Total sort overflows                        = 0

Data pages copied to extended storage       = 0
Index pages copied to extended storage      = 0
Data pages copied from extended storage     = 0
Index pages copied from extended storage    = 0
Bufferpool data logical reads               = 0
```

Example 10.4
Application snapshot. (Continued)

```
Bufferpool data physical reads                = 0
Bufferpool data writes                        = 0
Bufferpool index logical reads                = 0
Bufferpool index physical reads               = 0
Bufferpool index writes                       = 0
Total bufferpool read time (ms)               = 0
Total bufferpool write time (ms)              = 0
Time waited for prefetch (ms)                 = 0
Unread prefetch pages                         = 0
Direct reads                                  = 0
Direct writes                                 = 0
Direct read requests                          = 0
Direct write requests                         = 0
Direct reads elapsed time (ms)                = 0
Direct write elapsed time (ms)                = 0

Number of SQL requests since last commit      = 0
Commit statements                             = 0
Rollback statements                           = 0
Dynamic SQL statements attempted              = 0
Static SQL statements attempted               = 0
Failed statement operations                   = 0
Select SQL statements executed                = 0
Update/Insert/Delete statements executed      = 0
DDL statements executed                       = 0
Internal automatic rebinds                    = 0
Internal rows deleted                         = 0
Internal rows inserted                        = 0
Internal rows updated                         = 0
Internal commits                              = 1
Internal rollbacks                            = 0
Internal rollbacks due to deadlock            = 0
Binds/precompiles attempted                   = 0
Rows deleted                                  = 0
Rows inserted                                 = 0
Rows updated                                  = 0
Rows selected                                 = 0
Rows read                                     = 0
Rows written                                  = 0

UOW log space used (Bytes)                    = 0
Previous UOW completion timestamp             = 03-17-2003 20:56:52.943182
Elapsed time of last completed uow (sec.ms)= 0.000000
UOW start timestamp                           = 03-17-2003 20:56:52.943182
UOW stop timestamp                            = 03-17-2003 20:56:52.943182
UOW completion status                         =
```

Example 10.4
Application snapshot. (Continued)

```
Open remote cursors                          = 0
Open remote cursors with blocking            = 0
Rejected Block Remote Cursor requests        = 0
Accepted Block Remote Cursor requests        = 0
Open local cursors                           = 0
Open local cursors with blocking             = 0
Total User CPU Time used by agent (s)        = 0.000000
Total System CPU Time used by agent (s)      = 0.000000
Host execution elapsed time                  = 0.000000

Package cache lookups                        = 0
Package cache inserts                        = 0
Application section lookups                  = 0
Application section inserts                  = 0
Catalog cache lookups                        = 2
Catalog cache inserts                        = 0
Catalog cache overflows                      = 0
Catalog cache high water mark                = 0

Workspace Information

 Shared high water mark                      = 0
 Total shared overflows                      = 0
 Total shared section inserts                = 0
 Total shared section lookups                = 0
 Private high water mark                     = 0
 Total private overflows                     = 0
 Total private section inserts               = 0
 Total private section lookups               = 0

Most recent operation                        = None
Most recent operation start timestamp        =
Most recent operation stop timestamp         =
Agents associated with the application       = 1
Number of hash joins                         = 0
Number of hash loops                         = 0
Number of hash join overflows                = 0
Number of small hash join overflows          = 0
Statement type                               =
Statement                                    = Unknown
Section number                               = 0
Application creator                          =
Package name                                 =
Consistency Token                            =
Cursor name                                  =
Statement database partition number          = 0
```

Example 10.4
Application snapshot. (Continued)

```
Statement start timestamp                     =
Statement stop timestamp                      =
Elapsed time of last completed stmt(sec.ms)= 0.000000
Total user CPU time                           = 0.000000
Total system CPU time                         = 0.000000
SQL compiler cost estimate in timerons        = 0
SQL compiler cardinality estimate             = 0
Degree of parallelism requested               = 0
Number of agents working on statement         = 0
Number of subagents created for statement     = 0
Statement sorts                               = 0
Total sort time                               = 0
Sort overflows                                = 0
Rows read                                     = 0
Rows written                                  = 0
Rows deleted                                  = 0
Rows updated                                  = 0
Rows inserted                                 = 0
Rows fetched                                  = 0
Blocking cursor                               = NO

Memory usage for application:

  Agent process/thread ID                     = 1680
    Memory Pool Type                          = Application Heap
       Current size (bytes)                   = 65536
       High water mark (bytes)                = 65536
       Maximum size allowed (bytes)           = 1277952

  Agent process/thread ID                     = 1680
    Memory Pool Type                          = Application Control Heap
       Current size (bytes)                   = 16384
       High water mark (bytes)                = 16384
       Maximum size allowed (bytes)           = 2277376
```

Example 10.4
Application snapshot. (Continued)

Use application snapshots (Example 10.4) to monitor details of application activity. This snapshot enables you to identify applications consuming large amounts of CPU and memory. Locking, bufferpool, and agent activity are provided for each active application. This information can be used in conjunction with the `LIST APPLICATION SHOW DETAILS` command.

Dynamic SQL Snapshot

```
                        Dynamic SQL Snapshot Result

Database name                          = SAMPLE

Database path                          = C:\DB2\NODE0000\SQL00002\

Number of executions                   = 23
 Number of compilations                = 1
 Worst preparation time (ms)           = 8
 Best preparation time (ms)            = 8
 Internal rows deleted                 = 0
 Internal rows inserted                = 0
 Rows read                             = 2783
 Internal rows updated                 = 0
 Rows written                          = 0
 Statement sorts                       = 138
 Total execution time (sec.ms)         = 0.052168
 Total user cpu time (sec.ms)          = 0.030000
 Total system cpu time (sec.ms)        = 0.000000
 Statement text                        = SELECT ACCT_NAME, ACCT_ID,
                                         ACCT_AGENT_TYPE, ACCT_AGENT_ID,
                                         AGENT_NAME, CNT_EDIT, TP_EDIT,
                                         ACCT_STATUS_NUM, ACCT_STATUS,
                                         MINOR_ERRORS, T_ACCT.DATE_CREATED
                                         FROM T_ACCT LEFT OUTER JOIN T_AGENT
                                         ON T_ACCT.ACCT_AGENT_ID =
                                         T_AGENT.AGENT_ID  WHERE USER_ID
                                         <> 99999 AND  ACCT_AGENT_ID IN
                                         ('072303','072303001','072303002',
                                         '072303101') AND  PERIOD_ID  = 55
                                         AND  IS_CURRENT_VERSION = 'Y'
                                         ORDER BY ACCT_NAME
```

Example 10.5
Dynamic SQL snapshot

Dynamic SQL snapshots (Example 10.5) add overhead to the database manager and should be used only as needed. Output should be written to a file for detailed analysis. I have used Dynamic SQL snapshots to identify and tune rogue SQL. Review `Rows Read`, `Rows Written`, `Statement sorts`, `execution` and `cpu` times, `Number of compilations`, and of course the SQL statement for indications of abnormal activity and take action as necessary.

Resetting Monitor Switches

An application can reset monitor switches, which in effect resets the counters to 0 for the application issuing the reset command. Note: An application in this respect could be the CLP, Command Center, Third Party Vendor Tool, or a user-written application. This can be accomplished by an application issuing the `RESET MONITOR FOR DATABASE <database name>` command. The `GET MONITOR SWITCH` command can be used to display the current status of monitoring switches. The `RESET MONITOR ALL` command can be used to reset the monitor switches for all databases in an instance.

> **NOTE**
> Every application has its own copy of the snapshot monitor values. Resetting the monitor switches only affects the counters of the application that issues the reset.

SNAPSHOTS THROUGH NEW SQL FUNCTIONS

New in v8 is the ability to issue snapshot commands via SQL functions. These 20 new functions make it easy for you to write programs or scripts that issue snapshot commands and process the snapshot data. They can also be issued via the CLP. Previously this was only available via the administrative API. These new functions also provide you with the opportunity to store snapshot data in tables for historical performance analysis and reporting. Table 10.5 contains a list of the new functions and a description of data returned.

Table 10.5 Functions and Description of Data Returned

Function	Definition of Output Data
SNAPSHOT_AGENT	Application information associated with agents
SNAPSHOT_APPL_INFO	General application level identification for each application connected to the database
SNAPSHOT_APPL	Application information. Counters, status information and most recent SQL statement (statement monitor switch must be on)
SNAPSHOT_BP	Physical and logical reads, asynchronous and synchronous writes, counters
SNAPSHOT_CONTAINER	Tablespace container information
SNAPSHOT_DATABASE	Database information, counters, sorts, lock escalations, memory heaps
SNAPSHOT_DBM	Database Manager information, sort overflows, `dbheap`, `locklist` heap, other memory heaps
SNAPSHOT_FCM	Database manager level information regarding FCM resources
SNAPSHOT_DYN_SQL	Dynamic SQL from SQL statement cache

Table 10.5 Functions and Description of Data Returned (Continued)

Function	Definition of Output Data
SNAPSHOT_FCMNODE	Database manager information regarding FCM for a particular partition
SNAPSHOT_LOCK	Information at the database level and application level for each application connected to the database
SNAPSHOT_LOCKWAIT	Lock wait information for applications
SNAPSHOT_STATEMENT	Application and statement information including most recent SQL statement executed
SNAPSHOT_SUBSECT	Application information regarding the subsections of access plans for the applications connected to the database
SNAPSHOT_TABLE	Table activity information at the database and application level for each application connected to the database. Table activity information at the table level for each table that was accessed by an application connected to the database
SNAPSHOT_TBS	Information about tablespace activity at the database level, the application level for each application connected to the database, and the tablespace level for each tablespace that has been accessed by an application connected to the database
SNAPSHOT_SWITCHES	Database manager monitor switch settings
SNAPSHOT_QUIESCER	Information about quiescers at the tablespace level
SNAPSHOT_ RANGES	Information about ranges for a tablespace map
SNAPSHOT_TBS_CFG	Information about tablespace configuration

Working with SQL Snapshot Functions

SQL snapshot functions provide you with another way to monitor DB2 and to be able to store the snapshot data in DB2 tables. Again, this gives you the capability to save historical data so that you can use this data to identify performance problems over time. You can write customized SQL and produce reports for your items of interest.

An SQL snapshot function is issued as follows:

```
SELECT TABLESPACE_ID, BUFFERPOOL_ID
FROM TABLE (SNAPSHOT_TBS_CFG('GUNNDB', -1) as PGUN;
```

After issuing the above command from a command line, the data from the snapshot function is returned to the screen; if using an application, it is returned to the application. The SQL snapshot functions are user defined functions (UDFs) stored in the SYSIBM. SYSROUTINEPARMS catalog table (SYSCAT.ROUTINEPARMS view).

You can query the snapshot UDF definitions in the SYSCAT.ROUTINEPARMS catalog table. The UDF name begins with SNAPSHOT followed by the function name. For example, the bufferpool snapshot function is defined as SNAPSHOT_BP. By reviewing the parameters for this function, you can obtain the column name and data types to use in creating a table with which to store the associated snapshot data. Table 10.6 contains an example of column definitions and data types that can be used to store SNAPSHOT_BP function output.

Table 10.6 BP_SNAP Sample Table Layout for Storing Snapshot Data

Column	Data Type
SNAPSHOT_TIMESTAMP	TIMESTAMP
POOL_DATA_L_READS	BIGINT
POOL_DATA_P_READS	BIGINT
POOL_DATA_WRITES	BIGINT
POOL_INDEX_L_READS	BIGINT
POOL_INDEX_P_READS	BIGINT
POOL_INDEX_WRITES	BIGINT
POOL_READ_TIME	BIGINT
POOL_WRITE_TIME	BIGINT
POOL_ASYNC_DATA_RD	BIGINT
POOL_ASYNC_DT_WRT	BIGINT
POOL_ASYNC_IX_WRT	BIGINT
POOL_ASYNC_READ_TM	BIGINT
POOL_ASYNC_WR_TIME	BIGINT
POOL_ASYNC_DT_RDRQ	BIGINT
DIRECT_READS	BIGINT
DIRECT_WRITES	BIGINT
DIRECT_READ_REQS	BIGINT
DIRECT_WRITE_REQS	BIGINT
DIRECT_READ_TIME	BIGINT
DIRECT_WRITE_TIME	BIGINT
POOL_ASYNC_IX_RDS	BIGINT
POOL_DATA_ESTORE	BIGINT
POOL_INDEX_ESTORE	BIGINT

Table 10.6 `BP_SNAP` Sample Table Layout for Storing Snapshot Data (Continued)

Column	Data Type
POOL_INDEX_ESTORE	BIGINT
POOL_DATA_ESTORE	BIGINT
UNREAD_PREF_PGS	BIGINT
FILES_CLOSED	BIGINT
BP_NAME	CHAR (18)
DB_NAME	CHAR (8)
DB_PATH	VARCHAR (255)
INPUT_DB_ALIAS	CHAR (8)

After you create the table for storing the snapshot, you have to enable the correct monitor switches and then you can issue an SQL snapshot function and insert the output right into the associated table. In our case, the BP_SNAP table (Table 10.6).

By issuing the following statement, you take a snapshot and insert the results into the associated table as follows:

```
INSERT INTO BP_SNAP
Select * from TABLE(SNAPSHOT_BP('GUNNDB', -1)) as PGUN;
```

All the other snapshot tables can be created using the procedures outlined. You can then develop an historical repository which you can use to analyze performance and identify trends over time. You can also analyze this data through user-written queries and use the information to solve performance problems.

For additional information on SQL Snapshot Functions, Refer to the *DB2 UDB v8.1 SQL Reference, Volume 2,* and the *DB2 UDB v8.1 System Monitor Guide and Reference.*

Event Monitoring

As discussed, snapshot monitoring shows us performance data at a point in time. With snapshots, we may or may not capture the information of interest depending on the time we take the snapshot; whether or not the event we are trying to capture is running or has completed; and the frequency of the snapshot taken. Many times snapshot data gives you enough data to identify a suspected problem and then an event monitor is required to capture the complete picture. Hence event monitors should be used when snapshot data is inconclusive and further data capture is required.

> **NOTE**
> New in v8, event monitors can write output directly to event monitor tables. Event monitor tables are created when the Event monitor is created, or you can use the `DB2EVTBL` tool to create and customize event monitor output and tables.

Event monitors capture and record data as events complete. DB2 provides eight types of event monitors. They are:

- Database
- Tables
- Deadlocks
- Tablespaces
- Bufferpools
- Connections
- Statements
- Transactions

Database Events

Database event monitors record an event record when the last application disconnects from the database.

> **NOTE**
> Event monitors can be customized to capture events based on `APPL_ID`, `AUTH_ID`, and `APPL_NAME` event conditions.

Table Events

Table event monitors record an event record for each active table when the last application disconnects from the database. An active table is a table that has changed since the first connection to the database.

Deadlock Events

Deadlock event monitors record an event record for each deadlock event. When the `WITH DETAILS` option is used, the event monitor will generate a more complete deadlock connection event for each application involved. Additional details include:

- The statement text from the application that was executing when the deadlock occurred.

- The locks held by the application when the deadlock occurred. In a partitioned database environment, the locks are only included for the database partition where the application was waiting for its lock when the deadlock occurred.

> **NOTE**
> In v8, DB2 provides more details for help in resolving deadlock situations. Additional information provided is statement text from the application involved in the deadlock, connection event information for the connections involved, and more detail on locks held.

> **TIP**
> When using the `WITH DETAILS` option of the `DEADLOCK` event monitor, additional overhead is incurred by the Database Manager. Do not use this option unless specifically troubleshooting deadlock problems. Turn the event monitor off when no longer needed.

Tablespace Events

Records an event record for each active tablespace when the last application disconnects from the database.

Bufferpools Events

Bufferpool event monitor records an event record for bufferpools when the last application disconnects from the database.

Connection Events

Connection event monitors record an event record for each database connection event when an application disconnects for the database.

Statement Events

Statement event monitors record an event for every SQL statement issued by an application (for both dynamic and static SQL).

Transactions Events

Transaction event monitors record an event record for every transaction when it completes (indicated by a `COMMIT` or `ROLLBACK` statement).

Event Monitor Creation

Event monitors are created via the CLP or Control Center as a database event object. Event monitor can write event records to pipes, files, or tables. The type of output mechanism is indicated in the Create Event monitor SQL statement. Use the following criteria to determine what type of output mechanism you should use:

- Transaction volume
- Planned use for the event data
- Throughput required
- CPU capacity
- Disk storage available
- Use of third-party vendor tools

To create an event monitor, you must have either DBADM or SYSADM authority.

The following command can be used to create a connection event monitor that uses default values and writes-to tables:

```
CREATE EVENT MONITOR PGUNN
  FOR CONNECTIONS
  WRITE TO TABLE
```

> **NOTE**
> Event monitors are started and stopped by setting the STATE to 1 or 0, respectively.
> ```
> SET EVENT MONITOR <event monitor name> STATE = 1
> SET EVENT MONITOR PGUN2 STATE = 0
> ```

CREATE EVENT MONITOR OPTIONS

Options can be specified on the CREATE EVENT MONITOR statement to control the amount of information collected, to determine how the event monitor stops and starts, to specify the location and size of output files or pipes, types and size of buffers, and scope of the event monitor (local or global).

We have already discussed the various types of event monitors that can be created. We will now focus on major event monitor options and associated details.

WHERE *event condition*

WHERE *event condition* is used to specify one of three possible event conditions as follows:

> **APPL_ID**—Specifies that the application ID of each connection should be compared with the *comparison-string* in order to determine if the connection should generate CONNECTION, STATEMENT, or TRANSACTION events, if specified.

This option can also be used for specific AUTH_IDs or APPL_NAMES. The *comparison-string* is a character string that is compared with the APPL_ID, AUTH_ID, or APPL_NAME of each application that connects to the database. If the specific event condition is met, event data is captured.

WRITE TO

WRITE TO identifies the target output mechanism that will hold the event monitor data. An event monitor can write to a table, pipe, or file. I will briefly describe how DB2 event monitors write to files and pipes, and then go into much more detail using DB2 event monitors that write to the new event monitor WRITE TO TABLE capability in DB2 v8. When writing event monitors to a PIPE, the event monitor writes the data to the pipe in a single stream, as if it were a single, infinitely long file. When writing data to a pipe, an event monitor does not perform blocked writes. This is important because if there is no room in the pipe buffer, the event monitor will discard the data. The monitoring application using the pipe must read the data without delay to ensure no loss of data.

> **NOTE**
> It is uncommon for DBAs to use pipes for event monitors. This is because an application is required to read the data from a pipe; and the application must be started in advance of writing data to a pipe. However, it is common for ISV tools to use pipes, as they provide an application as part of the tool to read the pipe and process the data.

Using a pipe is very efficient and incurs the lowest amount of overhead on the database. However, as indicated, an application is required to read and process the data.

When writing event monitor data to a file (or set of files), the event data streams to files, which follow the following naming convention:

00000000.evt, 00000001.evt, 00000002.evt ... nnnnnnn.evt

unless limited by the MAXFILES option.

Even though multiple files may be used, the data is treated as one logical file.

TABLE OPTIONS

Table options are used to specify what logical data group data elements are written to event monitor tables. If not specified, all data elements are written. The evmGroupInfo and evmGroup options can be used to customize and limit the amount of data written to target tables.

NOTE

Event monitors separate the data stream into one or more logical data groups and insert each group into a separate table. Data or groups having a target table are kept, whereas data is discarded for groups without tables. Each monitor element is mapped to a table column with the same name. Elements without corresponding table columns are discarded.

Event Monitor Scope

An event monitor can have one of two scopes, depending on the database configuration used. The following are valid scopes.

Global

A global event monitor reports on all database partitions. As of DB2 v8, only event monitors defined on `DEADLOCKS` and `DEADLOCKS WITH DETAILS` can be defined as `GLOBAL`.

Local

A local event monitor reports only on the database partition that is running. Thus, it only gives you information on that particular partition.

Event Monitor Catalog Tables

Once an event monitor is created, information is stored in the following SYSCAT views:

- `SYSCAT.EVENT MONITORS`—Records event monitor definition
- `SYSCAT.EVENT`—Records event monitor events
- `SYSCAT.EVENTTABLES`—Records the names of the event monitor target tables when the `WRITE TO TABLE` option is used

You can query these tables to check on the status of an event monitor or to get event monitor definition data.

Write-to-Table Event Monitors

As indicated previously, write-to-table event monitors are new in v8. The power of this capability is the ability of DB2 to capture and store event monitor data in a 24 × 7 × 365 environment. You can then use this data to conduct performance analysis and retain this data for historical and trending purposes. You can also create event monitors to run during off-hours in an unattended mode. This can be done via a user written script and the data can be analyzed the next day. This fills a void that has existed in DB2 until v8. When a write-to-table event monitor is created, by default the following 13 event monitor tables are created:

- CONNHEADER
- DEADLOCK
- DLCONN
- CONTROL
- DLLOCK
- STMT
- SUBSECTION
- XACT
- CONN
- DB
- BUFFERPOOL
- TABLESPACE
- TABLE

If only a subset of events are specified on the CREATE EVENT MONITOR statement, then DB2 will only create tables needed for those events. DB2 uses the following naming convention when creating event monitor tables:

```
schemaname.table name_event_monitor_name
```

For example, if a DBA with a user id of PRODBA issued the following create event monitor statement:

```
CREATE EVENT MONITOR PGUN2 FOR CONNECTIONS WRITE TO TABLE
```

then the event monitor tables will be created with a schema of PRODDBA and with a table suffix of PGUN2 appended to the event monitor table name. The event monitor tables would be created as follows:

```
proddba.conn_pgun2
proddba.connheader_pgun2
proddba.control_pgun2
```

If not specified, the tables will be created in tablespaces as specified by the IN tablespaceName clause. If specified, the tablespaces must already exist. The CREATE EVENT MONITOR statement does not create tablespaces.

See Table 10.7 for a list of event monitor types and associated table names.

Table 10.7 Write-to-Table Event Monitor Target Tables

Event type	Target Table Names	Available information
DEADLOCKS	CONNHEADER	Connection metadata
	DEADLOCK	Deadlock data
	DLCONN	Applications and locks involved in deadlock
	CONTROL	Event monitor metadata
DEADLOCKS WITH DETAILS	CONNHEADER	Connection metadata
	DEADLOCK	Deadlock data
	DLCONN	Applications involved in deadlock
	DLLOCK	Locks involved in deadlock
	CONTROL	Event monitor metadata
STATEMENTS	CONNHEADER	Connection metadata
	STMT	Statement data
	SUBSECTION	Statement data specific to subsection
	CONTROL	Event monitor metadata
TRANSACTIONS	CONNHEADER	Connection metadata
	XACT	Transaction data
	CONTROL	Event monitor metadata
CONNECTIONS	CONNHEADER	Connection metadata
	CONN	Connection data
	CONTROL	Event monitor metadata
DATABASE	DB	Database manager data
	CONTROL	Event monitor metadata
BUFFERPOOLS	BUFFERPOOL	Bufferpool data
	CONTROL	Event monitor metadata
TABLESPACES	TABLESPACE	Tablespace data
	CONTROL	Event monitor metadata
TABLES	TABLE	Table data
	CONTROL	Event monitor metadata

General Consideration for Write-to-Table Event Monitors

When the CREATE EVENT MONITOR statement is issued, all event monitor target tables are created. If the creation of a table fails for any reason, an error is passed back to the application program and the CREATE EVENT MONITOR statement fails. During CREATE EVENT MONITOR processing, if a table already exists, but is *not defined* for use by another event monitor, no table is created, and processing continues. A warning is passed back to the application program.

> **NOTE**
> For the write-to-table event monitor, the LOCAL and GLOBAL keywords are ignored because an event monitor output process or thread is started on each database partition in the instance, and each of these processes reports data only for the database partition on which it is running.

A target table can only be used by one event monitor. During CREATE EVENT MONITOR processing, if a target table is found to have already been defined for use by another event monitor, the CREATE EVENT MONITOR statement fails and an error is passed back to the application program. You can tell if a table is already defined for use by another event monitor if the table name matches a value found in the SYSCAT.EVENTTABLES catalog view.

> **NOTE**
> DB2 does not drop target tables as part of the DROP EVENT MONITOR statement.

While an event monitor is running it inserts event records into target tables. If an insert fails, uncommitted changes are rolled back, a message is written to the administration notification log, and the event monitor is *deactivated*.

> **TIP**
> Make sure the tablespaces being used for your event monitor target tables have enough space to handle your requirements. For DMS tablespaces, the PCTDEACTIVATE option can specify as a percentage how full the tablespace can be before the event monitor automatically deactivates.

DB2 Event Analyzer (db2eva)

The db2eva event analyzer tool can be used to analyze event monitor data that has been written to tables using the write-to-table option. It can be used with or without parameters.

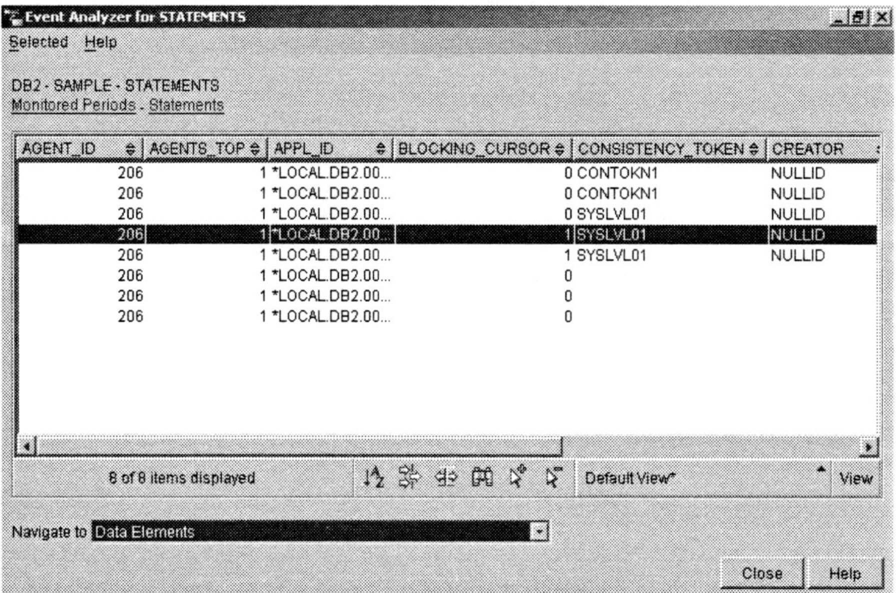

Figure 10.1
`db2eva` Analyze Statements view.

The `db2eva` command is issued from the command line and if no parameters are specified, the Open Event Analyzer dialog box opens to let you choose the database and event monitor names from a drop-down list. See Figure 10.1 for an example of a `db2eva` view.

The event analyzer can also be used to analyze the data of an active event monitor; however, data captured after the event analyzer has been invoked might not be shown. Event monitor data can also be viewed using the Control Center by right-clicking on the Control Center Event Monitors object.

Health Monitor and Health Center

New in v8, the Health monitor is a lightweight server-side agent (implemented in the Database Administration Server) and the Health Center is a GUI interface used to configure the Health Monitor and to present monitor data returned from the Health Monitor.

> **NOTE**
> The Health Monitor uses new monitoring technology in v8 that incurs very little overhead in the Database Manager. You should use the Health Monitor and Health Center as your initial source of monitoring information and then use snapshots and event monitors as needed.

The Health Center can be launched from the Control Center, as indicated in Figure 10.2.

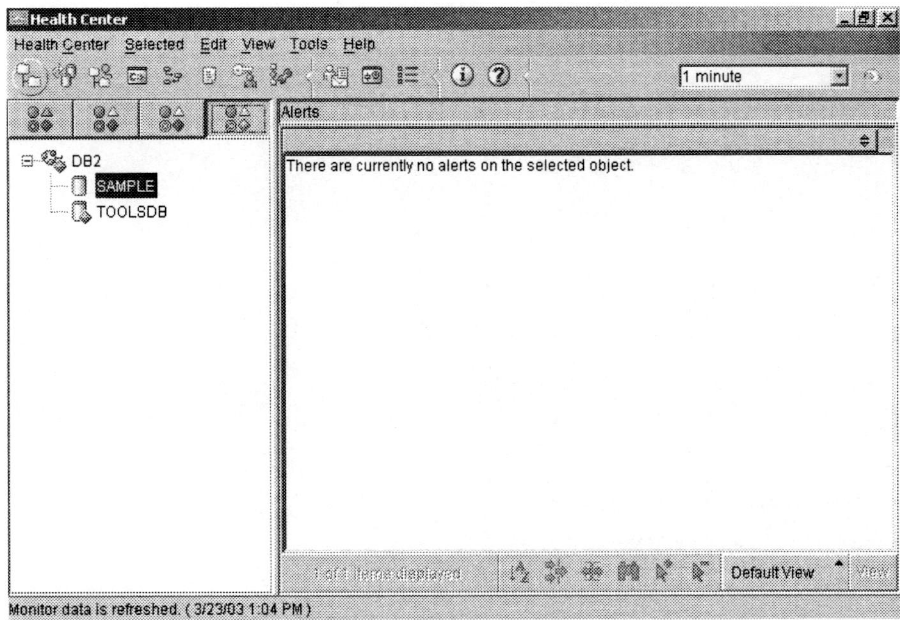

Figure 10.2
Health Center.

The Health Center can be used to make online changes to database configuration parameters and to set monitoring thresholds for configuration parameters. In conjunction with the Health Monitor, the Health Center reports on threshold violations via Health Beacons located on the toolbar of most DB2 tools launched from the Control Center. Threshold breaches are recorded by the Health Center and definitions of the breached parameters are provided along with the tuning recommendations, as seen in Figures 10.3 and 10.4.

After reviewing the alert and tuning recommendation, you can launch the Memory Visualizer to examine and graph DB2 memory usage. See Figure 10.5 for an example of the Memory Visualizer.

Memory usage can be tracked over time and the results used to make memory heap parameter configuration changes. It can then be used to track the effects of those changes. Lastly, the Health Monitor can be configured to provide emails and pager notifications to a DBA or group of DBAs. This new capability goes a long way in enabling DB2 to provide 24 × 7 × 365 monitoring capability. For additional information on the Health Center and monitoring in general, refer to the *System Monitor Guide and Reference.*

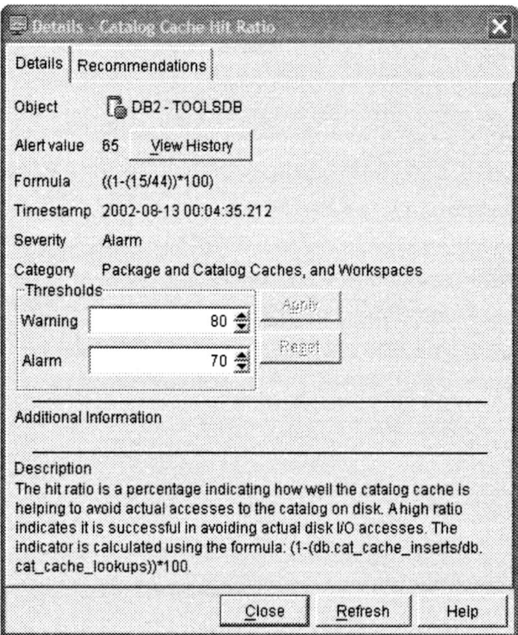

Figure 10.3
Health Center alert details.

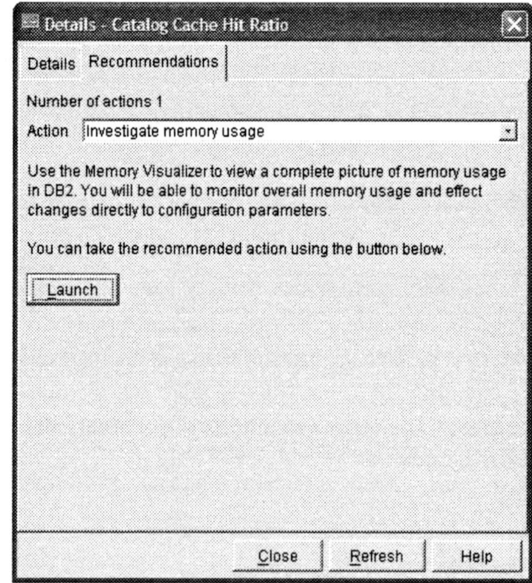

Figure 10.4
Health Center alert and recommendations.

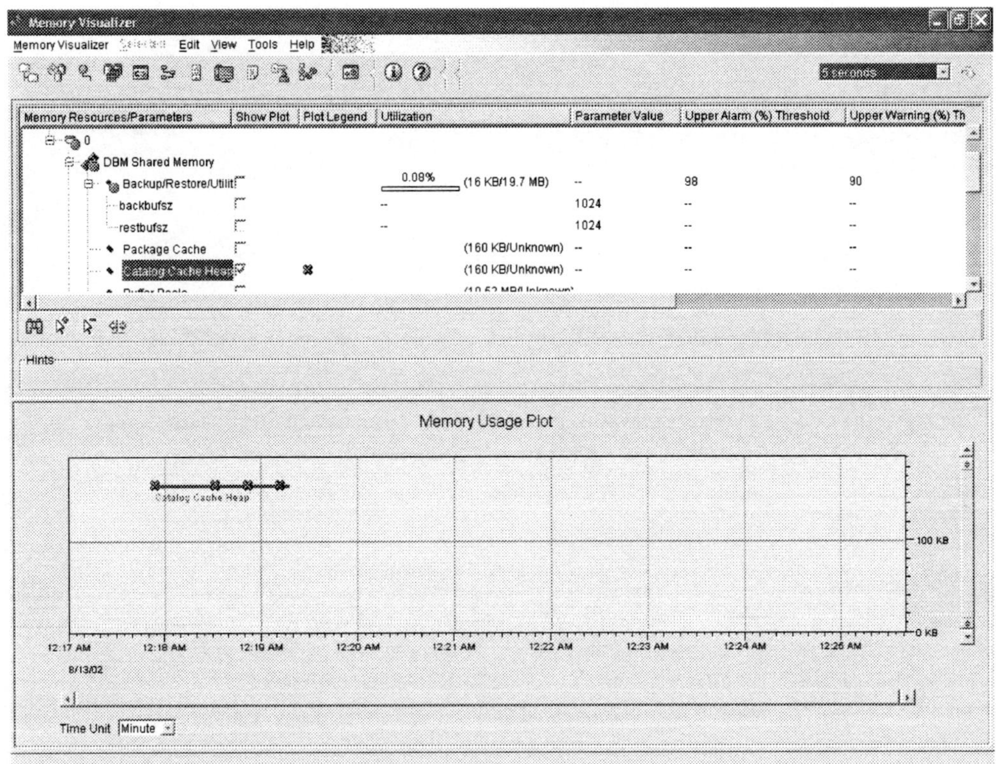

Figure 10.5
Memory Visualizer.

SUMMARY

Monitoring is one of the most important functions you perform as a DBA. Many new features and enhancements have been included in DB2 v8.

SMART and Autonomic Computing initiatives enable DB2 to be "self-monitoring" and "self-healing." We looked at this in Chapter 9.

New SQL snapshot functions make taking snapshots much easier for DBAs and applications and provide a way to write snapshot output to tables for historical reporting purposes. Additionally, write-to-table event monitors also provide you with a way to monitor DB2 and capture data for operational and historical purposes. The Health Monitor is a new lightweight server-side agent that provides 24 × 7 monitoring capability in conjunction with the Health Center. It provides "monitoring by exception" capability by providing for the notification of DBAs via emails and pager notifications. This is a major requirement at most large companies today.

Version 8 manageability and monitoring improvements make DB2 much easier to manage for today's DBA, in an ever increasing manpower and resource constrained environment.

C H A P T E R 11

Problem Determination

Good problem determination skills are required for you to be a successful DBA. Even with continued improvements in DB2 and client applications, problems still occur and you will need to know how to identify and locate problems quickly.

You should develop standard troubleshooting procedures for your environment. If you document and practice these procedures when investigating problems, you will be able to routinely identify and solve problems in a short amount of time. This will enable you to help your company maintain or improve their competitive advantage. Remember, downtime costs money and reflects negatively on your company.

There are several categories that we can use to categorize problems. They are:

- Connectivity problems
- Performance problems
  - stall, hang, or loop
- Application problems
  - Inefficient SQL
  - Unsupported functions being used
  - Application changes
- DB2 code (defect) problems

Connectivity Problems

Connectivity problems are by far the most common problems you will experience. They can usually be isolated to either the client or the server. Some of the most common problems are:

- Client can't connect to the database
- UserID and password problems
- Communication errors

- Database not cataloged
- Lack of authorization
- network changes
- Driver problems
- Intermittent connectivity problems
- Database down
- Instance down
- DB2COMM environmental variable not set properly
- DB2 TCP/IP Service Name (svcename) DBM CFG parameter not set
- Network changes made and not communicated throughout the organization
- Connections hanging or being interrupted

When investigating these types of problems, ask the following questions to help isolate the problem:

- Is this the first time you have had this problem?
- Can anyone else using the same application connect to the database?
- Can you connect or run the application from another PC?
- Are other people using the same applications able to connect or are they experiencing the same problems?
- Does the problem happen all the time or is it intermittent?
- Can you recreate the problem? If not, how frequently does it occur?
- Can it be recreated in a test environment?

After asking these questions, you should have obtained enough information to isolate the problem to the client, application, or database. Also, during this fact finding, you can be testing connections to the database in question, verifying that the instance is up and that the database is available. If your quick tests do not reveal any problems, immediately check the *db2diag.log* and administration notification log on the server for errors.

If errors are found, investigate those errors using the Information Center and messages and codes manual. If no errors are found, then look at the *db2diag.log* on the client. You will typically find errors on the client since we eliminated the server as the problem. Look up error messages in the Information Center or messages and codes manual. Take action as indicated. If this still does not point you to the problem, you will need to run a CLI/ODBC/JDBC trace on the client. An example of how to enable a CLI trace can be found later in this chapter.

NOTE

CLI traces are very valuable in identifying all types of problems. For additional information refer to the DB2 problem determination tutorial on the Web.

As of DB2 v8, the *DB2 Troubleshooting Guide* is no longer a separately published manual. Much of the former manual as well as DB2 internal return codes have been incorporated into the new DB2 Information Center and are available on the Web.

Performance and Application Problems

Performance problems are the second most often type of problem reported. The most common performance problems are usually the result of some type of change to the application, lack of RUNSTATS, change to the database configuration, or possibly the application was never tuned in the first place. I have included application problems in this section because many times performance and application problems are interrelated. Additional typical problem areas are long-running SQL, sort overflows, OS paging, high I/O wait times, and undersized bufferpools. When investigating performance problems ask the following questions:

- When did the problem occur?
- What is the nature of the problem?
- Can it be reproduced?
- Is the problem related to a specific PC or server?
- How long did the query normally run in the past?
- Were there any changes made to the application? If so, what changes were made?
- Is the problem related to a single table or tablespace?
- Was the query explained and if so what access path is it using? Has it changed?
- Did performance degrade suddenly, or was it a gradual progression to an unacceptable level?

To identify long-running or suboptimal SQL, use snapshots and event monitoring. Refer to Chapter 10 for specific details on snapshots and event monitoring. Once the SQL is identified, use Design Advisor and Visual Explain to determine if the access path can be improved with either index changes, additional indexes, or through changes to the SQL. By using Visual Explain (or any other type of DB2 explain) and Design Advisor, all problems of these types should be able to be resolved. Additionally, a combination of snapshot and event monitoring data can be used to identify sort problems and provide bufferpool performance data. Many times sort problems can be eliminated by tuning SQL and by creating or modifying indexes.

To ensure that RUNSTATS are current for the objects involved, you can use the Control Center to review whether or not RUNSTATS are current or to determine if they have ever been run. RUNSTATS can be executed from the Control Center, Command Center, or CLP.

DB2 Code (Defect) Problems

At times, you may experience any of the categories of problems highlighted at the beginning of this chapter due to DB2 defects. These are relatively infrequent, but you need to know where to look for information concerning your particular problem.

These errors were typically written to the *db2diag.log* file. DB2 support maintains a DB2 support page on the Internet at *www.3.ibm.com/cgi-bin/db2www/data/udb/wino>2unit/support/index.d2w/report*. See Figure 11.1 for a view of the DB2 support site.

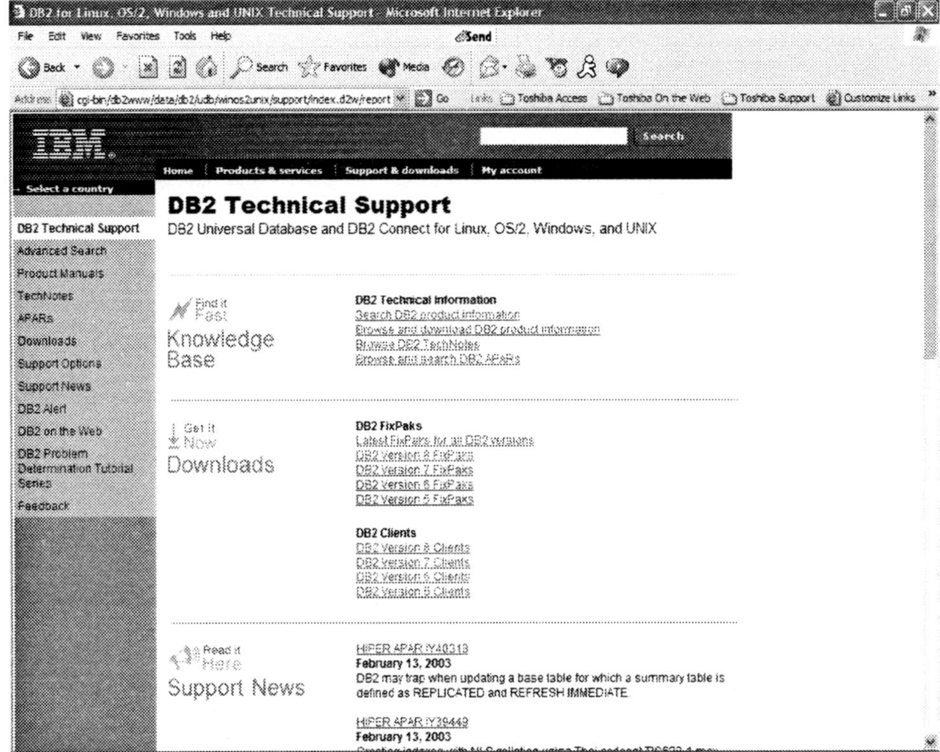

Figure 11.1
DB2 Support site.

Take the problem string from the *db2diag.log* and use it to search the support site for a possible fix. If your search finds a fix for the defect you are experiencing, you can download the fixpak, test it in a test environment, and apply it to production during a maintenance window. Always test a fixpak in a test environment before putting it on production.

> **NOTE**
>
> New in v8 is the DB2 Information Center. It contains most of the DB2 manuals and it is shipped with the product. HTML updates are available via HTML fixpaks, which can be installed via the Information Centers—Update Local Documentation menu item.
>
> To manually install HTML fixpaks on Windows, double load the fixpak into an empty directory and run the setup command. On UNIX, the fixpak is a tar.Z file. Uncompress and untar the file. It will create a directory command `delta_install` and a script called `install-docfix`. Just run the script to install the documentation fixpak.

DB2 PROBLEM DETERMINATION AIDS

In v8, diagnostic information is now written to two separate files; the *db2diag.log* and administration notification log. The *db2diag.log* was split into two files because too much information was being written to the *db2diag.log* file and it was causing "information overload," as it contained a mix of informational and severe errors. So, as a result of this and feedback from customers, DB2 Development decided to create a separate file for recording application errors, administrative errors, and miscellaneous error information. That way, the *db2diag.log* file can be dedicated for only severe-level errors.

DB2DIAG.LOG FILE

The *db2diag.log* file is located in the SQLLIB directory. It is an ASCII file that can be viewed with a text editor. Entries are written by DB2 to the *db2diag.log* file when the following events occur:

- Severe errors
- DB2 internal errors

The `DIAGLEVEL DBM CFG` parameter controls the amount of information that is written to the *db2diag.log* file. The default value for this parameter is 3. This will ensure that DB2 records all severe errors that occur. I recommend that you use this setting. Only set it to 4 when you are trying to debug a particular problem and you haven't been able to identify the problem through other means. As soon as you have captured the additional information, set this parameter back to 3.

All entries written to the *db2diag.log* file are written at the end of the file. So, you should look at the end of the file if investigating current errors. As entries are written to the end of the *db2diag.log* file, it continues to grow in size. It will continue to grow until it runs out of disk space or uses up all available space in the filesystem. Most DBAs copy the *db2diag.log* file nightly and delete it. DB2 will automatically create a new file when needed. If you copy it nightly, that will also give you an historical record for subsequent analysis, if needed. With only severe errors being written to the *db2diag.log* file these procedures may not be as important as in prior releases, but should still be done so you have a copy of the *db2diag.log* file for each day. It can aid you in troubleshooting later.

DB2 uses a naming convention for naming its modules. See Table 11.1 for a complete list.

The letter in the fourth position of the function name indicates what DB2 function was involved. This is helpful to know when searching for a fix or talking to DB2 support.

Format

Entries written to the *db2diag.log* file will be in First Failure Data Capture (FFDC) format. See Example 11.1 for a sample *db2diag.log* FFDC entry.

Table 11.1 Module Naming Conventions

Letter in fourth position	Function involved
B	Bufferpool management and manipulation
C	Communications between clients and servers
D	Data management
E	Database engine process
O	Operating system calls (privileged instructions)
P	Data protection
R	Relational database services
S	Sorting operations
X	Indexing operations

```
1 2003-01-22-15.55.51.437000   2 Instance:DB2   3 Node:000
4 PID:1680(db2syscs.exe)   5 TID:1608   6 Appid:*LOCAL.DB2.0092C2202617
7 database monitor  8 sqm.start_evmon  9 Probe:32   10 Database:SAMPLE

11 DIA0001E An internal error occurred. Report the following error code :
12 "ZRC=0x840D000C".
```

Example 11.1
Sample *db2diag.log* FFDC entry.

Although the primary purpose of the *db2diag.log* is to record severe errors for problem determination analysis by DB2 development, if you learn how to interpret FFDC information you can use this information to help solve problems that are within your capability. And if not, you'll at least be in a good position to provide information to DB2 level II support. We can break down the data elements in Example 11.1 as follows:

1. Message timestamp
2. Name of instance
3. For a partitioned database, the database partition number of the partition generating the message
4. Identification of the process generating the message
5. The unique transaction identifier of the transaction that generated the entry
6. Identification of the application for which the process is working; in this example the process generating the message is working on behalf of an application with the ID `*Local.DB2.0092C2202617`
7. The DB2 component that is writing the message
8. The module reporting the error

9. The function ID within the module reporting the error; used by DB2 support to locate the section of code that generated the error
10. The database where the error is occurring
11. The diagnostic error code and message text
12. The DB2 internal error code in hex

The key data elements you need to be concerned with in Example 11.1 are the DB2 internal return code (12) and the DB2 module reporting the error (8). DB2 internal return codes, 0x840D000C in our example, can be found on the Web using the Information Center.

> **NOTE**
> Due to the changing nature of DB2 internal return codes, they are not recorded in the manuals. DB2 Support has decided to make these available on the Web via the Information Center.

See Figure 11.2 for an overview of the DB2 Information Center. We can use it to search for our return code in this example. As indicated in Figure 11.3, internal return code 0x840D000C means "path not found." In our case, we were attempting to use an event monitor with an invalid path.

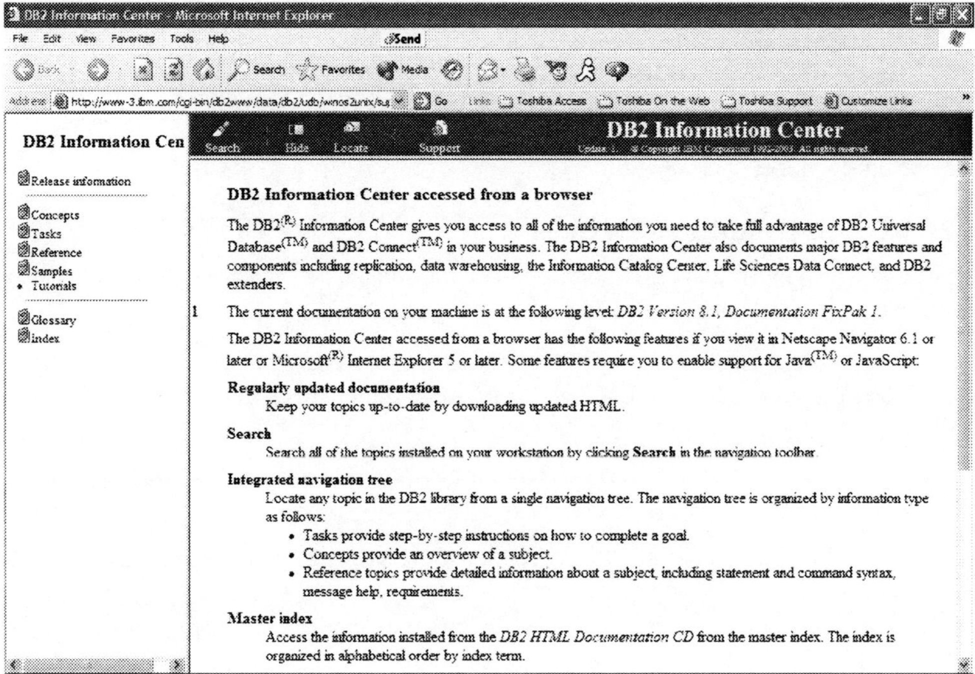

Figure 11.2
DB2 Information Center.

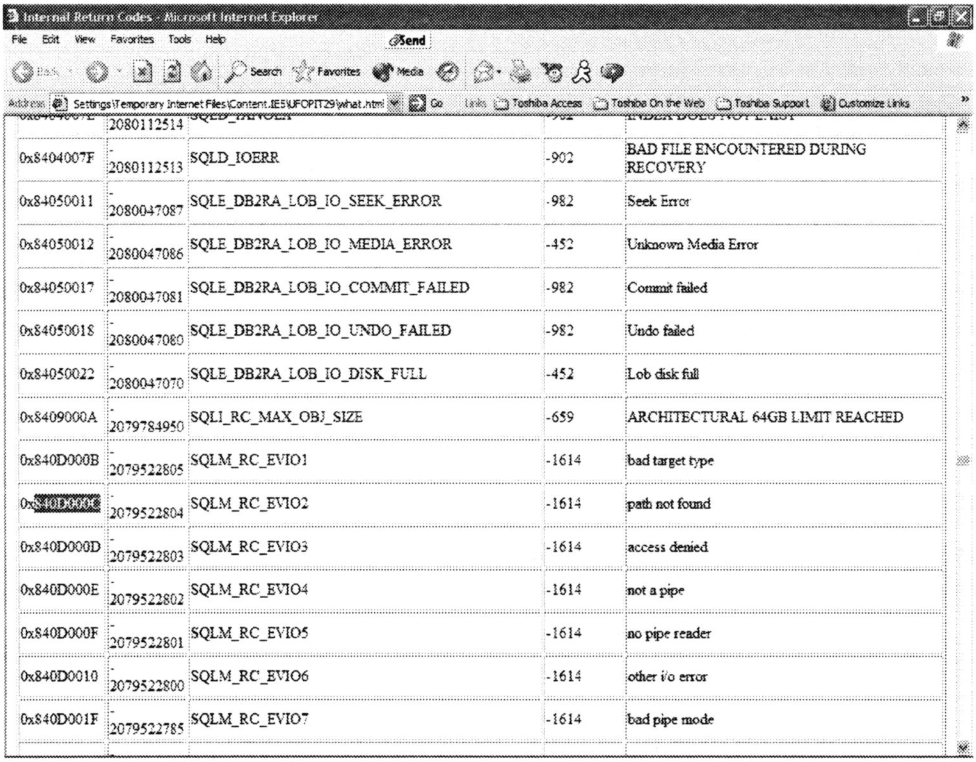

	-2080112514			
0x8404007F	-2080112513	SQLD_IOERR	-902	BAD FILE ENCOUNTERED DURING RECOVERY
0x84050011	-2080047087	SQLE_DB2RA_LOB_IO_SEEK_ERROR	-982	Seek Error
0x84050012	-2080047086	SQLE_DB2RA_LOB_IO_MEDIA_ERROR	-452	Unknown Media Error
0x84050017	-2080047081	SQLE_DB2RA_LOB_IO_COMMIT_FAILED	-982	Commit failed
0x84050018	-2080047080	SQLE_DB2RA_LOB_IO_UNDO_FAILED	-982	Undo failed
0x84050022	-2080047070	SQLE_DB2RA_LOB_IO_DISK_FULL	-452	Lob disk full
0x8409000A	-2079784950	SQLI_RC_MAX_OBJ_SIZE	-659	ARCHITECTURAL 64GB LIMIT REACHED
0x840D000B	-2079522805	SQLM_RC_EVIO1	-1614	bad target type
0x840D000C	-2079522804	SQLM_RC_EVIO2	-1614	path not found
0x840D000D	-2079522803	SQLM_RC_EVIO3	-1614	access denied
0x840D000E	-2079522802	SQLM_RC_EVIO4	-1614	not a pipe
0x840D000F	-2079522801	SQLM_RC_EVIO5	-1614	no pipe reader
0x840D0010	-2079522800	SQLM_RC_EVIO6	-1614	other i/o error
0x840D001F	-2079522785	SQLM_RC_EVIO7	-1614	bad pipe mode

Figure 11.3
Internal return code Ox840D000C.

DB2DIAG.LOG SQLCA ENTRIES

The SQLCA is used by DB2 to pass information from one program to another, to record the status of a call, and to return the status of results to the working application.

DB2 may record the contents of an SQLCA associated with severe errors in the *db2diag.log*. As such it is very useful in helping you to investigate application errors and other types of errors. See Example 11.2 for a sample *db2diag.log* SQLCA entry.

```
2003-02-08-23.31.37.307935 Instance:db2inst1 Node:000
PID:2640(asnapply) TID:8192 Appid:none
DRDA Application Requester sqljrDrdaArExecute Probe:90

DIA0001E An internal error occurred. Report the following error code :
"ZRC=0x8037006D".
```

Example 11.2
Sample *db2diag.log* SQLCA entry.

```
1 PID:2640  2 TID:8192  3 Node:000  4 Title: SQLCA
5 sqlcaid : SQLCA sqlcabc: 136 6 sqlcode: -518 sqlerrml: 0
sqlerrmc:
7 sqlerrp : SQLRAGSN~
8 sqlerrd : (1) 0x8012007E (2) 0x00000000 (3) 0x00000000
(4) 0x00000000 (5) 0x00000000 (6) 0x00000000
sqlwarn : (1) (2) (3) (4) (5) (6)
(7) (8) (9) (10) (11)
9 sqlstate: 07003

2003-02-08-23.31.37.332392 Instance:db2inst1 Node:000
PID:2640(asnapply) TID:8192 Appid:none
oper system services sqlofica Probe:10
```

Example 11.2
Sample *db2diag.log* SQLCA entry. (Continued)

The SQLCA uses the standard FFDC format. SQLCA field definitions are as follows:

1. Process ID
2. Unique transaction ID
3. Node where the error occurred
4. Title
5. Eye catcher that identifies the beginning of the SQLCA data structure entries
6. The SQL return code value
7. Reason codes, if provided
8. A hexadecimal value of up to six entries that caused the final SQL return code value generated—These codes are recorded in the sequence of events as they occurred
9. `SQLSTATE`—the `ANSI STANDARD SQLSTATE` value

In our example, we have a return code of 0x8012007E and an SQLCODE of -518. Using the DB2 Information Center, we search on these codes and find that a -518 SQL code or a 07003 `SQLSTATE` means that "a statement named in the `EXECUTE` statement is not in a prepared state or is a `SELECT` or `VALUES` statement." You can use this information to help a developer solve an application problem.

DB2 Administration Notification Log

New in v8, the Administration Notification log is used to record errors of interest to DBAs and application developers. In Windows 2000, DB2 uses the Windows event log as the Administration Notification log. It can be viewed with the Windows Event Viewer tool.

> **NOTE**
> The `NOTIFYLEVEL` Database Manager parameter controls the level of administration notification messages written to the administration notification log. The default value is 3. This parameter must be set to a value of 2 or higher to enable the Health Monitor to send notifications to contacts defined in its configuration.

See Figures 11.4 and 11.5 for typical administration notification log entries.

As indicated in Figure 11.4, the initial entry record shown using Event Viewer in Windows 2000 Server gives us a high-level view of the problem.

By double-clicking on this entry, we can get additional details, as shown in Figure 11.5. A description of the problem is provided along with a recommended solution.

For other operating systems, the log is created as an ASCII file with a file name of the format of <instance_name.nfy>.

Event Viewer

Action View

Tree: Event Viewer (Local) — Application Log, Security Log, System Log, DNS Server

Application Log 912 event(s)

Type	Date	Time	Source	Category	Event
Information	1/22/2003	3:25:48 PM	DB2	None	1
Warning	1/22/2003	3:25:48 PM	DB2	None	5
Information	1/22/2003	3:25:31 PM	DB2	None	1
Warning	1/22/2003	3:25:31 PM	DB2	None	5
Information	1/22/2003	3:25:17 PM	DB2	None	1
Information	1/22/2003	3:25:13 PM	DB2	None	1
Warning	1/22/2003	3:24:51 PM	DB2	None	5
Error	1/22/2003	3:23:06 PM	DB2	None	4
Error	1/22/2003	2:25:07 PM	DB2	None	4
Error	1/22/2003	2:25:06 PM	DB2	None	4
Information	1/22/2003	1:39:42 PM	DB2	None	1
Warning	1/22/2003	1:39:42 PM	DB2	None	5
Information	1/22/2003	1:39:06 PM	DB2JDS	None	1
Information	1/22/2003	1:38:48 PM	ESENT	General	100
Information	1/22/2003	1:38:45 PM	ESENT	General	100
Information	1/22/2003	1:38:32 PM	DB2REMOTECMD	None	1
Information	1/22/2003	1:38:32 PM	DB2REMOTECMD	None	1
Information	1/22/2003	1:38:18 PM	MSDTC	SVC	4097
Warning	1/21/2003	11:44:08 ...	DB2	None	5
Error	1/21/2003	11:44:08 ...	DB2	None	4
Warning	1/21/2003	11:44:08 ...	DB2	None	5

Figure 11.4
The Event Viewer Application Log.

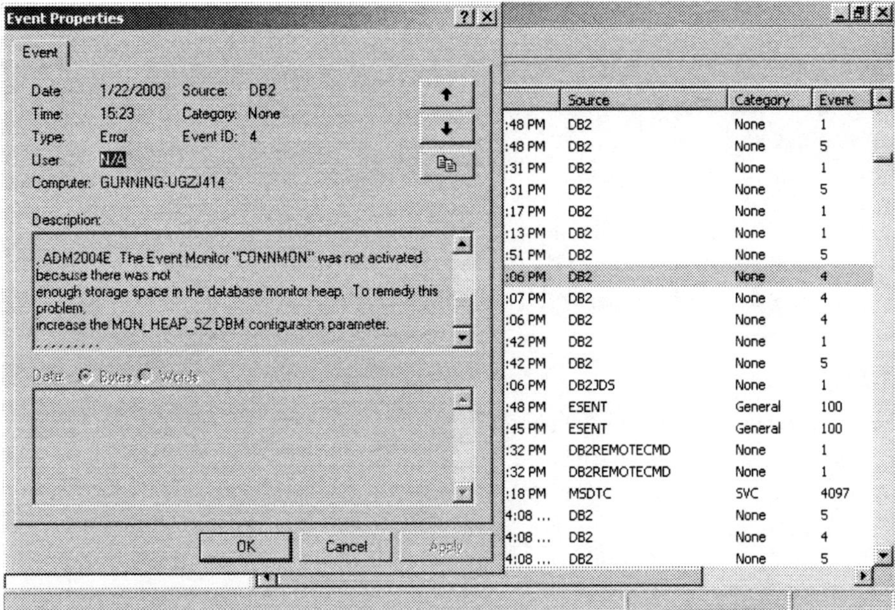

Figure 11.5
Event Properties.

SYSTEM LOGS

System logs are another important source of problem determination information. We have already discussed the Windows event log.

> **NOTE**
>
> The `DBM CFG DIAGPATH` parameter controls where FFDC information gets recorded. This parameter is null by default and FFDC data will be written to the db2diag.log on the following path: `C:\Program Files\IBM\SQLLIB\DB2\db2diag.log`.
>
> On UNIX by default, FFDC data is written to the following path: `$Home/sqllib/db2dump`.
> Example: `/prddb/sqllib/db2dump`, where `prddb` is the name of the instance owner.

On UNIX, operating system logs are used to record severe DB2 errors and warning conditions. Syslog can contain DB2 error information in the event of a DB2 crash. In this case, DB2 may not have been able to write to the *db2diag.log* before it crashes. Syslog will then be an important source of information.

Errors are added to the syslog based on priority and on what facility caused the error or warning condition. DB2 typically adds errors to the syslog under the following conditions:

- Agents have been killed
- DB2 architecture compromised
- I/O errors causing DB2 to panic

When conducting problem determination, information from the *db2diag.log*, administration notification logs, and syslog should be cross-checked so that all failure data is correlated. For additional information on using UNIX system logs, refer to specific operating system documentation.

CLI Trace

The output trace is typically what DB2 support will want. A DB2 CLI/ODBC trace shows the calls received from the ODBC Driver Manager, while an ODBC trace will show the calls made by the application to the driver manager. Enable the trace on the client by adding the following line to the DB2CLI.INI file:

```
[COMMON]
TRACE = 1
TRACEFILEMANE = C:\Traces\120202Prob.TXT
TRACEFLUSH = 1
```

The above example will cause a trace record to be written to disk after each entry. If using JDBC, a JDBC trace can also be used. The settings are similar. For additional information, refer to the Information Center.

DB2 Trace

The DB2 trace facility has been significantly improved in v8 and it can now be used as one of the primary tools for gathering information regarding a problem. However, the DB2 trace should only be used in conjunction with DB2 Support. DB2 trace records information about operations and formats it into a readable form. On UNIX, `sysadm`, `sysctrl`, or `sysmaint` authority is required. On Windows, no authorization is required.

> **NOTE**
> `db2trc` can be used to trace activity for an instance or for the DB2 Administration server.

A connection to the database is not required. `db2trc` is useful when other FFDC facilities have failed to provide you and DB2 Support with enough information to identify and solve the problem being investigated. The following is an example of the db2trc command:

```
db2trc on -p 20, 40, 60
```

The example command causes tracing to be enabled for processes 20, 40, and 60. Use the following command to dump the trace information to a file:

```
db2trc dmp dbtrc.dmp
```

After you have dumped the trace to a file you must stop the trace as follows:

```
db2trc off
```

After you have turned the trace off, you can format it using the *flw* or *fmt* option.

Note that the `db2trc` command has to be issued multiple times to gather the information and format it to a text file. For further information, refer to the DB2 UDB v8 *Command Reference.*

DRDA Trace

The DB2 DRDA trace (`db2drdat`) allows you to capture the DRDA data stream between a client and the DB2 UDB Server. Key outputs from this trace are the number of sends and receives that are required to execute an application. It can also aid in performance and tuning of client/server applications. The trace can be invoked from a CLP as follows:

```
db2drdat on
```

which turns on all as trace events. To stop collecting trace data, issue the *db2drdat off* command. With DB2 clients now using the DRDA protocol in v8, you will probably find this trace very useful. Do not run this trace while running a DB2 trace. Refer to the *DB2 UDB v8 Command Reference* for additional information.

Dumps

DB2 creates dump files when it determines internal information needs to be collected. DB2 creates two types of dumps: Type 1, Binary dump files, and Type 2, Locklist dump files.

The format and naming conventions for these files on UNIX are as follows:

Type 1 Binary Dump Files

- UNIX—`pppppp.nn`
  where `pppppp` is the process ID (PID)
  `nnn` is the node where the problem occurred
  Example: `323646.000`
- Windows—`pppttt.nnn`
  where `ppp` is the process ID (PID)
  `ttt` is the thread ID (TID)
  `nnn` is the node where the problem occurred
  Example: `323646.000`

Type 2 Locklist Dump Files

- UNIX—`lpppppp.nnn`

  where `pppppp` is the process ID (PID)
  `nnn` is the node where the problem occurred
  Example: `l323646.000`

- Windows—`lppptttt.nnn`

  where `ppp` is the process ID (PID)
  `ttt` is the thread ID (TID)
  `nnn` is the node where the problem occurred
  Example: `l323646.000`

Information written to dump files consists of internal DB2 control blocks and other diagnostic information. Each data item written to a dump file has a timestamp associated with it to aid in problem determination.

When a dump file is created or appended to, an entry is made in the *db2diag.log* indicating the time and type of data written. The fully qualified path for the dump file is also recorded.

For UNIX-based systems, dump files might be created in core dump directories. These files are called DB2 core files and are specific to DB2.

> **NOTE**
> The `db2support` tool will collect these core files for further analysis.

DB2 Core files are located in the path `$HOME/db2dump/core_directory`, where `core_directory` is the core path directory name. There is one directory for each process. Directory names start with the letter "c," followed by the process identifier (pid) number of the affected process. A name extension provides the partition for multipartition databases.

These core files are intended for use by DB2 Support. Use the `db2support` tool to develop a support bundle that can be sent to DB2 Support.

Dr. Watson

The Dr. Watson log on Windows 2000 Server (*drwtsn32.log*) contains a list of all exceptions that have occurred. This log is useful for developing a good picture of overall system stability and contains information regarding DB2 traps.

The default path for the log is `<installation_drive>:\Documents and Settings\All Users\Documents\DrWatson`

TRAPS

When certain severe errors are encountered, DB2 will issue a signal (on UNIX platforms) or an exception to itself. These are also known as segment violations or traps, depending on the operating system.

Signals or exceptions initiated by DB2 are reported in a trap file, which contains a function flow of the last steps that were executed before the system stopped. Trap files are used by DB2 Support to assist them in resolving problems.

Trap files reside in the directory specified by the `DIAGPATH` database manager configuration parameter. Trap files use the following naming convention:

```
t39336.000
t39338.006
```

Where

> `t`—identifies this as a trap file
>
> `39336.000`—is the name of the process with pid 39336
>
> `39336.010`—is the name of the process with pid 39338.006; with 006 signifying the database partition on which the process was running.

> **NOTE**
> DB2 does not remove *trap, dump, core,* or *trace* files. You should delete these files on a periodic basis.

CALL STACK TRACES

Call stack traces can be useful in providing DB2 Support with a detailed trace of internal DB2 functions in the order they were called. It can be used by DB2 Support to pinpoint the actual lines of code that were being executed and help them to either eliminate or identify the module involved as the source of the problem.

On UNIX operating systems, DB2 can generate a stack traceback when you intentionally stop a DB2 process. Each file (trap file) reports the signal or exception that was issued by DB2 to stop or interrupt the process. There is one file per process. In a partitioned database environment, these files reside on each partition for each process involved. To activate a call stack trace, use the following commands:

1. Issue the `db2_call_stack` command
2. Stop the DB2 instance

> **NOTE**
> The `db2_call_stack` command should be run by the instance owner only. Before running the command, make sure that a `/tmp/ $DB2INSTANCE` directory exists at each mode. If not, create it by issuing the following command: `db2_all "mkdir /tmp/ DB2INSTANCE"`.

SENDING INFORMATION TO DB2 SUPPORT

New in v8, the `db2support` Problem Analysis and Environment Collection tool can be used to provide a "support bundle" for you to provide to DB2 Support. This tool can be run with or without prompting. See Figure 11.6 for an example invoking `db2support` from a CLP.

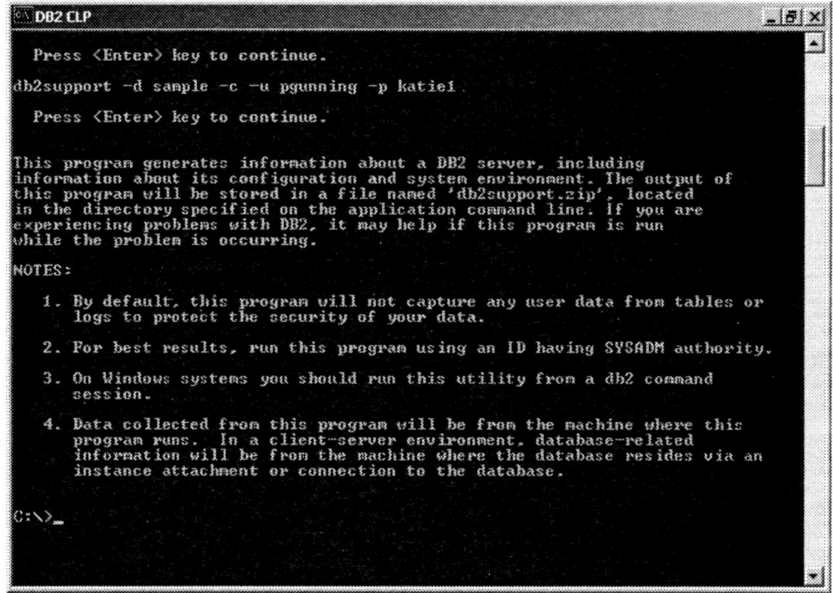

Figure 11.6
Invoking `db2support` from a CLP.

To invoke this utility, issue the following from the command line:

```
db2support output path/tmp/db2support_output/ -f -a -d -c -u -p
```

where:

> `output path`—specifies the path where the archived library is to be created. This is the directory where user-created files must be placed for inclusion in the archive.

`-f` or `-flow`—ignores pauses when requests are made for the user for Press<Enter> key to continue. This option is useful when running or calling the `db2support` tool via a script or some other automated procedure where unattended execution is desired.

`-a` or `-all_core`—specifies that all core files are to be captured.

`-r` or `-recent_core`—specifies that the most recent core files are to be captured. This option is ignored if the `-a` option is specified.

`-d database_name` or `-database database_name`—specifies the name of the database for which data is being collected.

`-c` or `-connect`—specifies that an attempt be made to connect to the specified database.

`-u userid` or `-user userid`—specifies the user ID to connect to the database.

`-p password` or `-password password`—specifies the password for the user ID.

`-g` or `-get_dump`—specifies that all files in a dump directory, excluding core files, are to be captured.

`-h` or `-help`—displays help information. When this option is specified, all other options are ignored, and only the help information is displayed.

`-l` or `-logs`—specifies that active logs are to be captured.

`-n` or `-number`—specifies the problem management (PMR) number or identifier for the current problem.

`-q` or `-question_response`—specifies that interactive problem analysis mode is to be used.

`-s` or `-system_detail`—specifies that detailed hardware and operating system information is to be gathered.

`-v` or `-verbose`—specifies that verbose output is to be used while this tool is running.

`-x` or `-xml_generate`—specifies that an XML document containing the entire decision tree logic used during the interactive problem analysis mode (`-q` mode) is to be generated.

Depending on the options selected, the `db2support` tool will build a support bundle in a compressed format consisting of the following files:

- Core files
- Database Manage and Database Configuration files
- *db2diag.log*
- Trap files
- Operating system environment information
- Bufferpool and tablespace information
- Active logs
- Recovery history file
- Log control file
- *DB2CLI.INI* file
- Database directory

- Node directory
- Node backup directory
- Archive log
- JDK level
- DB2 release information
- Tablespace history recovery file
- Disk, CPU, memory configuration

Upon completion of running `db2support`, which can include the PMR number as an option, the output can be sent to DB2 Support for analysis and further problem determination.

SUMMARY

In this chapter, we have focused on problem determination. We have highlighted troubleshooting methods and the associated problem determination aids, files, and tools available to assist you in resolving all DB2 problems.

New in v8, the `db2support` tool is very useful for gathering all available diagnostic and environmental information into a format that can be easily sent to DB2 Support.

Various traces were discussed that can help you identify and solve problems. Detailed examples on how to interpret *db2diag.log* and administration notification log entries were provided. And finally, the use of DB2 Information Center was documented and presented as the primary source to use when analyzing return codes and error messages.

CHAPTER 12

Understanding and Tuning DB2 Sort

To answer business questions and solve business problems, data for reports and online queries are required to be presented in an ordered sequence. Plus, generally, we humans need information in an orderly manner. Consequently, many SQL queries contain SQL statements such as `ORDER BY`, `GROUP BY`, `DISTINCT`, or other features such as `UNIONS` or `JOINS`. DB2 provides extensive sort capability and the DB2 designers continue to improve the efficiency of DB2 sort operations in each release of DB2. Many times DB2 has to perform a sort because of inadequate physical design (inadequate or incorrect indexes), inefficient SQL, or a combination of both of these problems. Or perhaps DB2 just needs to perform a sort on an intermediate result set or RID list to accomplish efficient join operations or list prefetch. In most of my consulting engagements, I find SQL queries spending 70% or more of their time performing sorts. They are usually consuming a significant amount of processing resources. Consequently, by tuning SQL, which causes unnecessary sort operations, most of these sorts can be eliminated and significant CPU resources made available for other resources. Usually, these unnecessary sort operations can be easily eliminated by changing an existing index, changing the SQL, or creating a new index to eliminate the sort. These are just some of the options available to us. In this chapter we will discuss the following:

- DBM and DB CFG parameters that control sort resources
- Memory areas
- Sort operations
- Monitoring
- Tuning
- Sizing
- Eliminating sorts

Most sort problems are not caused by the DB2 engine but by external resources over which DB2 has little control. One thing you can be sure of, sort is probably a problem with your applications currently in production at your shop.

> **NOTE**
> While sorts are needed, the actual sort operation can be avoided via the use of indexes and properly clustered tables.

DB2 Sort Memory Areas

DB2 reserves special memory areas for sort operations. They are reserved at the instance and database level. At the instance level, sort memory is controlled by the `SHEAPTHRES` `DBM` configuration parameter, which controls the amount of shared memory that can be allocated for private and shared sorts across an instance. The `SHEAPTHRES_SHR` and `SORTHEAP` `DB CFG` parameters control sort memory allocation at the database level.

> **NOTE**
> New in v8, the `SHEAPTHRES_SHR` database configuration parameter specifies how much database shared memory can be allocated for shared sorts *at the database level.* This new capability lets DBAs place a hard limit on the amount of shared sort memory a database can use when using intrapartition parallelism or connection concentration.

SORTHEAP

This parameter defines the maximum amount of shared sort or agent private `sortheap` that can be allocated. Private `sortheap` is allocated out of agent private memory and shared `sortheap` is allocated out of database shared memory. DB2 uses `sortheap` to perform sorts.

> **WARNING**
> DB2 v8 enables hash joins by default. Since hash joins use `SORTHEAP`, you should monitor `SORTHEAP` usage to make sure your previous settings are adequate.

Types of Sorts

Sorting in DB2 can be categorized as shared or private, and depending on the type of sort, either shared memory or agent private memory will be allocated.

The determining factors on whether or not shared sorts are used is the setting of the `intra_parallel` DBM configuration parameter or if connection concentration is enabled.

Shared Sort

Databases with intrapartition parallelism enabled use shared sorts and these sorts use database shared memory instead of agent private memory.

SHARED sort memory is allocated out of database shared memory.

DB2 sort operations consist of two steps: A Sort Phase and Return Sort Results Phase.

Additionally during the sort phase, a sort can be *overflowed* or *nonoverflowed*. Sort resource utilization at the database level can be monitored with the `GET SNAPSHOT FOR DBM` and `GET SNAPSHOT FOR DATABASE ON <database name>` where `<database name>` is the name of the database to be monitored. See Examples 12.1 and 12.2 for examples of the output provided by these commands.

```
Database Manager Snapshot

Node name                                          =
Node type                                          = Enterprise Server
Edition with local and remote clients
Instance name                                      = DB2
Number of database partitions in DB2 instance      = 1
Database manager status                            = Active

Product name                                       = DB2 v8.1.0.36
Service level                                      = s021023

Private Sort heap allocated                        = 0
Private Sort heap high water mark                  = 277
Post threshold sorts                               = 0
Piped sorts requested                              = 9
Piped sorts accepted                               = 9

Start Database Manager timestamp                   = 01-26-2003
22:17:59.069892
Last reset timestamp                               =
Snapshot timestamp                                 = 01-26-2003
22:26:00.641457
```

Example 12.1
Database Manager Snapshot output.

We can use the output from the Database Manager snapshot in Example 12.1 to review the amount of private `sortheap` allocated and associated high water mark to determine if we are close to our private sort limit. We can then take action to determine if sorts are consuming an abnormal amount of sort memory. If we observe post-threshold sorts, this is an indication that

```
Database Snapshot

Database name                                  = GNPRODDB
Database path                                  = /gardp01/gnprod/cat/
gnprod/NODE0000/SQL00001/
Input database alias                           =
Database status                                = Active
Catalog node number                            = 0
Catalog network node name                      =
Operating system running at database server = AIX
Location of the database                       = Local
First database connect timestamp               = 07-05-2002
03:02:59.580933
Last reset timestamp                           =
Last backup timestamp                          = 07-05-2002
03:02:45.829763
Snapshot timestamp                             = 07-05-2002
14:02:06.814058

High water mark for connections                = 38
Application connects                           = 11096
Secondary connects total                       = 0
Applications connected currently               = 34
Appls. executing in db manager currently       = 1
Agents associated with applications            = 34
Maximum agents associated with applications = 38
Maximum coordinating agents                    = 38

Locks held currently                           = 690
Lock waits                                     = 1
Time database waited on locks (ms)             = 1599
Lock list memory in use (Bytes)                = 46008
Deadlocks detected                             = 0
Lock escalations                               = 1
Exclusive lock escalations                     = 1
Agents currently waiting on locks              = 0
Lock Timeouts                                  = 0

Total Private Sort heap allocated              = 0
Total Shared Sort heap allocated               = 0
Shared Sort heap high water mark               = 0
Total sort heap allocated                      = 0
Total sorts                                    = 88705
Total sort time (ms)                           = 5030
```

Example 12.2
Output from Database Snapshot.
Note: This output has been edited to remove irrelevant information.

```
Sort overflows                              = 10
Active sorts                                = 0

Number of hash joins                        = 0
Number of hash loops                        = 0
Number of hash join overflows               = 0
Number of small hash join overflows         = 0
```

Example 12.2
Output from Database Snapshot. (Continued)
Note: This output has been edited to remove irrelevant information.

SHEAPTHRES has been reached and sorts are running in degraded mode. We will discuss post-threshold sorts later in this chapter. If the number of piped sorts requested is not the same as the number of piped sorts accepted, this means that the piped sorts requested by the optimizer are being rejected. This happens when post threshold sorts occur or when some other unanticipated DB2 event has occurred. Example 12.2 contains additional details on sort resource consumption.

The data elements of interest to us in Example 12.2 are as follows:

- Total sortheap allocated
- Total sorts
- Total sort time (ms)
- Sort overflows
- Active sorts

By analyzing these elements we can determine how sorts are performing. Of primary interest to us is the existence of sort overflows. Sort overflows should be less than 10% of total sorts. For top performance 3% or less is even better. These six elements also give us a "picture" of sort activity in our database. We can record this information over time and use it to determine what our normal sort activity is, and also be able to realize when abnormal sort activity is occurring. We can then conduct further analysis to determine the source of the abnormal sort activity. Thus, using database snapshots over time, we can tell at any point in time when sort activity is abnormal and take appropriate action.

Corrective action consists of identifying and capturing rogue SQL, or increasing or decreasing DBM and DB CFG sort-related parameters. Generally, SQL is the first place you should look. By doing proper SQL tuning to eliminate sorts, you will eliminate most sort problems. This will result in a decrease in sort overflows. If, after tuning offending SQL, sort overflows still occur, then increase SORTHEAP until either no sort overflows occur (if enough memory is available) or at least try and keep sort overflows to less than 3% of total sorts. In order to tune sort overflows, we need to understand how and when sorts overflow.

- **Overflowed**—A sort overflows from SORTHEAP if the data being sorted cannot entirely fit in the sortheap allocated. It overflows into temporary tables in the bufferpool and possibly to disk.
- **Nonoverflowed**—A nonoverflowed sort completes in the sortheap and does not overflow to the bufferpool or disk.

Furthermore, sorts can be categorized as piped or nonpiped.

- **Piped**—A piped sort is a sort that can return data directly without requiring a temporary table and therefore completes in the allocated sortheap.
- **Non-piped**—A nonpiped sort requires the use of a temporary table to return sort results.

> **HINT**
> A piped sort always performs better than a nonpiped sort.

See Figure 12.1 for an example of a nonoverflowed, piped sort.
As illustrated in Figure 12.1, the sortheap is adequate in this example and the sort can complete in memory. This is the ideal sort if one is necessary.

> **HINT**
> In OLTP and Web-based environments, sort overflows should be kept to a minimum as queries in these environments typically return one row or a small number of rows and response time is key.

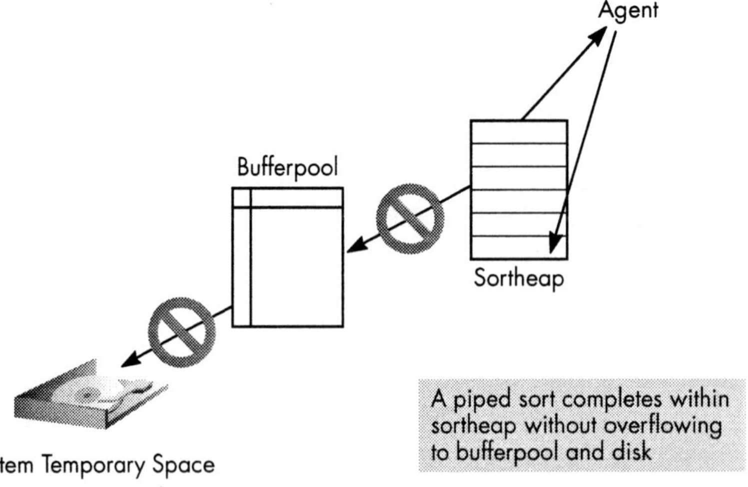

Figure 12.1
Nonoverflowed sort.

Figure 12.2 is an example of an overflowed sort. Overflowed sorts can seriously impact your ability to meet response time goals. Overflowed sorts overflow to the bufferpool and then possibly to temporary tables in a system temporary tablespace on disk. To make things worse, the sort results have to be read back from disk to the bufferpool or just possibly from the bufferpool if the temporary table was fully held in the bufferpool. Overflowed sorts use thousands of additional CPU instructions and possible disk reads. In a data warehouse environment with gigabytes or terabytes of data, it may not be possible to prevent sort overflows. In that case we need to tune the tablespace container placement for the system temporary tablespace. It should have multiple containers spread across multiple physical disks. This enables DB2 to use parallel I/O operations.

NOTE

With the arrival of 64-bit addressability in DB2 v8 and large main memories, even large environments will be able to minimize sort overflows by allocating much larger sort heaps. So help is on the way.

In either case, if the sort being performed cannot *completely* fit into `SORTHEAP`, the entire sort overflows through the bufferpool to system temporary space on disk.

CAUTION

If a sort overflows, the entire sort overflows through the bufferpool and system temporary space to disk. Therefore, sort overflows should be avoided where possible and even more so in OLTP environments.

See Figure 12.2 for an example of how sorts overflow.

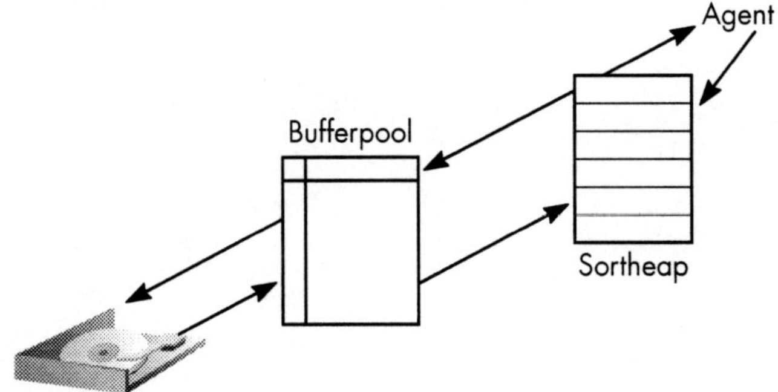

Figure 12.2
Sort overflow.

Sort overflows are more difficult to prevent in BI/DW environments with large result sets requiring large sorts and therefore large amounts of sort memory. This problem is obviated to some extent by the availability of 64-bit addressing (larger SORTHEAPs) and the onset of larger main memories, but sort overflows still may not be totally eliminated in these environments, due to just the sheer amount of data involved and other constraints.

NOTE
Database Index ANDing or ORing cause bitmaps to be built in sortheap. Use DB2 explain to determine if these types of index access are occurring and monitor sortheap and adjust as necessary.

SHEAPTHRES

As previously discussed SHEAPTHRES controls the amount of memory available for sort operations across the entire instance. When this threshold is reached, it has additional adverse effects on shared and private sorts:

- For shared sorts, it serves as a *hard limit* and additional shared sorts are not allowed until the total sort consumption falls below the SHEAPTHRES values.
- For private sorts, it serves as a *soft limit* and as agents request private sortheap, DB2 reduces the amount allocated (relative to the initial private SORTHEAP value) and continues to allocate smaller sortheaps to requesting agents. This of course causes degradation in response time but it does allow the sort to continue instead of the sort being terminated. These are known as *Post Threshold* sorts and can be monitored using snapshot monitoring.

Obviously, since the efficiency of sort operations are so important to us, how can we tell if they are performing satisfactorily? DB2 provides extensive capability to monitor sort performance through snapshot and event monitoring.

SIZING SORT MEMORY AREAS

Although DB2 provides default values for the various sort memory areas, these values are only intended for initial configuration and should be set based on monitoring information or benchmark testing.

You should calculate the initial settings for DB2 sort memory areas as follows:

SORTHEAP—use the default for your OS platform initially but monitor using database snapshots and if sort overflows are observed, then increase the value of the SORTHEAP parameter until few or no sort overflows are observed. While you are doing this you also need to consider whether or not the SHEAPTHRES parameter needs to be adjusted. If only private sorts are being used, the following formula can be used to provide a good estimate for SHEAPTHRES:

Total number of concurrent agents × database sortheap value

Take the product of the above results and use this for your initial SHEAPTHRES setting. This calculation takes into account the SORTHEAP requirements across an instance. This will be a good starting point but continuous monitoring is required to ensure that the value is adequate. Adjustments may be necessary if the workload is different than expected or if it changes over time.

Agent Private Sort (SORTHEAP DB CFG parameter)

DB2 explain output provides information regarding sorts such as the number of rows to be sorted, the width of the row, number of columns involved, and whether or not the sort is piped or if sort overflow is expected.

To determine the amount of sortheap required use the following formula:

# of rows to be sorted × row width = size of sortheap required.

Also, you can use the following formula to determine the number of concurrent ÷ private sorts that can be performed.

SHEAPTHRES ÷ average sortheap size =
maximum number of private sorts that can be active before post threshold sorts will occur

For shared sorts:

If post-threshold sorts are occurring, then either the SHEAPTHRES needs to be increased or SORTHEAP parameters reduced unless effective sort tuning is done. There are many methods available to reduce the amount of SORTHEAP required. We will discuss these in the next section.

So, what size is good for SHEAPTHRES? Well, it depends on your environment. What you don't want to do is make SORTHEAP and SHEAPTHRES so large that it causes OS paging. OS paging, in general, is worse than sort overflows and should be avoided whenever possible. I have seen SHEAPTHRES set to between 200–350 MB at many installations for both OLTP and DW environments. Typically, DW environments require larger SHEAPTHRES because of the nature of DW environments. You should use the previously provided formula for calculating SHEAPTHRES, but the aforementioned examples based on my experience are meant to give you an idea of the SHEAPTHRES setting that other companies may be using. At another client, SHEAPTHRES was set at 800 MB, and the total amount of space allocated to bufferpools was only 200 MB. This was an extreme case and these values should have been reversed. The problem in this case was that a third-party vendor package was being used and the DBAs had not looked at the SQL being run. Instead, they just kept increasing the values of `SHEAPTHRES` and `SORTHEAP`. The first place to look for a problem is the SQL! A quick snapshot of SQL being run indicated that applications were spending 90% of their time sorting and consuming all of the CPU on a 12-way S-80. One statement was captured and run through Index Advisor and some additional indexes were recommended. Visual Explain was used to review the access plan and it revealed eight separate sorts were being performed. A combination of Design Advisor recommendations and the Bonnie Baker method (local, `ORDER BY`, join predicates) was used to modify existing indexes and create two new ones. This eliminated five of the eight original sorts and reduced overall CPU consumption by 33%.

As a result of this tuning effort, `SHEAPTHRES` memory was able to be reduced. In addition to the example given, 30 additional SQL statements that were doing sorts were identified. Most of these sorts could have been eliminated using the techniques just discussed.

> **HINT**
> Look for statements with high amounts of CPU and sort time. These will typically be the resource consumers in a system. Eliminating these sorts will provide the biggest improvements to database performance.

MONITORING SORT PERFORMANCE

Database performance needs to be monitored on an ongoing basis. As part of that effort, `SORT` performance information must be gathered and analyzed. Two methods of monitoring sort performance are snapshot and event monitoring. First we'll discuss snapshot monitoring. We can use snapshot data to gather information on sort performance and resource consumption at the instance, database, and application level.

> **NOTE**
> New in v8 is the Health Center and Health Monitor. These can be used to monitor sort activity and generate alerts and recommendations when an automatic or user-calculated configuration setting has been breached.

Snapshot Monitoring

In addition to the previously discussed database snapshot, we can observe sort activity using application and table snapshot commands. Example 12.3 contains output from the `GET SNAPSHOT FOR APPLICATION on <database name>` command.

```
  Application Id: *LOCAL.genrod.020716203916
  Sequence number: 0001
Statement Identification:
  Statement Type: Dynamic
  Operation: Close
  Section number: 7
  Application creator: NULLID
  Package name: SQLLF200
  Cursor Name: SQLCUR7

Timestamps
  Start Time: 07-16-2002 19:29:47.310137
  Stop Time: 07-16-2002 19:29:47.310413
  CPU time: 2701.270000 seconds

Statement Activity

  Statement count: 13411

                  Metric      Total          Average       Min       Max
            Fetch Count:     256054            19.09         0        11
                  Sorts:          0             0.00         0         0

        Total Sort time:          0             0.00         0         0
         Sort Overflows:          0             0.00         0         0
              Rows Read:  733970392         54728.98         0    138888
           Rows Written:          0             0.00         0         0
  Internal Rows Deleted:          0             0.00         0         0
  Internal Rows Dpdated:          0             0.00         0         0
 Internal Rows Inserted:          0             0.00         0         0
               CPU Time:   2701.270             0.20     0.000     0.520
           Elapsed Time:   2731.921             0.20     0.000     0.574

  Application creator: NULLID
  Package name: SQLLF200
  # Agents created: 1
  Agents ID: 14
  SQLCA ...
  sqlcode: 100
  sqlstate: 02000
```

Example 12.3
Application Snapshot output.

Output from the application snapshot can be used to identify packages containing SQL that are performing sorts. This information can then be used to review the package for sections causing sorts to be performed. Once identified, action can be taken to eliminate them.

Unlike the database snapshot, which is very useful, the application and table snapshots contain little sort information. Therefore, you will find connection and statement event monitors much more useful.

> **HINT**
> You can use the `GET SNAPSHOT FOR DYNAMIC SQL` snapshot to take a snapshot of dynamic SQL. You can then sort through the output looking for statements that require sorts and tune and eliminate them using the techniques discussed.

Event Monitors

Event monitors are your key tool for identifying both top sort users and top sort SQL statements. This information can be gathered by creating an event monitor for *connections* and statements. The creation and use of event monitors will be covered in detail in Chapter 11. Example 12.4 contains output from a connection event monitor, which has been formatted using the `db2evmon` formatting tool.

In Example 12.4, the data elements we are interested in are listed under Sort and Hash Statistics.

```
3) Connection Header Event ...
 Appl Handle: 3
 Appl Id: *LOCAL.DB2.0092C2202617
 Appl Seq number: 000f
 DRDA AS Correlation Token: *LOCAL.DB2.0092C2202617
 Program Name : db2bp.exe
 Authorization Id: PGUNNING
 Execution Id : PGUNNING
 Codepage Id: 1252
 Territory code: 1
 Client Process Id: 2056
 Client Database Alias: SAMPLE
 Client Product Id: SQL08010
 Client Platform: Unknown
 Client Communication Protocol: Local
 Client Network Name:
 Connect timestamp: 01-22-2003 15:26:17.411636
```

Example 12.4
Connection Event Monitor output.
Note: This snapshot has been edited to remove unneccesary information.

```
4) Connection Event
 Appl Handle: 3
 Appl Id: *LOCAL.DB2.0092C2202617
 Appl Seq number: 0012

 Record is the result of a flush: FALSE

 Application Status: SQLM_DISCONNECTPEND

 Lock Statistics:
 Lock Waits: 0
 Total time waited on locks (milliseconds): 0
 Deadlocks: 0
 Lock escalations: 0
 X lock escalations: 0
 Lock timeouts: 0

 Sort Statistics:
 Sorts: 0
 Total sort time (milliseconds): 0
 Sort overflows: 0

 Hash Statistics:
 Hash Joins: 0
 Hash Loops: 0
 Hash Join Small Overflows: 0
 Hash Join Overflows: 0

 CPU times
 User CPU time used: Not Available
 System CPU time used: Not Available

 Disconnection Time: 01-22-2003 15:56:47.197122
```

Example 12.4
Connection Event Monitor output. (Continued)
Note: This snapshot has been edited to remove unneccesary information.

We can use the connection event monitor output to identify users consuming the most sort resources. Connection events show the true cost of sorts associated with the connection and application. We can use this information to contact users and investigate the high use of sort resources if necessary. We can then review statement event monitor data to identify the SQL statements causing the sorts. See Example 12.5 for an example of statement event monitor output.

```
718) Statement Event ...
 Appl Handle: 23
 Appl Id: *LOCAL.DB2.00F4C2203608
 Appl Seq number: 0002

 Record is the result of a flush: FALSE
 -------------------------------------------
 Type   : Dynamic
 Operation: Close
 Section : 5
 Creator : NULLID
 Package : SYSSH200
 Consistency Token : SYSLVL01
 Package Version ID :
 Cursor : SQL_CURSH200C5
 Cursor was blocking: TRUE
 Text   : select * from sysibm.syscolumns order by 1
 -------------------------------------------
 Start Time: 01-22-2003 15:37:09.100197
 Stop Time: 01-22-2003 15:37:15.322350
 Exec Time: 6.222153 seconds
 Number of Agents created: 1
 User CPU: Not Available
 System CPU: Not Available
 Fetch Count: 3144
 Sorts: 1
 Total sort time: 158
 Sort overflows: 1
 Rows read: 6288
 Rows written: 3144
 Internal rows deleted: 0
 Internal rows updated: 0
 Internal rows inserted: 0
 SQLCA:
 sqlcode: 100
 sqlstate: 02000
```

Example 12.5
Statement Event Monitor output.

We can use the output from Example 12.5 to identify and associate SQL statements with sort overflows, high number of sorts, and long sort elapsed time. We can then tune the SQL if needed to eliminate the sorts where possible.

ELIMINATING SORTS

Sorts can be eliminated by identifying appropriate indexes and ordering the columns in the indexes in the order required by the SQL statement being tuned.

However, when seeking out and eliminating sorts, we can't just take a blanket "create indexes" approach. When making the decision to create an index or not, you need to identify all the types of SQL activity performed on the table or tables involved. Putting an index on a 900 million now table that is heavily updated would not be a wise choice as DB2 would incur significant overhead updating all the index entries. Now, if this same table is read only, then it would make perfect sense to create the index to eliminate the sort if the query is important and run frequently enough to justify it. The only other considerations to analyze in this case are index rebuild time during utility operations. If the additional time required for index rebuild is acceptable, and improving response time through sort elimination is the business priority, then the index in this case is justified.

> **NOTE**
> An index can be used to obtain rows in an ordered sequence, eliminating the need for the database manager to sort the rows after they are read from the table.

While we are discussing using indexes to eliminate sorts, we should address who is responsible for the decision to add or modify an index. Well, it is clearly the DBA's responsibility, but the DBA cannot do this blindly. The DBA needs to work with application developers and business architects to identify the *business priorities.* After business priorities have been identified, then and only then can a DBA create or modify an index. The ultimate decision to create or modify an index rests solely with the DBA after conducting the appropriate coordination and fact finding we just outlined.

The reason I address this issue is because I have been in situations where the application development department had the final say. This approach cannot work because application developers are not trained in physical database design. The DBAs are the ones that have the skills and tools necessary to make an educated decision based on business priorities. Ultimately, the failure to meet business objectives with new applications usually falls back on the DBAs!

Example 12.6 is an example of an SQL statement (that was using lots of CPU time doing sorts) that was captured and used as input to the new Design Advisor (formerly Index Advisor).

```
 SELECT  DISTINCT  FILE_NAME FROM  PGUNN.T_SENT WHERE  COLLECTION_ID
= 1 AND  FILE_NAME IN ( SELECT  FILE_NAME FROM  PGUNN.T_RECE_DEFINED
WHERE  USER_ID = 1 AND  AGENT_ID = '?');
```

Example 12.6
SQL statement requiring a sort.

In Example 12.6, we have a SELECT DISTINCT SQL statement that will require a sort to eliminate duplicates if the rows we are interested in have duplicates. This statement was captured on a system that was suffering serious performance problems due to uncontrolled sorts and fully consumed sort resources. It was used as input to Design Advisor and amazing results were achieved.

```
execution started at timestamp 2002-08-12-16.23.39.356577
  found [1] SQL statements from the input file

Calculating initial cost (without recommmended indexes)
[23827.033203] timerons
Initial set of proposed indexes is ready.
Found maximum set of [2] recommended indexes
Cost of workload with all indexes included [143.370483] timerons
total disk space needed for initial set [  15.916] MB
total disk space constrained to         [  -1.000] MB
  2  indexes in current solution
 [23827.0332] timerons  (without indexes)
 [125.1684] timerons  (with current solution)
 [%99.47] improvement

 Trying variations of the solution set.
--
-- execution finished at timestamp 2002-08-12-16.23.39.735776
--
--
-- LIST OF RECOMMENDED INDEXES
-- ===========================
-- index[1],    15.821MB
   CREATE INDEX WIZ42 ON "PGUNN    "."T_SENT" ("COLLECTION_ID" DESC,
"FILE_NAME" DESC) ;
-- index[2],     0.095MB
   CREATE INDEX I_FILE_SELECTED ON "PGUNN    "."T_RECE_DEFINED"
("USER_ID" ASC, "AGENT_ID" ASC) ;
-- ===========================
--
DB2 Workload Performance Advisor tool is finished.
```

Example 12.7
Design Advisor output.

As illustrated in Example 12.7, Design Advisor output indicates that the cost of the SQL statement can be reduced by 99% if an index is provided. At the bottom of the output we can see the index and columns recommended by Design Advisor. Note that the 99% cost reduction is for one execution of this statement. If this statement is executed 1,000 times per hour, then the addition of the index to eliminate the sort will result in a significant reduction in CPU consumption! In our example, the indexes were created and significant CPU savings and sort memory reduction were achieved. This was just one of approximately 60 such statements that were performing unecessary sorts.

SQL Explain Tools

These are several SQL explain tools available for use in evaluating access plans. You can use the SQL explain tool of your choice to evaluate access plans in conjunction with Design Advisor.

SQL explain tools provided with DB2 UDB v8 are:

- `dynexpln`—Can be used from a command line to explain dynamic SQL statements.
- `db2expln`—Can be used from a command line to explain both static and dynamic SQL.
- `db2exfmt`—Can be used from a command line to format the contents of the explain tables.
- `DB2 Visual Explain`—Visual Explain can analyze both static and dynamic SQL statements and presents the results graphically. Refer to Figure 12.3 for an example of DB2 Visual Explain output.

Irrespective of the explain tool used, you will want to use the output to analyze the access plan of interest. DB2 explain tools display such items as the indexes being used, join methods used, timerons, index and table statistics, order of join operations, number and type of sort operations being

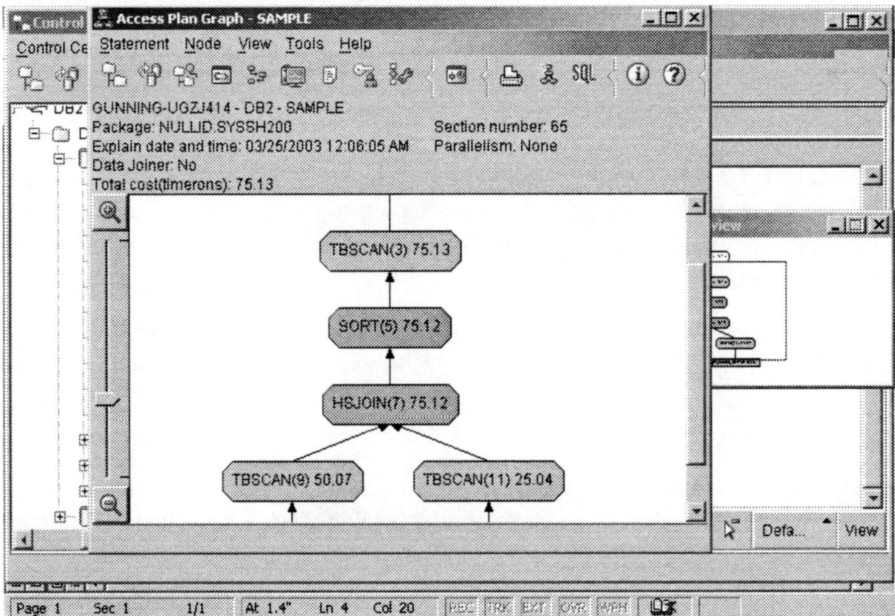

Figure 12.3
Visual Explain Input window.

performed, and optimization class used along with many other important details concerning the SQL being analyzed. Refer to the *DB2 UDB v8 Administration Guide: Performance* for additional details. For details on Visual Explain, refer to the *DB2 v8 Visual Explain Tutorial* manual.

If the SQL can be changed to eliminate the sort, then the SQL should be changed in conjunction with application development. If not, then use the index recommendations from Design Advisor to eliminate the sort.

Follow these steps for identifying, tuning, and eliminating sorts:

1. Identify SQL statements causing sorts using connection and statement event monitors.
2. Use Design Advisor to assist in identifying index improvements.
3. Use Visual Explain and change SQL if possible.
4. Modify or create indexes to eliminate sorts.
5. Repeat steps 1 thru 4 until all sort problems have been eliminated.

Use these five steps to tuning and eliminating sorts and you will significantly increase the performance of your databases.

Changing SQL

Changing SQL to eliminate sorts is one of the options available to us but it is generally not very effective. The reason for this is because applications and ad hoc queries usually contain `ORDER BY`, `UNION`, `DISTINCT`, or `GROUP BY SQL` statements that return results in a sorted order for use in developing reports for management or for returning ordered results to online applications.

A `UNION` can be changed to a `UNION ALL` to eliminate a sort if the application program can handle duplicates. A `DISTINCT SQL` statement can also be eliminated if the application can handle duplicates; however, `ORDER BY` and `GROUP BY` statements cannot be rewritten because the application must return results in an ordered manner. Therefore, you will have to use indexes to eliminate the sorts caused by these SQL statements.

Consider using predicates with good selectivity. Generally, try to use predicates with a selectivity of .01 or lower. Selectivity is used by DB2 to determine the number of rows that will be examined.

Allow Reverse Scans

The create index option `ALLOW REVERSE SCANS` can be used to enable a single index to be used to resolve sorts that require data in an ascending or descending order. This option is very effective at eliminating sorts required by `MIN` and `MAX` functions, fetch, and previous key, and eliminates the need for temporary tables for reverse scans. It is most effective when used on indexes on tables that already have several or many indexes defined on them and upon which the creation of additional indexes would cause inserts, updates, or deletes to slow down such that unacceptable performance would occur.

> **NOTE**
> The use of `ALLOW REVERSE SCANS` does use more CPU than indexes not defined with this option. If few indexes are on a table and business priorities dictate the fastest response time, do not use `ALLOW REVERSE SCANS` and create the required index with columns in the proper order.

SUMMARY

In this chapter we have discussed one of the top tuning areas in DB2, Sorts. Sorts are used to return data either to online forms or applications in an ordered manner. Sometimes using a sort is the best method, but often sorts cause the biggest application performance problems. DB2 can use indexes to eliminate sorts if the columns being sorted are defined in the index in the appropriate order. DB2 v8 gives us a new DB CFG parameter, `SHEAPTHRES_SHR`, with which to control the amount of shared memory available for shared sorts. This gives us the ability to control shared sorts at the database level instead of at the instance level.

Database snapshots provide us with details on overall sort performance at the database level. Additional snapshots are available to provide us with additional information on sorts. Connection and statement event monitors are the primary means available to us for gathering data on sort consumption and aid us in tuning and eliminating sorts.

The Design Advisor and Visual Explain are primary tools for us to use in tuning and eliminating sorts. Examples were provided where significant performance improvements were made, simply by using Design Advisor and knowledge of the application, to create or modify indexes to eliminate sorts.

Sort performance is probably a problem at your workplace. You can use the procedures and techniques outlined in this chapter to eliminate sorts and significantly enhance the performance of databases under your control.

C H A P T E R 13

Enterprise Server Edition—Database Partitioning Feature

DB2 v8.1 Enterprise Server Edition (ESE) is shipped with database partitioning as part of the base ESE product which enables the logical partitioning of data across many servers. In prior releases this was known as Enterprise Extended Edition (EEE). In order to use this option, you must license the Database Partitioning Feature (DPF). DB2 ESE uses a shared-nothing architecture. The shared-nothing architecture is very scalable. Unlike the Symmetric Multiprocessor (SMP) architecture, where scalability is limited by the amount of real memory that can be added and the overhead involved in managing multiple CPUs, shared-nothing architecture can scale by adding additional servers. DB2 provides mechanisms for extending data to these new servers. They will be covered later in this chapter.

My goal in this chapter is to provide you with an overview of database partitioning and with the details you will need to know to implement, support, and maintain a DB2-partitioned database.

WHEN SHOULD YOU USE PARTITIONED DATABASES?

This section is included because this is a question many of us have had to ponder, and arriving at a decision is not very easy unless you know what characteristics your application should have to work well with a partitioned database environment.

Besides the need for scalability, which is a basic feature of a partitioned database, we need to understand how DB2 uses parallelism so we can then determine if we should choose a partitioned or nonpartitioned database environment.

In a partitioned database environment, DB2 uses *interpartition parallelism,* where a single SQL statement is broken into a number of subset queries and each subset query works on a subset of the data. Each subset query is dispatched to the appropriate database partition, runs in parallel on a subset of the data, and returns results to the coordinating agent. The coordinator partition returns the results to the application. For example, a simple SELECT statement, such as "SELECT COLOR, STORE, SIZE FROM SKUDTL WHERE COLOR = 'BLUE'" in a four-partition database, would be decomposed into four subset queries across a subset of the data on the four partitions involved. These subset queries run in parallel, simultaneously, on the partitions involved. Since they run in parallel, the results can be returned much faster than if run on a uniprocessor. Partitioned databases also can process complex queries better than nonpartitioned databases. So with complex queries such as queries that use aggregations, multiple dimensions, and various time-dependent predicates, a partitioned database can process much of the work in parallel across multiple partitions and multiple servers, simultaneously. Again, this type of query runs well in a partitioned database environment. If your activity is primarily real-time inserts, updates, and deletes, then a nonpartitioned database would be a better choice as these operations don't lend themselves to high degrees of parallelism.

Finally, *interpartition parallelism* can be combined with *intrapartition parallelism* to return results even faster. When using both types of parallelism, DB2 can run subset queries across multiple database partitions and servers, and within these database partitions run additional sub-agents to scan, join, and sort data simultaneously. This powerful combination of two types of parallelism returns the results to the application very fast. Since each environment is different, you need to apply these guidelines to your requirements and then make the decision on whether or not to use DB2's partitioned database option.

The DB2 ESE Partitioning Option can be run on SMP servers or on a special server, referred to as a Scalar Power Parallel (SP) Complex. Many DPF environments start out on an SMP server with multiple processors and large memory and then scale to an SP complex as the data grows. See Figure 13.1 for an overview of SMP shared-everything architecture.

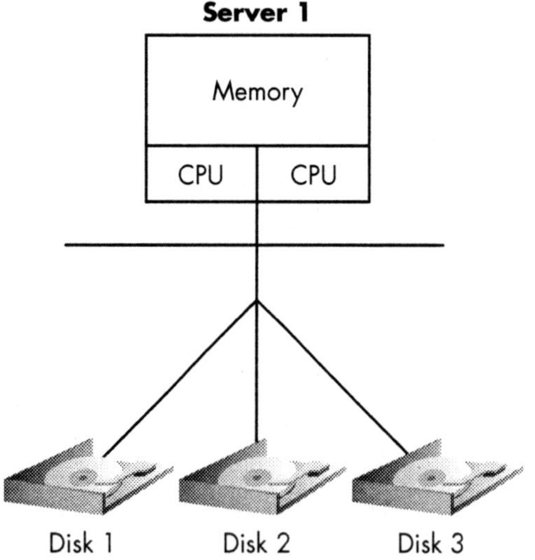

Figure 13.1
SMP (shared-everything) architecture.

Shared-everything architecture is very common, found mostly in OLTP environments. Its scalability is limited, however, by the overhead involved in managing multiple CPUs and bus and disk contention. The shared-nothing DPF of ESE solves this problem by providing the capability to partition data across multiple physical servers while at the same time presenting a single-database logical view to the end-user. This option provides massive SQL parallelism and can scale almost linearly. Figure 13.2 provides an overview of the shared-nothing architecture.

Shared-nothing architecture consists of a high-speed interconnect, used for sending SQL subqueries to multiple physical partitions and for returning query results, and usually a backup communications mechanism, in this case an Ethernet network. Each server in a shared-nothing architecture is usually using an SMP architecture with at least four CPUs.

Although it has become common to use DB2 on Linux running on blade servers with 1–2 CPUs. Having four CPUs enables CPU and I/O parallelism on each SMP server. In the DB2 ESE Partitioning Option, up to 999 partitions can be attached via the high-speed interconnect or network. Shared-nothing architecture is IBM's strategy for implementing massively parallel parallelism (MPP) via the ESE Partitioning Option. The DB2 ESE Partitioning Option is the DB2 configuration of choice for large data warehousing implementations. It is primarily used for decision support, business intelligence, and data warehousing applications. However, it is being used more and more in OLTP applications.

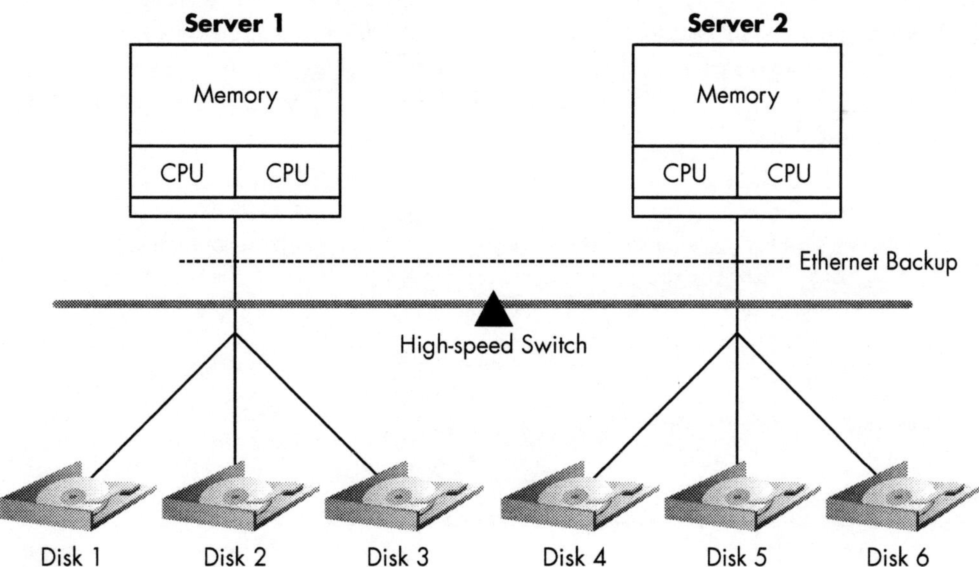

Figure 13.2
Shared-nothing architecture.

DB2 v8.1 ESE Improvements

DB2 v8.1 includes several Partitioning Option improvements. Improvements have been made in the following areas:

- Autoloader functionality has been included in the LOAD utility
- Local Catalog caching on each partition
- Identity Column Support with local cache
- Identity columns can form part of partitioning key
- Event Monitoring Enhancements

The following commands or functions have been integrated into the Control Center

- Multipartition control integrated into Control Center
- Redistribute Partitiongroup (Nodegroup)
- Create Table Wizard
- Add/Drop Partition (Node)
- MDC Creation

New Partitioning Terminology

With the introduction of v8.1, many terms have changed with partitioned databases. Most notably is the change from *node* and *nodegroup* to *database partition* and *database partition group.* This should eliminate the confusion from the past where at various times a node was referred to as a partition while at the same time it was also used to refer to a physical server. This change should help those new to DB2 a lot!

> **NOTE**
> Version 8.1 still supports these old terms, so you don't have to immediately change scripts that refer to the old names. However, have a plan to change them as they will probably not be supported in a future release or fixpack.

See Table 13.1 for a comparison of old and new terms.

Table 13.1 Old and New Partitioning Terms

DB2 v7.2 and Prior	DB2 v8.1
`LIST NODES`	`LIST DBPARTITIONNUMS`
`NODE`	`PARTITION`
`ADD NODE`	`ADD DBPARTITIONNUM`
`LIST NODEGROUPS`	`LIST DATABASE PARTITION GROUPS`

Table 13.1 Old and New Partitioning Terms (Continued)

REDISTRIBUTE NODEGROUP	REDISTRIBUTE DATABASE PARTITION GROUP
DROP NODE VERIFY	DROP DBPARTITIONNUM VERIFY

Database Partitioning

Sometimes it is hard to understand just what makes up a database partition. So I present a high-level view in Figure 13.3.

As illustrated in Figure 13.3, each database partition has its own:

- Data
- Database Configuration File (DB CFG)
- Log files
- Bufferpools
- Local caches (not pictured) for storing table descriptor information, authentication information, and local cache of identity column values

As you can see, there is no Database Manager Configuration (DBM CFG) file pictured. That's because there is 1 DBM CFG file per instance, not database. All partitions in the same instance share the same DBM CFG file.

> **NOTE**
> Generally, DB CFG parameters should be set the same across all partitions. All things being equal this helps to provide similar performance across all partitions.

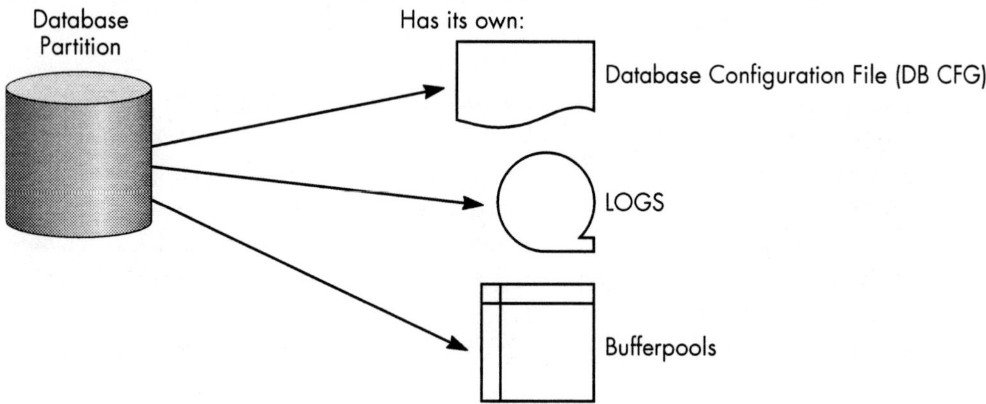

Figure 13.3
Database partition view.

DB2NODES.CFG File

Key to a successful DB2 installation is the *db2nodes.cfg* file. This file indicates to DB2 what partitions are defined and contains important port and communications information. This file must be created in the DB2 instance owner's home directory ($INSTHOME/SQLLIB). There is one file per DB2 instance and it contains one entry for each database partition per DB2 instance. It must be created before an instance can be created. The *db2nodes.cfg* file cannot be updated while DB2 is running. It is locked by DB2 during normal operation. It can be updated when DB2 is not running and as part of the `ADD DBPARTITIONNUM` option of the `DB2START` command. This will be covered in more detail later in this chapter. See Table 13.2 for a list of *db2nodes.cfg* field definitions.

Table 13.2 *db2nodes.cfg* File Field Definitions

File Entries			
DB Partition Num	**hostname**	**Logical Port**	**netname**
1	host1	0	switch1
2	host1	1	switch1
3	host2	0	switch2
4	host2	1	switch2
5	host3	0	switch3

The *db2nodes.cfg* file contains one entry for each database partition per DB2 instance, which DB2 uses for configuration information as follows:

- `DB PARTITIONNUM` is a required field. Each entry must be unique. The range of numbers must be between 0–999. The first value does not have to be 0. Entries must be in ascending order. Gaps can exist in the sequence for future growth.
- `HOSTNAME`—Name of the host network interface.
- `LOGICAL PORT`—Used by DB2 to distinguish between multiple database partitions on a single host (server). If not specified it defaults to 0. Each entry must be unique per host (server). If using a single database partition per host, if the logical port is specified it must be 0. If using multiple database partitions on a single host (server), the logical port number must start at 0 and 1, 2, 3, 4 and so forth for each host (server). If multiple database partitions are on a single host (server), the number of logical ports defined is the maximum number of database partitions for that particular host.
- `NETNAME`—If a high speed switch is being used, the `NETNAME` field is used for communications.

A range of ports must be reserved in the */etc/services* file with one port per database partition per host server.

In Figure 13.4, we have multiple database partitions on multiple servers.

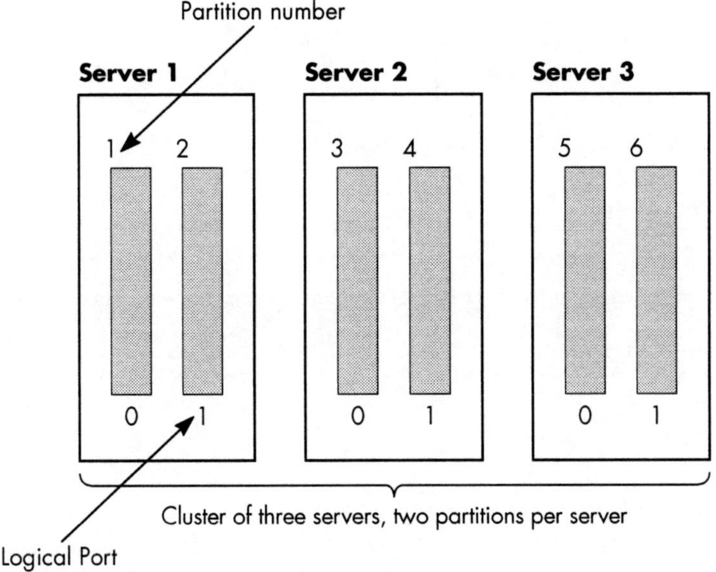

Figure 13.4
Server with multiple partitions (2) per server.

As we can see in Figure 13.5, a logical port has been assigned to each database partition on each server.

/etc/services

```
DB2_ATG           30000/tcp  # comment
DB2_ATG_END       30001/tcp  # comment
```

Figure 13.5
/etc/services multiple database partitions (2) per host.

The first port name must be the name of the instance, preceded by DB2_. In this example, our instance name is ATG, therefore our entry in the */etc/services* file is DB2_ATG. The last port name entry must be the name of the instance, preceded by DB2_ and suffixed by _END. So in our example we are using DB2_ATG_END and we define two ports, one for each database partition per server. The rule for reserving ports is as follows:

> Number of ports reserved (last port number – initial port number + 1) must be greater than or equal to the maximum number of database partitions on any individual host. *The same ports must be reserved on all hosts.*

In Figure 13.6, we have an example with two hosts and one database partition per server.

db2nodes.cfg	*/etc/services*
1 server1 2 server2	DB2_ATG 30000/tcp

Figure 13.6
Two hosts (servers) and one database per partition.

In this example we have entries for each partition (1 and 2) and a hostname, server1 and server2, in this case.

> **NOTE**
> If using netname you must specify a logical port.

We also show an entry reserving a TCP/IP port in the */etc/services* file (`DB2_ATG 30000/tcp`). It should be noted that the `HOSTNAME`, not the `SWITCH NAME`, is used for `DB2START` and `DB2STOP` processing. In our last example, Figure 13.7, we have an example of multiple database partitions per host and multiple hosts, with the associated entries for the *db2nodes.cfg* and */etc/services* files.

In Figure 13.7, we show that the first logical port on each server must be 0. This example shows two database partitions per host in a three-host configuration. Note that the port range reserved in /etc/services is for two ports per host (server).

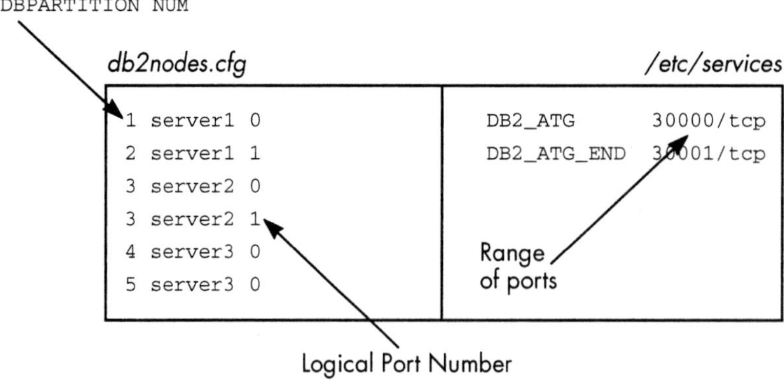

Figure 13.7
Three Hosts with two database partitions each.

Partitioning Keys

DB2 uses a partitioning key and a hashing function to evenly distribute data across tables in database partitions. The partitioning key is defined using the `CREATE TABLE` command. Criteria that you should use for selecting partitioning keys are:

- Frequently used join columns
- Columns that have a proportion of different values
- Integer columns are more efficient than character columns
- Equi-join columns
- Use the smallest number of columns possible

There are rules associated with creating partitioning keys. Most of these rules are designed to enable DB2 to provide good performance. The following rules apply to partitioning keys:

- Primary key or unique index must include the partitioning key
- Long varchar and LOB columns cannot be part of the partitioning key
- If no partitioning key is specified, the first column that is not a long field is used
- Tables containing only long fields cannot have partitioning keys and can only be placed into single-partition database partition groups

> **NOTE**
> New in v8.1, Identity Columns are supported and can be part of the partitioning key.

Partitioning Map Concepts

As depicted in Figure 13.8, the value of the partitioning key is input to a hashing algorithm that determines what partition will contain the data.

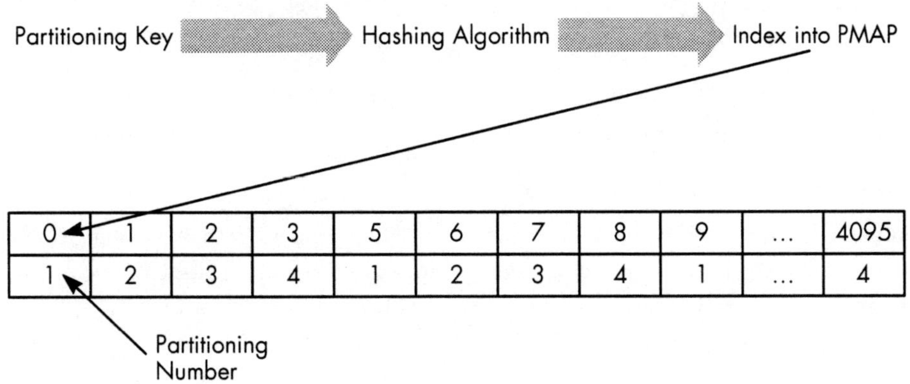

Figure 13.8
Partitioning map process.

The following steps describe the flow in Figure 13.8:

1. Data is being inserted into a table in the database and the value of the partitioning key is provided.
2. The partitioning key is provided to the hashing algorithm. The hashing algorithm transfers the partitioning key value into a number between 0 and 4095 and that new value is used as an index into the partitioning map.
3. The Partitioning Map (PMAP) contains a value at the index that indicates the database partition number where the row is to be stored.

DB2 keeps track of PMAP entries in the DB2 catalog, which is accessible through the `SYSCAT.PARTITIONMAPS` catalog view. The `PARTITIONMAP` column contains the PMAP for a particular database partition stored as a Long `VARCHAR` data type. We will see later in this chapter how we can extract the contents of the PMAP using the *db2gpmap* utility.

If we look at the partition number in Figure 13.8, we see that it is being assigned in a round-robin fashion. Partition numbers are assigned in ascending order from 1 to 4 in this example (because we have four partitions). This is the DB2 default partition assignment method. The default partition assignment is generally adequate and will provide an even distribution in most cases. A customized PMAP can be created if data skew is a problem. Refer to the *DB2 UDB v8.1 Administration Guide: Implementation* for further details. Now that we have looked at database partitioning and partitioning maps, we need to discuss another aspect of database partitioning called a Database Partition Group.

Database Partition Group

A database partition group is a grouping of database partitions within a database. A database partition can be a member of more than one database partition group. A database partition group has a database PMAP associated with it. We can use database partition groups to specify which partitions will contain a particular table's data. There are two types of database partition groups:

- Single–Partition Database Partition Group—Contains only one database partition
- Multipartition Database Partition Group—Contains more than one database partition

See Figure 13.9 for an example of a database partition group.

As we can see in Figure 13.9 we have two database partition groups. Both are multipartition databases, with the `INV_MATCH` database partition group comprising all the database partitions, and the `ATGW_P` database partition group, which does not include database partition #1. We will see the importance of database partition groups under the next section on collocated joins. The following commands were used to create the database partition groups in the previous example:

```
db2 create database partition group INV_MATCH on all DBPARTITIONUMS
db2 create database partition group ATGW_P on DBPARTITIONNUMS (2,3,4)
```

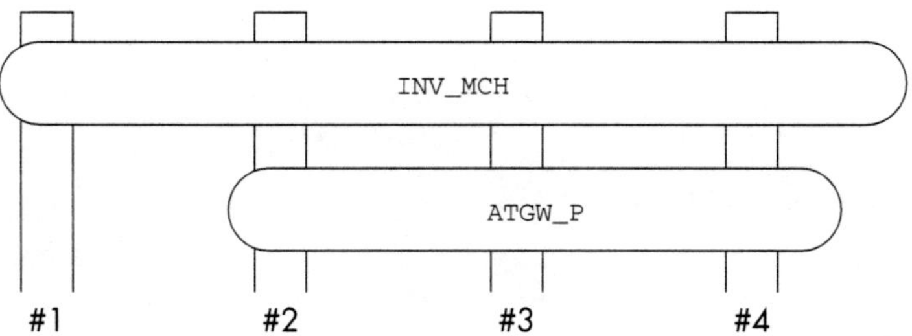

Figure 13.9
Database partition group.

Collocated Joins

Collocated joins are used by DB2 wherever possible so that data does not have to be shipped from partition to partition. Collocation between two joining tables means having the matching rows of the two tables always in the same database partition. If data is not collocated, DB2 has to move data through the network, whether over the SP switch or through an Ethernet or similar network. Since network transfer speeds are relatively slow, this results in poor performance.

Collocated joins can be used if the tables involved meet the following rules (for tables in multi-partition database groups):

- The tables must reside in the same database partition group

The following rules apply to both single and multipartition database partition groups:

- The database partition groups of both tables must have the same partitioning map.
- Corresponding partitioning key columns must be partition compatible (the same or similar base data type).
- The partitioning key from both tables must have the same number of columns.

In Figure 13.10 we can see that when tables T1 and T2 are joined, the rows from both tables reside in the same database partition and therefore can be joined without having to send the data between database partitions.

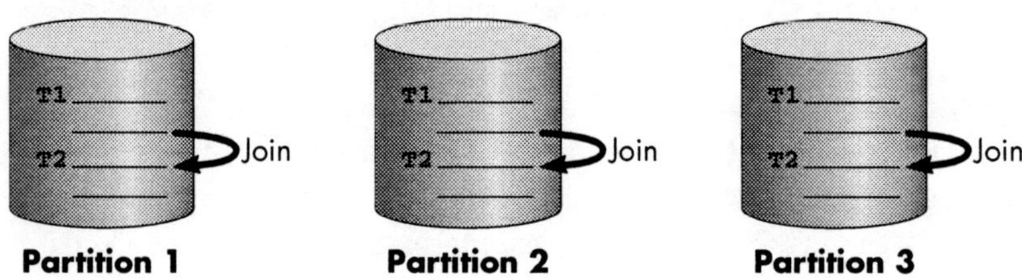

Figure 13.10
Collocated join example.

TIP
Always use collocated tables for good performance.

PARTITIONED DATABASE JOIN STRATEGIES

Chapter 3 discussed join concepts and strategies for nonpartitioned databases. In this section we'll discuss partitioned database join strategies. As shown in Table 13.3, there are six basic partitioned join strategies.

Table 13.3 Partitioned Database Join Attributes

Join Strategy	Outer Table	Inner Table
Collocated Table Join	Temporary Table	Temporary Table
Directed Inner Table Join	Temporary Table	Table Queue Hashed
Directed Outer Table Join	Table Queue Hashed	Table Queue Hashed
Directed Inner and Outer Table Join	Table Queue Hashed	Table Queue Hashed
Broadcast Inner Table Join	Temporary Table	Table Queue Broadcast
Broadcast Outer Table Join	Table Queue Broadcast	Temporary Table

We'll discuss each one in detail and look at the associated performance impacts of each strategy.

Directed Inner Table Join Strategy

With the *directed inner join strategy*, it may only be chosen as the join strategy when there are equijoin predicates on all partitioning key columns of the two partitioned tables. With the *directed inner join strategy*, the rows of the inner table are directed to the set of database partitions based on the hashed values of the joining columns. Once the rows are relocated to the target database partitions, the join between the two tables occurs on these database partitions. In Figure 13.11, we can examine sequence and flow of the *directed inner join strategy*.

The sequence of activity in a *directed inner table join strategy* is as follows:

1. The coordinator node receives the request from the application.
2. The coordinator node sends the request to all partitions involved.
3. The partitions scan the outer table and apply any predicates to the intermediate result set.
4. The partitions hash the join columns of the inner table that correspond to the outer table's partitioning key.
5. Based on the hashed values, the rows are then sent via a table queue to the partitions involved.

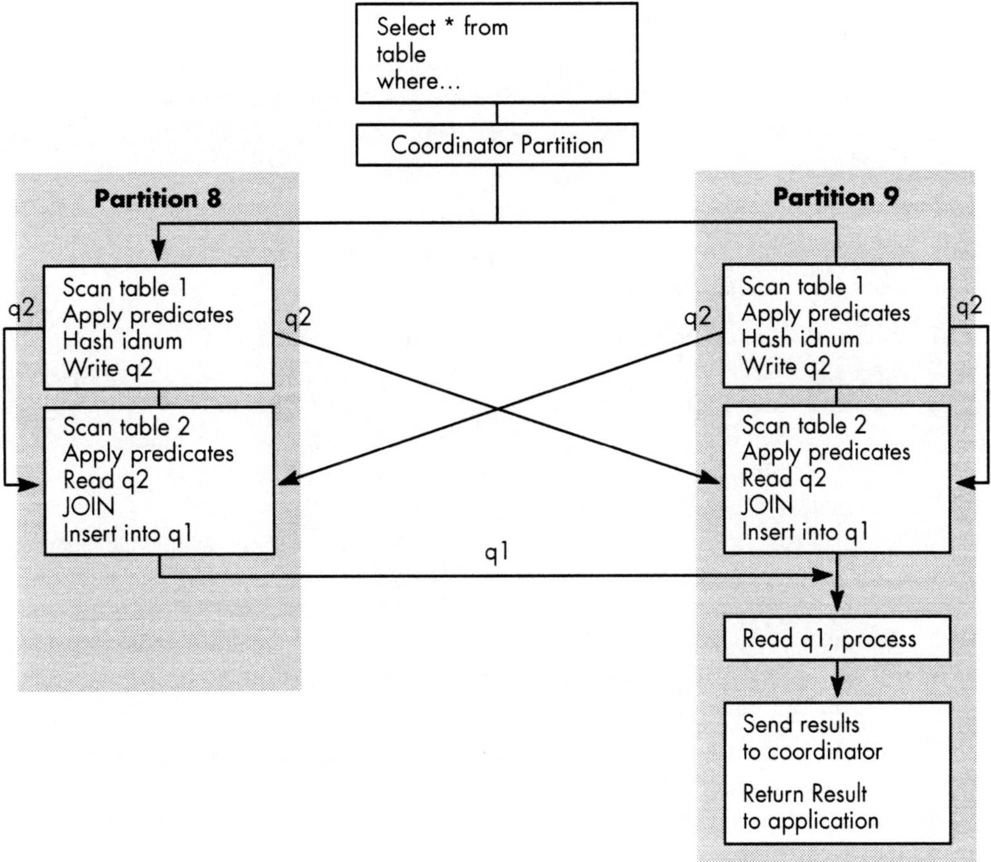

Figure 13.11
Directed inner table join strategy.

6. The target partitions receive the inner rows via a table queue.
7. The receiving partitions scan the outer table and apply any predicates.
8. The partitions then perform a join of the received inner table rows and the outer table.
9. The partitions then send the results of the join back to the coordinator partition.
10. The coordinator partition performs any final processing and returns the results to the requesting application.

An explain of the *directed inner table join strategy* will always show the outer table as a temporary table and the inner table as a table queue that has been hashed to the target partitions. With a *directed outer table join strategy*, the processing is the same except that the table that was directed to the target database partitions based on the hashed value of the joining columns is taken by DB2 as the outer table of the join.

Directed Inner and Outer Table Joins

The *directed inner and outer table join strategy* is a combination of a directed inner and directed outer table join strategy. In this case, rows from both the outer and inner tables are directed to a set of database partitions. The join then occurs on those database partitions. This join strategy may be chosen by the optimizer when the following conditions exist:

- The partitioning keys of both tables are different from the join columns.
- At least one equijoin predicate exists between the tables being joined.
- Both tables are relatively large.

The following sequence of operations occurs during a *directed inner and outer join*:

1. The initial request is received by the coordinator database partition.
2. The coordinator database partition sends the request to all involved partitions.
3. The outer table will be scanned on all the partitions that contain the table chosen as the outer table of the join. Predicates will be applied.
4. The inner table will be scanned on all database partitions that contain the table chosen as the inner table of the join. Predicates will be applied.
5. The outer table database partitions will hash each selected row from the outer table using the join columns specified in the query.
6. The inner table database partitions will hash each selected row from the inner table using the join columns specified in the query.
7. Each database partition involved will send the hashed rows to the appropriate database partition via hashed table queues.
8. The selected database partitions will receive the hashed table queues for the outer table rows.
9. The selected database partitions will receive the hashed table queues for the inner table rows.
10. The database partitions perform the join of the received outer table rows to the received inner table rows. Predicates will be applied.
11. The results of the join are then sent from the database partitions to the coordinator partition. The coordinator partition then completes any processing and returns the results to the applicaton.

Figure 13.12 depicts the *directed inner and outer table join sequence.*

You can recognize a directed inner and outer table join by the presence of the local join of two hashed table queues, in this example, q2 and q3.

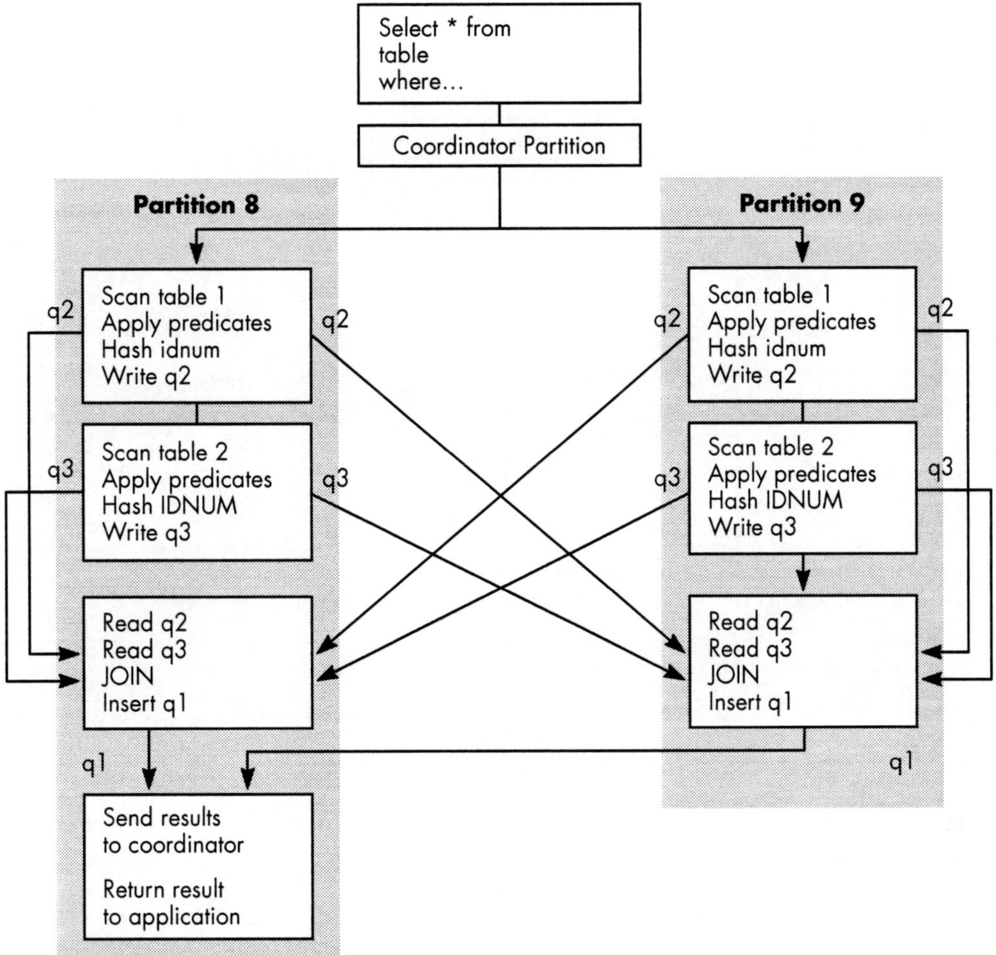

Figure 13.12
Directed inner and outer table join sequence.

Broadcast Table Joins—Inner and Outer

Broadcast table joins may be used when there is one very large table and one very small table involved in the join. *Broadcast table joins* may be used by the optimizer when the following conditions exist:

- No equijoin predicates exist between the joined tables.
- When the optimizer determines it is the most efficient method.
- When it is cheaper to broadcast the smaller table to all the database partitions where the larger table resides, rather than relocating the data in both tables.
- When the results of applying predicates to a large table results in a very small table.

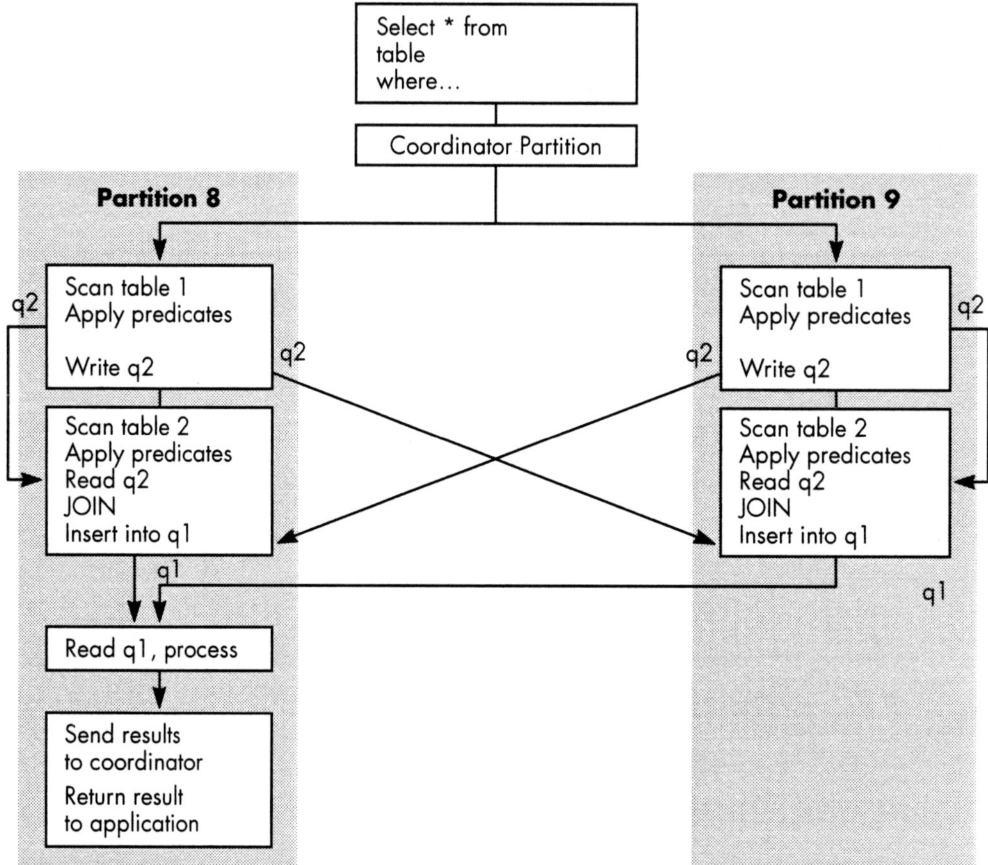

Figure 13.13
Broadcast table join sequence.

Figure 13.13 depicts the sequence of events in a *broadcast table join.*

The sequence of activity for a *broadcast outer table join* as depicted in Figure 13.13:

1. The coordinator partition receives the request.
2. The coordinator partition sends the request to all involved partitions.
3. The database partitions scan the table that was chosen as the outer table and apply any predicates to the intermediate result set.
4. The database partitions transmit the full resultant outer table to all involved partitions via table queues.
5. The database partitions receive the full resultant outer table via a table queue.
6. The receiving database partitions scan the inner table and apply any predicates. The output from this step is placed in a temporary table.

7. The database partitions then perform a join of the received outer table and local temporary inner table.
8. The database partitions then send the results of the join back to the coordinator partition.
9. The coordinator partition performs any final aggregation or other processing and returns the results to the application.

Similar to a directed inner and outer join, the broadcast inner and outer join are similar in operation where the rows from the outer table are broadcast to partitions where the inner table has rows, and the rows from the inner table are broadcast to partitions where the outer table has rows.

The End Result—Performance

Collocated table joins are the preferred join method when using the ESE Partitioning Option, as this precludes data from having to be shipped from partition to partition. Additionally, when joining very small and very large tables where no equijoin predicates exist, it is beneficial to define the small table to a separate database partition group so the optimizer will choose to broadcast the small table to the database partitions where the larger table resides.

Dynamic Bitmap Index Anding (DBIA)

Dynamic bitmap index ANDing (DBIA) is a powerful feature that results in significant performance improvement for queries when chosen by the optimizer. DBIA may be chosen by the optimizer when processing queries containing multiple AND predicates in which the columns specified in the AND predicates are contained in one or more indexes. Figure 13.14 is an example of how DBIA works.

In Step 1, DB2 performs an index scan to identify the qualifying RIDs for the first table and then

- hashes the RIDs to a location in the bitmap,
- sets the bit in the hashed location of the bitmap to 1, and
- repeats where all qualifying RIDs are located in the index scan.

In Step 2, DB2 proceeds to the next table and

- performs an index scan to identify the qualifying RIDs from the current table,
- initiates a probe of the bitmap to which the new RID will be hashed in the previous generated bitmap, and
- if the value in the bitmap location is one, then this indicates that the previous scan also found a qualifying RID and that this position in the bitmap is to be carried forward to the new bitmap being generated by the current scan.

No locations will be carried forward that do not have a qualifying bitmap slot in both the current and previous steps.

```
SELECT PO_NUM FROM INVOICE WHERE PO_QTY
> 100 AND PO_ECO_REORD_QTY
> 25
(SQL Select statement used in Figure 13.16.)
```

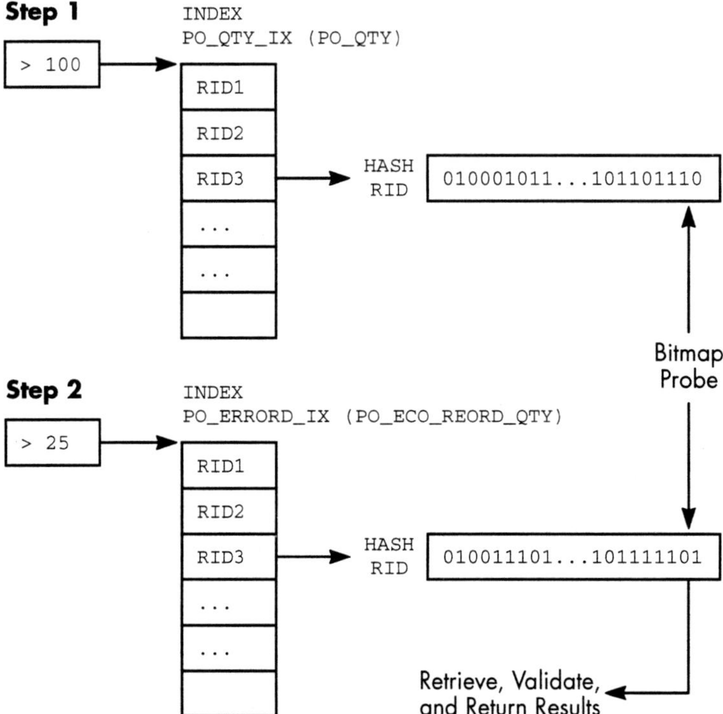

Figure 13.14
Dynamic bitmap index ANDing.

- This step will be repeated until all index entries are processed.

In Step 3, data is validated and returned to the requesting application as follows:

- For each bit location set to 1 in the bitmap, return the RID, retrieve the row, and validate it based on the predicates involved.
- Continue retrieving and validating all qualifying rows.
- Returned validated rows to the requesting application.

NOTE
You can determine if DB2 is using DBIA by using DB2 Explain and looking for `INDEX ANDING` and `INDEX ANDING BITMAP BUILD` in the explain output.

It is important to have accurate statistics for the optimizer to use in evaluating the use of DBIA during optimization. To provide the optimizer with adequate statistics you can execute the RUNSTATS command as follows:

```
RUNSTATS on table PO_INVOICE
    with DISTRIBUTION
    and DETAILED INDEXES ALL;
```

To just execute RUNSTATS on indexes, use:

```
RUNSTATS on table PO_INVOICE
    with DISTRIBUTION
    and DETAILED INDEX PO_QTY_IX
```

CAUTION
The database manager uses sortheap when creating the Dynamic Bitmap. Based on index cardinality, DB2 will estimate the amount of sortheap required. If DB2 shows frequent use of DBIA in your environment, take this into consideration when specifying the SORTHEAP DB CFG parameter.

DBIA can also be very beneficial to queries in Data Warehouse environments.

Index Considerations in a DPF Environment

In DPF, when an index is created, it is created across all database partitions for the target table. Like tables, index and data are spread across all database partitions where the table resides.

OLTP Environments

A good rule of thumb to follow would be a maximum of 3–5 indexes on a table. However, each environment is different, and the business priorities of the corporation should help to provide guidelines on what's important and what's not. Then you can use that information to help you to decide whether or not to create an index. Additionally, the type of application access must be considered when deciding on whether or not to create an index. If a table is heavily updated or inserted into, then additional indexes would slow down these operations and a new index would not be advised. However, if the opposite was true, where selects (reads) were the priority, then creating a new index would be beneficial. DBAs need to work with business architects and developers to arrive at the best solutions.

BI/DW Environments

A good rule of thumb in this environment is 5–10 indexes, depending on the maintenance window for the ETL process, space considerations, and again, business priorities. Since BI/DW tables are generally read only, more indexes can be used to provide the desired access paths to eliminate table scans and costly sorts. Ensuring that the periodic load of ETL data completes in the time allotted is usually one of the driving factors affecting the number of indexes in BI/DW environments.

For both OLTP and BI/DW, when in doubt, use an index. But you should really understand how the data is accessed and what the business priorities are. This general rule should only be used intermittently, when business priorities are not provided.

LOAD UTILITY CONSIDERATIONS IN A DPF ENVIRONMENT

In DB2 v8, the load utility incorporates all functions of the former Autoloader Utility. Pre-v8 autoloader behavior is still supported. Pre-v8 autoloader behavior can be used by setting the `DB2_PARTITIONEDLOAD__DEFAULT` MPP Configuration variable to NO, which will cause the default MODE to be set to `LOAD_ONLY`. This needs to be used if you were loading data into a single partition using the former `SPLIT_ONLY` mode of Autoloader and don't want to change existing scripts. However, have a plan in place to change them as this support will probably be dropped in a Fixpack or future release. The *db2atld* executable can still be used and it still accepts a configuration file. In v8, however, only one connection will be established when loading data into a multipartition database. Pre-v8, *db2atld* established one connection per output partition. The `LOAD_ONLY_VERIFY_PART` mode and any other new features of the v8 `LOAD` utility cannot be used when using the *db2atld* executable.

LOAD UTILITY OPERATIONS

Before data can be loaded in a partitioned database environment, the data must be "partitioned" so that the load utility can load the table data over the correct database partitions using the associated partitioning keys and PMAP. Prior to v8, this was referred to as "splitting" the data. Splitting is no longer applicable and we will use "partition or partitioning" to refer to the separation of data in accordance with the output from the hash function.

Before starting a load operation, a connection must be made to the database. By default, the partition that you connect to becomes the coordinator partition. Typically, this is partition 0, which is where the `CREATE DATABASE` command was issued from when you initially created the database. A partitioned database load operation has two phases: *setup* and *load*. During the setup phase, resources and locks are acquired. During the load phase, the data is loaded into the appropriate partitions. The `ISOLATE_PART_ERRS` option of the `LOAD` command determines how errors are handled during either of these phases. A description of this option can be found later in this chapter.

There can be only one coordinator partition per load operation. The coordinator partition can be changed by issuing the `SET CLIENT CONNECT_NODE` command via the CLP before issuing the `LOAD` command.

A load can have several types of agents associated with it:

- Prepartitioning agent—reads user input data and distributes it in a round-robin fashion to partitioning agents.

- Partitioning agent—receives data from the prepartitioning agent and partitions the data.
- Load agents—run on each output partition and coordinate the loading of data on that partition.
- Load-to-file agents—receive data from partitioning agents and write to a file on their partition.
- File transfer command agents—run on the *coordinator* partition and execute file transfer commands.

NOTE

Prepartitioning and partitioning agents run on the *coordinator partition.* A maximum of one partitioning agent is allowed per partition for any load operation. The data file to be loaded is assumed to reside on the coordinator partition unless the CLIENT option is specified.

Figure 13.15 is an example of loading data using `PARTITION` and `LOAD` in a partitioned database environment.

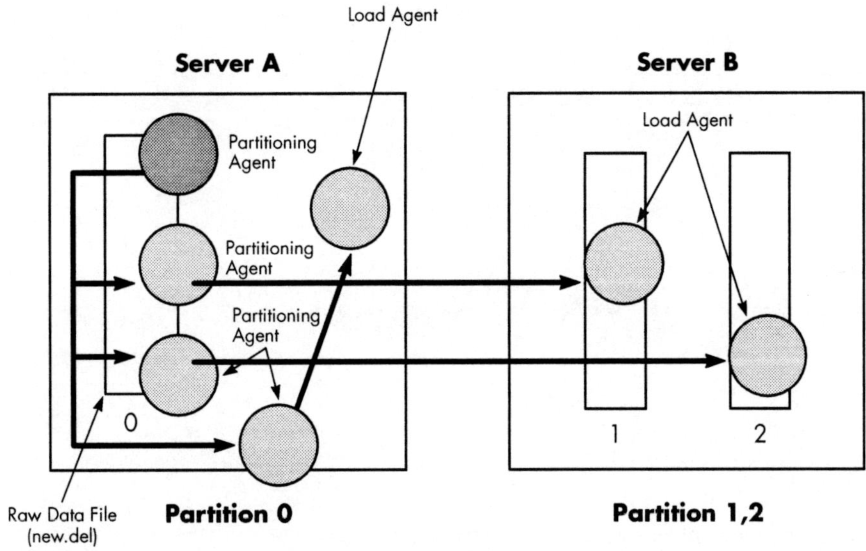

Command: `LOAD FROM new.del OF DEL REPLACE INTO TABLEY`

Note: This command illustrates the default load behavior if options are not specified. The `MODE` option will default to `PARTITION AND LOAD`, and the `OUTPUT_DBPARTNUMS` option will default to all nodes on which `TABLEY` is defined, `PARTITIONING_DBPARTNUMS` will default to the set of nodes selected according to `LOAD` command defaults to achieve optimal load performance.

Figure 13.15
Partition and load example using default options.

In Figure 13.15 the load operation proceeds as follows. A connection is made to the database, which defaults to Partition 0, and Partition 0 is the coordinator node. The file new.del resides on Server A in the working directory. A prepartitioning agent is created on Partition 0 along with partitioning agents since the PARTITIONING_DBPARTNUMS option was not specified. And finally, load agents are created on all partitions to coordinate the loading of data.

Figure 13.16 is an example of a load operation using PARTITION ONLY.

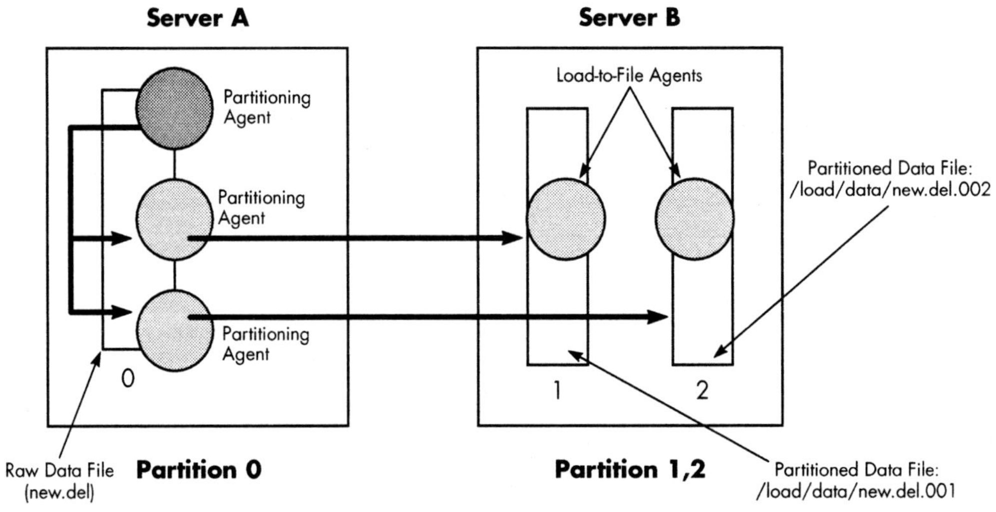

Command: LOAD FROM new.del OF DEL REPLACE INTO TABLEY PARTITION_ONLY PART_FILE_LOCATION /load/data OUTPUT_DBPARTNUMS (1,2)

Note: This command illustrates the PARTITION_ONLY mode, Data will be partitioned for partitions 1 and 2, and files placed on these partitions in accordance with the OUTPUT_DBPARTNUMS option.

Figure 13.16
Example of LOAD USING PARTITION ONLY.

Table 13.4 contains a useful comparison of pre-v8 and v8 LOAD MODE option behavior.

Table 13.4 Comparison of Pre-v8 and v8 LOAD MODE Options

Load Options	Pre-v8.1 Equivalent	Description
PARTITION_AND_LOAD	SPLIT_AND_LOAD	Data is partitioned and loaded simultaneously on corresponding database partitions.
PARTITION_ONLY	SPLIT_ONLY	Data is partitioned and output written to files on each partition.

Table 13.4 Comparison of Pre-v8 and v8 LOAD MODE Options (Continued)

Load Options	Pre-v8.1 Equivalent	Description
LOAD_ONLY	LOAD_ONLY	Data is assumed to be already partitioned; the partitioning process is skipped and the data is simultaneously loaded.
LOAD_ONLY_VERIFY_PART	Use input file with no partition header information.	Data is assumed to be partitioned and the data file does not contain a header. Partitioning is skipped and data loaded on designated partitions.
ANALYZE	ANALYZE	An optimal partitioning map with even distribution across all partitions is generated.

The former autoloader configuration options are now options on the PARTITIONED DB CONFIG load parameter of the LOAD command. Details on each option follows.

Partitioned DB CONFIG Options

HOSTNAME

Indicates where the file containing data resides. It may be a z/OS host or another server or workstation. This option is only applicable when used in conjunction with the FILE_TRANSFER_CMD. If this option is not specified, the hostname *nohost* will be used.

FILE_TRANSFER_CMD

Specifies an executable file, batch file, or script that will be called before data is loaded onto any partition. The value specified must be a fully qualified path. The command is invoked using the following syntax:

```
<COMMAND> <logpath> <hostname> <basepipename> <nummedia> <source media list>
```

Where:

<COMMAND> is the command specified by the FILE:TRANSFER:CMD modifier.

<logpath> is the log-in path for the file from which the data is being loaded. Diagnostic or temporary data may be written to this path.

<hostman> is the value of the HOSTNAME configuration option.

<basepipename> is the base name for named pipes that the load operation will create and expect to receive data from. One pipe is created for every source file on the LOAD command. Each of these files ends with .xxx, where xxx is the index of the source file for the LOAD command and the <basepipename>. In pipe 119, two named pipes would be created: pipe 119.000 and pipe 119.001. The <COMMAND> file will populate these named pipes with user data.

<nummedia> specifies the number of media arguments that follow.

<source media list> is the list of source files specified in the LOAD command. Each source file must be placed inside double quotation marks.

OUTPUT_DBPARNUMS

Represents a list of partition numbers. The partition numbers represent the database partitions on which the LOAD operation is to be performed. The partition numbers must be a subset of the database partitions on which the table is defined. The default is that all database partitions will be selected. The list must be enclosed in parentheses and the items in the list must be separated by commas. Ranges are permitted (e.g., (0,2 to 6,20)).

PARTITIONING_DBPARTNUMS

Designates a list of partition numbers that will be used in the partitioning process. The list must be enclosed in parentheses and the items in the list must be separated by commas (e.g., (0,2 to 6,20)). Ranges are permitted. The partitioning nodes specified can be different from the database partitions being loaded. If not specified, the LOAD command will determine how many partitions are needed and which partitions to use in order to achieve optimal performance.

If the ANYORDER modifier is not specified as part of the LOAD command, only one partition agent will be used in the load session. Furthermore, if there is only one partition specified for the OUTPUT_DBPARTNUMS option, or the *coordinator node* of the LOAD operation is not an element of OUTPUT:DBPARTNUMS, the coordinator node of the LOAD operation is used as the partitioning partition. Otherwise, the first partition (not the coordinator node) in OUTPUT_DBPARTNUMS is used as the partitioning partition.

If the ANYORDER modifier is specified, the number of partitioning nodes is determined as follows:

$$\frac{\text{number of partitions in OUTPUT\_DBRATNUMS}}{4+1}$$

Then the number of partitioning nodes is chosen from the OUTPUT_DBPARTNUMS value, excluding the partition being used to load the data.

PART_FILE_LOCATION

In PARTITION_ONLY mode, PART_FILE_LOCATION designates the fully qualified location of the partitioned files. In LOAD_ONLY mode, it designates the fully qualified location of the partitioned files. This location must exist on each partition specified by the OUTPUT_DBPARTNUMS option. In PARTITION_ONLY mode, if this value is not specified, an error will be returned. In LOAD_ONLY and LOAD_ONLY_VERIFY_PART modes, their parameters must be specified whenever the data file name specified in the LOAD command is not fully qualified. The following notes apply when using the PART_FILE_LOCATION option:

- This parameter is not valid when the `CLIENT` parameter is specified and the `LOAD` operation is taking place in the `LOAD_ONLY_VERIFY_PART` modes.
- For all file types other than `CURSOR`, the location refers to the path where the partitioned files exist or are to be created. For the `CURSOR` file type, the location does not refer to a path, but to a fully qualified file name. This will be the fully qualified base file name of the partitioned files that are created on each output partition. Multiple files may be created with the specified base name if there are LOB columns in the target table.

`MODE`

Designates one of five load options and controls the type of load operations taking place. Valid values are:

- `PARTITION_AND_LOAD`—Data is partitioned and loaded simultaneously on the corresponding database partitions. This option can also be used to partition and load data in parallel.
- `PARTITION_ONLY`—Data is partitioned and the output is written to files in a *specified location* on *each loading partition.*
- `LOAD_ONLY`—Data is assumed to be already partitioned: the partition process is skipped, and the data is loaded simultaneously on the corresponding database partitions.
- `LOAD_ONLY_VERIFY_PART`—Data is expected to be already partitioned, but the data file does not contain a partition header. The partitioning process is skipped and the data is loaded simultaneously on the corresponding database partitions. During the `LOAD` operation, each row is checked to verify that it is on the correct partition. Rows containing partition violations are placed in a dumpfile if the *dumpfile* file type modifier is specified. Otherwise, the rows are discarded. If partition violations exist on a particular loading partition, a *single warning will be written to the load message file for that partition.*
- `ANALYZE`—An optimal partitioning map with even distribution across all database partitions is generated.

`MAX_NUM_PART_AGENTS`

Specifies the maximum number of partitioning agents to be used in a `LOAD` session. The default is 25.

`ISOLATE_PART_ERRS`

Specifies how the `LOAD` operation will react to errors that occur on individual partitions. The default is `LOAD_ERRS_ONLY`. Valid values are:

- `SETUP_ERRS_ONLY`—Errors that occur on a partition during setup, such as problems accessing a partition, or problems accessing a tablespace or table on a partition, will cause the `LOAD` operation to stop on the failing partitions but to continue on the remaining partitions. Errors that occur on a partition while data is being loaded will cause the entire operation to fail and roll back to the last point of consistency on each partition.

- LOAD_ERRS_ONLY—Errors that occur on a partition during setup will cause the entire LOAD operation to fail. When an error occurs while data is being loaded, the partition with errors will be rolled back to their last point of consistency. The LOAD operation will continue on the remaining partition until a failure occurs or until all data is loaded. On the partition where all the data was loaded, the data will not be visible following the LOAD operation. Because of the errors in the other partitions, the transaction will be aborted. Data on all of the partitions will remain invisible until a LOAD restart operation is performed. This will make the newly loaded data visible on the partitions where the LOAD operation completed and will resume the LOAD operation on partitions that experienced an error.

> **NOTE**
> The LOAD_ERRS_ONLY modifier of the ISOLATE_PART_ERRS option cannot be used with the ALLOW, READ ACCESS, or COPY YES options of the LOAD command.

- SETUP_AND_LOAD_ERRS—In this mode, partition-level errors during setup or loading data cause processing to stop only on the affected partitions. As with the LOAD_ERRS_ONLY mode, when partition errors do occur while data is being loaded, the data on all partitions will remain invisible until a LOAD restart operation is performed.

> **NOTE**
> The SETUP_AND_LOAD_ERRS modifier of the ISOLATE_PART_ERRS option cannot be used with the ALLOW_READ_ACCESS or COPY YES options of the LOAD command.

- NO_ISOLATION—Any error during the LOAD operation causes the transaction to fail.

STATUS_INTERVAL

Specifies how often you will be notified of the volume of data that has been read. The unit of measurement is megabytes (MB). The default is 100 MB. Valid values are whole numbers from 1 to 4000.

PORT_RANGE

Specifies the range of TCP ports used to create sockets for interval communications. The default range is from 6000 to 6063. If defined at the time of invocation, the value of the DB2ATLD_PORTS DB2 registry variable will replace the value of the PORT_RANGE load configuration option. For the DB2ATLD_PORTS registry variable, the range should be provided in the following format:

```
<lower-port-number>:< highest-port-number>
CLP format is slightly different:
<lower-port-number, highest-port-number>
```

> **NOTE**
> The default PORT_RANGE is only adequate for small workloads. You should use 150 ports as a starting point to avoid excessive communication errors.

CHECK_TRUNCATION

Specifies that the program should check the truncation of data records at input/output. The default behavior is that data will not be checked for truncation at input/output.

MAP_FILE_INPUT

Specifies the input file name for the partitioning map. This parameter must be specified if the partitioning map is customized.

MAP_FILE_OUTPUT

Specifies the output filename for the partitioning map. This parameter should be used when the ANALYZE mode is specified. An optional partitioning map with even distribution across all database partitions is generated. If this modifier is not specified and the ANALYZE mode is specified, the program exits with an error.

TRACE

Specifies the number of records to trace when you require a review of a dump of the data conversion process and the output of the basking values. The default is 0.

NEWLINE

Specifies when the input data file is an ASCII file with each record and delimited by a new line character and the RECLEN parameter of the LOAD command is specified. When this option is specified, each record will be checked for a new line character. The record length, as specified in the RECLEN parameter, will also be checked.

DISTFILE

Specified the name of the partition distribution file. The default is DISTFILE.

OMIT_HEADER

Specified that a partition map header should not be included in the partition file. If not specified, a header will be generated.

RUN_STAT_DBPARTNUM

If the STATISTICS YES parameter has been specified in the LOAD command, statistics will be collected only on one database partition. This parameter specifies on which database partition to collect statistics. If the value is –1 or not specified at all, statistics will be collected on the first database partition in the output partition list.

Monitoring Load Operations

LOAD operations on partitioned databases can be monitored using the LOAD QUERY command while connected to the partition of interest. To accomplish this, issue the following commands from the CLP for the partition of interest:

```
set client connect_node 3
connect to ATGW_P
load query table tabley
```

This command will display the contents of all message files that currently reside on the partition of interest for the table name specified. In conjunction with this command, remember to check the *db2diag.log* for load errors. If errors are detected, then corrective action must be taken to correct the problem or *restart* or *terminate* the load operation.

Restarting or Terminating a Failed Load Operation

Now that we know how to load data and monitor the status of a load operation, we need to be prepared to respond to failed load operations. Since downtime is very costly and most companies have tight maintenance or batch windows in which to accomplish database loads, we as DBAs must be very familiar with load restart procedures. In fact, they should be documented as part of your shop standards and practiced prior to first use.

The ISOLATE_PART_ERRORS option of the LOAD utility controls how errors are handled when loading data into a partitioned database. In general, failures during the *setup stage* do not require a restart or terminate. A failure during the *load stage* will require a LOAD RESTART or LOAD TERMINATE on all partitions involved. These can be broken down to actions and procedures to take when a failure occurs during either one of these stages. Before action can be taken, a failed setup or load must be detected, as described in the previous section.

Failures During the Setup Stage

When LOAD_ERRS_ONLY or NO_ISOLATION has been specified for the LOAD operation, and a LOAD operation fails on at least one partition during the setup stage, the entire LOAD operation will be aborted and the state of the table on each partition will be rolled back to the state it was in prior to the LOAD operation. In these instances, there is no need to issue a LOAD RESTART or LOAD TERMINATE command.

When SETUP_ERRS_ONLY or SETUP_AND_LOAD_ERRS has been specified for the LOAD operation, and a LOAD operation fails on at least one partition during the setup stage, the LOAD operation will continue on the partitions where the setup stage was successful, but the table on each of the failing partitions is rolled back to the state it was in prior to the LOAD operation. In this case, there is no need to perform a LOAD RESTART or LOAD TERMINATE operation, unless there is also a failure during the load stage.

To complete the LOAD process on the partitions where the LOAD operation failed during the setup stage, a LOAD REPLACE or LOAD INSERT operation must be run and the OUTPUT_DBPARTNUMS option specified so that only the partition numbers of the partitions that failed are completed. Let's use the following example:

> TABLEY is defined on partitions 0 through 4.
> The following LOAD command is issued:

```
load from new.del of del replace into tabley partitioned db config
isolate_part_errs setup_load_errs
```

> The LOAD operation fails during the *setup stage* on partitions 1 and 4. Since *setup stage* errors are being isolated, the LOAD operation will complete successfully and data will be loaded on partitions 0, 2, and 3. To complete the LOAD operation on partitions 1 and 4, the following command should be issued:

```
load from new.del of del replace into tabley partitioned db config
output_dbpartnums (1,4)
```

Failure During the Load Stage

If a LOAD operation fails on at least one partition during the load stage, a LOAD RESTART or LOAD TERMINATE command must be issued on all partitions involved in the LOAD operation, irregardless of whether or not they encountered errors during the LOAD operation. This is because the loading of data in a partitioned environment is done through a single transaction. When the LOAD RESTART operation is initiated, loading will continue where it left off on all partitions.

Let's use the following example:

> Tableny is defined on partitions 0 through 4. The following command is issued:

```
load from newy.del of del replace into tableny partitioned db
config isolate_part_errs no_isolation
```

> The LOAD operation fails during the *load stage* on partitions 1 and 4. To resume the LOAD operation, issue the LOAD RESTART command and specify the same set of output options as the original command since the LOAD operation must be restarted on all partitions:

```
load from newy.del of del restart into tableny partitioned db
config isolate_part_errs no _isolation
```

> **NOTE**
> For LOAD RESTART operations, the options specified in the LOAD RESTART command will be honored, so it is important that they are identical to the ones specified in the original LOAD command. If they are not the same the restart will fail.

When the LOAD TERMINATE command is issued after LOAD operation failure during the *load stage,* all work done in the previous LOAD operation will be lost and the table on each partition will be returned to the state it was in prior to the initial LOAD operation.

Going back to our first load example, if the PARTIONED DB CONFIG ISOLATE_PART_ERRS and NO_ISOLATION modifiers are specified and a failure occurs in the load stage, the LOAD operation can be terminated with the LOAD TERMINATE command that specifies the same output parameters as the original command:

```
Load from newy.del of del terminate into tableny partitioned db config
isolate_part_errs no_isolation
```

Adding a Database Partition

As corporations grow and new accounts, policies, and so on are acquired or if mergers and acquisitions occur, the data in the corporation will grow and the partitioned DB2 database will have to grow with the changing corporate requirements. Luckily, DB2 provides mechanisms to add database partitions and redistribute the data over the new partitions. New partitions can be added using existing servers or new servers can be added. There are two ways to add new partitions to a partitioned database:

1. Edit the *db2nodes.cfg* file and manually add the new database partition.
2. Use the db2start command with the ADDDBPARTIONNUM option.

After the new partition has been added, the REDISTRIBUTE DATABASE PARTITION GROUP command must be issued to rebalance the data across all partitions. For detailed information on adding partitions and redistributing data, refer to the *DB2 Administration Guide: Implementation.*

Improving Import Performance with Buffered Inserts

Although not specific to DPF, the IMPORT utility can take advantage of buffered inserts to improve insert performance. Buffered inserts reduce the amount of network message traffic required to accomplish inserts across a network.

Nonbuffered INSERT processing is serialized across all database partitions, which means there are waits involved. With buffered INSERTS, each row is hashed to an insert buffer at the coordinator partition (it is the size of the communication block) with one buffer for each partition.

After each buffer is filled, it is sent to the target partition. Since `INSERTS` are buffered, significantly fewer network messages are exchanged, resulting in improved performance.

The `INSERT BUF` option of the `PREP` and `BIND` commands can be used to enable buffered inserts. The `IMPORT` package must be rebound. This can be accomplished by binding the *db2uimpm.bnd* bind file against the database in question. This bind file is found in the *$INSTHOME/sqllib/bnd* directory.

Although buffered inserts will provide improved `IMPORT` performance, an error during the import will result in the entire block being rolled back. The `ROLLBACK` will be reported asynchronously, and the offending record will not be identified and a partial loss of data could occur. Make sure that the input data is valid before using `BUFFERED INSERTS`.

SUMMARY

In this chapter we have discussed partitioned database concepts. Central to DB2's partitioning strategy are partitioning keys and a hashing function. The shared-nothing architecture was discussed and presented as the architecture of choice for large partitioned databases.

Version 8 enhancements and new terminology were presented and discussed, and comparisons made between new and old commands to ease your transition to v8.

Partitioned database concepts such as partitions, database partition groups, partitioning keys, partitioning maps, and basic partitioned database performance concepts were presented.

Design for performance was emphasized in our discussion on collocated tables and the various parallel join strategies were highlighted. By following the concepts presented in this chapter, you should be able to design and support a partitioned database environment.

APPENDIX 

DB2 Catalog Views

The DB2 catalog in v8 contains 86 catalog views with a schema of SYSCAT and five user-updateable views with a schema of SYSSTAT. These views are defined on tables with a schema of SYSIBM in the SYSCATSPACE tablespace. Select privileges are granted to group PUBLIC by default on SYSCAT views. Update privileges are granted to group PUBLIC by default on SYSSTAT views, as columns in these views can be updated with production statistics or "artificial" statistics to replicate a production or test database environment.

This appendix will serve as a quick reference for DBAs and application developers. You can use this appendix to develop ad-hoc queries to help solve questions, such as What tablespace is a certain table contained in? What indexes are defined but not being used? Who has what privileges on a certain package?

This appendix provides the name for each view, and contains column names, data types, and descriptions.

SYSCAT.ATTRIBUTES

Contains one row for each attribute (including inherited attributes where applicable) that is defined for a user-defined structured data type.

Column Name	Data Type	Nullable	Description
TYPESCHEMA	VARCHAR(128)		Qualified name of the structured data type that includes the attribute.
TYPENAME	VARCHAR(128)		Qualified name of the structured data type that includes the attribute.

Column Name	Data Type	Nullable	Description
ATTR_NAME	VARCHAR(128)		Attribute name.
ATTR_TYPESCHEMA	VARCHAR(128)		Qualified name of the type of the attribute.
ATTR_TYPENAME	VARCHAR(128)		Qualified name of the type of the attribute.
TARGET_TYPESCHEMA	VARCHAR(128)	Yes	Qualified name of the target type, if the type of the attribute is REFERENCE. Null value if the type of the attribute is not REFERENCE.
TARGET_TYPENAME	VARCHAR(128)	Yes	Qualified name of the target type, if the type of the attribute is REFERENCE. Null value if the type of the attribute is not REFERENCE.
SOURCE_TYPESCHEMA	VARCHAR(128)		Qualified name of the data type in the data type hierarchy where the attribute was introduced. For noninherited attributes, these columns are the same as TYPE-SCHEMA and TYPENAME.
SOURCE_TYPENAME	VARCHAR(128)		Qualified name of the data type in the data type hierarchy where the attribute was introduced. For non-inherited attributes, these columns are the same as TYPE-SCHEMA and TYPENAME.
ORDINAL	SMALLINT		Position of the attribute in the definition of the structured data type, starting with zero.
LENGTH	INTEGER		Maximum length of data; 0 for distinct types. The LENGTH column indicates precision for DECIMAL fields.
SCALE	SMALLINT		Scale for DECIMAL fields; 0 if not DECIMAL.
CODEPAGE	SMALLINT		Code page of the attribute. For character-string attributes not defined with FOR BIT DATA, the value is the database code page. For graphic-string attributes, the value is the DBCS code page implied by the (composite) database code page. Otherwise, the value is 0.

Column Name	Data Type	Nullable	Description
LOGGED	CHAR(1)		Applies only to attributes whose type is LOB or distinct based on LOB; otherwise, blank. Y = Attribute is logged. N = Attribute is not compacted.
COMPACT	CHAR (1)		Applies only to attributes whose type is LOB or distinct based on LOB; otherwise, blank. Y = Attribute is logged. N = Attribute is not compacted.
DL_FEATURES	CHAR(10)		Applies to DATALINK type attributes only. Blank for REFERENCE type attributes; otherwise, null. Encodes various DATALINK features such as linktype, control mode, recovery, and unlink properties.

SYSCAT.BUFFERPOOLDBPARTITIONS

Contains a row for each database partition in the bufferpool for which the size of the bufferpool on the database partition is different from the default size in SYSCAT.BUFFERPOOLS column NPAGES.

Column Name	Data Type	Nullable	Description
BUFFERPOOLID	INTEGER		Internal bufferpool identifier.
DBPARTITIONNUM	SMALLINT		Database partition number.
NPAGES	INTEGER		Number of pages in this bufferpool on this database partition.

SYSCAT.BUFFERPOOLS

Contains a row for every bufferpool in every database partition group.

Column Name	Data Type	Nullable	Description
BPNAME	VARCHAR(128)		Name of the bufferpool.
BUFFERPOOLID	INTEGER		Internal bufferpool identifier.
NGNAME	VARCHAR(128)	Yes	Database partition group name (NULL if the bufferpool exists on all database partitions in the database).

Column Name	Data Type	Nullable	Description
NPAGES	INTEGER		Number of pages in the bufferpool.
PAGESIZE	INTEGER		Page size for this bufferpool.
ESTORE	CHAR(1)		N = This bufferpool does not use extended storage. Y = This bufferpool uses extended storage.

SYSCAT.CASTFUNCTIONS

Contains a row for each cast function. It does not include built-in cast functions.

Column Name	Data Type	Nullable	Description
FROM_TYPESCHEMA	VARCHAR(128)		Qualified name of the data type of the parameter.
FROM_TYPENAME	VARCHAR(18)		Qualified name of the data type of the parameter.
TO_TYPESCHEMA	VARCHAR(128)		Qualified name of the data type of the result after casting.
TO_TYPENAME	VARCHAR(18)		Qualified name of the data type of the result after casting.
FUNCSCHEMA	VARCHAR(128)		Qualified name of the function.
FUNCNAME	VARCHAR(18)		Qualified name of the function.
SPECIFICNAME	VARCHAR(18)		The name of the function instance.
ASSIGN_FUNCTION	CHAR(1)		Y = Implicit assignment function N = Not an assignment function

SYSCAT.CHECKS

Contains one row for each CHECK constraint.

Column Name	Data Type	Nullable	Description
CONSTNAME	VARCHAR(18)		Name of the check constraint (unique within a table).
DEFINER	VARCHAR(128)		Authorization ID under which the check constraint was defined.

Column Name	Data Type	Nullable	Description
TABSCHEMA	VARCHAR(128)		Qualified name of the table to which this constraint applies.
TABNAME	VARCHAR(128)		Qualified name of the table to which this constraint applies.
CREATE_TIME	TIMESTAMP		The time at which the constraint was defined. Used in resolving functions that are used in this constraint. No functions will be chosen that were created after the definition of the constraint.
QUALIFIER	VARCHAR(128)		Value of the default schema at time of object definition. Used to complete any unqualified references.
TYPE	CHAR(1)		Type of check constraint: A = System generated check constraint for GENERATED ALWAYS column C = Check constraint
FUNC_PATH	VARCHAR(254)		The current SQL path that was used when the constraint was created.
TEXT	CLOB(64K)		The text of the CHECK clause.

SYSCAT.COLAUTH

Contains one or more rows for each user or group who is granted a column-level privilege, indicating the type of privilege and whether or not it is grantable.

Column Name	Data Type	Nullable	Description
GRANTOR	VARCHAR(128)		Authorization ID of the user who granted the privileges or SYSIBM.
GRANTEE	VARCHAR(128)		Authorization ID of the user or group who holds the privileges.
GRANTEETYPE	CHAR(1)		U = Grantee is an individual user. G = Grantee is a group.
TABSCHEMA	VARCHAR(128)		Qualified name of the table or view.
TABNAME	VARCHAR(128)		Qualified name of the table or view.
COLNAME	VARCHAR(128)		Name of the column to which this privilege applies.

Column Name	Data Type	Nullable	Description
COLNO	SMALLINT		Number of this column in the table or view.
PRIVTYPE	CHAR(1)		Indicates the type of privilege held on the table or view: U = Update privilege R = Reference privilege
GRANTABLE	CHAR(1)		Indicates if the privilege is grantable. G = Grantable N = Not grantable

SYSCAT.COLCHECKS

Each row represents some column that is referenced by a CHECK constraint.

Column Name	Data Type	Nullable	Description
CONSTNAME	VARCHAR(18)		Name of the check constraint (unique within a table; may be system generated).
TABSCHEMA	VARCHAR(128)		Qualified name of table containing referenced column.
TABNAME	VARCHAR(128)		Qualified name of table containing referenced column.
COLNAME	VARCHAR(128)		Name of column.
USAGE	CHAR(1)		R = Column is referenced in the check constraint S = Column is a source column in the system-generated check constraint that supports a generated column T = Column is a target column in the system-generated check constraint that supports a generated column

SYSCAT.COLDIST

Contains detailed column statistics for use by the optimizer. Each row describes the Nth-most-frequent value of some column.

Column Name	Data Type	Nullable	Description
TABSCHEMA	VARCHAR(128)		Qualified name of the table to which this entry applies.

Column Name	Data Type	Nullable	Description
TABNAME	VARCHAR(128)		Qualified name of the table to which this entry applies.
COLNAME	VARCHAR(128)		Name of the column to which this entry applies.
TYPE	CHAR(1)		F = Frequency (most frequent value) Q = Quantile value
SEQNO	SMALLINT		If TYPE = F, then N in this column identifies the Nth most frequent value If TYPE = Q, then N in this column identifies the Nth quantile value
COLVALUE	VARCHAR(254)	Yes	The data value, as a character literal or a null value.
VALCOUNT	BIGINT		If TYPE = F, then VALCOUNT is the number of occurrences of COLVALUE in the column If TYPE = Q, then VALCOUNT is the number of rows whose value is less than or equal to COLVALUE
DISTCOUNT	BIGINT	Yes	If TYPE = Q, this column records the number of distinct values that are less than or equal to COLVALUE (null if unavailable).

SYSCAT.COLGROUPDIST

Contains a row for every value of a column in a column group that makes up the nth most frequent value of the column group or the nth quantile of the column group.

Column Name	Data Type	Nullable	Description
COLGROUPID	INTEGER		Internal identifier of the column group.
TYPE	CHAR(1)		F = Frequency value Q = Quantile value
ORDINAL	SMALLINT		Ordinal number of the column in the group.
SEQNO	SMALLINT		Sequence number *n* representing the *n*th TYPE value.
COLVALUE	VARCHAR(254)	Yes	Data value as a character literal or a null value.

SYSCAT.COLGROUPDISTCOUNTS

Contains a row for the distribution statistics that apply to the nth most frequent value of a column group, or the nth quantile of a column group.

Column Name	Data Type	Nullable	Description
COLGROUPID	INTEGER		Internal identifier of the column group.
TYPE	CHAR(1)		F = Frequency value Q = Quantile value
SEQNO	SMALLINT		Sequence number *n* representing the *n*th TYPE value.
VALCOUNT	BIGINT		If TYPE = F, VALCOUNT is the number of occurrences of COLVALUE for the column group with this SEQNO. If TYPE = Q, VALCOUNT is the number of rows whose value is less than or equal to COLVALUE for the column group with this SEQNO.
DISTCOUNT	BIGINT	Yes	If TYPE = Q, this column records the number of distinct values that are less than or equal to COLVALUE for the column group with this SEQNO (null if unavailable).

SYSCAT.COLGROUPS

Contains a row for every column group and statistics that apply to the entire column group.

Column Name	Data Type	Nullable	Description
COLGROUPSCHEMA	VARCHAR(128)		Qualified name of the column group.
COLGROUPNAME	VARCHAR(128)		Qualified name of the column group.
COLGROUPID	INTEGER		Internal identifier of the column group.
COLGROUPCARD	BIGINT		Cardinality of the column group.
NUMFREQ_VALUES	SMALLINT		Number of frequent values collected for the column group.
NUMQUANITLES	SMALLINT		Number of quantiles collected for the column group.

SYSCAT.COLOPTIONS

Each row contains column-specific option values.

Column Name	Data Type	Nullable	Description
TABSCHEMA	VARCHAR(128)		Qualified nickname for the column.
TABNAME	VARCHAR(128)		Qualified nickname for the column.
COLNAME	VARCHAR(128)		Local column name.
OPTION	VARCHAR(128)		Name of the column option.
SETTING	VARCHAR(255)		Value for the column option.

SYSCAT.COLUMNS

Contains one row for each column (including inherited columns where applicable) that is defined for a table or view. All of the catalog views have entries in the SYSCAT.COLUMNS table.

Column Name	Data Type	Nullable	Description
TABSCHEMA	VARCHAR(128)		Qualified name of the table or view that contains the column.
TABNAME	VARCHAR(128)		Qualified name of the table or view that contains the column.
COLNAME	VARCHAR(128)		Column name.
COLNO	SMALLINT		Numerical place of column in table or view, beginning at zero.
TYPESCEMA	VARCHAR(128)		Contains the qualified name of the type, if the data type of the column is distinct. Otherwise, TYPESCHEMA contains the value SYSIBM and TYPENAME contains the data type of the column (in long form, for example, CHARACTER). If FLOAT or FLOAT(n) with n greater than 24 is specified, TYPENAME is renamed to DOUBLE. If FLOAT(n) with n less than 25 is specified, TYPENAME is renamed to REAL. Also, NUMERIC is renamed to DECIMAL.

Column Name	Data Type	Nullable	Description
TYPENAME	VARCHAR(18)		Contains the qualified name of the type, if the data type of the column is distinct. Otherwise, TYPESCHEMA contains the value SYSIBM and TYPENAME contains the data type of the column (in long form, for example, CHARACTER). If FLOAT or FLOAT(n) with n greater than 24 is specified, TYPENAME is renamed to DOUBLE. If FLOAT(n) with n less than 25 is specified, TYPENAME is renamed to REAL. Also, NUMERIC is renamed to DECIMAL.
LENGTH	INTEGER		Maximum length of data, 0 for distinct types. The LENGTH column indicates precision for DECIMAL fields.
SCALE	SMALLINT		Scale for DECIMAL fields, 0 if not DECIMAL.
DEFAULT	VARCHAR(254)	Yes	Default value for the column of a table expressed as a constant, special register, or cast-function appropriate for the data type of the column. May also be the keyword NULL. Values may be converted from what was specified as a default value. For example, date and time constants are presented in ISO format and cast-function names are qualified with schema name and the identifiers are delimited. Null value if a DEFAULT clause was not specified or the column is a view column.
NULLS	CHAR(1)		Y = Column is nullable N = Column is not nullable The value can be N for a view column that is derived from an expression or function. Nevertheless, such a column allows nulls when the statement using the view is processed with warnings for arithmetic errors.

Column Name	Data Type	Nullable	Description
CODEPAGE	SMALLINT		Code page on the column. For character-string columns not defined with the FOR BIT DATA attribute, the value is the database code page. For graphic-string columns, the value is the DBCS code page implied by the (composite) database code page. Otherwise, the value is 0.
LOGGED	CHAR(1)		Applies only to columns whose type is LOB or distinct based on LOB (blank otherwise). Y = Column is logged N = Column is not logged
COMPACT	CHAR(1)		Applies only to columns whose type is LOB or distinct based on LOB (blank otherwise). Y = Column is compacted in storage N = Column is not compacted
COLCARD	BIGINT		Number of distinct values in the column; –1 if statistics are not gathered; –2 for inherited columns and columns of H-tables.
HIGH2KEY	VARCHAR(254)	Yes	Second highest value of the column. This field is empty if statistics are not gathered and for inherited columns and columns of H-tables.
LOW2KEY	VARCHAR(254)	Yes	Second lowest value of the column. This field is empty if statistics are not gathered and for inherited columns and columns of H-tables.
AVGCOLLEN	INTEGER		Average space required for the column length. –1 if a long field or LOB, or statistics have not been collected; –2 for inherited columns and columns of H-tables.
KEYSEQ	SMALLINT	Yes	The column's numerical position within the table's primary key. This field is null for subtables and hierarchy tables.

Column Name	Data Type	Nullable	Description
PARTKEYSEQ	SMALLINT	Yes	The column's numerical position within the table's partitioning key. This field is null or 0 if the column is not part of the partitioning key. This field is also null for subtables and hierarchy tables.
NQUANTILES	SMALLINT		Number of quantile values recorded in SYSCAT.COLDIST for this column; –1 if no statistics; –2 for inherited columns and columns of H-tables.
NMOSTFREQ	SMALLINT		Number of most-frequent values recorded in SYSCAT.COLDIST for this column; –1 if no statistics; –2 for inherited columns and columns of H-tables.
NUMNULLS	BIGINT		Contains the number of nulls in a column. –1 if statistics are not gathered.
TARGET_TYPESCHEMA	VARCHAR(128)	Yes	Qualified name of the target type, if the type of the column is REFERENCE. Null value if the type of the column is not REFERENCE.
TARGET_TYPENAME	VARCHAR(18)	Yes	Qualified name of the target type, if the type of the column is REFERENCE. Null value if the type of the column is not REFERENCE.
SCOPE_TABSCHEMA	VARCHAR(128)	Yes	Qualified name of the scope (target table), if the type of the column is REFERENCE. Null value if the type of the column is not REFERENCE or the scope is not defined.
SCOPE_TABNAME	VARCHAR(128)	Yes	Qualified name of the scope (target table), if the type of the column is REFERENCE. Null value if the type of the column is not REFERENCE or the scope is not defined.
SOURCE_TABSCHEMA	VARCHAR(128)		Qualified name of the table or view in the respective hierarchy where the column was introduced. For noninherited columns, the values are the same as TBCREATOR and TBNAME. Null for columns of nontyped tables and views.

Column Name	Data Type	Nullable	Description
SOURCE_TABNAME	VARCHAR(128)		Qualified name of the table or view in the respective hierarchy where the column was introduced. For noninherited columns, the values are the same as TBCREATOR and TBNAME. Null for columns of nontyped tables and views.
DL_FEATURES	CHAR(10)	Yes	Applies to DATALINK type columns only. Null otherwise. Each character position is defined as follows: • Link type (U for URL) • Link control (F for file, N for no) • Integrity (A for all, N for None) • Read permission (F for file system, D for database) • Write permission (F for file system, B for blocked, A for admin requiring token for update, N for admin not requiring token for update) • Recovery (Y for yes, N for no) • On unlink (R for restore, D for delete, N for not applicable) • Characters 8 through 10 are reserved for future use.
SPECIAL_PROPS	CHAR(8)	Yes	Applies to REFERENCE type columns only. Null otherwise. Each character position is defined as follows: • Object identifier (OID) column (Y for yes, N for no) • User generated or system generated (U for user, S for system)
HIDDEN	CHAR(1)		Type of hidden column S = System managed hidden column Blank if column is not hidden
INLINE_LENGTH	INTEGER		Length of structured type column that can be kept with base table row. 0 if no value explicitly set by ALTER/CREATE TABLE statement.

Column Name	Data Type	Nullable	Description
IDENTITY	CHAR(1)		Y indicates that the column is an identity column; N indicates that the column is not an identity column.
GENERATED	CHAR(1)		Type of generated column A = Column value is always generated D = Column value is generated by default Blank if column is not generated
COMPRESS	CHAR(1)		S = Compress system default values O = Compress off
TEXT	CLOB(64K)		Contains the text of the generated column, starting with the keyword AS.
REMARKS	VARCHAR(254)	Yes	User-supplied comment.
AVGDISTINCTPERPAGE	DOUBLE	Yes	For future use.
PAGEVARIANCERATIO	DOUBLE	Yes	For future use.
SUB_COUNT	SMALLINT		Average number of subelements. Only applicable for character columns. For example, consider the following string: `database simulation analytical business intelligence` In this example, SUB_COUNT = 5, because there are 5 sub-elements in the string.
SUB_DELIM_LENGTH	SMALLINT		Average length of each delimiter separating each subelement. Only applicable for character columns. For example, consider the following string: `database simulation analytical business intelligence` In this example, SUB_DELIM_LENGTH = 1, because each delimiter is a single blank.

SYSCAT.COLUSE

Contains a row for every column that participates in the DIMENSIONS clause of the CREATE TABLE statement.

Column Name	Data Type	Nullable	Description
TABSCHEMA	VARCHAR(128)		Qualified name of the table containing the column.
TABNAME	VARCHAR(128)		Qualified name of the table containing the column.
COLNAME	VARCHAR(128)		Name of the column.
DIMENSION	SMALLINT		Dimension number, based on the order of dimensions specified in the DIMENSONS clause (initial position = 0). For a composite dimension, this value will be the same for each component of the dimension.
COLSEQ	SMALLINT		Numeric position of the column in the dimension to which it belongs (initial position = 0). The value is 0 for the single column in a noncomposite dimension.
TYPE	CHAR(1)		Type of dimension. C = clustering/multidimensional clustering (MDC)

SYSCAT.CONSTDEP

Contains a row for every dependency of a constraint on some other object.

Column Name	Data Type	Nullable	Description
CONSTNAME	VARCHAR(18)		Name of the constraint.
TABSCHEMA	VARCHAR(128)		Qualified name of the table to which the constraint applies.
TABNAME	VARCHAR(128)		Qualified name of the table to which the constraint applies.
BTYPE	CHAR(1)		Type of object that the constraint depends on. Possible values: F = Function instance I = Index instance R = Structured type

Column Name	Data Type	Nullable	Description
BSCHEMA	VARCHAR(128)		Qualified name of object that the constraint depends on.
BNAME	VARCHAR(18)		Qualified name of object that the constraint depends on.

SYSCAT.DATATYPES

Contains a row for every data type, including built-in and user-defined types.

Column Name	Data Type	Nullable	Description
TYPESCHEMA	VARCHAR(128)		Qualified name of the data type (for built-in types, TYPESCHEMA is SYSIBM).
TYPENAME	VARCHAR(18)		Qualified name of data type (for built-in types, TYPESCHEMA is SYSIBM).
DEFINER	VARCHAR (128)		Authorization ID under which type was created.
SOURCESCHEMA	VARCHAR(128)	Yes	Qualified name of the source type for distinct types. Qualified name of the built-in type used as the reference type that is used as the representation for references to structured types. Null for other types.
SOURCENAME	VARCHAR(18)	Yes	Qualified name of the source type for distinct types. Qualified name of the built-in type used as the reference type that is used as the representation for references to structured types. Null for other types.
METATYPE	CHAR(1)		S = System predefined type T = Distinct type R = Structured type
TYPEID	SMALLINT		The system generated internal identifier of the data type.

Column Name	Data Type	Nullable	Description
SOURCETYPEID	SMALLINT	Yes	Internal type ID of source type (null for built-in types). For user-defined structured types, this is the internal type ID of the reference representation type.
LENGTH	INTEGER		Maximum length of the type. 0 for system predefined parameterized types (for example, DECIMAL and VARCHAR). For user-defined structured types, this indicates the length of the reference representation type.
SCALE	SMALLINT		Scale for distinct types or reference representation types based on the system predefined DECIMAL type.0 for all other types (including DECIMAL itself). For user-defined structured types, this indicates the length of the reference representation type.
CODEPAGE	SMALLINT		Code page for character and graphic distinct types or reference representation types; 0 otherwise.
CREATE_TIME	TIMESTAMP		Creation time of the data type.
ATTRCOUNT	SMALLINT		Number of attributes in data type.
INSTANTIABLE	CHAR(1)		Y = Type can be instantiated N = Type can not be instantiated
WITH_FUNC_ACCESS	CHAR(1)		Y = All the methods for this type can be invoked using function notation. N = Methods for this type can not be invoked using function notation.
FINAL	CHAR(1)		Y = User-defined type can not have subtypes. N = User-defined type can have subtypes.
INLINE_LENGTH	INTEGER		Length of structured type that can be kept with base table row. 0 if no value explicitly set by CREATE TYPE statement.

Column Name	Data Type	Nullable	Description
NATURAL_INLINE_LENGTH	INTEGER		System-calculated inline length of the structured type.
REMARKS	VARCHAR(254)	Yes	User-supplied comment, or null.

SYSCAT.DBAUTH

Records the database authorities held by users.

Column Name	Data Type	Nullable	Description
GRANTOR	VARCHAR(128)		SYSIBM or authorization ID of the user who granted the privileges.
GRANTEE	VARCHAR(128)		Authorization ID of the user or group who holds the privileges.
GRANTEETYPE	CHAR(1)		U = Grantee is an individual user G = Grantee is a group
DBADMAUTH	CHAR(1)		Whether grantee holds DBADM authority over the database: Y = Authority is held N = Authority is not held
CREATETABAUTH	CHAR(1)		Whether grantee can create tables in the database (CREATETAB): Y = Privilege is held N = Privilege is not held
BINDADDAUTH	CHAR(1)		Whether grantee can create new packages in the database (BINDADD): Y = Privilege is held N = Privilege is not held
CONNECTAUTH	CHAR(1)		Whether grantee can connect to the database (CONNECT): Y = Privilege is held N = Privilege is not held
NOFENCEAUTH	CHAR(1)		Whether grantee holds privilege to create nonfenced functions. Y = Privilege is held N = Privilege is not held

Column Name	Data Type	Nullable	Description
IMPLSCHEMAAUTH	CHAR(1)		Whether grantee can implicitly create schemas in the database (IMPLICIT_SCHEMA): Y = Privilege is held N = Privilege is not held
LOADAUTH	CHAR(1)		Whether grantee holds LOAD authority over the database: Y = Authority is held N = Authority is not held
EXTERNATLROUTINEAUTH	CHAR(1)		Whether grantee can create external routines (CREATE_EXTERNAL_ROUTINE): Y = Authority is held N = Authority is not held
QUIESCECONNECTAUTH	CHAR(1)		Whether grantee can connect to a database (QUIESCE_CONNECT): Y = Authority is held N = Authority is not held

SYSCAT.DBPARTITIONGROUPDEF

Contains a row for each partition that is contained in a database partition group.

Column Name	Data Type	Nullable	Description
DBPGNAME	VARCHAR(18)		The name of the database partition group that contains the database partition.
DBPARTITIONNUM	SMALLINT		The partition number of a partition contained in the database partition group. A valid partition number is between 0 and 999 inclusive.
IN_USE	CHAR(1)		Status of the database partition. A = The newly added partition is not in the partitioning map but the containers for the tablespaces in the database partition group are created. The partition is added to the partitioning map when a redistribute database partition group operation is successfully completed. D = The partition will be dropped when a redis-

Column Name	Data Type	Nullable	Description
			tribute database partition group operation is completed. T = The newly added partition is not in the partitioning map and it was added using the WITHOUT TABLESPACES clause. Containers must be specifically added to the table spaces for the database partition group. Y = The partition is in the partitioning map.

SYSCAT.DBPARTITIONGROUPS

Contains a row for each database partition group.

Column Name	Data Type	Nullable	Description
DBPGNAME	VARCHAR(18)		Name of the database partition group.
DEFINER	VARCHAR(128)		Authorization ID of the database partition group definer.
PMAP_ID	SMALLINT		Identifier of the partitioning map in SYSCAT.PARTITIONMAPS.
REDISTRIBUTE_PMAP_ID	SMALLINT		Identifier of the partitioning map currently being used for redistribution. Value is –1 if redistribution is currently not in progress.
CREATE_TIME	TIMESTAMP		Creation time of database partition group.
REMARKS	VARCHAR(254)	Yes	User-provided comment.

SYSCAT.EVENTMONITORS

Contains a row for every event monitor that has been defined.

Column Name	Data Type	Nullable	Description
EVMONNAME	VARCHAR(128)		Name of event monitor.
DEFINER	VARCHAR(128)		Authorization ID of definer of event monitor.

Column Name	Data Type	Nullable	Description
TARGET_TYPE	CAHR(1)		The type of target to which event data is written. Values: F = File P = Pipe T = Table
TARGET	VARCHAR(246)		Name of the target to which event data is written. Absolute pathname of file, or absolute name of pipe.
MAXFILES	INTEGER	Yes	Maximum number of event files that this event monitor permits in an event path. Null if there is no maximum, or if the target-type is not FILE.
MAXFILESIZE	INTEGER	Yes	Maximum size (in 4K pages) that each event file can reach before the event monitor creates a new file. Null if there is no maximum, or if the target-type is not FILE.
BUFFERSIZE	INTEGER	Yes	Size of buffers (in 4K pages) used by event monitors with file targets; otherwise, null.
IO_MODE	CHAR(1)	Yes	Mode of file I/O B = Blocked N = Not blocked Null if target-type is not FILE
WRITE_MODE	CHAR(1)	Yes	Indicates how this monitor handles existing event data when the monitor is activated. A = Append R = Replace Null if target-type is not FILE.
AUTOSTART	CHAR(1)		The event monitor will be activated automatically when the database starts. Y = Yes N = No
DBPARTITIONNUM	SMALLINT		The number of the database partition on which the event monitor runs and logs events.

Column Name	Data Type	Nullable	Description
MONSCOPE	CHAR(1)		Monitoring scope: L = Local G = Global T = Per node where tablespace exists A blank character, valid only for WRITE TO TABLE event monitors.
EVMON_ACTIVATES	INTEGER		The number of times this event monitor has been activated.
REMARKS	VARCHAR(254)	Yes	Reserved for future use.

SYSCAT.EVENTS

Contains a row for every event that is being monitored. An event monitor, in general, monitors multiple events.

Column Name	Data Type	Nullable	Description
EVMONNAME	VARCHAR(18)		Name of event monitor that is monitoring this event.
TYPE	VARCHAR(18)		Type of event being monitored Possible values: DATABASE CONNECTIONS TABLES STATEMENTS TRANSACTIONS DEADLOCKS DETAILDEADLOCKS TABLESPACES
FILTER	CLOB(32K)	Yes	The full text of the WHERE-clause that applies to this event.

SYSCAT.EVENTTABLES

Contains a row for every target table of an event monitor that writes to SQL tables.

Column Name	Data Type	Nullable	Description
EVMONNAME	VARCHAR(128)		Name of event monitor.

Column Name	Data Type	Nullable	Description
LOGICAL_GROUP	VARCHAR(18)		Name of the logical data group. This can be one of: BUFFERPOOL CONN CONNHEADER CONTROL DB DEADLOCK DLCONN DLLOCK STMT SUBSECTION TABLE TABLESPACE XACT
TABSCHEMA	VARCHAR(128)		Qualified name of the target table.
TABNAME	VARCHAR(128)		Qualified name of the target table.
PCTDEACTIVATE	SMALLINT		A percent value that specifies how full a DMS tablespace must be before an event monitor automatically deactivates. Set to 100 for SMS tablespaces.

SYSCAT.FULLHIERARCHIES

Each row represents the relationship between subtable and a supertable, a subtype and a supertype, or a subview and a superview. All hierarchical relationships, including immediate ones, are included in this view.

Column Name	Data Type	Nullable	Description
METATYPE	CHAR(1)		Encodes the type of relationship: R = Between structured types U = Between typed tables W = Between typed views
SUB_SCHEMA	VARCHAR(128)		Qualified name of subtype, subtable, or subview.
SUB_NAME	VARCHAR(128)		Qualified name of subtype, subtable, or subview.
SUPER_SCHEMA	VARCHAR(128)		Qualified name of supertype, supertable, or superview.

Column Name	Data Type	Nullable	Description
SUPER_NAME	VARCHAR(128)		Qualified name of supertype, supertable, or superview.
ROOT_SCHEMA	VARCHAR(128)		Qualified name of the table, view, or type that is at the root of the hierarchy.
ROOT_NAME	VARCHAR(128)		Qualified name of the table, view, or type that is at the root of the hierarchy.

SYSCAT.FUNCMAPOPTIONS

Each row contains function mapping option values.

Column Name	Data Type	Nullable	Description
FUNCTION_MAPPING	VARCHAR(18)		Function mapping name.
OPTION	VARCHAR(128)		Name of the function mapping option.
SETTING	VARCHAR(255)		Value of the function mapping option.

SYSCAT.FUNCMAPPARMOPTIONS

Each row contains function mapping parameter option values.

Column Name	Data Type	Nullable	Description
FUNCITON_MAPPING	VARCHAR(18)		Name of function mapping.
ORDINAL	SMALLINT		Position of parameter.
LOCATION	CHAR(1)		L = Local R = Remote
OPTION	VARCHAR(128)		Name of the function mapping parameter option.
SETTING	VARCHAR(255)		Value of the function mapping parameter option.

SYSCAT.FUNCMAPPINGS

Each row contains function mappings.

Column Name	Data Type	Nullable	Description
FUNCTION_MAPPING	VARCHAR(18)		Name of function mapping (may be system generated).
FUNCSCHEMA	VARCHAR(128)	Yes	Function schema. Null if system built-in function.
FUNCNAME	VARCHAR(1024)	Yes	Name of the local function (built-in or user-defined).
FUNCID	INTEGER	Yes	Internally assigned identifier.
SPECIFICNAME	VARCHAR(18)	Yes	Name of the local function instance.
DEFINER	VARCHAR(128)		Authorization ID under which this mapping was created.
WRAPNAME	VARCHAR(128)	Yes	Wrapper name to which the mapping is applied.
SERVERNAME	VARCHAR(128)	Yes	Name of the data source.
SERVERTYPE	VARCHAR(30)	Yes	Type of data source to which mapping is applied.
SERVERVERSION	VARCHAR(18)	Yes	Version of the server type to which mapping is applied.
CREATE_TIME	TIMESTAMP	Yes	Time at which the mapping is created.
REMARKS	VARCHAR(254)	Yes	User-supplied comment, or null.

SYSCAT.HIERARCHIES

Each row represents the relationship between subtable and its immediate supertable, a subtype and its immediate supertype, or a subview and its immediate superview. Only immediate hierarchical relationships are included in this view.

Column Name	Data Type	Nullable	Description
METATYPE	CHAR(1)		Encodes the type of relationship: R = Between structured types U = Between typed tables W = Between typed views.

Column Name	Data Type	Nullable	Description
SUB_SCHEMA	VARCHAR(128)		Qualified name of subtype, subtable, or subview.
SUB_NAME	VARCHAR(128)		Qualified name of subtype, subtable, or subview.
SUPER_SCHEMA	VARCHAR(128)		Qualified name of supertype, supertable, or superview.
SUPER_NAME	VARCHAR(128)		Qualified name of supertype, supertable, or superview.
ROOT_SCHEMA	VARCHAR(128)		Qualified name of the table, view, or type is at the root of the hierarchy.
ROOT_NAME	VARCHAR(128)		Qualified name of the table, view, or type is at the root of the hierarchy.

SYSCAT.INDEXAUTH

Contains a row for every privilege held on an index.

Column Name	Data Type	Nullable	Description
GRANTOR	VARCHAR(128)		Authorization ID of the user who granted the privileges.
GRANTEE	VARCHAR(128)		Authorization ID of the user or group who holds the privileges.
GRANTEETYPE	CHAR(1)		U = Grantee is an individual user G = Grantee is a group
INDSCHEMA	VARCHAR(128)		Qualified name of the index.
INDNAME	VARCHAR(18)		Qualified name of the index.
CONTROLAUTH	CHAR(1)		Whether grantee holds CONTROL privilege over the index: Y = Privilege is held N = Privilege is not held

SYSCAT.INDEXCOLUSE

Lists all columns that participate in an index.

Column Name	Data Type	Nullable	Description
INDSCHEMA	VARCHAR(128)		Qualified name of the index.

Column Name	Data Type	Nullable	Description
INDNAME	VARCHAR(18)		Qualified name of the index.
COLNAME	VARCHAR(128)		Name of the column.
COLSEQ	SMALLINT		Numeric position of the column in the index (initial position = 1)
COLORDER	CHAR(1)		Order of the values in this column in the index. Values: A = Ascending D = Descending I = INCLUDE column (ordering ignored)

SYSCAT.INDEXDEP

Each row represents a dependency of an index on some other object.

Column Name	Data Type	Nullable	Description
INDSCHEMA	VARCHAR(128)		Qualified name of the index that has dependencies on another object.
INDNAME	VARCHAR(18)		Qualified name of the index that has dependencies on another object.
BTYPE	CHAR(1)		Type of object on which the index depends. A = Alias F = Function instance O = Privilege dependency on all subtables or subviews in a table or view hierarchy R = Structured type S = Materialized query table T = Table U = Typed table V = View W = Typed view X = Index extension
BSCHEMA	VARCHAR(128)		Qualified name of the object on which the index has a dependency.
BNAME	VARCHAR(128)		Qualified name of the object on which the index has a dependency.

Column Name	Data Type	Nullable	Description
TABAUTH	SMALLINT	Yes	If BTYPE = O, S, T, U, V, or W; encodes the privileges on the table or view that are required by the dependent index; otherwise, null.

SYSCAT.INDEXES

Contains one row for each index (including inherited indexes, where applicable) that is defined for a table.

Column Name	Data Type	Nullable	Description
INDSCHEMA	VARCHAR(128)		Name of the index.
INDNAME	VARCHAR(18)		Name of the index.
DEFINER	VARCHAR(128)		User who created the index.
TABSCHEMA	VARCHAR(128)		Qualified name of the table or nickname on which the index is defined.
TABNAME	VARCHAR(128)		Qualified name of the table or nickname on which the index is defined.
COLNAMES	VARCHAR(640)		List of column names, each preceded by + or – to indicate ascending or descending order, respectively. Warning: This column will be removed in the future. Use SYSCAT.INDEXCOLUSE for this information.
UNIQUERULE	CHAR(1)		Unique rule: D = Duplicates allowed P = Primary index U = Unique entries only allowed

Column Name	Data Type	Nullable	Description
MADE_UNIQUE	CHAR(1)		Y = Index was originally nonunique but was converted to a unique index to support a unique or primary key constraint. If the constraint is dropped, the index will revert to nonunique. N = Index remains as it was created.
COLCOUNT	SMALLINT		Number of columns in the key, plus the number of include columns, if any.
UNIQUE_COLCOUNT	SMALLINT		The number of columns required for a unique key. Always <=COLCOUNT. <COLCOUNT only if there are include columns. –1 if the index has no unique key (permits duplicates).
INDEXTYPE	CHAR(4)		Type of index. CLUS = Clustering REG = Regular DIM = Dimension block index BLOK = Block index
ENTYTYPE	CHAR(1)		H = An index on hierarchy table (H-table) L = Logical index on a typed table Blank if an index on an untyped table
PCTFREE	SMALLINT		Percentage of each index leaf page to be reserved during initial building of the index. This space is available for future inserts after the index is built.

Column Name	Data Type	Nullable	Description
IID	SMALLINT		Internal index ID.
NLEAF	INTEGER		Number of leaf pages; –1 if statistics are not gathered.
NLEVELS	SMALLINT		Number of index levels; –1 if statistics are not gathered.
FIRSTKEYCARD	BIGINT		Number of distinct first key values; –1 if statistics are not gathered.
FIRST2KEYCARD	BIGINT		Number of distinct keys using the first two columns of the index; –1 if no statistics, or if not applicable.
FIRST3KEYCARD	BIGINT		Number of distinct keys using the first three columns of the index; –1 if no statistics, or if not applicable.
FIRST4KEYCARD	BIGINT		Number of distinct keys using the first four columns of the index; –1 if no statistics, or if not applicable.
FULLKEYCARD	BIGINT		Number of distinct full key values; –1 if statistics are not gathered.
CLUSTERRATIO	SMALLINT		Degree of data clustering with the index; –1 if statistics are not gathered, or if detailed index statistics are gathered (in which case, CLUSTERFACTOR will be used instead).
CLUSTERFACTOR	DOUBLE		Finer measurement of degree of clustering, or –1 if detailed index statistics have not been gathered, or if the index is defined on a nickname.

Column Name	Data Type	Nullable	Description
SEQUENTIAL_PAGES	INTEGER		Number of leaf pages located on disk in index key order with few or no large gaps between them; –1 if no statistics are available.
DENSITY	INTEGER		Ratio of SEQUENTIAL_PAGES to number of pages in the range of pages occupied by the index, expressed as a percent (integer between 0 and 100; –1 if no statistics are available).
USER_DEFINED	SMALLINT		1 if this index was defined by a user and has not been dropped; otherwise, 0.
SYSTEM_REQUIRED	SMALLINT		Valid values are: 1 if one or the other of the following conditions is met: • This index is required for a primary or unique key constraint, or this index is a dimension block index or composite block index for a multidimensional clustering (MDC) table. • This is an index on the (OID) column of a typed table. 2 if both of the following conditions are met: • This index is required for a primary or unique key constraint, or this index is a dimension block index or composite block index for an

Column Name	Data Type	Nullable	Description
			MDC table. • This is an index on the (OID) column of a typed table. 0 otherwise.
CREATE_TIME	TIMESTAMP		Time when the index was created.
STATS_TIME	TIMESTAMP	Yes	Last time when any change was made to recorded statistics for this index. Null if no statistics available.
PAGE_FETCH_PAIRS	VARCHAR(254)		A list of pairs of integers, represented in character form. Each pair represents the number of pages in a
			hypothetical buffer, and the number of page fetches required to scan the table with this index using that hypothetical buffer. (Zero-length string if no data available.)
MINPCTUSED	SMALLINT		If not zero, online index defragmentation is enabled, and the value is the threshold of minimum used space before merging pages.
REVERSE_SCANS	CHAR(1)		Y = Index supports reverse scans N = Index does not support reverse scans

Column Name	Data Type	Nullable	Description
INTERNAL_FORMAT	SMALLINT		Valid values are: • 1 if the index does not have backward pointers • >= 2 if the index has backward pointers • 6 if the index is a composite block index
REMARKS	VARCHAR(254)	Yes	User-supplied comment or null.
IESCHEMA	VARCHAR(128)	Yes	Qualified name of index extension. Null for ordinary indexes.
IENAME	VARCHAR(18)	Yes	
IEARGUMENTS	CLOB(32K)	Yes	External information of the parameter specified when the index is created. Null for ordinary indexes.
INDEX_OBJECTID	INTEGER		Index object identifier for the table.
NUMRIDS	BIGINT		Total number of row identifiers (RIDs) in the index.
NUMRIDS_DELETED	BIGINT		Total number of row identifiers in the index that are marked as deleted, excluding those row identifiers on leaf pages on which all row identifiers are as marked deleted.
NUM_EMPTY_LEAFS	BIGINT		Total number of index leaf pages that have all of their row identifiers marked as deleted.

Column Name	Data Type	Nullable	Description
AVERAGE_RANDOM_FETCH_PAGES	DOUBLE		Average number of random table pages between sequential page accesses when fetching using the index; –1 if it is not known.
AVERAGE_RANDOM_PAGES	DOUBLE		Average number of random index pages between sequential index page accesses; –1 if it is not known.
AVERAGE_SEQUENCE_GAP	DOUBLE		Gap between index page sequences. Detected through a scan of index leaf pages, each gap represents the average number of index pages that must be randomly fetched between sequences of index pages; –1 if it is not known.
AVERAGE_SEQUENCE_FETCH_GAP	DOUBLE		Gap between table page sequences when fetching using the index. Detected through a scan of index leaf pages, each gap represents the average number of table pages that must be randomly fetched between sequences of table pages; –1 if it is not known.
AVERAGE_SEQUENCE_PAGES	DOUBLE		Average number of index pages accessible in sequence (that is, the number of index pages that the prefetchers would detect as being in sequence); –1 if it is not known.

Column Name	Data Type	Nullable	Description
AVERAGE_SEQUENCE_FETCH_PAGES	DOUBLE		Average number of table pages accessible in sequence (that is, the number of index pages that the prefetchers would detect as being in sequence) when fetching using the index; –1 if it is not known.
TBSPACEID	INTEGER		Internal identifier for the index table space.

SYSCAT.INDEXEXPLOITRULES

Each row represents an index exploitation.

Column Name	Data Type	Nullable	Description
FUNCID	INTEGER		Function ID.
SPECID	SMALLINT		Number of the predicate specification in the CREATE FUNCTION statement.
IESCHEMA	VARCHAR(128)		Qualified name of index extension.
IENAME	VARCHAR(128)		Qualified name of index extension.
RULEID	SMALLINT		Unique exploitation rule ID.
SEARCHMETHODID	SMALLINT		The search method ID in the specific index extension.
SEARCHKEY	VARCHAR(320)		Key used to exploit index.
SEARCHARGUMENT	VARCHAR(1800)		Search arguments used in the index exploitation.

SYSCAT.INDEXEXTENSIONDEP

Contains a row for each dependency that index extensions have on various database objects.

Column Name	Data Type	Nullable	Description
IESCHEMA	VARCHAR(128)		Qualified name of the index extension that has dependencies on another object.
IENAME	VARCHAR(18)		Qualified name of the index extension that has dependencies on another object.
BTYPE	CHAR(1)		Type of object on which the index extension is dependent: A = Alias F = Function instance or method instance J = Server definition O = "Outer" dependency on hierarchic SELECT privilege R = Structured type S = Materialized query table T = Table (not typed) U = Typed table V = View (not typed) W = Typed view X = Index extension
BSCHEMA	VARCHAR(128)		Qualified name of the object on which the index extension depends. (If BTYPE = F, this is the specific name of a function.)
BNAME	VARCHAR(128)		Qualified name of the object on which the index extension depends. (If BTYPE = F, this is the specific name of a function.)
TABAUTH	SMALLINT	Yes	If BTYPE = O, T, U, V, or W; encodes the privileges on the table (or view) that are required by a dependent trigger; otherwise, null.

SYSCAT.INDEXEXTENSIONMETHODS

Each row represents a search method. One index extension may include multiple search methods.

Column Name	Data Type	Nullable	Description
METHODNAME	VARCHAR(18)		Name of search method.

Column Name	Data Type	Nullable	Description
METHODID	SMALLINT		Number of method in the index extension.
IESCHEMA	VARCHAR(128)		Qualified name of index extension.
IENAME	VARCHAR(18)		Qualified name of index extension.
RANGEFUNCSCHEMA	VARCHAR(128)		Qualified name of range-through function.
RANGEFUNCNAME	VARCHAR(18)		Qualified name of range-through function.
RANGESPECIFICNAME	VARCHAR(18)		Range-through function specific name.
FILTERFUNCSCHEMA	VARCHAR(128)		Qualified name of filter function.
FILTERFUNCNAME	VARCHAR(18)		Qualified name of filter function.
FILTERSPECIFICNAME	VARCHAR(18)		Function-specific name of filter function.
REMARKS	VARCHAR(254)	Yes	User-supplied or null.

SYSCAT.INDEXEXTENSIONPARMS

Each row represents an index extension instance parameter or source key definition.

Column Name	Data Type	Nullable	Description
IESCHEMA	VARCHAR(128)		Qualified name of index extension.
IENAME	VARCHAR(18)		Qualified name of index extension.
ORDINAL	SMALLINT		Sequence number of parameter or source key.
PARMNAME	VARCHAR(18)		Name of parameter or source key.
TYPESCHEMA	VARCHAR(128)		Qualified name of the instance parameter or source key data type.
TYPENAME	VARCHAR(18)		Qualified name of the instance parameter or source key data type.
LENGTH	INTEGER		Length of the instance parameter or source key data type.
SCALE	SMALLINT		Scale of the instance parameter or source key data type. Zero (0) when not applicable.

Column Name	Data Type	Nullable	Description
PARMTYPE	CHAR(1)		Type represented by the row: P = Index extension parameter K = Key column
CODEPAGE	SMALLINT		Code page of the index extension parameter. Zero if not a string type.

SYSCAT.INDEXEXTENSIONS

Contains a row for each index extension.

Column Name	Data Type	Nullable	Description
IESCHEMA	VARCHAR(128)		Qualified name of index extension.
IENAME	VARCHAR(18)		Qualified name of index extension.
DEFINER	VARCHAR(128)		Authorization ID under which the index extension was defined.
CREATE_TIME	TIMESTAMP		Time at which the index extension was defined.
KEYGENFUNCSCHEMA	VARCHAR(128)		Qualified name of key generation function.
KEYGENFUNCNAME	VARCHAR(18)		Qualified name of key generation function.
KEYGENSPECIFICNAME	VARCHAR(18)		Key generation function-specific name.
TEXT	CLOB(64K)		The full text of the CREATE INDEX EXTENSION statement.
REMARKS	VARCHAR(254)		User-supplied comment, or null.

SYSCAT.INDEXOPTIONS

Each row contains index-specific option values.

Column Name	Data Type	Nullable	Description
INDSCHEMA	VARCHAR(128)		Schema name of the index.
INDNAME	VARCHAR(18)		Local name of the index.
OPTION	VARCHAR(128)		Name of the index option.
SETTING	VARCHAR(255)		Value.

SYSCAT.KEYCOLUSE

Lists all columns that participate in a key (including inherited primary or unique keys where applicable) defined by a unique, primary key, or foreign key constraint.

Column Name	Data Type	Nullable	Description
CONSTNAME	VARCHAR(18)		Name of the constraint (unique within a table).
TABSCHEMA	VARCHAR(128)		Qualified name of the table containing the column.
TABNAME	VARCHAR(128)		Qualified name of the table containing the column.
COLNAME	VARCHAR(128)		Name of the column.
COLSEQ	SMALLINT		Numeric position of the column in the key (initial position = 1).

SYSCAT.NAMEMAPPINGS

Each row represents the mapping between logical objects and the corresponding implementation objects that implement the logical objects.

Column Name	Data Type	Nullable	Description
TYPE	CHAR(1)		C =Column I = Index U = Typed table
LOGICAL_SCHEMA	VARCHAR(128)		Qualified name of the logical object.
LOGICAL_NAME	VARCHAR(128)		Qualified name of the logical object.
LOGICAL_COLNAME	VARCHAR(128)	Yes	If TYPE = C, then the name of the logical column. Otherwise, null.
IMPL_SCHEMA	VARCHAR(128)		Qualified name of the implementation object that implements the logical object.
IMPL_NAME	VARCHAR(128)		Qualified name of the implementation object that implements the logical object.
IMPL_COLNAME	VARCHAR(128)	Yes	If TYPE = C, then the name of the implementation column. Otherwise, null.

SYSCAT.PACKAGEAUTH

Contains a row for every privilege held on a package.

Column Name	Data Type	Nullable	Description
GRANTOR	VARCHAR(128)		Authorization ID of the user who granted the privileges.
GRANTEE	VARCHAR(128)		Authorization ID of the user or group who holds the privileges.
GRANTEETYPE	CHAR(1)		U = Grantee is an individual user G = Grantee is a group
PKGSCHEMA	VARCHAR(128)		Name of the package on which the privileges are held.
PKGNAME	CHAR(8)		Name of the package on which the privileges are held.
CONTTOLAUTH	CHAR(1)		Indicates whether grantee holds CONTROL privilege on the package: Y = Privilege is held N = Privilege is not held
BINDAUTH	CHAR(1)		Indicates whether grantee holds BIND privilege on the package: Y = Privilege is held N = Privilege is not held G = Privilege is held and grantable
EXECUTEAUTH	CHAR(1)		Indicates whether grantee holds EXECUTE privilege on the package: Y = Privilege is held N = Privilege is not held G = Privilege is held and grantable

SYSCAT.PACKAGEDEP

Contains a row for each dependency that packages have on indexes, tables, views, triggers, functions, aliases, types, and hierarchies.

Column Name	Data Type	Nullable	Description
PKGSCHEMA	VARCHAR(128)		Name of the package

Column Name	Data Type	Nullable	Description
PKGNAME	CHAR(8)		
UNIQUED	CHAR(8)		Internal date and time information indicating when the package was first created. Useful for identifying a specific package when multiple packages having the same name exist.
PKGVERSION	VARCHAR(64		Version identifier of the package.
BINDER	VARCHAR(128)	Yes	Binder of the package.
BTYPE	CHAR(1)		Type of object BNAME: A = Alias B = Trigger D = Server definition F = Function instance I = Index M = Function mapping N = Nickname O = Privilege dependency on all subtables or sub-views in a table or view hierarchy P = Page size R = Structured type S = Materialized query table T = Table U = Typed table V = View W = Typed view
BSCHEMA	VARCHAR(128)		Qualified name of an object on which the package depends.
BNAME	VARCHAR(128)		Qualified name of an object on which the package depends.
TABAUTH	SMALLINT	Yes	If BTYPE is O, S, T, U, V, or W; then it encodes the privileges that are required by this package (Select, Insert, Delete, Update).

SYSCAT.PACKAGES

Contains a row for each package that has been created by binding an application program.

Column Name	Data Type	Nullable	Description
PKGSCHEMA	VARCHAR(128)		Name of the package.
PKGNAME	CHAR(18)		
PKGVERSION	VARCHAR(64)		Version identifier of the package.
BOUNDBY	VARCHAR(128)		Authorization ID (OWNER) of the binder of the package.
DEFINER	VARCHAR(128)		User ID under which the package was bound.
DEFAULT_SCHEMA	VARCHAR(128)		Default schema (QUALIFIER) name used for unqualified names in static SQL statements.
VALID	CHAR(1)		Y = Valid N = Not valid X = Package is inoperative because some function instance on which it depends has been dropped. Explicit rebind is needed. (If a function instance with dependencies is dropped, the package is put into an "inoperative" state, and it must be explicitly rebound. If any other object with dependencies is dropped, the package is put into an "invalid" state, and the system will attempt to rebind the package automatically when it is first referenced.)
UNIQUE_ID	CHAR(8)		Internal date and time information indicating when the package was first created. Useful for identifying a specific package when multiple packages having the same name exist.
TOTAL_SECT	SMALLINT		Total number of sections in the package.
FORMAT	CHAR(1)		Date and time format associated with the package: 0 = Format associated with the territory code of the client 1 = USA date and time

Column Name	Data Type	Nullable	Description
			2 = EUR date, EUR time 3 = ISO date, ISO time 4 = JIS date, JIS time 5 = LOCAL date, LOCAL time
ISOLATION	CHAR(2)	Yes	Isolation level: RR = Repeatable read RS = Read stability CS = Cursor stability UR = Uncommitted read
BLOCKING	CHAR(1)	Yes	Cursor blocking option: N = No blocking U = Block unambiguous cursors B = Block all cursors
INSERT_BUF	CHAR(1)		Insert option used during BIND: Y = Inserts are buffered N = Inserts are not buffered
LANG_LEVEL	CHAR(1)	Yes	LANGLEVEL value used during BIND: 0 = SAA1 1 = SQL92E or MIA
FUNC_PATH	VARCHAR(254)		The SQL path used by the last BIND command for this package. This is used as the default path for REBIND.SYSIBM for pre-Version 2 packages.
QUERYOPT	INTEGER		Optimization class under which this package was bound. Used for REBIND. The classes are: 0, 1, 3, 5, and 9.
EXPLAIN_LEVEL	CHAR(1)		Indicates whether Explain was requested using the EXPLAIN or EXPLSNAP bind option. P = Plan Selection level Blank if 'No' Explain requested
EXPLAIN_MODE	CHAR(1)		Value of EXPLAIN bind option: Y = Yes (static) N = No A = All (static and dynamic)

Column Name	Data Type	Nullable	Description
EXPLAIN_SNAPSHOT	CHAR(1)		Value of EXPLSNAP bind option: Y = Yes (static) N = No A = All (static and dynamic)
SQLWARN	CHAR(1)		Are positive SQLCODEs resulting from dynamic SQL statements returned to the application? Y = Yes N = No, they are suppressed
SQLMATHWARN	CHAR(1)		Value of the database configuration parameter DFT_SQLMATHWARN at the time of bind. Are arithmetic errors and retrieval conversion errors in static SQL statements handled as nulls with a warning? Y = Yes N = No, they are suppressed
EXPLICIT_BIND_TIME	TIMESTAMP		The time at which this package was last explicitly bound or rebound. When the package is implicitly rebound, no function instance will be selected that was created later than this time.
LAST_BIND_TIME	TIMESTAMP		Time at which the package last explicitly or implicitly bound or rebound.
CODEPAGE	SMALLINT		Application code page at bind time (–1 if not known).
DEGREE	CHAR(5)		Indicates the limit on intrapartition parallelism (as a bind option) when package was bound. 1 = No intrapartition parallelism 2-32767 = Degree of intrapartition parallelism ANY = Degree was determined by the database manager
MULTINODE_PLANS	CHAR(1)		Y = Package was bound in a multiple partition environment N = Package was bound in a single partition environment

Column Name	Data Type	Nullable	Description
INTRA_PARALLEL	CHAR(1)		Indicates the use of intrapartition parallelism by static SQL statements within the package. Y = One or more static SQL statements in package uses intrapartition parallelism. N = No static SQL statements in package uses intrapartition parallelism F = One or more static SQL statements in package can use intrapartition parallelism; this parallelism has been disabled for use on a system that is not configured for intrapartition parallelism.
VALIDATE	CHAR(1)		B = All checking must be performed during BIND R = Reserved
DYNAMICRULES	CHAR(1)		B = BIND. Dynamic SQL statements are executed with bind behavior D = DEFINEBIND. When the package is run within a routine context, dynamic SQL statements in the package are executed with define behavior. When the package is not run within a routine context, dynamic SQL statements in the package are executed with bind behavior. E = DEFINERUN. When the package is run within a routine context, dynamic SQL statements in the package are executed with define behavior. When the package is not run within a routine context, dynamic SQL statements in the package are executed with run behavior. H = INVOKEBIND. When the package is run within a routine context, dynamic SQL statements in the package are executed with invoke behavior. When the package is not run within a routine context, dynamic SQL statements in the package are executed with bind behavior. I = INVOKERUN. When the package is run within a routine context, dynamic SQL statements in the package are executed with invoke behavior. When the

Column Name	Data Type	Nullable	Description
			package is not run within a routine context, dynamic SQL statements in the package are executed with run behavior. R = RUN. Dynamic SQL statements are executed with run behavior. This is the default.
SQLERROR	CHAR(1)		Indicates SQLERROR option on the most recent subcommand that bound or rebound the package. C = Reserved N = No package
REFRESHAGE	DECIMAL(20,6)		Timestamp duration indicating the maximum length of time between when a REFRESH TABLE statement is run for a materialized query table and when the materialized query table is used in place of a base table.
TRANSFORMGROUP	CHAR(1024)	Yes	String containing the transform group bind option.
REMARKS	VARCHAR(254)	Yes	User-supplied comment, or null.

SYSCAT.PARTITIONMAPS

Contains a row for each partitioning map that is used to distribute table rows among the partitions in a database partition group, based on hashing the table's partitioning key.

Column Name	Data Type	Nullable	Description
PMAP_ID	SMALLINT		Identifier of the partitioning map.
PARTITIONMAP	LONG VARCHAR FOR BIT DATA		The actual partitioning map, a vector of 4 096 two-byte integers for a multiple partition database partition group. For a single partition database partition group, there is one entry denoting the partition number of the single partition.

SYSCAT.PASSTHRUAUTH

This catalog view contains information about authorization to query data sources in pass-through sessions. A constraint on the base table requires that the values in SERVER correspond to the values in the SERVER column of SYSCAT.SERVERS. None of the fields in SYSCAT.PASSTHRUAUTH are nullable.

Column Name	Data Type	Nullable	Description
GRANTOR	VARCHAR(128)		Authorization ID of the user who granted the privilege.
GRANTEE	VARCHAR(128)		Authorization ID of the user or group who holds the privilege.
GRANTEETYPE	CHAR(1)		A letter that specifies the type of grantee: U = Grantee is an individual user G = Grantee is a group
SERVERNAME	VARCHAR(128)		Name of the data source that the user or group is being granted authorization to.

SYSCAT.PREDICATESPECS

Each row represents a predicate specification.

Column Name	Data Type	Nullable	Description
FUNCSCHEMA	VARCHAR(128)		Qualified name of function.
FUNCNAME	VARCHAR(18)		Qualified name of function.
SPECIFICNAME	VARCHAR(18)		The name of the function instance.
FUNCID	INTEGER		Function ID.
SPECID	SMALLINT		ID of this predicate specification.
CONTEXTOP	CHAR(8)		Comparison operator is one of the built-in relational operators (=, <, >=, and so on).
CONTEXTEXP	CLOB(32K)		Constant, or an SQL expression.
FILTERTEXT	CLOB(32K)	Yes	Text of data filter expression.

SYSCAT.PROCOPTIONS

Each row contains procedure-specific option values.

Column Name	Data Type	Nullable	Description
PROCSCHEMA	VARCHAR(128)		Qualifier for the stored procedure name or nickname.
PROCNAME	VARCHAR(128)		Name or nickname of the stored procedure.
OPTION	VARCHAR(128)		Name of the stored procedure option.
SETTING	VARCHAR(255)		Value of the stored procedure option.

SYSCAT.PROCPARMOPTIONS

Each row contains procedure parameter-specific option values.

Column Name	Data Type	Nullable	Description
PROSCHEMA	VARCHAR(128)		Qualified procedure name or nickname.
PROCNAME	VARCHAR(128)		Qualified procedure name or nickname.
ORDINAL	SMALLINT		The parameter's numerical position within the procedure signature.
OPTION	VARCHAR(128)		Name of the stored procedure parameter option.
SETTING	VARCHAR(255)		Value of the stored procedure parameter option.

SYSCAT.REFERENCES

Contains a row for each defined referential constraint.

Column Name	Data Type	Nullable	Description
CONSTNAME	VARCHAR(18)		Name of the constraint.
TABSCHEMA	VARCHAR(128)		Qualified name of the table.
TABNAME	VARCHAR(128)		Qualified name of the table.
DEFINER	VARCHAR(128)		User who created the constraint.
REFKEYNAME	VARCHAR(18)		Name of the parent key.
REFTABSCHEMA	VARCHAR(128)		Qualified name of the parent table.
REFTABNAME	VARCHAR(128)		Qualified name of the parent table.
COLCOUNT	SMALLINT		Number of columns in the foreign key.
DELETERULE	CHAR(1)		Delete rule: A = NO ACTION C = CASCADE N = SET NULL R = RESTRICT
UPDATERULE	CHAR(1)		Update rule: A = NO ACTION R = RESTRICT

Column Name	Data Type	Nullable	Description
CREATE_TIME	TIMESTAMP		The timestamp when the referential constraint was defined.
FK_COLNAMES	VARCHAR(640)		List of foreign key column names. *Warning:* This column will be removed in the future. Use of SYSCAT.KEYCOLUSE for this information.
PK_COLNAMES	VARCHAR(640)		List of parent key column names. *Warning:* This column will be removed in the future. Use SYSCAT.KEYCOLUSE for this information.

SYSCAT.REVTYPEMAPPINGS

Each row contains reverse data type mappings (mappings from data types defined locally to data source data types). No data in this version. Defined for possible future use with data type mappings.

Column Name	Data Type	Nullable	Description
TYPE_MAPPING	VARCHAR(18)		Name of the reverse type mapping (may be system generated).
TYPESCHEMA	VARCHAR(128)	Yes	Schema name of the type. Null for system built-in types.
TYPENAME	VARCHAR(18)		Name of the local type in a reverse type mapping.
TYPEID	SMALLINT		Type identifier.
SOURCETYPEID	SMALLINT		Source type identifier.
DEFINER	VARCHAR(128)		Authorization ID under which this type mapping was created.
LOWER_LEN	INTEGER	Yes	Lower bound of the length/precision of the local type.
UPPER_LEN	INTEGER	Yes	Upper bound of the length/precision of the local type. If null then the system determines the best length/precision attribute.
LOWER_SCALE	SMALLINT	Yes	Lower bound of the scale for local decimal data types.
UPPER_SCALE	SMALLINT	Yes	Upper bound of the scale for local decimal data types. If null, then the system determines the best scale attribute.

Column Name	Data Type	Nullable	Description
S_OPR_P	CHAR(2)	Yes	Relationship between local scale and local precision. Basic comparison operators can be used. A null indicates that no specific relationship is required.
BIT_DATA	CHAR(1)	Yes	Y = Type is for bit data N = Type is not for bit data NULL = This is not a character data type or the system determines the bit data attribute
WRAPNAME	VARCHAR(128)	Yes	Mapping applies to this data access protocol.
SERVERNAME	VARCHAR(128)	Yes	Name of the data source.
SERVERTYPE	VARCHAR(30)	Yes	Mapping applies to this type of data source.
SERVERVERSION	VARCHAR(18)	Yes	Mapping applies to this version of SERVERTYPE.
REMOTE_TYPESCHEMA	VARCHAR(128)	Yes	Schema name of the remote type.
REMOTE_TYPENAME	VARCHAR(128)		Name of the data type as defined on the data source(s).
REMOTE_META_TYPE	CHAR(1)	Yes	S = Remote type is a system built-in type T = Remote type is a distinct type
REMOTE_LENGTH	INTEGER	Yes	Maximum number of digits for remote decimal type, and maximum number of characters for remote character type. Otherwise, null.
REMOTE_SCALE	SMALLINT	Yes	Maximum number of digits allowed to the right of the decimal point (for remote decimal types). Otherwise, null.
REMOTE_BIT_DATA	CHAR(1)	Yes	Y = Type is for bit data N = Type is not for bit data NULL = This is not a character data type or that the system determines the bit data attribute
USER_DEFINED	CHAR(1)		Defined by user.
CREATE_TIME	TIMESTAMP		Time when this mapping was created.
REMARKS	VARCHAR(254)	Yes	User-supplied comments, or null.

SYSCAT.ROUTINEAUTH

Contains one or more rows for each user or group who is granted EXECUTE privilege on a particular routine in the database.

Column Name	Data Type	Nullable	Description
GRANTOR	VARCHAR(128)		Authorization ID of the user who granted the privilege or SYSIBM.
GRANTEE	VARCHAR(128)		Authorization ID of the user or group who holds the privilege.
GRANTEETYPE	CHAR(1)		U = Grantee is an individual user G = Grantee is a group
SCHEMA	VARCHAR(128)		Qualifier of the routine.
SPECIFICNAME	VARCHAR(128)	Yes	Specific name of the routine. If SPECIFICNAME is null and ROUTINETYPE is not M, the privilege applies to all routines in the schema of the type specified in ROUTINETYPE. If SPECIFICNAME is null and ROUTINETYPE is M, the privilege applies to all methods in the schema of subject type TYPENAME.
TYPESCHEMA	VARCHAR(128)	Yes	Qualifier of the type name for the method. If ROUTINETYPE is not M, TYPESCHEMA is null.
TYPENAME	VARCHAR(18)	Yes	Type name for the method. If ROUTINETYPE is not M, TYPENAME is null. If TYPENAME is null and ROUTINETYPE is M, the privilege applies to subject types in the schema TYPESCHEMA.
ROUTINETYPE	CHAR(1)		Type of routine: F = Function M = Method P = Procedure
EXECUTEAUTH	CHAR(1)		Indicates whether grantee holds EXECUTE privilege on the function or method: Y = Privilege is held G = Privilege is held and grantable N = Privilege is not held
GRANT_AUTH	TIMESTAMP		Time at which the EXECUTE privilege is granted.

SYSCAT.ROUTINEDEP

Each row represents a dependency of a routine on some other object. (This catalog view supercedes SYSCAT.FUNCDEP. The other view exists, but will remain as it was in DB2 version 7.1.)

Column Name	Data Type	Nullable	Description
ROUTINESCHEMA	VARCHAR(128)		Qualified name of the routine that has dependencies on another object.
ROUTINENAME	VARCHAR(128)		Qualified name of the routine that has dependencies on another object.
BTYPE	CHAR(1)		Type of object on which the routine depends. A = Alias F = Routine instance O = Privilege dependency on all subtables or subviews in a table or view hierarchy R = Structured type S = Materialized query table T = Table U = Typed table V = View W = Typed view X = Index extension
BSCHEMA	VARCHAR(128)		Qualified name of the object on which the function or method depends (if BTYPE = F, this is the specific name of a routine).
BNAME	VARCHAR(128)		Qualified name of the object on which the function or method depends (if BTYPE = F, this is the specific name of a routine).
TABAUTH	SMALLINT	YES	If BTYPE = O, S, T, U, V, or W, it encodes the privileges on the table or view that are required by the dependent routine. Otherwise, null.

SYSCAT.ROUTINEPARMS

Contains a row for every parameter or result of a routine defined in SYSCAT.ROUTINES. (This catalog view supercedes SYSCAT.FUNCPARMS and SYSCAT.PROCPARMS. The other views exist, but will remain as they were in DB2 version 7.1.)

Column Name	Data Type	Nullable	Description
ROUTINESCHEMA	VARCHAR(128)		Qualified routine name.

Column Name	Data Type	Nullable	Description
ROUTINENAME	VARCHAR(18)		Qualified routine name.
SPECIFICNAME	VARCHAR(18)		The name of the routine instance (may be system generated).
PARMNAME	VARCHAR(128)	Yes	Name of parameter or result column, or null if no name exists.
ROWTYPE	CHAR(1)		B = Both input and output parameter C = Result after casting O = Output parameter P = Input parameter R = Result before casting
ORDINAL	SMALLINT		If ROWTYPE = B, O, or P, the parameter's numerical position within the routine signature. If ROWTYPE = R, and the routine is a table function, the column's numerical position within the result table. Otherwise, 0.
TYPESCHEMA	VARCHAR(128)		Qualified name of data type of parameter or result.
TYPENAME	VARCHAR(18)		Qualified name of data type of parameter or result.
LOCATOR	CHAR(1)		Y = Parameter or result is passed in the form of a locator. N = Parameter or result is not passed in the form of a locator.
LENGTH	INTEGER		Length of parameter or result. 0 if parameter or result is a distinct type.
SCALE	SMALLINT		Scale of parameter or result. 0 if parameter or result is a distinct type.
CODEPAGE	SMALLINT		Code page of parameter or result. 0 denotes either not applicable, or a parameter or result for character data declared with the FOR BIT DATA attribute.
CAST_FUNCSCHEMA	VARCHAR(128)	Yes	Qualified name of the function used to cast an argument or a result. Applies to sourced and external functions; otherwise, null.

Column Name	Data Type	Nullable	Description
CAST_FUNCSPECIFIC	VARCHAR(18)	Yes	Qualified name of the function used to cast an argument or a result. Applies to sourced and external functions; otherwise, null.
TARGET_TYPESCHEMA	VARCHAR(128)	Yes	Qualified name of the target type, if the type of the parameter or result is REFERENCE. Null value if the type of the parameter or result is not REFERENCE.
TARGET_TYPENAME	VARCHAR(18)	Yes	Qualified name of the target type, if the type of the parameter or result is REFERENCE. Null value if the type of the parameter or result is not REFERENCE.
SCOPE_TABSCHEMA	VARCHAR(128)	Yes	Qualified name of the scope (target table), if the type of the parameter or result is REFERENCE. Null value if the type of the parameter or result is not REFERENCE, or the scope is not defined.
SCOPE_TABNAME	VARCHAR(128)	Yes	Qualified name of the scope (target table), if the type of the parameter or result is REFERENCE. Null value if the type of the parameter or result is not REFERENCE, or the scope is not defined.
TRANSFORM_GRPNAME	VARCHAR(18)	Yes	Name of transform group for a structured type parameter or result.
REMARKS	VARCHAR(254)	Yes	Parameter remarks.

SYSCAT.ROUTINES

Contains a row for each user-defined function (scalar, table, or source), system-generated method, user-defined method, or procedure. Does not include built-in functions. (This catalog view supercedes SYSCAT.FUNCTIONS and SYSCAT.PROCEDURES. The other views exist, but will remain as they were in DB2 version 7.1.)

Column Name	Data Type	Nullable	Description
ROUTINESCHEMA	VARCHAR(128)		Qualified routine name.
ROUTINENAME	VARCHAR(18)		Qualified routine name.
ROUTINETYPE	CHAR(1)		F = Function M = Method P = Procedure

Column Name	Data Type	Nullable	Description
DEFINER	VARCHAR(128)		Authorization ID of routine definer.
SPECIFICNAME	VARCHAR(18)		The name of the routine instance (may be system generated).
ROUTINEID	INTEGER		Internally-assigned routine ID.
RETURN_TYPESCHEMA	VARCHAR(128)	Yes	Qualified name of the return type for a scalar function or method.
RETURN_TYPENAME	VARCHAR(128)	Yes	Qualified name of the return type for a scalar function or method.
ORIGIN	CHAR(1)		B = Built-in E = User-defined, external M = Template Q = SQL-bodied U = User-defined, based on a source S = System generated T = System-generated transform
FUNCTIONTYPE	CHAR(1)		C = Column function R = Row function S = Scalar function or method T = Table function Blank = Procedure
PARM_COUNT	SMALLINT		Number of parameters.
LANGUAGE	CHAR(8)		Implementation language of routine body. Possible values are C, COBOL, JAVA, OLE, OLEDB, or SQL. Blank if ORIGIN is not E or Q.
SOURCESCHEMA	VARCHAR(128)	Yes	If ORIGIN = U and the routine is a user-defined function, contains the qualified name of the source function. If ORIGIN = U and the source function is built in, SOURCESCHEMA is SYSIBM and SOURCESPECIFIC is N/A for built-in. Null if ORIGIN is not U.

Column Name	Data Type	Nullable	Description
SOURCESPECIFC	VARCHAR(18)	Yes	If ORIGIN = U and the routine is a user-defined function, contains the qualified name of the source function. If ORIGIN = U and the source function is built in, SOURCESCHEMA is SYSIBM and SOURCESPECIFIC is N/A for built-in. Null if ORIGIN is not U.
DETERMINISTIC	CHAR(1)		Y = Deterministic (results are consistent) N = Nondeterministic (results may differ) Blank if ORIGIN is not E or Q.
EXTERNAL_ACTION	CHAR(1)		E = Function has external side effects (number of invocations is important) N = No side effects Blank if ORIGIN is not E or Q.
NULLCALL	CHAR(1)		Y = CALLED ON NULL INPUT N = RETURNS NULL ON NULL INPUT (result is implicitly null if operand(s) are null). Blank if ORIGIN is not E or Q.
CAST_FUNCTION	CHAR(1)		Y = This is a cast function N = This is not a cast function
ASSIGN_FUNCTION	CHAR(1)		Y = Implicit assignment function N = Not an assignment function
SCRATCHPAD	CHAR(1)		Y = This routine has a scratch pad N = This routine does not have a scratch pad Blank if ORIGIN is not E or ROUTINETYPE is P.
SCRATCHPAD_LENGTH	SMALLINT		n = Length of the scratch pad in bytes 0 = SCRATCHPAD is N -1 = LANGUAGE is OLEDB
FINALCALL	CHAR(1)		Y = Final call is made to this function at runtime end-of-statement N = No final call is made Blank if ORIGIN is not E.

Column Name	Data Type	Nullable	Description
PARALLEL	CHAR(1)		Y = Function can be executed in parallel N = Function cannot be executed in parallel. Blank if ORIGIN is not E.
PARAMETER_STYLE	CHAR(8)		Indicates the parameter style declared when the routine was created. Values: DB2SQL SQL DB2GENRL GENERAL JAVA DB2DARI GNRLNULL Blank if ORIGIN is not E.
FENCED	CHAR(1)		Y = Fenced N = Not fenced Blank if ORIGIN is not E.
SQL_DATA_ACCESS	CHAR(1)		C = CONTAINS SQL: Only SQL that does not read or modify SQL data is allowed. M = MODIFIES SQL DATA: All SQL allowed in routines is allowed. N = NO SQL: SQL is not allowed. R = READS SQL DATA: Only SQL that reads SQL data is allowed.
DBINFO	CHAR(1)		Y = DBINFO is passed N = DBINFO is not passed
PROGRAMTYPE	CHAR(1)		M = Main S = Subroutine
COMMIT_ON_RETURN	CHAR(1)		N = Changes are not committed after the procedure completes. Blank if ROUTINETYPE is not P.
RESULT_SETS	SMALLINT		Estimated upper limit of returned result sets.

Column Name	Data Type	Nullable	Description
SPEC_REG	CHAR(1)		I = INHERIT SPECIAL REGISTERS: Special registers start with their values from the invoking statement. Blank if ORIGIN is not E or Q.
FEDERATED	CHAR(1)		Y = Routine can access federated objects. N = Routine may not access federated objects. Blank if ORIGIN is not E or Q.
THREADSAFE	CHAR(1)		Y = Routine can run in the same process as other routines N = Routine must be run in a separate process from other routines Blank if ORIGIN is not E.
VALID	CHAR(1)		Y = SQL procedure is valid N = SQL procedure is invalid X = SQL procedure is inoperative because some object it requires has been dropped. The SQL procedure must be explicitly dropped and recreated. Blank if ORIGIN is not Q.
METHODIMPLEMENTED	CHAR(1)		Y = Method is implemented N = Method specification without an implementation. Blank if ROUTINETYPE is not M.
METHODEFFECT	CHAR(2)		MU = Mutator method OB = Observer method CN = Constructor method Blanks if FUNCTIONTYPE is not T.
TYPE_PRESERVING	CHAR(1)		Y = Return type is governed by a "type-preserving" parameter. All system-generated mutator methods are type-preserving. N = Return type is the declared return type of the method. Blank if ROUTINETYPE is not M.

Column Name	Data Type	Nullable	Description
WITH_FUNC_ACCESS	CHAR(1)		Y = This method can be invoked by using functional notation. N = This method cannot be invoked by using functional notation. Blank if ROUTINETYPE is not M.
OVERRIDEN_METHODID	INTEGER	Yes	Reserved for future use.
SUBJECT_TYPESCHEMA	VARCHAR(128)	Yes	Subject type for method.
SUBJECT_TYPENAME	VARCHAR(18)	Yes	
CLASS	VARCHAR(128)	Yes	If LANGUAGE = JAVA, identifies the class that implements this routine; otherwise, null.
JAR_ID	VARCHAR(128)	Yes	If LANGUAGE = JAVA, identifies the jar file that implements this routine; otherwise, null.
JARSCHEMA	VARCHAR(128)	Yes	If LANGUAGE = JAVA, identifies the schema of the jar file that implements this routine; otherwise, null.
JAR_SIGNATURE	VARCHAR(128)	Yes	If LANGUAGE = JAVA, identifies the signature of the JAVA method that implements this routine; otherwise, null.
CREATE_TIME	TIMESTAMP		Timestamp of routine creation. Set to 0 for version 1 functions.
ALTER_TIME	TIMESTAMP		Timestamp of most recent routine alteration. If the routine has not been altered, set to CREATE_TIME.
FUNC_PATH	VARCHAR(254)	Yes	SQL path at the time the routine was defined.
QUALIFIER	VARCHAR(128)		Value of default schema at object definition time.
IOS_PER_INVOC	DOUBLE		Estimated number of I/Os per invocation; –1 if not known (0 default).
INSTS_PER_INVOC	DOUBLE		Estimated number of instructions per invocation; –1 if not known (450 default).

Column Name	Data Type	Nullable	Description
IOS_PER_ARGBYTE	DOUBLE		Estimated number of I/Os per input argument byte; –1 if not known (0 default).
INSTS_PER_ARGBYTE	DOUBLE		Estimated number of instructions per input argument byte; –1 if not known (0 default).
PERCENT_ARGBYTES	SMALLINT		Estimated average percent of input argument bytes that the routine will actually read; –1 if not known (100 default).
INITIAL_IOS	DOUBLE		Estimated number of I/Os performed the first/last time the routine is invoked; –1 if not known (0 default).
INITIAL_INSTS	DOUBLE		Estimated number of instructions executed the first/last time the routine is invoked; –1 if not known (0 default).
CARDINALITY	BIGINT		The predicted cardinality of a table function; –1 if not known, or if the routine is not a table function.
SELECTIVITY	DOUBLE		Used for user-defined predicates; –1 if there are no user-defined predicates.
RESULT_COLS	SMALLINT		For a table function (ROUTINETYPE = F and TYPE = T), contains the number of columns in the result table. For other functions and methods (ROUTINETYPE = F or M), contains 1. For procedures (ROUTINETYPE = P), contains 0.
IMPLEMENTATION	VARCHAR(254)	Yes	If ORIGIN = E, identifies the path/module/function that implements this function. If ORIGIN = U and the source function is built-in, this column contains the name and signature of the source function; otherwise, null.
LIB_ID	INTEGER	Yes	Reserved for future use.
TEXT_BODY_OFFSET	INTEGER		If LANGUAGE = SQL, the offset to the start of the SQL procedure body in the full text of the CREATE statement; 0 if LANGUAGE is not SQL.

Column Name	Data Type	Nullable	Description
TEXT	CLOB(1M)	Yes	If LANGUAGE = SQL, the text of the CREATE FUNCTION, CREATE METHOD, or CREATE PROCEDURE statement.
NEWSAVEPOINTLEVEL	CHAR(1)		Indicates whether the routine initiates a new savepoint level when it is invoked. Y = A new savepoint level is initiated when the routine is invoked. N = A new savepoint level is not initiated when the routine is invoked. The routine uses the existing savepoint level. Blank = not applicable.
DEBUG_MODE	CHAR(1)		0 = Debugging is off for this routine 1 = Debugging is on for this routine
TRACE_LEVEL	CHAR(1)		Reserved for future use.
DIAGNOSTIC_LEVEL	CHAR(1)		Reserved for future use.
CHECKOUT_USERID	VARCHAR(128)	Yes	User ID of the user who performed a checkout of the object. Null if not checked out.
PRECOMPILE_OPTIONS	VARCHAR(1024)	Yes	Precompile options specified for the routine.
COMPILE_OPTIONS	VARCHAR(1024)	Yes	Compile options specified for the routine.
REMARKS	VARCHAR(254)	Yes	User-supplied comment, or null.

SYSCAT.SCHEMAAUTH

Contains one or more rows for each user or group who is granted a privilege on a particular schema in the database. All schema privileges for a single schema granted by a specific grantor to a specific grantee appear in a single row.

Column Name	Data Type	Nullable	Description
GRANTOR	VARCHAR(128)		Authorization ID of the user who granted privileges or SYSIBM.
GRANTEE	VARCHAR(128)		Authorization ID of the user or group who holds the privileges.

Column Name	Data Type	Nullable	Description
GRANTEETYPE	CHAR(1)		U = Grantee is an individual user G = Grantee is a group
SCHEMANAME	VARCHAR(128)		Name of the schema.
ALTERINAUTH	CHAR(1)		Indicates whether grantee holds ALTERIN privilege on the schema: Y = Privilege is held G = Privilege is held and grantable N = Privilege is not held
CREATEINAUTH	CHAR(1)		Indicates whether grantee holds CREATEIN privilege on the schema: Y = Privilege is held G = Privilege is held and grantable N = Privilege is not held
DROPINAUTH	CHAR(1)		Indicates whether grantee holds DROPIN privilege on the schema: Y = Privilege is held G = Privilege is held and grantable N = Privilege is not held

SYSCAT.SCHEMATA

Contains a row for each schema.

Column Name	Data Type	Nullable	Description
SCHEMANAME	VARCHAR(128)		Name of the schema.
OWNER	VARCHAR(128)		Authorization id of the schema. The value for implicitly created schemas is SYSIBM.
DEFINER	VARCHAR(128)		User who created the schema.
CREATE_TIME	TIMESTAMP		Timestamp indicating when the object was created.
REMARKS	VARCHAR(254)	Yes	User-provided comment.

SYSCAT.SEQUENCEAUTH

Contains a row for each authorization ID that can be used to use or to alter a sequence.

Column Name	Data Type	Nullable	Description
GRANTOR	VARCHAR(128)		SYSIBM or authorization ID that granted the privilege.
GRANTEE	VARCHAR(128)		Authorization ID that holds the privilege.
GRANTEETYPE	CHAR(1)		Type of authorization ID that holds the privilege. U = Grantee is an individual user.
SEQSCHEMA	VARCHAR(128)		Qualified name of the sequence.
SEQNAME	VARCHAR(128)		Qualified name of the sequence.
USAGEAUTH	CHAR(1)		Y = Privilege is held N = Privilege is not held G = Privilege is held and is grantable
ALTERAUTH	CHAR(1)		Y = Privilege is held N = Privilege is not held G = Privilege is held and is grantable

SYSCAT.SEQUENCES

Contains a row for each sequence defined in the database. This catalog view is updated during normal operations, in response to SQL data definition statements, environment routines, and certain utilities. Data in the catalog view is available through normal SQL query facilities. Columns have consistent names based on the type of objects that they describe.

Column Name	Data Type	Nullable	Description
SEQSCHEMA	VARCHAR(128)		Qualified name of the sequence (generated by DB2 for an identify column).
SEQNAME	VARCHAR(128)		Qualified name of the sequence (generated by DB2 for an identify column).
DEFINER	VARCHAR(128)		Definer of the sequence.
OWNER	VARCHAR(128)		Owner of the sequence.
SEQID	INTEGER		Internal ID of the sequence.

Column Name	Data Type	Nullable	Description
SEQTYPE	CHAR(1)		Sequence type: S = Regular sequence I = Identity sequence
INCREMENT	DECIMAL(31,0)		Increment value
START	DECIMAL(31,0)		Starting value
MAXVALUE	DECIMAL(31,0)		Maximal value
MINVALUE	DECIMAL(31,0)		Minimum value
CYCLE	CHAR(1)		Whether cycling will occur when a boundary is reached: Y = Cycling will occur N = Cycling will not occur
CACHE	INTEGER		Number of sequence values to preallocate in memory for faster access. 0 indicates that values are not preallocated.
ORDER	CHAR(1)		Whether or not sequence numbers must be generated in order of request: Y = Sequence numbers must be generated in order of request N = Sequence numbers are not required to be generated in order of request
DATATYPED	INTEGER		For built-in types, the internal ID of the built-in type. For distinct types, the internal ID of the distinct type.
SOURCETYPEID	INTEGER		For a built-in type, this has a value of 0. For a distinct type, this is the internal ID of the built-in type that is the source type for the distinct type.
CREATE_TIME	TIMESTAMP		Time when the sequence was created.
ALTER_TIME	TIMESTAMP		Time when the last ALTER SEQUENCE statement was executed for this sequence.
PRECISION	SMALLINT		The precision of the data type of the sequence. Values are: 5 for a SMALLINT, 10 for INTEGER, and 19 for BIGINT. For DECIMAL, it is the precision of the specified DECIMAL data type.

Column Name	Data Type	Nullable	Description
ORIGIN	CHAR(1)		Sequence Origin U = User-generated sequence S = System-generated sequence
REMARKS	VARCHAR(254)	Yes	User-supplied comments, or null.

SYSCAT.SERVEROPTIONS

Each row contains configuration options at the server level.

Column Name	Data Type	Nullable	Description
WRAPNAME	VARCHAR(128)	Yes	Wrapper name.
SERVERNAME	VARCHAR(128)	Yes	Name of the server.
SERVERTYPE	VARCHAR(30)	Yes	Server type.
SERVERVERSION	VARCHAR(18)	Yes	Server version.
CREATE_TIME	TIMESTAMP		Time when entry is created.
OPTION	VARCHAR(128)		Name of the server option.
SETTING	VARCHAR(2084)		Value of the server option.
SERVEROPTIONKEY	VARCHAR(18)		Uniquely identifies a row.
REMARKS	VARCHAR(254)	Yes	User-supplied comments, or null.

SYSCAT.SERVERS

Each row represents a data source. Catalog entries are not necessary or tables that are stored in the same instance that contains this catalog table.

Column Name	Data Type	Nullable	Description
WRAPNAME	VARCHAR(128)		Wrapper name.
SERVERNAME	VARCHAR(128)		Name of data source as it is known to the system.
SERVERTYPE	VARCHAR(30)	Yes	Type of data source (always uppercase).
SERVERVERSION	VARCHAR(18)	Yes	Version of data source.
REMARKS	VARCHAR(254)	Yes	User-supplied comments, or null.

SYSCAT.STATEMENTS

Contains one or more rows for each SQL statement in each package in the database.

Column Name	Data Type	Nullable	Description
PKGSCHEMA	VARCHAR(128)		Name of the package.
PKGNAME	CHAR(8)		
UNIQUEID	CHAR(8)		Internal date and time information indicating when the package was first created. Useful for identifying a specific package when multiple packages having the same name exist.
PKGVERSION	VARCHAR(64)		Version identifier of the package.
STMTNO	INTEGER		Line number of the SQL statement in the source module of the application program.
SECTNO	SMALLINT		Number of the package section containing the SQL statement.
SEQNO	SMALLINT		Always 1.
TEXT	CLOB(64K)		Text of the SQL statement.

SYSCAT.TABAUTH

Contains one or more rows for each user or group who is granted a privilege on a particular table or view in the database. All the table privileges for a single table or view granted by a specific grantor to a specific grantee appear in a single row.

Column Name	Data Type	Nullable	Description
GRANTOR	VARCHAR(128)		Authorization ID of the user who granted the privileges or SYSIBM.
GRANTEE	VARCHAR(128)		Authorization ID of the user or group who holds the privileges.
GRANTEETYPE	CHAR(1)		U = Grantee is an individual user G = Grantee is a group
TABSCHEMA	VARCHAR(128)		Qualified name of the table or view.
TABNAME	VARCHAR(128)		Qualified name of the table or view.

Column Name	Data Type	Nullable	Description
CONTROLAUTH	CHAR(1)		Indicates whether grantee holds CONTROL privilege on the table or view: Y = Privilege is held N = Privilege is not held
ALTERAUTH	CHAR(1)		Indicates whether grantee holds ALTER privilege on the table: Y = Privilege is held N = Privilege is not held G = Privilege is held and grantable
DELETEAUTH	CHAR(1)		Indicates whether grantee holds DELETE privilege on the table or view: Y = Privilege is held N = Privilege is not held G = Privilege is held and grantable
INDEXAUTH	CHAR(1)		Indicates whether grantee holds INDEX privilege on the table or view: Y = Privilege is held N = Privilege is not held G = Privilege is held and grantable
INSERTAUTH	CHAR(1)		Indicates whether grantee holds INSERT privilege on the table or view: Y = Privilege is held N = Privilege is not held G = Privilege is held and grantable
SELECTAUTH	CHAR(1)		Indicates whether grantee holds SELECT privilege on the table or view: Y = Privilege is held N = Privilege is not held G = Privilege is held and grantable
REFAUTH	CHAR(1)		Indicates whether grantee holds REFERENCE privilege on the table or view: Y = Privilege is held N = Privilege is not held G = Privilege is held and grantable
UPDATEAUTH	CHAR(1)		Indicates whether grantee holds UPDATE privilege on the table or view: Y = Privilege is held N = Privilege is not held G = Privilege is held and grantable

SYSCAT.TABCONST

Each row represents a table constraint of type CHECK, UNIQUE, PRIMARY KEY, or FOREIGN KEY.

Column Name	Data Type	Nullable	Description
CONSTNAME	VARCHAR(18)		Name of the constraint (unique within a table).
TABSCHEMA	VARCHAR(128)		Qualified name of the table to which this constraint applies.
TABNAME	VARCHAR(128)		Qualified name of the table to which this constraint applies.
DEFINER	VARCHAR(128)		Authorization ID under which the constraint was defined.
TYPE	CHAR(1)		Indicates the constraint type: F = FOREIGN KEY K = CHECK P = PRIMARY KEY U = UNIQUE
REMARKS	VARCHAR(254)	Yes	User-supplied comment, or null.
ENFORCED	CHAR(1)		Y = Enforce constraint N = Do not enforce constraint
CHECKEXISTINGDATA	CHAR(1)		D = Defer checking of existing data I = Immediately check existing data N = Never check existing data
ENABLEQUERYOPT	CHAR(1)		Y = Query optimization is enabled N = Query optimization is disabled

SYSCAT.TABDEP

Contains a row for every dependency of a view or a materialized query table on some other object. Also encodes how privileges on this view depend on privileges on underlying tables and views. (The VIEWDEP catalog view is still available, but only at the v7 level.)

Column Name	Data Type	Nullable	Description
TABSCHEMA	VARCHAR(128)		Name of the view or materialized query table with dependencies on a base table.

Column Name	Data Type	Nullable	Description
TABNAME	VARCHAR(128)		Name of the view or materialized query table with dependencies on a base table.
DTYPE	CHAR(1)		S = Materialized query table V = View (untyped) W = Typed view
DEFINER	VARCHAR(128)		Authorization ID of the creator of the view.
BTYPE	CHAR(1)		Type of object BNAME: A = Alias F = Function instance N = Nickname O = Privilege dependency on all subtables or subviews in a table or view hierarchy I = Index if recording dependency on a base table R = Structured type S = Materialized query table T = Table U = Typed table V = View W = Typed view
BSCHEMA	VARCHAR(128)		Qualified name of the object on which the view depends.
BNAME	VARCHAR(128)		Qualified name of the object on which the view depends.
TABAUTH	SMALLINT	Yes	If BTYPE = O, S, T, U, V, W, encodes the privileges on the underlying table or view on which this table depends. Otherwise, null.

SYSCAT.TABLES

Contains one row for each table, view, nickname or alias that is created. All of the catalog tables and views have entries in the SYSCAT.TABLES catalog view.

Column Name	Data Type	Nullable	Description
TABSCHEMA	VARCHAR(128)		Qualified name of the table, view, nickname, or alias.
TABNAME	VARCHAR(128)		Qualified name of the table, view, nickname, or alias.

Column Name	Data Type	Nullable	Description
DEFINER	VARCHAR (128)		User who created the table, view, nick-name, or alias.
TYPE	CHAR(1)		The type of object: A = Alias H = Hierarchy table N = Nickname S = Materialized query table T = Table U = Typed table V = View W = Typed view
STATUS	CHAR(1)		The check pending status of the object: N = Normal table, view, alias, or nick-name C = Check pending on table or nick-name X = Inoperative view or nickname
DROPRULE	CHAR(1)		N = No rule R = Restrict rule applies on drop
BASE_TABSCHEMA	VARCHAR(128)	Yes	If TYPE = A, these columns identify the table, view, alias, or nickname that is referenced by this alias; otherwise, they are null.
BASE_TABNAME	VARCHAR(128)	Yes	If TYPE = A, these columns identify the table, view, alias, or nickname that is referenced by this alias; otherwise, they are null.
ROWTYPESCHEMA	VARCHAR(128)	Yes	Contains the qualified name of the row-type of this table, where applicable; otherwise, null.
ROWTYPENAME	VARCHAR(18)		Contains the qualified name of the row-type of this table, where applicable; otherwise, null.
CREATE_TIME	TIMESTAMP		The timestamp indicating when the object was created.

Column Name	Data Type	Nullable	Description
STATS_TIME	TIMESTAMP	Yes	Last time when any change was made to recorded statistics for this table. Null if no statistics available.
COLCOUNT	SMALLINT		Number of columns in the table.
TABLEID	SMALLINT		Internal table identifier.
TBSPACEID	SMALLINT		Internal identifier of primary tablespace for this table.
CARD	BIGINT		Total number of rows in the table. For tables in a table hierarchy, the number of rows at the given level of the hierarchy; –1 if statistics are not gathered, or the row describes a view or alias; –2 for hierarchy tables (H-tables)
NPAGES	INTEGER		Total number of pages on which the rows of the table exist; –1 if statistics are not gathered, or the row describes a view or alias; –2 for subtables or H-tables.
FPAGES	INTEGER		Total number of pages; –1 if statistics are not gathered, or the row describes a view or alias; –2 for subtables or H-tables.
OVERFLOW	INTEGER		Total number of overflow records in the table; –1 if statistics are not gathered, or the row describes a view or alias; –2 for subtables or H-tables.
TBSPACE	VARCHAR(18)	Yes	Name of primary tablespace for the table. If no other tablespace is specified, all parts of the table are stored in this tablespace. Null for aliases and views.
INDEX_TBSPACE	VARCHAR(18)	Yes	Name of tablespace that holds all indexes created on this table. Null for aliases and views, or if the INDEX IN clause was omitted or specified with the same value as the IN clause of the CREATE TABLE statement.

Column Name	Data Type	Nullable	Description
LONG_TBSPACE	VARCHAR(18)	Yes	Name of tablespace that holds all long data (LONG or LOB column types) for this table. Null for aliases and views, or if the LONG IN clause was omitted or specified with the same value as the IN clause of the CREATE TABLE statement.
PARENTS	SMALLINT	Yes	Number of parent tables of this table (the number of referential constraints in which this table is a dependent).
CHILDREN	SMALLINT	Yes	Number of dependent tables of this table (the numbered of referential constraints in which this table is a parent).
SELFREFS	SMALLINT	Yes	Number of self-referencing referential constraints for this table (the number of referential constraints in which this table is both a parent and a dependent).
KEYCOLUMNS	SMALLINT	Yes	Number of columns in the primary key of the table.
KEYINDEXID	SMALLINT	Yes	Index ID of the primary index. This field is null or 0 if there is no primary key.
KEYUNIQUE	SMALLINT		Number of unique constraints (other than primary key) defined on this table.
CHECKCOUNT	SMALLINT		Number of check constraints defined on this table.
DATACAPTURE	CHAR(1)		Y = Table participates in data replication N = Does not participate L = Table participates in data replication, including replication of LONG VARCHAR and LONG VARGRAPHIC columns.
CONST_CHECKED	CHAR(32)		Byte 1 represents foreign key constraints. Byte 2 represents check constraints. Byte 5 represents materialized query table. Byte 6 represents generated columns. Byte 7 represents staging table. Other bytes are reserved. Encodes constraint information on checking. Values: Y = Checked by system

Column Name	Data Type	Nullable	Description
			U = Checked by user N = Not checked (pending) W = Was in a U state when the table was placed in check pending (pending) F = In byte 5, the materialized query table cannot be refreshed incrementally. In byte 7, the content of the staging table is incomplete and cannot be used for incremental refresh of the associated materialized query table.
PMAP_ID	SMALLINT	Yes	Identifier of the partitioning map used by this table. Null for aliases and views.
PARTITION_MODE	CHAR(1)		Mode used for tables in a partitioned database. H = Hash on the partitioning key R = Table replicated across database partitions Blank for aliases, views, and tables in single partition database partition groups with no partitioning key defined. Also blank for nicknamed.
LOG_ATTRIBUTE	CHAR(1)		0 = Default logging 1 = Table created not logged initially
PCTFREE	SMALLINT		Percentage of each page to be reserved for future inserts. Can be changed by ALTER TABLE.
APPEND_MODE	CHAR(1)		Controls how rows are inserted on pages: N = New rows are inserted into existing spaces if available Y = New rows are appended at end of data Initial value is N.
REFRESH	CHAR(1)		Refresh mode: D = Deferred I = Immediate O = Once Blank if not a materialized query table.

Column Name	Data Type	Nullable	Description
REFRESH_TIME	TIMESTAMP	Yes	For REFRESH = D or O, timestamp of the REFRESH TABLE statement that last refreshed the data. Otherwise, null.
LOCKSIZE	CHAR(1)		Indicates preferred lock granularity for tables when accessed by DML statements. Only applies to tables. Possible values are: R = Row T = Table Blank if not applicable. Initial value is R.
VOLATILE	CHAR(1)		C = Cardinality of the table is volatile Blank if not applicable.
ROW_FORMAT	CHAR(1)		Version of the row format. Possible values are: 0 = Object does not physically exist on disk (for example, a view) 1 = Row format starting with DB2 v8 2 = Row format prior to DB2 v8
PROPERTY	VARCHAR(32)		Properties for the table. A single blank indicates that the table has no properties.
STATISTICS_PROFILE	CLOB(32K)	Yes	RUNSTATS command used to register a statistical profile of the table.
COMPRESSION	CHAR(1)		V = Value compression is activated, and a row format that supports compression is used N = No compression; a row format that does not support compression is used
ACCESS_MODE	CHAR(1)		Access mode of the object. This access mode is used in conjunction with the STATUS field to represent one of four states. Possible values are: N = No access (corresponds to a status value of C) R = Read-only (corresponds to a status value of C)

Column Name	Data Type	Nullable	Description
			D = No data movement (corresponds to a status value of C) F = Full access (corresponds to a status value of C)
CLUSTERED	CHAR(1)	Yes	Y = Multidimensional clustering (MDC) table Null for a non-MDC table
ACTIVE_BLOCKS	INTEGER	Yes	Total number of in-use blocks in an MDC table; –1 if statistics are not gathered.
REMARKS	VARCHAR(254)	Yes	User-provided comment.

SYSCAT.TABLESPACES

Contains a row for each tablespace.

Column Name	Data Type	Nullable	Description
TBSPACE	VARCHAR(18)		Name of tablespace
DEFINER	VARCHAR(128)		Authorization ID of tablespace definer.
CREATE_TIME	TIMESTAMP		Creation time of tablespace.
TBSPACEID	INTEGER		Internal tablespace identifier.
TBSPACETYPE	CHAR(1)		The type of the tablespace: S = System-managed space D = Database-managed space
DATATYPE	CHAR(1)		Type of data that can be stored: A = All types of permanent data L = Large data—long data or index data T = System temporary tables only U = Declared temporary tables only
EXTENTSIZE	INTEGER		Size of extent, in pages of size PAGESIZE. This many pages are written to one container in the table space before switching to the next container.

Column Name	Data Type	Nullable	Description
PREFETCHSIZE	INTEGER		Number of pages of size PAGESIZE to be read when prefetch is performed.
OVERHEAD	DOUBLE		Controller overhead and disk seek and latency time in milliseconds.
TRANSFERRATE	DOUBLE		Time to read one page of size PAGESIZE into the buffer.
PAGESIZE	INTEGER		Size (in bytes) of pages in the tablespace.
DBPGNAME	VARCHAR(18)		Name of the database partition group or the tablespace.
BUFFERPOOLID	INTEGER		ID of bufferpool used by this tablespace (1 indicates default bufferpool).
DROP_RECOVERY	CHAR(1)		N = Table is not recoverable after a DROP TABLE statement Y = Table is recoverable after a DROP TABLE statement
REMARKS	VARCHAR(254)	Yes	User-provided comment.

SYSCAT.TABOPTIONS

Each row contains option associated with a remote table.

Column Name	Data Type	Nullable	Description
TABSCHEMA	VARCHAR(128)		Qualified name of table, view, alias, or nickname.
TABNAME	VARCHAR(128)		Qualified name of table, view, alias, or nickname.
OPTION	VARCHAR(128)		Name of the table, view, alias, or nickname option.
SETTING	VARCHAR(255)		Value

SYSCAT.TBSPACEAUTH

Contains one row for each user or group who is granted USE privilege on a particular tablespace in the database.

Column Name	Data Type	Nullable	Description
GRANTOR	CHAR(128)		Authorization ID of the user who granted the privileges or SYSIBM.

Column Name	Data Type	Nullable	Description
GRANTEE	CHAR(128)		Authorization ID of the user or group who holds the privileges.
GRANTEETYPE	CHAR(1)		U = Grantee is an individual user G = Grantee is a group
TBSPACE	VARCHAR(18)		Name of the tablespace.
USEAUTH	CHAR(1)		Indicates whether grantee holds USE privilege on the tablespace: G = Privilege is held and grantable N = Privilege is not held Y = Privilege is held

SYSCAT.TRANSFORMS

Contains a row for each transform function type within a user-defined type contained in a named transform group.

Column Name	Data Type	Nullable	Description
TYPEID	SMALLINT		Internal type ID as defined in SYSCAT.DATATYPES
TYPESCHEMA	VARCHAR(128)		Qualified name of the given user-defined structured type.
TYPENAME	VARCHAR(18)		Qualified name of the given user-defined structured type.
GROUPNAME	VARCHAR(18)		Transform group name.
FUNCID	INTEGER	Yes	Internal function ID for the associated transform function, as defined in SYSCAT.FUNCTIONS. Null only for internal system function.
FUNSCHEMA	VARCHAR(128)		Qualified name of the associated transform functions.
FUNCNAME	VARCHAR(18)		Qualified name of the associated transform functions.
SPECIFICNAME	VARCHAR(18)		Function-specific (instance) name.
TRANSFORMTYPE	VARCHAR(8)		From SQL = Transform function transforms a structured type from SQL To SQL = Transform function transforms a structured type to SQL

Column Name	Data Type	Nullable	Description
FORMAT	CHAR(1)		U = User-defined
MAXLENGTH	INTEGER	Yes	Maximum length (in bytes) of output from the FROM SQL transform. Null for TO SQL transforms.
ORIGIN	CHAR(1)		O = Original transform group (user- or system-defined) R = Redefined
REMARKS	VARCHAR(254)	Yes	User-supplied comment or null.

SYSCAT.TRIGDEP

Contains a row for every dependency of a trigger on some other object.

Column Name	Data Type	Nullable	Description
TRIGSCHEMA	VARCHAR(128)		Qualified name of the trigger.
TRIGNAME	VARCHAR(18)		Qualified name of the trigger.
BTYPE	CHAR(1)		Type of object BNAME: A = Alias B = Trigger F = Function instance N = Nickname O = Privilege dependency on all subtables or subviews in a table or view hierarchy R = Structured type S = Materialized query table T = Table U = Typed table V = View W = Typed view X = Index extension
BSCHEMA	VARCHAR(128)		Qualified name of object depended on by a trigger
BNAME	VARCHAR(128)		Qualified name of object depended on by a trigger.
TABAUTH	SMALLINT	Yes	If BTYPE = O, S, T, U, V, or W encodes the privileges on the table or view that are required by this trigger; otherwise, null.

SYSCAT.TRIGGERS

Contains one row for each trigger. For table hierarchies, each trigger is recorded only at the level of the hierarchy where it was created.

Column Name	Data Type	Nullable	Description
TRIGSCHEMA	VARCHAR(128)		Qualified name of the trigger.
TRIGNAME	VARCHAR(18)		Qualified name of the trigger.
DEFINER	VARCHAR(128)		Authorization ID under which the trigger was defined.
TABSCHEMA	VARCHAR(128)		Qualified name of the table or view to which this trigger applies.
TABNAME	VARCHAR(128)		
TRIGTME	CHAR(1)		Time when triggered actions are applied to the base table, relative to the event that fired the trigger: A = Trigger applied after event B = Trigger applied before event I = Trigger applied instead of event
TRIGEVENT	CHAR(1)		Event that fires the trigger: I = Insert D = Delete U = Update
GRANULARITY	CHAR(1)		Trigger is executed once per: S = Statement R = Row
VALID	CHAR(1)		Y = Trigger is valid X = Trigger is inoperative; must be recreated.
CREATE_TIME	TIMESTAMP		Time at which the trigger was defined. Used in resolving functions and types.
QUALIFIER	VARCHAR(128)		Contains value of the default schema at the time of object definition.
FUNC_PATH	VARCHAR(254)		Function path at the time the trigger was defined. Used in resolving functions and types.
TEXT	CLOB(64K)		The full text of the CREATE TRIGGER statement, exactly as typed.
REMARKS	VARCHAR(254)	Yes	User-supplied comment, or null.

SYSCAT.TYPEMAPPINGS

Each row contains a user-defined mapping of a remote built-in data type to a local built-in data type.

Column Name	Data Type	Nullable	Description
TYPE_MAPPING	VARCHAR(18)		Name of the type mapping (may be system-generated).
TYPESCHEMA	VARCHAR(128)	Yes	Schema name of the type. Null for system built-in types.
TYPENAME	VARCHAR(18)		Name of the local type in a data type mapping.
TYPEID	SMALLINT		Type identifier.
SOURCETYPEID	SMALLINT		Source type identifier.
DEFINER	VARCHAR(128)		Authorization ID under which this type mapping was created.
LENGTH	INTEGER	Yes	Maximum length or precision of the data type. If null, the system determines the best length/precision.
SCALE	SMALLINT	Yes	Scale for DECIMAL fields. If null, the system determines the best scale attribute.
BIT_DATA	CHAR(1)	Yes	Y = Type is for bit data N = Type is not for bit data NULL = This is not a character data type or that the system determines the bit data attribute
WRAPNAME	VARCHAR(128)	Yes	Mapping applies to this data access protocol.
SERVERNAME	VARCHAR(128)	Yes	Name of the data source.
SERVERTYPE	VARCHAR(30)	Yes	Mapping applies to this type of data source.
SERVERVERSION	VARCHAR(18)	Yes	Mapping applies to this version of SERVERTYPE
REMOTE_TYPESCHEMA	VARCHAR(128)	Yes	Schema name of the remote type.
REMOTE_TYPENAME	VARCHAR(128)		Name of the data type as defined on the data source(s).

Column Name	Data Type	Nullable	Description
REMOTE_META_TYPE	CHAR(1)	Yes	S = Remote type is a system built-in type T = Remote type is a distinct type
REMOTE_LOWER_LEN	INTEGER	Yes	Lower bound of the length/precision of the remote decimal type. For character data types, this field indicates the number of characters.
REMOTE_UPPER_LEN	INTEGER	Yes	Upper bound of the length/precision of the remote decimal type. For character data types, this field indicates the number of characters.
REMOTE_LOWER_SCALE	SMALLINT	Yes	Lower bound of the scale of the remote type.
REMOTE_UPPER_SCALE	SMALLINT	Yes	Upper bound of the scale of the remote type.
REMOTE_S_OPR_P	CHAR(2)	Yes	Relationship between remote scale and remote precision. Basic comparison operators can be used. A null indicated that no specific relationship is required.
REMOTE_BIT_DATA	CHAR(1)	Yes	Y = Type is for bit data N = Type is not for bit data NULL = This is not a character data type or the system determines the bit data attribute
USER_DEFINED	CHAR(1)		Definition supplied by user.
CREATE_TIME	TIMESTAMP		Time when this mapping was created.
REMARKS	VARCHAR(254)	Yes	User-supplied comments, or null.

SYSCAT.USEROPTIONS

Each row contains server specific option values.

Column Name	Data Type	Nullable	Description
AUTHID	VARCHAR(128)		Local authorization ID (always uppercase).
SERVERNAME	VARCHAR(128)		Name of the server for which the user is defined.

Column Name	Data Type	Nullable	Description
OPTION	VARCHAR(128)		Name of the user options.
SETTING	VARCHAR(255)		Value

SYSCAT.VIEWS

Contains one or more rows for each view that is created.

Column Name	Data Type	Nullable	Description
VIEWSCHEMA	VARCHAR(128)		Qualified name of a view or the qualified name of a table that is used to define a materialized query table or a staging table.
VIEWNAME	VARCHAR(128)		Qualified name of a view or the qualified name of a table that is used to define a materialized query table or a staging table.
DEFINER	VARCHAR(128)		Authorization ID of the creator of the view.
SEQNO	SMALLINT		Always 1.
VIEWCHECK	CHAR(1)		States the type of view checking: N = No check option L = Local check option C = Cascaded check option
READONLY	CHAR(1)		Y = View is read-only because of its definition. N = View is not read-only
VALID	CHAR(1)		Y = View or materialized query table definition is valid X = View or materialized query table definition is inoperative; must be recreated.
QUALIFIER	VARCHAR(128)		Contains value of the default schema at the time of object definition.
FUNC_PATH	VARCHAR(254)		The SQL path of the view creator at the time the view was defined. When the view is used in data manipulation statements, this path must be used to resolve function calls in the view. SYSIBM for views created before v2.
TEXT	CLOB(64K)		Text of the CREATE VIEW statement.

SYSCAT.WRAPOPTIONS

Each row contains wrapper specific options.

Column Name	Data Type	Nullable	Description
WRAPNAME	VARCHAR(128)		Wrapper name
OPTION	VARCHAR(128)		Name of wrapper option.
SETTING	VARCHAR(255)		Value

SYSCAT.WRAPPERS

Each row contains information on the registered wrapper.

Column Name	Data Type	Nullable	Description
WRAPNAME	VARCHAR(128)		Wrapper name.
WRAPTYPE	CHAR(1)		N = Nonrelational R = Relational
WRAPVERSION	INTEGER		Version of the wrapper.
LIBRARY	VARCHAR(255)		Name of the file that contains the code used to communicate with the data sources associated with this wrapper.
REMARKS	VARCHAR(254)	Yes	User-supplied comment, or null

SYSSTAT.COLDIST

Each row describes the Nth-most-frequent value or Nth quantile value of some column. Statistics are not recorded for inherited columns of typed tables.

Column Name	Data Type	Nullable	Description	Updatable
TABSCHENMA	VARCHAR(128)		Qualified name of the table to which this entry applies.	
TABNAME	VARCHAR(128)		Qualified name of the table to which this entry applies.	
COLNAME	VARCHAR(128)		Name of the column to which this entry applies.	

Column Name	Data Type	Nullable	Description	Updatable
TYPE	CHAR(1)		Type of statistic collected: F = Frequency (most frequent value) Q = Quantile value	
SEQNO	SMALLINT		If TYPE = F, then N in this column identifies the Nth most frequent value. If TYPE = Q, then N in this column identifies the Nth quantile value.	
COLVALUE	VARCHAR(254)	Yes	The data value, as a character literal or a null value. This column can be updated with a valid representation of the value appropriate to the column that the statistic is associated with. If null is the required frequency value, the column should be set to NULL.	Yes
VALCOUNT	BIGINT		If TYPE = F, then VALCOUNT is the number of occurrences of COLVALUE in the column. If TYPE = Q, then VALCOUNT is the number of rows whose value is less than or equal to COVALUE. This column can be only updated with the following values: >=0 (zero)	Yes
DISTCOUNT	BIGINT		If TYPE = q, this column records the number of distinct values that are less than or equal to COLVALUE (null if unavailable.) the number of rows whose value is less than or equal to COLVALUE.	Yes

SYSSTAT.COLUMNS

Contains one row for each column for which statistics can be updated. Statistics are not recorded for inherited columns of typed tables.

Column Name	Data Type	Nullable	Description	Updatable
TABSCHEMA	VARCHAR(128)		Qualified name of the table that contains the column.	
TABNAME	VARCHAR(128)		Qualified name of the table that contains the column.	
COLNAME	VARCHAR(128)		Column name.	
COLCARD	BIGINT		Number of distinct values in the column; –1 if Statistics are not gathered; –2 for inherited columns and columns of H-tables. For any column, COLCARD cannot have a higher value than the cardinality of the table containing that column. This column can only be updated with the following values: -1 or >= 0 (zero)	Yes
HIGH2KEY	VARCHAR(33)	Yes	Second highest value of the column. This field is empty if statistics are not gathered and for inherited columns and columns of H-tables. This column can be updated with a valid representation of the value appropriate to the column that the statistic is associated with. LOW2KEY should not be greater than HIGH2KEY.	Yes

Column Name	Data Type	Nullable	Description	Updatable
LOW2KEY	VARCHAR(33)	Yes	Second lowest value of the column. Empty if statistics not gathered and for inherited columns and columns of H-tables. This column can be updated with a valid representation of the value appropriate to the column that the statistic is associated with.	Yes
AVGCOLLEN	INTEGER		Average column length. –1 if a long field or LOB, or statistics have not been collected; –2 for inherited columns and columns of H-tables. This column can only be updated with the following values: -1 or >= 0 (zero)	Yes
NUMNULLS	BIGINT		Contains the number of nulls in a column. –1 if statistics are not gathered. This column can only be updated with the following values: -1 or >= 0 (zero)	Yes
SUB_COUNT	SMALLINT		Average number of sub-elements. Only applicable for character columns. For example, consider the following string: database simulation analytical business intelligence. In this example, SUB_COUNT = 5, because there are 5 sub-elements in the string.	

Column Name	Data Type	Nullable	Description	Updatable
SUB_DELIM_LENGTH	SMALLINT		Average length of each delimeter separating each subelement. Only applicable for character columns. For example, consider the following string: `database simulation analytical business intelligence` In this example, SUB_DELIM_LENGTH = 1, because each delimeter is a single blank.	

SYSSTAT.INDEXES

Contains one row for each index that is defined for a table.

Column Name	Data Type	Nullable	Description	Updatable
INDSCHEMA	VARCHAR(128)		Qualified name of the index.	
INDNAME	VARCHAR(18)		Qualified name of the index.	
TABSCHEMA	VARCHAR(128)		Qualifier of the table name.	
TABNAME	VARCHAR(128)		Name of the table or nickname on which the index is defined.	
COLNAMES	CLOB(1M)		List of column names with + or – prefixes.	
NLEAF	INTEGER		Number of leaf pages; –1 if statistics are not gathered. This column can only be updated with the following values: -1 or > 0 (zero)	Yes
NLEVELS	SMALLINT		Number of index levels: –1 if statistics are not gathered. This column can only be updated with the following values: -1 or > 0 (zero)	Yes

Column Name	Data Type	Nullable	Description	Updatable
FIRSTKEYCARD	BIGINT		Number of distinct first key values; –1 if statistics are not gathered. This column can only be updated with the following values: -1 or >= 0 (zero)	Yes
FIRST2KEYCARD	BIGINT		Number of distinct keys using the first two columns of the index –1 if no statistics, or not applicable). This column can only be updated with the following values: -1 or >= 0 (zero)	Yes
FIRST3KEYCARD	BIGINT		Number of distinct keys using the first three columns of the index (–1 if no statistics, or not applicable). This column can only be updated with the following values: -1 or >= 0 (zero)	Yes
FIRST4KEYCARD	BIGINT		Number of distinct keys using the first four columns of the index (–1 if no statistics, or not applicable). This column can only be updated with the following values: -1 or >= 0 (zero)	Yes
FULLKEYCARD	BIGINT		Number of distinct full key values; –1 if statistics are not gathered. This column can only be updated with the following values: -1 or >= 0 (zero)	Yes

Column Name	Data Type	Nullable	Description	Updatable
CLUSTERRATIO	SMALLINT		This column is used by the optimizer. It indicates the degree of data clustering with the index; –1 if statistics are not gathered, or if detailed index statistics have been gathered. This column can only be updated with the following values: -1 or between 0 and 100	Yes
CLUSTERFACTOR	DOUBLE		This column is used by the optimizer. It is a finer measurement of degree of clustering, or –1 if detailed index statistics have not been gathered. This column can only be updated with the following values: -1 or between 0 and 1	Yes
SEQUENTIAL_PAGES	INTEGER		Number of leaf pages located on disk in index key order with few or no large gaps between them; –1 if no statistics are available. This column can only be updated with the following values: -1 or >= 0 (zero)	Yes
DENSITY	INTEGER		Ratio of SEQUENTIAL_PAGES to number of pages in the range of pages occupied by the index, expressed as a percent (integer between 0 and 100; –1 if no statistics are available.) This column can only be updated with the following values: -1 or between 0 and 100	Yes

Column Name	Data Type	Nullable	Description	Updatable
PAGE_FETCH_PAIRS	VARCHAR(254)		A list of pairs of integers, represented in character form. Each pair represents the number of pages in a hypothetical buffer, and the number of page fetches required to scan the index using that hypothetical buffer. (Zero-length string if no data available.) This column can be updated with the following input values: • The pair delimeter and pair separator characters are the only non-numeric characters accepted. • Blanks are the only characters recognized as a pair delimeter and pair separator. • Each number entry must have an accompanying partner number entry with the two being separated by the pair separator character. • Each pair must be separated from any other pairs by the pair delimeter character. • Each expected number entry must be between 0-9 (positive values only).	Yes
NUMRIDS	BIGINT		Number of RIDs in the index; –1 if statistics are not gathered.	Yes

Column Name	Data Type	Nullable	Description	Updatable
NUMRIDS_DELETED	BIGINT		Number of RIDs in the index that are marked deleted, excluding the ones on pages on which all RIDs are marked deleted; –1 if statistics are not gathered.	Yes
NUM_EMPTY_LEAFS	BIGINT		Number of leaf pages in the index on which all RIDs are marked deleted; –1 if statistics are not gathered.	Yes
AVERAGE_RANDOM _FETCH_PAGES	DOUBLE		Average number of random table pages between sequential page accesses when fetching using the index; –1 if it is not known.	
AVERAGE_RANDOM _PAGES	DOUBLE		Average number of random index pages between sequential index page accesses; –1 if it is not known.	
AVERAGE_SEQUENCE _GAP	DOUBLE		Gap between index page sequences. Detected through a scan of index leaf pages, each gap represents the average number of index pages that must be randomly fetched between sequences of index pages; –1 if it is not known.	
AVERAGE_SEQUENCE _FETCH_GAP	DOUBLE		Gap between table page sequences when fetching using the index. Detected through a scan of index leaf pages, each gap represents the average number of table pages that must be randomly fetched between sequences of table pages; –1 if it is not known.	

Column Name	Data Type	Nullable	Description	Updatable
AVERAGE_SEQUENCE _PAGES	DOUBLE		Average number of index pages accessible in sequence (that is, the number of index pages that the prefetchers would detect as being in sequence); –1 if it is not known.	
AVERAGE_SEQUENCE _FETCH_PAGES	DOUBLE		Average number of table pages accessible in sequence (that is, the number of table pages that the prefetchers would detect as being in sequence) when fetching using the index; –1 if it is not known.	

SYSSTAT.ROUTINES

Contains a row for each user-defined function (scalar, table, or source), system-generated method, user-defined method, or procedure. Does not include built-in functions. (This catalog view supercedes SYSSTAT.FUNCTIONS. The other view exists, but will remain as it was in DB2 version 7.1.)

Column Name	Data Type	Nullable	Description	Updatable
ROUTINESCHEMA	VARCHAR(128)		Qualified routine name.	
ROUTINENAME	VARCHAR(18)			
ROUTINETYPE	CHAR(1)		F = Function M = Method P = Procedure.	
SPECIFICNAME	VARCHAR(18)		The name of the routine instance (may be system generated).	
IOS_PER_INVOC	DOUBLE		Estimated number of I/Os per invocation; –1 if not known (0 default). This column can only be updated with -1 or >= 0 (zero).	Yes

Column Name	Data Type	Nullable	Description	Updatable
INSTS_PER_INVOC	DOUBLE		Estimated number of instructions per invocation; –1 if not known (450 default). This column can only be updated with -1 or >= 0 (zero).	Yes
IOS_PER_ARGBYTE	DOUBLE		Estimated number of I/Os per input argument byte; –1 if not known (0 default). This column can only be updated with -1 or >= 0 (zero).	Yes
INSTS_PER_ARGBYTE	DOUBLE		Estimated number of instructions per input argument byte; –1 if not known (0 default). This column can only be updated with -1 or >= 0 (zero).	Yes
PERCENT_ARGBYTE	SMALLINT		Estimated average percent of input argument bytes that the routine will actually read; –1 if not known (100 default). This column can only be updated with -1 or a number between 0 (zero) and 100.	Yes
INITIAL_IOS	DOUBLE		Estimated number of I/Os performed the first/last time the routine is invoked; –1 if not known (0 default). This column can only be updated with -1 or >= 0 (zero).	Yes
INITIAL_INSTS	DOUBLE		Estimated number of instructions executed the first/last time the routine is invoked; –1 if not known (0 default). This column can only be updated with -1 or >= 0 (zero).	Yes

Column Name	Data Type	Nullable	Description	Updatable
CARDINALITY	BIGINT		The predicted cardinality of a table function; –1 if not known, or if the routine is not a table or function. This column can only be updated with -1 or >= 0 (zero).	Yes
SELCTIVITY	DOUBLE		Used for user-defined predicates; –1 if there are no user-defined predicates.	

SYSSTAT.TABLES

Contains one row for each *base* table. Views or aliases are, therefore, not included. For typed tables, only the root table of a table hierarchy is included in this view. Statistics are not recorded for inherited columns of typed tables. The CARD value applies to the root table only while the other statistics apply to the entire table hierarchy.

Column Name	Data Type	Nullable	Description	Updatable
TABSCHEMA	VARCHAR(128)		Qualified name of the table.	
TABNAME	VARCHAR(128)			
CARD	BIGINT		Total number of rows in the table; –1 if statistics are not gathered. An update to CARD for a table should not attempt to assign it a value less than the COLCARD value of any of the columns in that table. A value of –2 cannot be changed and a column value cannot be directly set to –2. This column can only be updated with the following values: -1 or >= 0 (zero).	Yes

Column Name	Data Type	Nullable	Description	Updatable
NPAGES	INTEGER		Total number of pages on which the rows of the table exist; –1 if statistics are not gathered, and –2 for subtables and H-tables. A value of –2 cannot be changed and a column value cannot be directly set to –2. This column can only be updated with the following values: -1 or >= 0 (zero).	Yes
FPAGES	INTEGER		Total number of pages in the file; –1 if statistics are not gathered, and –2 for subtables and H-tables. A value of –2 cannot be changed and a column value cannot be directly set to –2. This column can only be updated with the following values: -1 or > 0 (zero).	Yes
ACTIVE_BLOCKS	INTEGER		Total number of in-use blocks in a multi-dimensional clustering (MDC) table; –1 if statistics are not gathered.	Yes
OVERFLOW	INTEGER		Total number of overflow records in the table; –1 if statistics are not gathered, and –2 for subtables and H-tables. A value of –2 cannot be changed and a column value cannot be directly set to –2. This column can only be updated with the following values: -1 or >= 0 (zero).	Yes

APPENDIX B

DB2 Information on the Web

There is a lot of valuable information on DB2 and related technologies on the Web. This appendix contains a listing of useful list servers, newsgroups, newsletters, e-zines, and Web sites.

DB2-L LISTSERVER

This list is dedicated to DB2 on all platforms. It is a very active list, with over 4,000 subscribers from around the world. You can subscribe to this list via the Web at *http://listserv.ylassoc.com/faq.asp*. Yours truly is a long-time associate list owner!

Postings are cross-posted to the *bit.listserv.db2-l* newsgroup.

NEWSGROUP

comp.database.ibm.db2

This group does not provide for newsgroup access from your email client. You can join this newsgroup and post or monitor discussion via Google at *www.google.com.*

NEWSLETTERS

BITPIPE

www.bitpipe.com
Information and white papers on information technology.

Data Warehousing

www.datawarehouse.com
Information on data warehouse news and technology.

ITWORLD

www.itworld.com
Information, articles, and white papers on information technology.

Sysopt

www.sysopt.com
Information on the UNIX operating system.

Tidal Wire

www.tidalwire.com/news/StorageReporter
Information on storage technology.

E-ZINES

www.dbazine.com

www.db2mag.com
(Also available in hard copy via subscription)

www.idug.org/idug/journal/index.cfm
(Also available in hard copy via subscription)

WEB SITES

Association for Computing Machinery (ACM) Transactions on Databases

www.informatik.uni-trier.de/~ley/db/journals/tods/index.html
www.ACM.org

International Society of Electrical and Electronic Engineers (IEEE) Computer Society

www.computer.org

DB2 Online Technical Support

www-3.ibm.com/cgi-bin/db2www/data/db2/udb/winos2unix/support/index.d2w/report

DB2 Zone

www.gunningts.com

DB-HQ

www.db-hq.net

IBM Redbooks

www.redbooks.ibm.com

DB2 UDB v8 for Linux, UNIX, and Windows Home Page

www.software.ibm.com/data/db2/udb

USER GROUP

International DB2 Users Group

www.idug.org
(Refer to this site for listings of Regional User Groups)

VENDOR WEB SITES

BMC Software

www.bmc.com

Embarcadero Technologies

www.embarcadero.com

Computer Associates

www.ca.com

Candle Corporation

www.candle.com

Compuware

www.compuware.com

Quest

www.quest.com

Veritas Software

www.veritas.com

APPENDIX C

DB2 Limits

This appendix on DB2 Limits contains a quick reference for information often sought after by DBAs and application developers alike on architectural limits in DB2. This appendix contains limit definitions in the following areas:

- Identifier length limits
- Numeric limits
- String limits
- Datetime limits
- Database Manager limits
- Database Manager page size-specific limits

Applications developed within these limits will enable applications to be developed that are easily portable across the DB2 family.

Table C.1 Identifier Length Limits

Description	Limit in bytes
Longest authorization name (can only be single-byte characters)	30
Longest constraint name	18
Longest correlation name	128
Longest condition name	64
Longest cursor name	18
Longest data source column name	128

Table C.1 Identifier Length Limits (Continued)

Description	Limit in bytes
Longest data source index name	128
Longest data source name	128
Longest data source table name (remote-table- name)	128
Longest external program name	8
Longest host identifier	255
Longest identifier of a data source user (remote-authorization-name)	30
Longest label name	64
Longest method name	18
Longest parameter name	128
Longest password to access a data source	32
Longest savepoint name	128
Longest schema name	30
Longest server (database alias) name	8
Longest SQL variable name	64
Longest statement name	18
Longest transform group name	18
Longest unqualified column name	30
Longest unqualified package name	8
Longest unqualified user-defined type, user-defined function, user-defined method, bufferpool, tablespace, database partition group, trigger, index, or index specification name	18
Longest unqualified table name, view name, stored procedure name, sequence name, nickname, or alias	128
Longest wrapper name	128

Notes:

1. Individual host language compilers may have a more restrictive limit on variable names.
2. Parameter names in an SQL procedure are limited to 64 bytes.
3. The schema name for a user-defined type is limited to 8 bytes.

Table C.2 Numeric Limits

Description	Limits
Smallest INTEGER value	–2,147,483,648
Largest INTEGER value	+2,147,483,647
Smallest BIGINT value	–9,223,372,036,854,775,808
Largest BIGINT value	+9,223,372,036,854,775,807
Smallest SMALLINT value	–32,768
Largest SMALLINT value	+32,767
Largest decimal precision	31
Smallest DOUBLE value	–1.79769E + 308
Largest DOUBLE value	+1.79769E + 308
Smallest positive DOUBLE value	+2.225E – 307
Largest negative DOUBLE value	–2.225E – 307
Smallest REAL value	–3.402E + 38
Largest REAL value	+3.402E + 38
Smallest positive REAL value	+1.175E – 37
Largest negative REAL value	–1.175E – 37

Table C.3 String Limits

Description	Limits
Maximum length of CHAR (in bytes)	254
Maximum length of VARCHAR (in bytes)	32,672
Maximum length of LONG VARCHAR (in bytes)	32,700
Maximum length of CLOB (in bytes)	2,147,483,647
Maximum length of GRAPHIC (in characters)	127
Maximum length of VARGRAPHIC (in characters)	16,336
Maximum length of LONG VARGRAPHIC (in characters)	16,350
Maximum length of DBCLOB (in characters)	1,073,741,823

Table C.3 String Limits (Continued)

Description	Limits
Maximum length of BLOB (in bytes)	2,147,483,647
Maximum length of character constant	32,672
Maximum length of graphic constant	16,336
Maximum length of concatenated character string	2,147,483,647
Maximum length of concatenated graphic string	1,073,741,823
Maximum length of concatenated binary string	2,147,483,647
Maximum number of hex constant digits	16,336
Maximum size of a catalog comment (in bytes)	254
Largest instance of a structured type column object at runtime	1 GB

Table C.4 Datetime Limits

Description	Limits
Smallest DATE value	0001-01-01
Largest DATE value	9999-12-31
Smallest TIME value	00:00:00
Largest TIME value	24:00:00
Smallest TIMESTAMP value	0001-01-01-00.00.00.000000
Largest TIMESTAMP value	9999-12-31-24.00.00.000000

Table C.5 Database Manager Limits

Description	Limits
Most columns in a table	1,012
Most columns in a view	5,000
Maximum length of a row including all overhead	32,677
Maximum size of a table per partition (in gigabytes)	512
Maximum size of an index per partition (in gigabytes)	512
Most rows in a table per partition	4 × 10^9

Table C.5 Database Manager Limits (Continued)

Description	Limits
Longest index key including all overhead (in bytes)	1,024
Most columns in an index key	16
Most indexes on a table	32,767 or storage
Most tables referenced in an SQL statement or a view	storage
Most host variable declarations in a precompiled program	storage
Most host variable references in an SQL statement	32,767
Longest host variable value used for insert or update (in bytes)	2,147,483,647
Longest SQL statement (in bytes)	65,535
Most elements in a select list	1,012
Most predicates in a `WHERE` or `HAVING` clause	storage
Maximum number of columns in a `GROUP BY` clause	1,012
Maximum total length of columns in a `GROUP BY` clause (in bytes)	32,677
Maximum number of columns in an `ORDER BY` clause	1,012
Maximum total length of columns in an `ORDER BY` clause (in bytes)	32,677
Maximum size of an SQLDA (in bytes)	storage
Maximum number of prepared statements	storage
Most declared cursors in a program	storage
Maximum number of prepared statements	storage
Most tables in an SMS tablespace	65,534
Maximum number of constraints on a table	storage
Maximum level of subquery nesting	storage
Maximum number of subqueries in a single statement	storage
Most values in an `INSERT` statement	1,012
Most `SET` clauses in a single `UPDATE` statement	1,012
Most columns in a `UNIQUE` constraint (supported via a `UNIQUE` index)	16

Table C.5 Database Manager Limits (Continued)

Description	Limits
Maximum combined length of columns in a `UNIQUE` constraint (supported via a `UNIQUE` index) (in bytes)	1,024
Most referencing columns in a foreign key	16
Maximum combined length of referencing columns in a foreign key (in bytes)	1,024
Maximum length of a check constraint specification (in bytes)	65,535
Maximum number of columns in a partitioning key	500
Maximum number of rows changed in a unit of work	storage
Maximum number of packages	storage
Most constants in a statement	storage
Maximum concurrent users of server	64,000
Maximum number of parameters in a stored procedure	32,767
Maximum number of parameters in a user-defined function	90
Maximum runtime depth of cascading triggers	16
Maximum number of simultaneously active event monitors	32
Maximum size of a regular DMS tablespace (in gigabytes)	512
Maximum size of a long DMS tablespace (in terabytes)	2
Maximum size of a temporary DMS tablespace (in terabytes)	2
Maximum number of databases per instance concurrently in use	256
Maximum number of concurrent users per instance	64,000
Maximum number of concurrent applications per database	60,000
Maximum number of connections per process within a DB2 client	512
Maximum depth of cascaded triggers	16
Maximum partition number	999
Most table objects in a DMS tablespace	51,000
Longest variable index key part (in bytes)	1,022 or storage

Table C.5 Database Manager Limits (Continued)

Description	Limits
Maximum number of columns in a data source table of view that is referenced by a nickname	5,000
Maximum `NPAGES` in a bufferpool for 32-bit releases	524,288
Maximum `NPAGES` in a bufferpool for 64-bit releases	2,147,483,647
Maximum total size of all bufferpool slots (4K)	2,147,483,646
Maximum number of nested levels for stored procedures	16
Maximum number of tablespaces in a database	4,096
Maximum number of attributes in a structured type	4,082
Maximum number of simultaneously opened LOB locators in a transaction	32,100

Notes:

1. This maximum can be achieved using a join in the `CREATE VIEW` statement. Selecting from such a view is subject to the limit of most elements in a select list.
2. The actual data for `BLOB`, `CLOB`, `LONG VARCHAR`, `DBCLOB`, and `LONG VARGRAPHIC` columns is not included in this count. However, information about the location of that data does take up some space in the row.
3. The numbers shown are architectural limits and approximations. The practical limits may be less.
4. The actual value will be the value of the `MAXAGENTS` configuration parameter.
5. This is an architectural limit. The limit on the most columns in an index key should be used as the practical limit.
6. Table objects include data, indexes, `LONG VARCHAR` or `VARGRAPHIC` columns, and LOB columns. Table objects that are in the same tablespace as the table data do not count extra toward the limit. However, each table object that is in a different tablespace than the table data does contribute one toward the limit for each table object type per table in the tablespace in which the table object resides.
7. For page size-specific values, see Database Manager Page Size-Specific Limits.
8. This is limited only by the longest index key, including all overhead (in bytes). As the number of index key parts increases, the maximum length of each key part decreases.

Table C.6 Database Manager Page Size-Specific Limits

Description	Page Size Limit			
	4K	8K	16K	32K
Most columns in a table	500	1,012	1,012	1,012
Maximum length of a row including all overhead	4,005	8,101	16,293	32,677
Maximum size of a table per partition (in gigabytes)	64	128	256	512
Maximum size of an index per partition (in gigabytes)	64	128	256	512

Table C.6 Database Manager Page Size-Specific Limits (Continued)

Description	Page Size Limit			
	4K	8K	16K	32K
Most elements in a select list	500	1,012	1,012	1,012
Maximum number of columns in a GROUP BY clause	500	1,012	1,012	1,012
Maximum total length of columns in a GROUP BY clause (in bytes)	4,005	8,101	16,293	32,677
Maximum number of columns in an ORDER BY clause	500	1,012	1,012	1,012
Maximum total length of columns in an ORDER BY clause (in bytes)	4,005	8,101	16,293	32,677
Most values in an INSERT statement	500	1,012	1,012	1,012
Most SET clauses in a single UPDATE statement	500	1,012	1,012	1,012
Maximum size of a regular DMS tablespace (in gigabytes)	64	128	256	512

APPENDIX D

DB2 Registry and Environmental Variables

This appendix contains a complete list of DB2 v8 Registry and Environmental variables. Also included are 16 variables that have become obsolete in v8. Additionally, eight new v8 variables are highlighted. Note that new variables are emphasized by a gray background.

To review a list of all supported registry variables, issue the `db2set-lr` command. Values can be changed for the current or default instance by using the following command:

```
db2set registry_variable_name=new_variable
```

On UNIX systems, the *export* command can be used instead of the *set* command.

Depending on your operating system, the `DB2INSTANCE`, `DB2PATH`, `DB2NODE`, and `DB2INSTPROF` may or may not be stored in the DB2 profile registries. See the *Administration Guide: Implementation* for additional details.

> **NOTE**
> If registry variables requires Boolean values as arguments, the values `YES`, `1`, and `ON` are all equivalent and the values `NO`, `0`, and `OFF` are also equivalent. For any variable, you can specify any of the appropriate equivalent values.

The following variables are obsolete in v8:

```
DB2_BLOCK_ON_LOG_DISK_FULL
DB2COUNTRY
DB2_STRIPED_CONTAINERS
DB2DIRPATHNAME
```

```
DB2CIENTADPT
DB2CLIENTCOMM
DB2ROUTE
DB2ATLD_PORTS
DB2CHGPWD_EEE
DB2_UPDATE_PART_KEY
DB2_AVOID_PREFETCH
DB2_NO_PKG_LOCK
DB2_RR_RS
DB2_FORCE_TRUNCATION
DB2_INDEX_2BYTEVARLEN
DB2UPMPR
```

You can use this appendix to make sure that systems you support are optimally configured.

> **NOTE**
> The default for the `DB2_HASH_JOIN` variable has been changed from `NO` to `YES` in v8.

General Registry Variables

Variable name	Operating system	Values
`DB2ACCOUNT`	All	Default = `null`
The accounting string that is sent to the remote host. Refer to the *DB2 Connect User's Guide* for details.		
`DB2BIDI`	All	Default = `NO` Values: `YES` or `NO`
This variable enables bidirectional support and the `DB2CODEPAGE` variable is used to declare the code page to be used. Refer to the National Language Support appendix for additional information on bidirectional support.		
`DB2CODEPAGE`	All	Default: derived from the language ID, as specified by the operating system.
Specifies the code page of the data presented to DB2 for database client application. The user should not set `DB2CODEPAGE` unless explicitly stated in DB2 documents, or asked to do so by the DB2 service. Setting `DB2CODEPAGE` to a value not supported by the operating system can produce unexpected results. Normally, you do not need to set `DB2CODEPAGE` because DB2 automatically derives the code page information from the operating system.		

Variable name	Operating system	Values
DB2DBMSADDR		Default = 0x20000000 for Windows NT Value: 0x20000000 to 0xB0000000 in increments of 0x10000

Specifies the default database manager shared memory address in hexadecimal format. If db2start fails due to a shared memory address collision, this registry variable can be modified to force the database manager instance to allocate its shared memory at a different address.

Variable name	Operating system	Values
DB2_DISABLE_FLUSH_LOG	All	Default = OFF Value: ON or OFF

Specifies whether to disable closing the active log file when the online backup is completed. When an online backup completes, the last active log file is truncated, closed, and made available to be archived. This ensures that your online backup has a complete set of archived logs available for recovery. You might disable closing the last active log file if you are concerned that you are wasting portions of the Log Sequence Number (LSN) space. Each time an active log file is truncated, the LSN is incremented by an amount proportional to the space truncated. If you perform a large number of online backups each day, you might disable closing the last active log file. You might also disable closing the last active log file if you find you are receiving log full messages a short time after the completion of the online backup. When a log file is truncated, the reserved active log space is incremented by the amount proportional to the size of the truncated log. The active log space is freed once the truncated log file is reclaimed. The reclamation occurs a short time after the log file becomes inactive. During the short interval between these two events you may receive log full messages.

Variable name	Operating system	Values
DB2DISCOVERYTIME	Windows operating systems	Default = 40 seconds Minimum = 20 seconds

Specifies the amount of time that SEARCH discovery will search for DB2 systems.

Variable name	Operating system	Values
DB2INCLUDE	All	Default = current directory

Specifies a path to be used during the processing of the SQL INCLUDE text-file statement during DB2PREP processing. It provides a list of directories where the INCLUDE file might be found. Refer to the *Application Development Guide* for descriptions of how DB2INCLUDE is used in different precompiled languages.

Variable name	Operating system	Values
DB2INSTDEF	Windows operating systems	Default = DB2

Sets the value to be used if DB2INSTANCE is not defined.

Variable name	Operating system	Values
DB2INSTOWNER	Windows NT	Default = null

The registry variable created in the DB2 profile registry when the instance is first created. This variable is set to the name of the instance-owning machine.

Variable name	Operating system	Values
DB2_LIC_STAT_SIZE	All	Default = null Range: 0 to 32,767

Variable name	Operating system	Values
The registry variable determines the maximum size (in MBs) of the file containing the license statistics for the system. A value of zero turns the license statistic gathering off. If the variable is not recognized or not defined, the variable defaults to unlimited. The statistics are displayed using the License Center.		
DB2DBDFT	All	Default = null
Specifies the database alias name of the database to be used for implicit connects. If an application has no database connection but SQL statements are issued, an implicit connect will be made if the DB2DBDFT environment variable has been defined with a default database.		
DB2LOCALE	All	Default = no Values: YES or NO
Specifies whether the default "C" locale of a process is restored to the default "C" locale after calling DB2 and whether to restore the process locale back to the original 'C' after calling a DB2 function. If the original locale was not 'C', then this registry variable is ignored.		
DB2NBDISCOVERRCVBUFS	All	Default = 16 buffers Minimum = 16 buffers
This variable is used for the NetBIOS search discovery. The variable specifies the number of concurrent discovery responses that can be received by a client. If the client receives more concurrent responses than are specified by this variable, then the excess responses are discarded by the NetBIOS layer. The default is (16) NetBIOS receive buffers. If a number less than the default value is chosen, then the default is used.		
DB2OPTIONS	All except Windows 3.1 and Macintosh	Default = null
Sets command line processor options.		
DB2SLOGON	Windows 3.x	Default = null Values: YES or NO
Enables a secure logon in DB2 for Windows 3.x. If DB2SLOGON = YES, DB2 does not write user IDs and passwords to a file, but instead uses a segment of memory to maintain them. When DB2SLOGON is enabled, the user must log on each time Windows 3.x is started.		
DB2TERRITORY	All	Default: derived from the language ID, as specified by the operating system.
Specifies the region or territory code of the client application, which influences date and time formats.		
DB2TIMEOUT	Windows 3.x and Macintosh	Default = (not set)
Used to control the timeout period for Windows 3.x and Macintosh clients during long SQL queries. After the timeout period has expired a dialog box pops up asking if the query should be interrupted or allowed to continue. The minimum value for this variable is 30 seconds. If DB2TIMEOUT is set to a value between 1 and 30, the default minimum value will be used. If DB2TIMEOUT is set to a value of 0, or a negative value, the timeout feature is disabled. This feature is disabled by default.		

Variable name	Operating system	Values
DB2TRACENAME	Windows 3.x and Macintosh	Default = DB2WIN.TRC (on Windows 3.x), DB2MAC.TRC (on Macintosh)
On Windows 3.x and Macintosh, specifies the name of the file where trace information is stored. The default for each system is saved in your current instance directory (for example, \sqllib\db2). It is strongly recommended that you specify the full path name when naming the trace file.		
DB2TRACEON	Windows 3.1x and Macintosh	Default = NO Values: YES or NO
On Windows 3.x and Macintosh, turns trace on to provide information to IBM in case of a problem. (It is not recommended that you turn trace on unless you encounter a problem you cannot resolve.) Troubleshooting information includes information about using the trace facility with clients.		
DB2TRCFLUSH	Windows 3.x and Macintosh	Default = NO Values: YES or NO
On Windows 3.x and Macintosh, DB2TRACEFLUSH can be used in conjunction with DB2TRACEON = YES. Setting DB2TRACEFLUSH = YES will cause each trace record to be written immediately into the trace file. This will slow down your DB2 system considerably, so the default setting is DB2TRACEFLUSH = NO. This setting is useful in cases where an application hangs the system and requires the system to be rebooted. Setting this keyword guarantees that the trace file and trace entries are not lost by the reboot.		
DB2TRCSYSERR	Windows 3.x and Macintosh	Default = 1 Values: 1 - 32,767
Specifies the number of system errors to trace before the client turns off tracing. The default value traces one system error, after which trace is turned off.		
DB2YIELD	Windows 3.x	Default = NO Values: YES or NO
Specifies the behavior of the Windows 3.x client while communicating with a remote server. When set to NO, the client will not yield the CPU to other Windows 3.x applications, and the Windows environment is halted while the client application is communicating with the remote server. You must wait for the communications operation to complete before you can resume any other tasks. When set to YES, your system functions as normal. It is recommended that you try to run your application with DB2YIELD = YES. If your system crashes, you will need to set DB2YIELD = NO. For application development, ensure your application is written to accept and handle Windows messages while waiting for a communications operation to complete.		

System Environment Variables

<table>
<tr><th>Variable name</th><th>Operating system</th><th>Values</th></tr>
<tr><td>DB2CONNECT_IN_APP_PROCESS</td><td>All</td><td>Default = YES
Values: YES or NO</td></tr>
<tr><td colspan="3">When you set this variable to NO, local DB2 Connect clients on a DB2 Connect Enterprise Edition machine are forced to run within an agent. Some advantages of running within an agent are that local clients can be monitored and that they can use SYSPLEX support.</td></tr>
<tr><td>DB2DOMAINLIST</td><td>Windows NT server only</td><td>Default = NULL
Values: A list of Windows NT domain names separated by commas (“,”).</td></tr>
<tr><td colspan="3">Defines one or more Windows NT domains. Only users belonging to these domains will have their connection or attachment requests accepted. This registry variable should only be used under a pure Windows NT domain environment with DB2 servers and clients running DB2 Universal Database Version 7.1 (or later).</td></tr>
<tr><td>DB2ENVLIST</td><td>UNIX</td><td>Default: null</td></tr>
<tr><td colspan="3">Lists specific variable names for either stored procedures or user-defined functions. By default, the db2start command filters out all user environment variables except those prefixed with DB2 or db2. If specific registry variables must be passed to either stored procedures or user-defined functions, you can list the variable names in the DB2ENVLIST registry variable. Separate each variable name by one or more spaces. DB2 constructs its own PATH and LIBPATH, so if PATH or LIBPATH is specified in DB2ENVLIST, the actual value of the variable name is appended to the end of the DB2-constructed value.</td></tr>
<tr><td>DB2INSTANCE</td><td>All</td><td>Default = DB2INSTDEF on Windows 32-bit operating systems.</td></tr>
<tr><td colspan="3">The environment variable used to specify the instance that is active by default. On UNIX, users must specify a value for DB2INSTANCE.</td></tr>
<tr><td>DB2INSTPROF</td><td>Windows operating systems</td><td>Default: null</td></tr>
<tr><td colspan="3">The environment variable used to specify the location of the instance directory on Windows operating systems, if different than DB2PATH.</td></tr>
<tr><td>DB2LIBPATH</td><td>UNIX</td><td>Default: null</td></tr>
<tr><td colspan="3">Specifies the value of LIBPATH in the DB2LIBPATH registry variable. The value of LIBPATH cannot be inherited between parent and child processes if the user ID has changed. Since the db2start executable is owned by the root, DB2 cannot inherit the LIBPATH settings of end-users. If you list the variable name, LIBPATH, in the DB2ENVLIST registry variable, you must also specify the value of LIBPATH in the DB2LIBPATH registry variable. The db2start executable then reads the value of DB2LIBPATH and appends this value to the end of the DB2-constructed LIBPATH.</td></tr>
<tr><td>DB2NODE</td><td>All</td><td>Default: null
Values: 1 to 999</td></tr>
</table>

Variable name	Operating system	Values
Used to specify the target logical node of a DB2 Enterprise Server Edition database partition server that you want to attach to or connect to. If this variable is not set, the target logical node defaults to the logical node which is defined with port 0 on the machine.		
DB2_PARALLEL_IO	All	Default: null Values: *(meaning every tablespace) or a comma-separated list of more than one defined tablespace
While reading or writing data from and to table space containers, DB2 may use parallel I/O for each table space value that you specify. The degree of parallelism is determined by the prefetch size and extent size for the containers in the tablespace. For example, if the prefetch size is four times the extent size, then there are four extent-sized prefetch requests. The number of containers in the tablespace does not affect the number of prefetchers. To enable parallel I/O for all tablespaces, use the wildcard character, "*". To enable parallel I/O for a subset of all tablespaces, enter the list of tablespaces. If there is more than one container, extent-size pieces of any full prefetch request are broken down into smaller requests executed in parallel based on the number of prefetches. When this variable is not enabled, the number of prefetcher requests created is based on the number of containers in the tablespace.		
DB2PATH	Windows operating systems	Default: varies by operating system
The environment variable used to specify the directory where the product is installed on Windows 32-bit operating systems.		
DB2_USE_PAGE_CONTAINER_TAG	All	Default: null Values: ON, null
By default, DB2 stores a container tag in the first extent of each DMS container, whether it is a file or a device. The container tag is the metadata for the container. Before DB2 version 8.1, the container tag was stored in a single page, and it thus required less space in the container. To continue to store the container tag in a single page, set DB2_USE_PAGE_CONTAINER_TAG to ON. However, if you set this registry variable to ON when you use RAID devices for containers, I/O performance might degrade. Because for RAID devices you create tablespaces with an extent size equal to or a multiple of the RAID stripe size, setting the DB2_USE_PAGE_CONTAINER_TAG to ON causes the extents not to line up with the RAID stripes. As a result, an I/O request might need to access more physical disks than would be optimal. Users are strongly advised against enabling this registry variable. To activate changes to this registry variable, issue a DB2STOP command and then enter a DB2START command.		

COMMUNICATIONS VARIABLES

Variable name	Operating system	Values
DB2CHECKCLIENTINTERVAL	AIX server only	Default = 0 Values: A numeric value greater than zero.

Used to verify the status of APPC client connections. Permits early detection of client termination, rather than waiting until after the completion of the query. When set to zero, no check will be made. When set to a numerical value greater than zero, the value represents DB2 internal work units. For guidance, the following check frequency values are given: low frequency use 300, medium frequency use 100, high frequency use 50. Checking more frequently for client status while executing a database request lengthens the time taken to complete the queries. If the DB2 workload is heavy (i.e., it involves many internal requests), then setting DB2CHECHCLIENTINTERVAL to a low value has a greater impact on performance than in a situation where the workload is light and most of the time DB2 is waiting.

Variable name	Operating system	Values
DB2COMM	All, server only	Default = null Values: any combination of APPC, IPXSPX, NETBIOS, NPIPE, TCPIP

Specifies the communication managers that are started when the database manager is started. If this is not set, no DB2 communications managers are started at the server.

Variable name	Operating system	Values
DB2_FORCE_NLS_CACHE	AIX, HP_UX, Solaris	Default = False Values: TRUE or FALSE

Used to eliminate the chance of lock contention in multithreaded applications. When this registry variable is "TRUE," the code page and territory code information is saved the first time a thread accesses it. From that point, the cached information is used for any other thread that requests this information. This eliminates lock contention and results in a performance benefit in certain situations. This setting should not be used if the application changes locale settings between connections. It is probably not needed in such a situation because multithreaded applications typically do not change their locale settings because it is not "thread-safe" to do so.

Variable name	Operating system	Values
DB2NBADAPTERS	Windows	Default = 0 Range: 0-15 Multiple values should be separated by commas

Used to specify which local adapters to use for DB2 NetBIOS LAN communications. Each local adapter is specified using its logical adapter number.

Variable name	Operating system	Values
DB2CHECKUPTIME	Windows server only	Default = 1 Values: 1-720

Specifies the time interval between each invocation of the NetBIOS protocol checkup procedure. Checkup time is specified in minutes. Lower values ensure that the NetBIOS protocol checkup runs more often, freeing up memory and other system resources left when unexpected agent/session termination occurs.

Variable name	Operating system	Values
DB2NBINTRLISTENS	Windows server only	Default = 1 Values: 1-10 Multiple values should be separated by commas

Specifies the number of NetBIOS listen send commands (NCBs) that are asynchronously issued in readiness for remote client interrupts. This flexibility is provided for "interrupt active" environments to ensure that interrupt calls from remote clients can establish connections when servers are busy servicing other remote interrupts. Setting DB2NBINTRLISTENS to a lower value conserves NetBIOS sessions and NCBs at the server. However, in an environment where client interrupts are common, you may need to set DB2INTRLISTENS to a higher value in order to be responsive to interrupting clients. *Note:* Values specified are position sensitive; they relate to the corresponding value positions for DB2NBADAPTERS.

Variable name	Operating system	Values
DB2NBRECVBUFFSIZE	Windows server only	Default = 4096 bytes Range: 4096–65536

Specifies the size of the DB2 NetBIOS protocol receive buffers. These buffers are assigned to the NetBIOS receive NCBs. Lower values conserve server memory, while higher values may be required when client data transfers are larger.

Variable name	Operating system	Values
DB2NBBRECVNCBS	Windows server only	Default = 10 Range: 1–99

Specifies the number of NetBIOS `receive_any` commands (NCBs) that the server issues and maintains during operation. This value is adjusted depending on the number of remote clients to which your server is connected. Lower values conserve server resources. *Note:* Each adapter in use can have its own unique receive NCB value specified by DB2NBBRECVNCBS. The values specified are position sensitive; they can relate to the corresponding value positions for DB2NBADAPTERS.

Variable name	Operating system	Values
DB2NBRESOURCES	Windows server only	Default = null

Specifies the number of NetBIOS resources to allocate for DB2 use in a multicontext environment. This variable is restricted to multicontext client operation.

Variable name	Operating system	Values
DB2NBSENDNCBS	Windows server only	Default = 6 Range: 1-720

Specifies the number of send NetBIOS commands (NCBs) that the server reserves for use. This value can be adjusted depending on the number of remote clients your server is connected to. Setting DB2NBSENDCBS to a lower value will conserve server resources. However, you might need to set it to a higher value to prevent the server from waiting to send to a remote client when all other send commands are in use.

Variable name	Operating system	Values
DB2NBSESSIONS	Windows server only	Default = null Range: 5-254

Variable name	Operating system	Values
Specifies the number of sessions that DB2 should request to be reserved for DB2 use. The value of DB2NBSESSIONS can be set to request a specific session for each adapter specified using DB2NBADAPTERS. *Note:* Values specified are position sensitive; they relate to the corresponding value positions for DB2NBADAPTERS.		
DB2NBXTRANCBS	Windows server only	Default = 5 per adapter Range: 5-254
Specifies the number of "extra" NetBIOS commands (NCBs) the server will need to reserve when the db2start command is issued. The value of DB2NBXTRANCBS can be set to request a specific session for each adapter specified using DB2NBADAPTERS.		
DB2NETREQ	Windows 3.x	Default = 3 Range: 0-25
Specifies the number of NetBIOS requests that can be run concurrently on Windows 3.x clients. The higher you set this value, the more memory below the 1MB level is used. When the concurrent number of requests to use NetBIOS services reaches the number you have set, subsequent incoming requests for NetBIOS services are held in a queue and become active as the current requests complete. If you enter 0 (zero) for DB2NETREQ, the Windows database client issues NetBIOS calls in synchronous mode using the NetBIOS wait option. In this mode, the database client allows only the current NetBIOS request to be active and does not process another one until the current request has completed. This can affect other application programs. The 0 value is provided for backward compatibility only. It is strongly recommended that 0 not be used.		
DB2RETRY	Windows	Default = 0 Range: 0-20,000
The number of times DB2 attempts to restart the APPC listener. If the SNA subsystem at the server/gateway is down, this profile variable, in conjunction with DB2RETRYTIME, can be used to automatically restart the APPC listener without disrupting client communications using other protocols. In such a scenario, it is no longer necessary to stop and restart DB2 to reinstate the APPC client communications.		
DB2RETRYTIME	Windows	Default = 1 minute Range: 0–7,200 minutes
In increments of one minute, the number of minutes that DB2 allows between performing successive retries to start the APPC listener. If the SNA subsystem at the server/gateway is down, this profile variable, in conjunction with DB2RETRY, can be used to automatically restart the APPC listener without disrupting client communications using other protocols. In such a scenario, it is no longer necessary to stop and restart DB2 to reinstate the APPC client communications.		
DB2SERVICETPINSTANCE	Windows, AIX, and Sun Solaris	Default = null
Used to solve the problem caused by: • more than one instance running on the same machine • a version 6 or version 7 instance running on the same machine attempting to register the same TP names.		

Variable name	Operating system	Values
When the `db2start` command is invoked, the instance specified will start the APPC listeners for the following TP names: • `DB2DRDA` • `X'07'6DB`		
`DB2SOSNDBUF`	Windows NT	Default = 32767
Specifies the value of TCP/IP send buffers on Windows NT operating systems		
`DB2SYSPLEX_SERVER`	Windows NT and UNIX	Default = `null`
Specifies whether `SYSPLEX` exploitation when connected to DB2 for OS/390 or z/OS is enabled. If this registry variable is not set (which is the default), or is set to a nonzero value, exploitation is enabled. If this registry variable is set to zero (0), exploitation is disabled. When set to zero, SYSPLEX exploitation is disabled for the gateway regardless of how the DCS database catalog entry has been specified. For more information, see the command-line processor `CATALOG DCS DATABASE` command.		
`DB2TCPCONNMGRS`	All	Default = 1 on serial machines; square root of the number of processors rounded up to a maximum of eight connection managers on symmetric multiprocessor machines. Values: 1 to 8
The default number of connection managers is created if the registry variable is not set. If the registry variable is set, the value assigned here overrides the default value. The number of TCP/IP connection managers specified up to a maximum of 8 is created. If less than one is specified then `DB2TCPCONNMGRS` is set to a value of one and a warning is logged that the value is out of range. If greater than eight is specified, then `DB2TCPCONNMGRS` is set to a value of eight and a warning is logged that the value is out of range. Values between one and eight are used as given. When there is greater than one connection manager created, connection throughput should improve when multiple client connections are received simultaneously. There may be additional TCP/IP connection manager processes (on UNIX) or threads (on Windows operating systems) if the user is running on a SMP machine, or has modified the `DB2TCPCONNMGRS` registry variable. Additional processes or threads require additional storage. *Note:* Having the number of connection managers set to one causes a drop in performance on remote connections in systems with a lot of users, frequent connects and disconnects, or both.		
`DB2_VI_ENABLE`	Windows NT	Default = `OFF` Values: `ON` or `OFF`
Specifies whether to use the Virtual Interface (VI) Architecture communication protocol or not. If this registry variable is `ON`, then FCM will use VI for internode communication. If this registry variable is `OFF`, then FCM will use TCP/IP for internode communication. *Note:* The value of this registry variable must be the same across all the database partitions in the instance.		
`DB2_VI_VIPL`	Windows NT	Default = `vipl.dll`

Variable name	Operating system	Values
Specifies the name of the Virtual Interface Provider Library (VIPL) that will be used by DB2. In order to load the library successfully, the library name used in this registry variable must be in the PATH user environment variable. The currently supported implementations all use the same library name.		
DB2_VI_DEVICE	Windows NT	Default = null Values: nic0 or VINIC
Specifies the symbolic name of the device or Virtual Interface Provider Instance associated with the Network Interface Card (NIC). Independent hardware vendors (IHVs) each produce their own NIC. Only one NIC is allowed per Windows NT machine; multiple logical nodes on the same physical machine will share the same NIC. The symbolic device name VINIC must be in uppercase and can only be used with Synfinity Interconnect. All other currently supported implementations use nic0 as the symbolic device name.		

COMMAND-LINE VARIABLES

Variable name	Operating system	Values
DB2BQTIME	All	Default = 1 second Maximum value: 1 second
Specifies the amount of time the command-line processor front end sleeps before it checks whether the back-end process is active and establishes a connection to it.		
DB2BQTRY	All	Default = 60 retries Minimum value: 0 retries
Specifies the number of times the command-line process tries to determine whether the back-end process is already active. It works in conjunction with DB2BQTIME.		
DB2IQTIME	All	Default = 5 seconds Minimum value: 1 second
Specifies the amount of time the command-line processor back-end process waits on the input queue for the front-end process to pass commands.		
DB2RQTIME	All	Default = 5 seconds Minimum value: 1 second
Specifies the amount of time the command-line processor back-end process waits for a request from the front-end process.		

MPP Configuration Variables

Variable name	Operating system	Values
DB2ATLD_PWFILE	DB2 UDB ESE on AIX, Solaris, and Windows NT	Default = null Value: a file path expression

Specifies a path to a file that contains a password used during AutoLoader authentication. If not set, AutoLoader either extracts the password from its configuration file or prompts you interactively. Using this variable addresses password security concerns and allows the separation of AutoLeader configuration information from authentication information.

This registry variable is no longer needed, but is retained for backward compatibility.

Variable name	Operating system	Values
DB2CHGPWD_ESE	DB2 UDB ESE on AIX and Windows NT	Default = null Values: YES or NO

Specifies whether you allow other users to change passwords on AIX or Windows NT ESE systems. You must ensure that the passwords for all partitions or nodes are maintained centrally using either a Windows NT domain controller on Windows NT, or NIS on AIX. If not maintained centrally, passwords may not be consistent across all partitions or nodes. This could result in a password being changed only at the database partition to which the user connects to make the change. In order to modify this global registry variable, you must be at the root directory and on the DAS instance.

This variable is required only if you use the old db2atld utility instead of the new LOAD utility.

Variable name	Operating system	Values
DB2_FORCE_FCM_BP	AIX	Default = NO Values: YES or NO

This registry variable is applicable to DB2 UDB ESE for AIX with multiple logical partitions. When DB2START is issued, DB2 allocates the FCM buffers either from the database global memory or from a separate shared memory segment, if there is not enough global memory available. These buffers are used by all FCM daemons for that instance on the same physical machine. The kind of memory allocated is largely dependent on the number of FCM buffers to be created, as specified by the fcm_num_buffers database manger configuration parameter.

If the DB2_FORCE_FCM_BP variable is set to Yes, the FCM buffers are always created in a separate memory segment so that communication between FCM daemons of different logical partitions on the same physical node occur through shared memory. Otherwise, FCM daemons on the same node communicate through UNIX sockets. Communicating through shared memory is faster, but there is one fewer shared memory segment available for other uses, particularly for database bufferpools. Enabling the DB2_FORCE_FCM_BP registry variable thus reduces the maximum size of database bufferpools.

Variable name	Operating system	Values
DB2_NUM_FAILOVER_NODES	All	Default: 2 Values: 0 to the number of logical nodes

Specifies the number of nodes that can be used as failover nodes in a high availability environment. With high availability, if a node fails, then the node can be restarted as a second logical node on a different host. The number used with this variable determines how much memory is reserved for FCM resources for failover nodes.

For example, host A has two logical nodes: 1 and 2; and host B has two logical nodes: 3 and 4. Assume

Variable name	Operating system	Values
DB2_NUM_FAILOVER_NODES is set to 2. During DB2START, both host A and B will reserve enough memory for FCM so that up to four logical nodes could be managed. Then if one host fails, the logical nodes for the failing host could be restarted on the other host.		
DB2_PARTITIONEDLOAD_DEFAULT	All supported ESE platforms	Default: YES Range of values: YES/NO
The DB2_PARTITIONEDLOAD_DEFAULT registry variable lets users change the default behavior of the Load utility in an ESE environment when no ESE-specific Load options are specified. The default value is YES, which specifies that in an ESE environment if you do not specify ESE-specific Load options, loading is attempted on all partitions on which the target table is defined. When the value is NO, loading is attempted only on the partition to which the Load utility is currently connected.		
DB2PORTRANGE	Windows NT	Values: nnnn:nnnn
This value is set to the TCP/IP port range used by FCM so that any additional partitions created on another machine will also have the same port range.		

SQL Compiler Variables

Variable name	Operating system	Values
DB2_ANTIJOIN	All	Default = NO in an ESE envrionment Default = YES in a non-ESE envrionment Values: YES or NO
For DB2 Universal Database ESE environments: when YES is specified, the optimizer searches for opportunities to transform NOT EXISTS subqueries into anti-joins, which can be processed more efficiently by DB2. For non-ESE environments: when NO is specified, the optimizer limits the opportunities to transform NOT EXISTS subqueries into anti-joins.		
DB2_CORRELATED_PREDICATES	All	Default = YES Values: YES or NO
The default for this variable is YES. When there are unique indexes on correlated columns in a join, and this registry variable is YES, the optimizer attempts to detect and compensate for correlation of join predicates. When this registry variable is YES, the optimizer uses the KEYCARD information of unique index statistics to detect cases of correlation, and dynamically adjusts the combined selectivities of the correlated predicates, thus obtaining a more accurate estimate of the join size and cost. Adjustment is also done for correlation of simple equality predicates like WHERE C1=5 AND C2=10 if there is an index on C1 and C2. The index need not be unique but the equality predicate columns must cover all the columns in the index.		

Variable name	Operating system	Values
DB2_HASH_JOIN	All	Default = YES Values: YES or NO

Specifies hash join as a possible join method when compiling an access plan.

Variable name	Operating system	Values
DB2_INLIST_TO_NLJN	All	Default = NO Values: YES or NO

In some situations, the SQL compiler can rewrite an IN list predicate to a join. For example, the following query:

```
SELECT *
FROM EMPLOYEE
WHERE DEPTNO IN
('D11', 'D21', 'E21')
```

could be written as

```
SELECT *
FROM EMPLOYEE,
(VALUES 'D11', 'D21', 'E21) AS V (DNO)
WHERE
DEPTNO = V.DNO
```

This revision might provide better performance if there is an index on DEPTNO. The list of values would be accessed first and joined to EMPLOYEE with a nested loop join using the index to apply the join predicate.

Sometimes the optimizer does not have accurate information to determine the best join method for the rewritten version of the query. This can occur if the IN list contains parameter markers or host variables that prevent the optimizer from using catalog statistics to determine the selectivity. This registry variable causes the optimizer to favor nested loop joins to join the list of values, using the table that contributes the IN list as the inner table in the join.

Variable name	Operating system	Values
DB2_LIKE_VARCHAR	All	Default = Y,N Values: Y, N, S, or a floating point constant between 0 and 6.2

Controls the collection and use of subelement statistics. These are about the content of data in columns when the data has a structure in the form of a series of subfields or subelements delimited by blanks.

This registry variable affects how the optimizer deals with a predicate of the form:

```
COLUMN LIKE
'%xxxxxx%'
```

where the xxxxxx is any string of characters.

The syntax showing how this registry variable is used is:

```
Db2set DB2_LIKE_VARCHAR=
[Y/N/S/num1] [,Y/N/S/num2]
```

where

- The term preceding the comma, or the only term to the right of the predicate, means the following but only for columns that do not have positive subelement statistics:
  - S—The optimizer estimates the length of each element in a series of elements concatenated

Variable name	Operating system	Values

together to form a column based on the length of the string enclosed in the % characters.

- Y—The default. Use a default value of 1.9 for the algorithm parameter. Use a variable-length subelement algorithm with the algorithm parameter.
- N—Use a fixed-length sub-element algorithm.
- num1—Use the value of num1 as the algorithm parameter with the variable length subelement algorithm.

- The term following the comma means the following:
  - N—The default. Do not collect or use sub-element statistics.
  - Y—Collect subelement statistics. Use a variable-length subelement algorithm that uses the collected statistics together with the 1.9 default value for the algorithm parameter in the case of columns with positive subelement statistics.
  - num2—Collect subelement statistics. Use a variable-length subelement algorithm that uses the collected statistics together with the value of num2 as the algorithm parameter in the case of columns with positive subelement statistics.

DB2_MINIMIZE_LIST_PREFETCH	All	Default = NO Values: YES or NO

List prefetch is a special table access method that involves retrieving the qualifying RIDs from the index, sorting them by page number and then prefetching the data pages. Sometimes the optimizer does not have accurate information to determine if list prefetch is a good access method. This might occur when predicate selectivities contain parameter markers or host variables that prevent the optimizer from using catalog statistics to determine the selectivity.

This registry variable prevents the optimizer from considering list prefetch in such situations.

DB2_SELECTIVITY	All	Default = NO Values: YES or NO

The registry variable controls where the SELECTIVITY clause can be used in search conditions in SQL statements.

When this registry variable is set to YES, the SELECTIVITY clause can be specified for the following predicates:

- A basic predicate in which at least one expression contains host variables
- A LIKE predicate in which the MATCH expression, predicate expression, or escape expression contains host variables

DB2_NEW_CORR_SQ_FF	All	Default = OFF Values: ON or OFF

Affects the selectivity value computed by the SQL optimizer for certain subquery predicates when it is set to ON. It can be used to improve the accuracy of the selectivity value of equality subquery predicates that use the MIN or MAX aggregate function in the SELECT list of the subquery. For example:

```
SELECT * FROM T WHERE
T.COL = (SELECT MIN (T.COL) FROM T WHERE ...)
```

Variable name	Operating system	Values
DB2_PRED_FACTORIZE	All	Default = NO Value: YES or NO

Specifies whether the optimizer searches for opportunities to extract additional predicates from disjuncts. In some circumstances, the additional predicates can alter the estimated cardinality of the intermediate and final result sets. With the following query:

```
SELECT n1.emppno,
    n1.lastname
FROM  employee n1,
    Employee n2
WHERE
((n1.lastname='SMITH'
AND n2.lastname='JONES')
OR (n1.lastname='JONES'
AND n2.lastname='SMITH))
```

the optimizer can generate the following additional predicates:

```
SELECT n1.empno,
    n1.lastname
FROM employee n1,
    Employee n2
WHERE n1.lastname IN
 ('SMITH', 'JONES')
AND n2.lastname IN

 ('SMITH', 'JONES')
AND
((n1.lastname='SMITH'
AND n2.lastname='JONES')
OR (n1.lastname='JONES'
AND n2.lastname='SMITH'))
```

Variable name	Operating system	Values
DB2_REDUCED_OPTIMIZATION	All	Default = NO Values: NO, YES, any integer, DISABLE

This registry variable lets you request either reduced optimization features or rigid use of optimization features at the specified optimization level. If you reduce the number of optimization techniques used, you also reduce time and resource use during optimization.

Note: Although optimization time and resource use might be reduced, the risk of producing a less than optimal data access plan is increased. Use this registry variable only when advised by IBM or one of its partners.

- If set to NO, the optimizer does not change its optimization techniques.
- If set to YES, if the optimization level is 5 (the default) or lower, the optimizer disables some optimization techniques that might consume significant prepare time and resources but do not usually produce a better access plan.

Variable name	Operating system	Values

- If the optimization level is exactly 5, the optimizer scales back or disables some additional techniques, which might further reduce optimization time and resource use, but also further increase the risk of a less than optimal access plan. For optimization levels lower than 5, some of these techniques might not be in effect in any case. If they are, however, they remain in effect.
- If set to any integer the effect is the same as YES, with the following additional behavior for dynamically prepared queries optimized at level 5. If the total number of joins in any query block exceeds the setting, then the optimizer switches to greedy join enumeration instead of disabling additional optimization techniques as described above for level 5 optimization levels, which implies that the query will be optimized at a level similar to optimization level 2.
- If set to DISABLE the behavior of the optimizer when unconstrained by this DB2_REDUCED_OPTIMIZATION variable is sometimes to dynamically reduce the optimization for dynamic queries at optimization level 5. This setting disables this behavior and requires the optimizer to perform full level 5 optimization.

Note that the dynamic optimization reduction at optimization level 5 takes precedence over the behavior described for optimization level of exactly 5 when DB2_REDUCED_OPTIMIZATION is set to YES as well as the behavior described for the integer setting.

PERFORMANCE VARIABLES

Variable name	Operating system	Values
DB2_APM_PERFORMANCE	All	Default = OFF Values: ON, OFF

Set this variable to ON to enable performance-related changes in the access plan manager (APM) that affect the behavior of SQL cache (package cache). These settings are not usually recommended for production systems. They introduce some limitations, such as the possibility of out-of-package cache errors or increased memory use or both.

Setting DB2_APM_PERFORMANCE to ON also enables the No Package Lock mode. This mode allows the Global SQL Cache to operate without the use of package locks, which are internal system locks that protect cached package entries from being removed. The No Package Lock mode might result in somewhat improved performance, but certain database operations are not allowed. These prohibited operations might include: operations that invalidate packages, operations that inoperate packages, and PRECOMPILE, BIND, and REBIND.

Variable name	Operating system	Values
DB2_AVOID_PREFETCH	All	Default = OFF Values: ON or OFF

Specifies whether prefetch should be used during crash recovery. If DB2_AVOID_PREFETCH=ON prefetch is not used.

Variable name	Operating system	Values
DB2_AWE	Windows 2000	Default = null Values: <entry>[,<entry>...] where <entry> = <bufferpool ID>, <number of physical pages>, <number of address windows>

Allows DB2 UDB on 32-bit Windows 2000 platforms to allocate bufferpools that use up to 64 GB of memory. Windows 2000 must be configured correctly to support Address Windowing Extensions (AWE) bufferpools. This includes associating the "lock pages in memory" right with the user, allocating the physical pages and the address window pages, and setting this registry variable. In setting this variable you need to know the bufferpool ID of the bufferpool that is used for AWE support. The ID of the bufferpool can be seen in the BUFFERPOOLID column of the SYSCAT.BUFFERPOOLS system catalog view.

Note: If AWE support is enabled, extended storage cannot be used for any of the bufferpools in the database. Also, bufferpools referenced with this registry variable must already exist in SYSCAT.SYSBUFFERPOOLS.

Variable name	Operating system	Values
DB2_BINSORT	All	Default = YES Value: YES or NO

Enables a new sort algorithm that reduces the CPU time and elapsed time of sorts. This new algorithm extends the extremely efficient integer sorting technique of DB2 UDB to all sort data types such as BIGINT, CHAR, VARCHAR, FLOAT, and DECIMAL, as well as combinations of these data types. To enable this new algorithm, use the following command:

```
Db2set DB2_BINSORT = yes
```

Variable name	Operating system	Values
DB2BPVARS	As specified for each parameter	Default = path

Two sets of parameters are available to tune bufferpools. One set of parameters, available only on Windows, specifies that bufferpools should use scatter read for specific types of containers. The other set of parameters, available on all platforms, affect prefetching behavior.

Parameters are specified in an ASCII file, one parameter on each line, in the form parameter = value. For example, a file named bpvars.vars might contain the following lines:

```
NO_NT_SCATTER=1
NUMPREFETCHQUEUES = 2
```

Assuming that *bpvars.vars* is stored in F:\vars\, to set these variables you execute the following command:

```
db2set DB2BPVARS=F:\vars\bpvars.vars
```

Scatter-read Parameters

The scatter-read parameters are recommended for systems with a large amount of sequential prefetching against the respective type of containers and for which you have already set DB2NTNOCACHE to ON. These parameters, available only on Windows platforms, are NT_SCATTER_DMSFILE, NT_SCATTER_DMSDEVICE, and NT_SCATTER_SMS. Specify the NO_NT_SCATTER parameter to explicitly disallow scatter read for any container. Specific parameters are used to turn scatter read on for all containers of the indicated type. For each of these parameters, the default is zero (or OFF); and the possible values include: zero (or OFF) and 1 (or ON).

Note: You can turn on scatter read only if DB2NTNOCACHE is set to ON to turn Windows file caching off.

Variable name	Operating system	Values

If DB2NTNOCACHE is set to OFF or not set, a warning message is written to the administration notification log if you attempt to turn on scatter read for any container, and scatter read remains disabled.

Prefetch-Adjustment Parameters

The prefetch-adjustment parameters are NUMPREFETCHQUEUES and PREFETCHQUEUESIZE. These parameters are available on all platforms and can be used to improve bufferpool data prefetching. For example, consider sequential prefetching in which the desired PREFETCHSIZE is divided into PREFETCHSIZE/EXTENTSIZE prefetch requests. In this case, requests are placed on prefetch queues from which I/O servers are dispatched to perform asynchronous I/O. By default, DB2 maintains one queue of size max (100,2*NUM_IOSERVERS) for each database partition. In some environments, performance improves with either more queues or queues of a different size or both. The number of prefetch queues should be at most one half of the number of I/O servers. When you set these parameters, consider other parameters such as PREFETCHSIZE, EXTENTSIZE, NUM_IOSERVERS, buffer-pool size, and DB2_BLOCK_BASED_BP, as well as workload characteristics such as the number of current users.

If you think the default values are too small for your environment, first increase the values only slightly. For example, you might set NUMPREFETCHQUEUES = 4 and PREFETCHQUEUESIZE = 200. Make changes to these parameters in a controlled manner so that you can monitor and evaluate the effects of the change.

For NUMPREFETCHQUEUES, the default is 1 and the range of values is 1 to NUM_IOSERVERS. If you set NUMPREFETCHQUEUES to less than 1, it is adjusted to 1. If you set it greater than NUM_IOSERVERS, it is adjusted to NUM_IOSERVERS.

For PREFETCHQUEUESIZE, the default value is max (100,2*NUM_IOSERVERS). The range of values is 1 to 32767. If you set PREFETCHQUEUESIZE to less than 1 it is adjusted to the default. If set greater than 32767, it is adjusted to 32767.

DB2CHKPTR	All	Default = OFF Values: ON or OFF

Specifies whether or not pointer checking for input is required

DB2_ENABLE_BUFPD	All	Default = OFF Values: ON or OFF

Specifies whether or not DB2 uses intermediate buffering to improve query performance. The buffering may not improve query performance in all environments. Testing should be done to determine individual query performance improvements.

DB2_EXTENDED_OPTIMIZATION	All	Default = OFF Values: ON or OFF

Specifies whether or not the query optimizer uses optimization extensions to improve query performance. The extensions may not improve query performance in all environments. Testing should be done to determine individual query performance improvements.

DB2MAXFSCRSEARCH	All	Default = 5 Values: –1, 1 to 33 554

Variable name	Operating system	Values
Specifies the number of free-space control records to search when adding a record to a table. The default is to search five free-space control records. Modifying this value allows you to balance insert speed with space reuse. Use large values to optimize for space reuse. Use small values to optimize for insert speed. Setting the value to –1 forces the database manager to search all free-space control records.		
DB2MEMDISCLAIM	AIX	Default = YES Value: YES or NO
On AIX, memory used by DB2 processes may have some associated paging space. This paging space may remain reserved even when the associated memory has been freed. Whether or not this is so depends on the AIX system's (tunable) virtual memory management allocation policy. The DB2MEMDISCLAIM registry variable controls whether DB2 agents explicitly request that AIX disassociate the reserved paging space from the freed memory. A DB2MEMDISCLAIM setting of YES results in smaller paging space requirements, and possibly less disk activity from paging. A DB2MEMDISCLAIM setting of NO will result in larger paging space requirements, and possibly more disk activity from paging. In some situations, such as if paging space is plentiful and real memory is so plentiful that paging never occurs, a setting of NO provides a minor performance improvement.		
DB2MEMMAXFREE	All	Default = 8,388,608 bytes Values: 0 to 2^{32}–1 bytes
Specifies the maximum number of bytes of unused private memory that is retained by DB2 processes before unused memory is returned to the operating system.		
DB2_MMAP_READ	AIX	Default = ON Values: ON or OFF
Used in conjunction with DB2_MMAP_WRITE to allow DB2 to use mmap as an alternate method of I/O. In most environments, mmap should be used to avoid operating system locks when multiple processes are writing to different sections of the same file. However, perhaps you migrated from Parallel Edition v1.2 where the default was OFF, allowing caching by AIX of DB2 data read from JFS file systems into memory (outside the bufferpool). If you want comparable performance with DB2 UDB, you can either increase the size of the bufferpool or change DB2_MMAP_READ and DB2_MMAP_WRITE to OFF.		
DB2_MMAP_WRITE	AIX	Default = ON Value: ON or OFF
Used in conjunction with DB2_MMAP_READ to allow DB2 to use mmap as an alternate method of I/O. In most environments, mmap should be used to avoid operating system locks when multiple processes are writing to different sections of the same file. However, perhaps you migrated from Parallel Edition v1.2 where the default was OFF, allowing AIX caching of DB2 data read from JFS file systems into memory (outside the bufferpool). If you want the comparable performance with DB2 UDB, you can either increase the size of the bufferpool, or change DB2_MMAP_READ and DB2_MMAP_WRITE to OFF.		
DB2NTMEMSIZE	Windows NT	Default = (varies by memory segment)
Windows NT requires that all shared memory segments be reserved at DLL initialization time in order to guarantee matching addresses across processes. DB2NTMEMSIZE permits the user to override the DB2		

Variable name	Operating system	Values

defaults on Windows NT if necessary. In most situations, the default values should be sufficient. The memory segments, default sizes, and override options are: (1) Database Kernel: default size is 16777216 (16 MB); override option is DBMS:<number of bytes>. (2) Parallel FCM Buffers: default size is 22020096 (21 MB); override option is FCM:<number of bytes>. (3) Database Admin GUI: default size is 33554432 (32 MB); override option is DBAT:<number of bytes>. (4) Fenced Stored Procedures: default size is 16777216 (16 MB); override option is APLD:<number of bytes>. More than one segment may be overridden by separating the override options with a semi-colon (;). For example, to limit the database kernel to approximately 256K, and the FCM buffers to approximately 64 MB use: db2set DB2NTMEMSIZE=DBMS:256000; FCM:64000000

`DB2NTNOCACHE`	Windows NT	Default = `OFF` Value: `ON` or `OFF`

Specifics whether DB2 opens database files with a `NOCACHE` option. If `DB2NTNOCACHE = ON`, file system caching is eliminated. If `DB2NTNOCACHE = OFF`, the operating system caches DB2 files. This applies to all data except for files that contain long fields or LOBs. Eliminating system caching allows more memory to be available to the database so that the bufferpool or sortheap can be increased.

In Windows NT, files are cached when they are opened, which is the default behavior. 1 MB is reserved from a system pool for every 1 GB in the file. Use this registry variable to override the undocumented 192 MB limit for the cache. When the cache limit is reached, an out-of-resource error is given.

`DB2NTPRICLASS`	Windows NT	Default = `null` Value: `R`, `H`, (any other value)

Sets the priority class for the DB2 instance (program `DB2SYSCS.EXE`). There are three priority classes:

- `NORMAL_PRIORITY_CLASS` (the default priority class)
- `REALTIME_PRIORITY_CLASS` (set by using `R`)
- `HIGH_PRIORITY_CLASS` (set by using `H`)

The variable is used in conjunction with individual thread priorities (set using `DB2PRIORITIES`) to determine the absolute priority of DB2 threads relative to other threads in the system.

Note: Care should be taken when using this variable. Misuse could adversely affect overall system performance.

For more information, please refer to the *SetPriorityClass()* API in the Win32 documentation.

`DB2NTWORKSET`	Windows NT	Default = 1,1

Used to modify the minimum and maximum working-set size available to DB2. By default, when Windows NT is not in a paging situation, the working set of a process can grow as large as needed. However, when paging occurs, the maximum working set that a process can have is approximately 1 MB. `DB2NTWORKSET` allows you to override this default behavior.

Specify `DB2NTWORKSET` for DB2 using the syntax `DB2NTWORKSET = min, max`, where `min` and `max` are expressed in megabytes.

`DB2_OVERRIDE_BPF`	All	Default = not set Values: a positive numeric number of pages

Specifies the size of the bufferpool, in pages, to be created at database activation, or first connection, time. It is useful when failures occur during database activation or first connection resulting from mem-

Variable name	Operating system	Values
ory constraints. Should even a minimal bufferpool of 16 pages not be brought up by the database manager, then the user can try again after specifying a smaller number of pages using this environment variable. The memory constraint could arise either because of a real memory shortage (which is rare); or, because of the attempt by the database manager to allocate large, inaccurately configured bufferpools. This value, if set, overrides the current bufferpool size.		
DB2_PINNED_BP	AIX, HP-UX	Default = NO Values: YES or NO

This variable is used to specify the database global memory (including bufferpools) associated with the database in the main memory on some AIX operation systems. Keeping this database global memory in the system main memory allows database performance to be more consistent.

For example, if the bufferpool is swapped out of the system main memory, database performance deteriorates. The reduction of disk I/O by having the bufferpools in system memory improves database performance. If other applications require more of the main memory, allow the database global memory to be swapped out of main memory depending on the system main memory requirements.

For HP-UX in a 64-bit environment, in addition to modifying this registry variable, the DB2 instance group must be given the MLOCK privilege. To do this, a user with root access rights performs the following actions:

1. Adds the DB2 instance group to the */etc/privgroup* file. For example, if the DB2 instance group belongs to db2iadm1 group then the following line must be added to the */etc/privgroup* file: db2iadm1 MLOCK.
2. Issuses the following command:

```
Setprivgrp -f /etc/privgroup
```

DB2PRIORITIES	All	Value setting is platform dependent.

Controls the priorities of DB2 processes and threads.

DB2_SORT_AFTER_TQ	All	Default = NO Values: YES or NO

Specifies how the optimizer works with directed table queues in a partitioned database when the receiving end requires the data to be sorted and the number of receiving nodes is equal to the number of sending nodes.

When DB2_SORT_AFTER_TQ = NO, the optimizer tends to sort at the sending end and merge the rows at the receiving end.

When DB2_SORT_AFTER_TQ = YES, the optimizer tends to transmit the rows unsorted, not merge at the receiving end, and sort the rows at the receiving end after receiving all the rows.

DB2_STPROC_LOOKUP_FIRST	All	Default = ON Values: ON or OFF

Formerly DB2_DARI_LOOKUP_ALL, this variable specifies whether or not the UDB server performs a catalog lookup for ALL DARIs and stored procedures before it looks in the function subdirectory of the sqllib subdirectory; and in the unfenced subdirectory of the sqllib subdirectory.

Note: For stored procedures of PARAMETER TYPE DB2DARI that are located in the directories mentioned above, setting this value to ON degrades performance because the catalog lookup might be performed on

Variable name	Operating system	Values

another node in an ESE configuration before the function directories are searched.

When you call a stored procedure, the default behavior for DB2 is to search for a shared library with the same name as the stored procedure in the function subdirectoy of the `sqllib` subdirectory and in the unfenced subdirectory of the function subdirectory of the `sqllib` subdirectory before it looks up the name of the shared library for the stored procedures in the system catalog. Only stored procedures of `PARAMETER TYPE DB2DARI` can have the same name as their shared library, so only `DB2DARI` stored procedures benefit from the default behavior of DB2. If you use stored procedures cataloged with a different `PARAMETER TYPE`, the time that DB2 spends searching the above directories degrades the performance of those stored procedures.

To enhance the performance of stored procedures that are not cataloged as `PARAMETER TYPE DB2DARI`, set the `DB2_STPROC_LOOKUP_FIRST` registry variable to `ON`. This registry variable forces DB2 to look up the name of the shared library for the stored procedure in the system catalog before searching the above directories.

Data-Links Variables

`DLFM_BACKUP_DIR_NAMR`	AIX, Windows NT	Default: `null` Values: TSM or any valid path

Specifies the backup device to use. If you change the setting of this registry variable between TSM and a path at runtime, the archived files are not moved. Only new backups are placed in the new location. Previously archived files are not moved.

`DLFM_BACKUP_LOCAL_MP`	AIX, Windows NT	Default: `null` Values: any valid path to the local mount point in the DFS system

Specifies the fully qualified path to a mount point in the DFS system. When a path is specified, it is used instead of the path specified with `DLFM_BACKUP_DIR_NAME`.

`DFLM_BACKUP_TARGET`	AIX, Windows NT	Default = `null` Values: `LOCAL`, `TSM`, `XBSA`

Specifies the type of backup used.

`DLFM_BACKUP_TARGET_LIBRARY`	AIX, Windows NT	Default = `null` Values: any valid path to the DLL or shared library name.

Specifies the fully qualified path to the DLL or shared library. This library is loaded using the *libdfmxbsa.a* library.

`DLFM_ENABLE_STRPOC`	AIX, Windows NT	Default: `NO` Values: `YES` or `NO`

Specifies whether a stored procedure is used to link groups of files.

DLFM_FS_ENVIRONMENT	AIX, Windows NT	Default: NATIVE Values: NATIVE or DFS

Specifies the environment in which Data Links servers operate. NATIVE indicates that the Data Links server is in a single machine environment in which the server can take over files on its own machine. DFS indicates that the Data Links server is in a distributed file system (DFS) environment in which the server can take over files throughout the file system. Mixing DFS file sets and native file systems is not allowed.

DLFM_GC_MODE	AIX, Windows NT	Default: PASSIVE Values: SLEEP, PASSIVE, or ACTIVE

Specifies the control of garbage file collection on the Data Links server. When set to SLEEP, no garbage collection occurs. When set to PASSIVE, garbage collection runs only if no other transactions are running. When set to ACTIVE, garbage collection runs even if other transactions are running.

DLFM_INSTALL_PATH	AIX, Windows NT	Default: On AIX: /usr/opt/db2_08_01/adm On NT: DB2PATH/bin Range: any valid path

Specifies the path where the Data Links executables are installed.

DLFM_LOG_LEVEL	AIX, Windows NT	Default: LOG_INFO Values: LOG_CRIT, LOG_DEBUG, LOG_ERR, LOG_INFO, LOG_NOTICE, LOG_WARNING

Specifies the level of diagnostic information to be recorded.

DLFM_PORT	All except Windows 3.n	Default: 50100 Values: any valid port number

Specifies the port number used to communicate with the Data Links servers running the DB2 Data Links Manager. This environment variable is only used when a table contains a "DATALINKS" column.

DLFM_TSM_MGMTCLASS	AIX, Windows NT, Solaris	Default: the default TSM management class Values: any valid TSM management class

Specifies which TSM management class to use to archive and retrieve linked files. If no value is set for this variable, the default TSM management class is used.

Miscellaneous Variables

Variable name	Operating system	Values
DB2ADMINSERVER	Windows and UNIX	Default = null

Specifies the DB2 Administration Server

DB2CLIINIPATH	All	Default = null

Used to override the default path of the DB2 CLI/ODBC configuration file (*db2cli.ini*) and specify a different location on the client. The value specified must be a valid path on the client system.

Variable name	Operating system	Values
DB2DEFPREP	All	Default = NO Values: ALL, YES, or NO

Simulates the runtime behavior of the DEFERRED_PREPARE precompile option for applications that were precompiled before this option was available. For example, if DB2 v2.1.1 or an earlier application were run in a DB2 v2.1.2 or later environment, DB2DEFPREP could be used to indicate the desired "deferred prepare" behavior.

Variable name	Operating system	Values
DB2_DJ_COMM	All	Default = null Values include: libdrda.a, libsqlnet.a, libnet8.a, libdrda.dll, libsqlnet.dll, libnet8.dll, and so on.

Specifies the wrapper libraries that are loaded when the database manager is started. Specifying this variable reduces the runtime cost of loading frequently used wrappers. Other values for other operating systems are supported (the .dll extension is for the Windows NT operating system; the .a extension is for the AIX operating system). Library names vary by protocol and operating system. This variable is not available unless the database manager parameter federated is set to YES.

Variable name	Operating system	Values
DB2DMNBCKCTLR	Windows NT	Default = null Values: ? or a domain name

If you know the name of the domain for which the DB2 server is the backup domain controller, set DB2DMNBCKCTLR = DOMAIN_NAME. The DOMAIN_NAME must be in upper case. To have DB2 determine the domain for which the local machine is a backup domain controller, set DB2DMNBCKCTLR = ? If the DB2DMNBCKCTLR profile variable is not set or is set to blank, DB2 performs authentication at the primary domain controller.

Note: DB2 does not use an existing backup domain controller by default because a backup domain controller can get out of synchronization with the primary domain controller, causing a security exposure. Getting out of synchronization can occur when the primary domain controller's security database is updated but the changes are not propagated to a backup domain controller. This could occur if there are network latencies or if the computer browser service is not operational.

Variable name	Operating system	Values
DB2_ENABLE_LDAP	All	Default = null Vaules: YES or NO

Specifies whether or not the Lightweight Directory Access Protocol (LDAP) is used. LDAP is an access method to directory services.

Variable name	Operating system	Values
DB2_FALLBACK	Windows NT	Default = ON Values: ON or OFF

This variable allows you to force all database connections off during the fallback processing. It is used in conjunction with the failover support in the Windows NT enviornment with Microsoft Cluster Server (MSCS). If DB2_FALLBACK is not set or is set to OFF, and database connection exists during the fallback, the DB2 resource cannot be brought offline. This will mean the fallback processing will fail.

<table>
<tr><th>Variable name</th><th>Operating system</th><th>Values</th></tr>
<tr><td>DB2_GRP_LOOKUP</td><td>Windows NT</td><td>Default = null
Values: LOCAL, DOMAIN</td></tr>
<tr><td colspan="3">This variable is used to tell DB2 where to validate user accounts and perform group member lookup. Set the variable to LOCAL to force DB2 to always enumerate groups and validate user accounts on the DB2 server. Set the variable to DOMAIN to force DB2 to always enumerate groups and validate user accounts on the Windows NT domain to which the user account belongs.</td></tr>
<tr><td>DB2LDAP_BASEDN</td><td>All</td><td>Default = null
Values: Any valid base domain name</td></tr>
<tr><td colspan="3">Specifies the base domain name for the LDAP directory.</td></tr>
<tr><td>DB2LDAPCACHE</td><td>All</td><td>Default = YES
Values: YES or NO</td></tr>
<tr><td colspan="3">Specifies that the LDAP cache is to be enabled. This cache is used to catalog the database, node, and DCS directories on the local machine.
To ensure that you have the latest entries in the cache, do the following:
REFRESH LDAP DB DIR
REFRESH LDAP NODE DIR
These commands update and remove incorrect entries from the database directory and the node directory.</td></tr>
<tr><td>DB2LDAP_CLIENT_PROVIDER</td><td>Windows 98/NT/2000 only</td><td>Default = null (Microsoft, if available, is used; otherwise, IBM is used)
Values: IBM or Microsoft</td></tr>
<tr><td colspan="3">When running in a Windows environment, DB2 supports using either Microsoft LDAP clients or IBM LDAP clients to access the LDAP directory. This registry variable is used to explicitly select the LDAP client to be used by DB2.
Note: To display the current value of this registry variable, use the db2set command:
Db2set DB2LDAP_CLIENT_PROVIDER</td></tr>
<tr><td>DB2LDAPHOST</td><td>All</td><td>Default = null
Values: Any valid hostname</td></tr>
<tr><td colspan="3">Specifies the hostname of the location for the LDAP directory.</td></tr>
<tr><td>DB2LDAP_SEARCH_SCOPE</td><td>All</td><td>Default = DOMAIN
Values: LOCAL, DOMAIN, GLOBAL</td></tr>
<tr><td colspan="3">Specifies the search scope for information found in partitions or domains in the Lightweight Directory Access Protocol (LDAP). *LOCAL* disables searching in the LDAP directory. *DOMAIN* only searches in LDAP for the current directory partition. *GLOBAL* searches in LDAP for the current directory partitions until the object is found.</td></tr>
<tr><td>DB2LOADREC</td><td>All</td><td>Default = null</td></tr>
<tr><td colspan="3">Used to override the location of the load copy during roll forward. If the user has changed the physical location of the load copy; DB2LOADREC must be set before issuing the roll forward.</td></tr>
</table>

Variable name	Operating system	Values
DB2LOCK_TO_RB	All	Default = null Values: Statement

Specifies whether lock timeouts cause the entire transaction to be rolled back, or only the current statement. If DB2LOCK_TO_RB is set to STATEMENT, locked timeouts cause only the current statement to be rolled back. Any other setting results in transaction rollback.

Variable name	Operating system	Values
DB2NEWLOGPATH2	UNIX	Default = 0 Values: 0 or 1

This parameter allows you to specify whether a secondary path should be used to implement dual logging. The secondary path name is generated by appending a "2" to the current value of the logpath database configuration parameter.

Variable name	Operating system	Values
DB2NOEXITLIST	All	Default = OFF Values: ON or OFF

If defined, this variable indicates to DB2 not to install an exit list handler in applications and not to perform a COMMIT. Normally, DB2 installs a process exit list handler in applications and the exit list handler performs a COMMIT operation if the application ends normally.

For applications that dynamically load the DB2 library and unload if before the application terminates, the invocation of the exit list handler fails because the handler routine is no longer loaded in the application. If your application operates in this way, you should set the DB2NOEXITLIST variable and ensure your application explicitly invokes all required COMMITs.

Variable name	Operating system	Values
DB2REMOTEPREG	Window NT	Default = null Value: any valid Windows 95 or Windows NT machine name

Specifies the remote machine name that contains the Win32 registry list of DB2 instance profiles and DB2 instances. The value for DB2REMOTEPREG should only be set once after DB2 is installed, and should not be modified. Use this variable with extreme caution.

Variable name	Operating system	Values
DB2ROUTINE_DEBUG	AIX and Windows NT	Default = OFF Values: ON, OFF

Specifies whether to enable the debug capability for Java stored procedures. If you are not debugging Java stored procedures, use the default, OFF. There is a performance impact to enable debugging.

Variable name	Operating system	Values
DB2SORCVBUF	Windows NT	Default = 32767

Specifies the value of TCP/IP receive buffers on Windows NT operating systems

Variable name	Operating system	Values
DB2SORT	All, server only	Default = null

Specifies the location of a library to be loaded at runtime by the LOAD utility. The library contains the entry point for functions used in sorting indexing data. Use DB2SORT to exploit vendor-supplied sorting products for use with the LOAD utility in generating table indexes. The path supplied must be relative to the database server.

Variable name	Operating system	Values
DB2SYSTEM	Windows and UNIX	Default = null

Specifies the name that is used by your users and database administrators to identify the DB2 server system. If possible, this name should be unique within your network.

This name is displayed in the system level of the Control Center's object tree to aid administrators in the identification of server systems that can be administered from the Control Center.

When using the "Search the Network" function of the Client Configuration Assistant, DB2 discovery returns this name and it is displayed at the system level in the resulting object tree. This name aids users in identifying the system that contains the database they wish to access. A value for `DB2SYSTEM` is set at installation time as follows:

- On Windows NT the setup program sets it equal to the computer name specified for the Windows system.
- On UNIX systems, it is set equal to the UNIX system's TCP/IP hostname.

Variable name	Operating system	Values
DB2_VENDOR_INI	AIX, HP-UX, Sun Solaris, and Windows	Default = null Values: any valid path and file

Points to a file containing all vendor-specific environment settings. The value is read when the database manager starts.

Variable name	Operating system	Values
DB2_XBSA_LIBRARY	AIX, HP-UX, Sun Solaris, and Windows	Default = null Value: any valid path and file

Points to the vendor-supplied XBSA library. On AIX, the setting must include the shared object if it is not named shr.o. HP-UX, Sun Solaris, and Windows NT do not require the shared object name. For example, to use Legato's NetWorker Business Suite Module for DB2, the registry variable must be set as follows:

```
db2set DB2_XSBA_LIBRARY="/usr/lib/libxdb2.a(bsashr10.o)"
```

The XBSA interface can be invoked through the BACKUP DATABASE or the RESTORE DATABASE commands. For example:

```
db2 backup db sample use XBSA
db2 restore db sample use XBSA
```

Bibliography

Advanced Computers & Network Corporation. 2002. "RAID 0+1: High Data Transfer Performance." RAID.edu. Accessible at *www.acnc.com/04_01_0p1.html.*

Advanced Computers & Network Corporation. 2002. "RAID 5: Independent Data Disks with Distributed Parity Blocks." RAID.edu. Accessible at *www.acnc.com/04_01_05.html.*

Advanced Computers & Network Corporation. 2002. "RAID 10: Very High Reliability Combined with High Performance." RAID.edu. Accessible at *www.acnc.com/04_01_10.html.*

Arellano, Michael, et al. 2001. "Ultra320 SCSI: New Technology—Still SCSI." SCSI Trade Association. Accessible at *www.SCSITA.org.*

Bernstein, Phil, et al. 2000. "The Asilomar Report on Database Research. Sigmod Record." Accessible at *acm.org/sigmond/record/issues.9812/asilomar.html.*

Bhatt, Ajay. 2002. "Creating a Third Generation I/O Interconnect." 3rd Generation I/O. Accessible at *www.intel.com/technology.*

Brathwaite, Ken. 1991. *Relational Databases: Concepts, Design, and Administration.* New York: McGraw-Hill.

Caruso, Jeff. 2002. "RDMA Compared to Other Technologies." Network World High Speed LANs Newsletter. Accessible at *www.nwfusion.com/cgi-bin/mailto/x.cgi.*

Cassells, Brad, et al. 2000. *DB2 UDB v7.1 Performance Tuning Guide.* IBM REDBOOKS: San Jose.

Codd, E.F. 1970. "A Relational Model of Data for Large Shared Data Bank." *CACM*, vol 13, no. 6, pp. 337–387.

Dawson, Philip. 2002. "InfiniBand Yields to PCI Express." Tech Update. Accessible at *www.zdnet.com/filters/printerfriendly/0,6061,2885009-92,00.html.*

DeRoest, James. 1997. *AIX Version 4: System and Administration Guide.* New York: McGraw-Hill.

Enterprise Storage Forum Staff. 2002. "Intel and Enterprise Industry Leaders Collaborate on InfiniBand Eval Progam." Enterprise Storage Forum. Accessible at *www.enterprisestorageforum.com/technology/news/print/0,,10563_1487221,00.html.*

Erlanger, Leon. 2001. "High-Performance Buses and Interconnects." Extreme Tech. Accessible at *www.extremetech.com/print_article/0,3998,a=18058,00.asp.*

Fagin, R. 1981. "A Normal Form for Relational Databases That is Based on Domains and Keys." *ACM Trans. On Database Systems*, vol. 6, no. 3, pp. 387–415.

Field, Gary, et al. *The Book of SCSI.* 2nd Edition. William Pollock, No Starch Press: San Francisco, 2000.

Fonseca, Brian, & Neel, Dan. 2002. "Serving the Holy Grail." InfoWorld. Lead with Knowledge. Accessible at *www.infoworld.com/articles/pl/xml/02/03/18/020318plblades.xml.*

Frisch, AEleen. 1995. *Essential System Administration.* O'Reilly & Associates: Sebastopol, CA.

Gibson, Garth, et al. 1988. "A Case for Redundant Arrays of Inexpensive Disks (RAID)." ACM Sigmod International Conference on Management of Data, pp. 109–116.

Goodwins, Rupert. 2002. "InfiniBand—Old Before its Time?" Tech Update. Accessible at *www.zdnet.com/filters/printerfriendly/0,6061,2880760-92,00.html.*

Grant, John. 1987. *Logical Introduction to Databases.* Orlando, FL: Harcourt Brace Jovanovich.

Gfroerer, Diana, et al. *Understanding IBM eServer pSeries Performance and Sizing*. IBM REDBOOK: San Jose.

Gulutzan, Peter, et al. 2003. *SQL Performance Tuning.* Pearson Education: New York.

Gunning, Philip. 2002. "Database Technology Leaps Ahead." *DB2 Magazine.* Accessible at *www.db2mag.com*

Gunning, Philip, et al. "Tuning Up for OLTP and Data Warehousing." *DB2 Magazine.* Accessible at *www.db2mag.com*

Halpin, Terry. 2001. *Information Modeling and Relational Databases.* Morgan Kauffman: San Francisco.

Hicks, Matt. 2002. "IBM Gets SMART about Managing DB2." *EWeek.* Accessible at *www.eweek.com/print_article/0,3668,a=27775,00.asp.*

IBM. 2002. "IBM Introduces Next-Generation Enterprise Storage Server ("Shark") that Outperform Competition." Accessible at *www.storage.ibm.com/press/announce/20020715.html.*

IBM. 2002. "SSA for Beginners." Accessible at *www.tek-tips.com/gfaqs.cfm/lev2/lev3/20/pid/52/fid/1727.*

IBTA. 2002. "About InfiniBand Trade Association: An InfiniBand Technology Overview." Accessible at *www.infinibandta.org/ibta.*

Intel Corporation. 2002. "InfiniBand Achitecture Moves Ahead." *Interoperability.* pp.1–17.

Irving, Allan, et al. 2003. *Database Performance Tuning on AIX.* IBM REDBOOK: San Jose.

JES Hardware Solutions. 1999. "What is RAID." Accessible at *www.4raid.com/raidlevels.htm.*

Krazit, Tom. 2002. "PCI-X 2.0, PCI Express Specs Released to Developers." *InfoWorld.* Lead with Knowledge. Accessible at *staging.infoworld.com/articles/hn.xml/02/07/24/020724hnpcispecs.xml.*

Krill, Paul. 2002. "IDF: Intel Envisions Modular Computing Future." *InfoWorld.* Lead with Knowledge. Accessible at *staging.infoworld.com/articles/hn/xml/02/09/20/020910hnmodular.xml.*

Kroenke, David. 2000. *Database Processing: Fundamentals, Design, and Implementation.* Upper Saddle River, NJ: Prentice Hall.

Menon, Jai, & Thomasian, Alexander. 1997. "RAID5 Performance with Distributed Sparing." IEEE. Accessible at *www.computer.org/tpds/td1997/10640abs.htm.*

Mellish, Barry. 2001. *IBM ESS and DB2 UDB Working Together*, IBM REDBOOKS: San Jose.

Mullins, Craig. 2002. *Database Administration: The Complete Guide to Practices and Procedures.* Boston: Addison-Wesley.

Neel, Dan. 2001. "Arapahoe Work Group Adds Industry Heavyweights." *InfoWorld.* Lead with Knowledge. Accessible at *staging.infoworld.com/articles/hn/xml/01/08/29/010829hnpci.xml*

Olson, Jack. 2002. "Working with Problem Databases." DataWarehouse.com. Accessible at *www.datawarehouse.com/iknowledge/articles/print.cfm?ContentID=3335.*

Performance Associates, Inc. 2000. "Open Systems I/O: Syllabus." Accessible at *www.perfassoc.com/opensystemsio_syllabus.html.*

Ranade, Jay, et al. 1991. *DB2: Concepts, Programming, and Design.* New York: McGraw-Hill.

Schlesinger, Lee. 2002. "Intel Exits, but InfiniBand Intact." Tech Update. Accessible at *www.zdnet.com/filters/printerfriendly/0,6061,2868287-92,00.html.*

Selinger, Pat, et al. 2002. "Access Path Selection in a Relational Database Management System." Sigmod Conference 1979. Accessible at *www.informatick.uni-trier.de/~ley/db/conf/sigmond/SelingerACLP79.html.*

Shafer, Scott Tyler. 2002. "iSCSI Faces Hazy Future." *InfoWorld.* Lead with Knowledge. Accessible at *staging.infoworld.com/articles/ne/xml/02/11/04/021104neipstore.xml.*

Shirai, Tetsuya, et al. 2001. *DB2 Universal Database in Applications Development Environments.* Upper Saddle River, NJ: Prentice-Hall.

Sobell, Mark. 1995. *Unix System V: A Practical Guide,* 3rd Edition. Addison-Wesley: Menlo Park, CA.

Solinap, Tom. 2001. "RAID: An In-Depth Guide to RAID Technology." SLCentral. Accessible at *sicentral.com/articles/01/1/raid.*

Stam, Nick. 2002. "Inside PCI Express." Extreme Tech. Accessible at *www.extremetech.com/print_article/0,3998,a=30763,00.asp.*

Underhill, Sandra. 2001. "InfiniBand Set to Speed Up Servers." *InfiniSource.* Accessible at *www.infinisource.com/features/infiniband-pf.html.*

Index

C

D

E

F

G

H

I

N

O

P

Q

R

S

T

U

V

W

X